The Communicator's Commentary

1,2 Chronicles

THE COMMUNICATOR'S COMMENTARY SERIES
OLD TESTAMENT

Lloyd J. Ogilvie

─────────── General Editor ───────────

The
Communicator's
Commentary

1,2 Chronicles

Leslie C. Allen

WORD BOOKS, PUBLISHER • WACO, TEXAS

To Allinson D.G. Walder
who in his largeheartedness
reminds me of the Chronicler

Library of Congress Cataloging in Publication Data
Main entry under title:

The Communicator's commentary.

   Bibliography: p.
   Contents: OT10. 1, 2 Chronicles/Leslie C. Allen
   1. Bible. O.T.—Commentaries.   I. Ogilvie, Lloyd
John.   II. Allen, Leslie C., 1935–
BS1151.2.C66   1987   221.7′7   86–11138
ISBN 0–8499–0415–3 (v. OT10)

Printed in the United States of America

5 6 7 8 9 9   AGF   9 8 7 6 5

Contents

94172

Editor's Preface

God has called all of His people to be communicators. Everyone who is in Christ is called into ministry. As ministers of "the manifold grace of God," all of us—clergy and laity—are commissioned with the challenge to communicate our faith to individuals and groups, classes and congregations.

The Bible, God's Word, is the objective basis of the truth of His love and power that we seek to communicate. In response to the urgent, expressed needs of pastors, teachers, Bible study leaders, church school teachers, small group enablers, and individual Christians, the Communicator's Commentary is offered as a penetrating search of the Scriptures of the Old and New Testament to enable vital personal and practical communication of the abundant life.

Many current commentaries and Bible study guides provide only some aspects of a communicator's needs. Some offer in-depth scholarship but no application to daily life. Others are so popular in approach that biblical roots are left unexplained. Few offer impelling illustrations that open windows for the reader to see the exciting application for today's struggles. And most of all, seldom have the expositors given the valuable outlines of passages so needed to help the preacher or teacher in his or her busy life to prepare for communicating the Word to congregations or classes.

This Communicator's Commentary series brings all of these elements together. The authors are scholar-preachers and teachers outstanding in their ability to make the Scriptures come alive for individuals and groups. They are noted for bringing together excellence in biblical scholarship, knowledge of the original Hebrew and Greek, sensitivity to people's needs, vivid illustrative material from biblical, classical, and contemporary sources, and lucid communication by the use of clear outlines of thought. Each has been selected to contribute to this series because of his Spirit-empowered ability to help people live in the skins of biblical characters and provide a "you-are-there" intensity to the drama of events of the Bible which have so much to say about our relationships and responsibilities today.

The design for the Communicator's Commentary gives the reader an overall outline of each book of the Bible. Following the introduction, which reveals the author's approach and salient background on the book, each chapter of the commentary provides the Scripture to be exposited. The New King James Bible has been chosen for the Communicator's Commentary because it combines with integrity the beauty of language, underlying Hebrew and Greek textual basis, and thought-flow of the 1611 King James Version, while replacing obsolete verb forms and other archaisms with their everyday contemporary counterparts for greater readability. Reverence for God is preserved in the capitalization of all pronouns referring to the Father, Son, or Holy Spirit. Readers who are more comfortable with another translation can readily find the parallel passage by means of the chapter and verse reference at the end of each passage being exposited. The paragraphs of exposition combine fresh insights to the Scripture, application, rich illustrative material, and innovative ways of utilizing the vibrant truth for his or her own life and for the challenge of communicating it with vigor and vitality.

It has been gratifying to me as Editor of this series to receive enthusiastic progress reports from each contributor. As they worked, all were gripped with new truths from the Scripture—God-given insights into passages, previously not written in the literature of biblical explanation. A prime objective of this series is for each user to find the same awareness: that God speaks with newness through the Scriptures when we approach them with a ready mind and a willingness to communicate what He has given; that God delights to give communicators of His Word "I-never-saw-that-in-that-verse-before" intellectual insights so that our listeners and readers can have "I-never-realized-all-that-was-in-that-verse" spiritual experiences.

The thrust of the commentary series unequivocally affirms that God speaks through the Scriptures today to engender faith, enable adventuresome living of the abundant life, and establish the basis of obedient discipleship. The Bible, the unique Word of God, is unlimited as a resource for Christians in communicating our hope to others. It is our weapon in the battle for truth, the guide for ministry, and the irresistible force for introducing others to God.

A biblically rooted communication of the Gospel holds in unity and oneness what divergent movements have wrought asunder. This commentary series courageously presents personal faith, caring for individuals, and social responsibility as essential, inseparable dimensions of biblical Christianity. It seeks to present the quadrilateral Gospel in its fullness which calls us to unreserved commitment to Christ, unrestricted self-esteem in His grace, unqualified love for others in personal evangelism, and undying efforts to work for justice and righteousness in a sick and suffering world.

A growing renaissance in the church today is being led by clergy and laity who are biblically rooted, Christ-centered, and Holy Spirit-empowered. They have dared to listen to people's most urgent questions and deepest needs and then to God as He speaks through the Bible. Biblical preaching is the secret of growing churches. Bible study classes and small groups are equipping the laity for ministry in the world. Dynamic Christians are finding that daily study of God's Word allows the Spirit to do in them what He wishes to communicate through them to others. These days are the most exciting time since Pentecost. The Communicator's Commentary is offered to be a primary resource of new life for this renaissance.

It has been very encouraging to receive the enthusiastic responses of pastors and teachers to the twelve New Testament volumes of the Communicator's Commentary series. The letters from communicators on the firing line in pulpits, classes, study groups, and Bible fellowship clusters across the nation, as well as the reviews of scholars and publication analysts, have indicated that we have been on target in meeting a need for a distinctly different kind of commentary on the Scriptures, a commentary that is primarily aimed at helping interpreters of the Bible to equip the laity for ministry.

This positive response has led the publisher to press on with an additional twenty-one volumes covering the books of the Old Testament. These new volumes rest upon the same goals and guidelines that undergird the New Testament volumes. Scholar-preachers with facility in Hebrew as well as vivid contemporary exposition have been selected as authors. The purpose throughout is to aid the preacher and teacher in the challenge and adventure of Old Testament exposition in communication. In each volume you will meet Yahweh, the "I AM" Lord who is Creator, Sustainer, and Redeemer in the unfolding drama of His call and care of Israel. He is the Lord who acts, intervenes, judges, and presses His people into the immense challenges and privileges of being a chosen people, a holy nation. And in the descriptive exposition of each passage, the implications of the ultimate revelation of Yahweh in Jesus Christ, His Son, our Lord, are carefully spelled out to maintain unity and oneness in the preaching and teaching of the Gospel.

I take great pleasure in introducing to you the author of this exceptional commentary on 1 and 2 Chronicles. Leslie C. Allen is Professor of Old Testament at Fuller Theological Seminary and author of numerous biblical studies and commentaries.

Dr. Allen comes to us from England where he received his education. Studying first at Cambridge University, he completed his theological training with a Ph.D. from London University. He taught for thirteen years at London Bible College before coming to Fuller Seminary in Pasadena, California.

It is likely that you will know Dr. Allen from his scholarly writings, especially his excellent commentaries on several Old Testament books. He is an outstanding scholar who is gaining increasing recognition in this country. Ironically, as I was finishing this preface, the latest edition of the *Journal of Biblical Literature* came to my attention. The lead article in this bastion of biblical academia is written by none other than Leslie Allen!

This commentary on Chronicles reflects throughout Dr. Allen's excellence in biblical scholarship. His profound and pristinely clear explanations reveal his expertise. As always, he bases his work upon mastery of Hebrew, of Israelite culture, and of Old Testament theology.

But this commentary will surprise you. For Dr. Allen shows himself to be far more than just a top-notch Old Testament scholar. First of all, this analysis of Chronicles continually makes deep and invaluable connections with the New Testament. Dr. Allen, for all of his Old Testament wisdom, writes as a Christian who knows and loves his New Testament. The biblical communicator will be greatly served by this thoroughly Christian interpretation of Chronicles.

Furthermore, in this commentary you will see not only Professor Allen the scholar, but equally Leslie Allen the churchman. With one foot solidly planted in the academic world and the other firmly set in the church, he addresses today's Christian in practical terms. You will enjoy Dr. Allen's rich illustration and application of

Chronicles and find it helpful as you communicate God's deeper truths.

This volume, like all in the *Communicator's Commentary* series, has been prepared especially for those who preach and teach the Bible. Leslie Allen regards Chronicles as particularly promising for communicators, since "the Chronicler was essentially a preacher of pastoral theology." This commentary explores the Chronicler's theological preaching—and helps us to communicate with the same sense of awe before God as the ancient writer felt.

Dr. Allen sagely notes: "The heartbeat of Chronicles is a concern for spirituality. In this respect its key word is to 'seek' God." Christians today are yearning for a revived spirituality. We are learning anew how to seek God, as individuals and as a church. There could be no better time for the timeless Word of Chronicles to be spoken. Leslie Allen speaks this Word with integrity and equips us to do the same.

LLOYD J. OGILVIE

Introduction

One could think of at least three reasons why not to study Chronicles. First, it is much too long. Second, its first nine chapters are off-putting, just lists of names. Third, most of it is a rehash of material already available in the books of Samuel and Kings. Yet there must be something of value in Chronicles for it to have survived as part of Scripture. Early Jewish readers realized that it was God's Word for them and worth preserving for posterity. It became part of the Hebrew canon of Scripture and thence part of the Old Testament for the church. So presumably one may not regard it as a white elephant to keep stored away in a religious attic. As part of the Bible, Chronicles confronts us with a challenge and dares us to discover its value for ourselves.

In this enterprise we are fortunate to be living when we do. Over the past two decades or so, Old Testament scholars have stopped regarding Chronicles as a poor relation of Samuel and Kings. They have done Chronicles the courtesy of letting it speak to them of its own concerns. The exciting result has been a plethora of positive insights into this literary work. Along with these investigations, there has been a new appreciation of the post-exilic period of Judah's history, when the Chronicler lived, and so a greater endeavor to understand his message and to differentiate it from the earlier messages of Samuel and Kings. If we can tune into this scholarly wavelength, we go halfway toward finding in Chronicles its contemporary significance. We have to see what it meant before we can see what it means. We need to look over the Chronicler's shoulder and appreciate what he was trying to do. We must overhear what he wanted to say to post-exilic Judaism before we can hear his message to the church.

There is always a temptation to pick out vital passages from biblical books and ignore the rest. Before I developed an interest in Chronicles, I used to prize in it only two chapters, 1 Chronicles 29 and 2 Chronicles 20. The former chapter I liked for its beautiful prayer of praise, while the second was dear to me because it presents a model of faith and survival. The rest of Chronicles was a relatively closed book, a mass of small print, except for the little prayer in 1 Chronicles 4:10, memorable perhaps because it was the text of a sermon delivered by the first woman preacher I ever heard! Since then I have grown to love Chronicles as a whole, and the Chronicler has become a good friend of mine, whose foibles I accept for the privilege of knowing him.

THE PLACE OF CHRONICLES IN THE CANON

It may come as a surprise to learn that in the Jewish Bible Chronicles occupies the final place. It belongs to the third and last part of the Hebrew canon, the Writings, after the Law and the Prophets. When Jesus spoke of a long history of martyrdom "from the blood of Abel to the blood of Zechariah who perished between the altar and the temple" (Luke 11:51), He was speaking of the biblical record of persecution from beginning to end, from Genesis to Chronicles (see 2 Chron. 24:20, 21). It was a good solid note for the Jewish canon to end on. Was it put last because it resembles Genesis in beginning with Adam and ending with hope of attaining the promised land? Out in the world, away from home! This has been the sad experience of Jews for much of their history, but a redeeming feature which has fostered their survival has been a sense of the purpose and promise of God. In the Christian canon the prophets from Isaiah to Malachi have been put at the end, with their much clearer image of divine promise, to enhance the role of the New Testament as its Christ-centered fulfillment. Chronicles, however, has suffered by being put at the back of Samuel and Kings as if it were some pale shadow of them, instead of being regarded as an epic work in its own right and the weighty climax of the first part of the canon.

HOW CHRONICLES IS STRUCTURED

Chronicles falls into four parts. 1 Chronicles 1–9 with its many long genealogies serves as an introduction. The reader—and the expositor!—is tempted to skip this hors d'oeuvre and to move on to the meat of the second part, the history of David and Solomon in 1 Chronicles 10 through 2 Chronicles 9. It is wiser to keep to the balanced diet of the whole meal as it has been prepared. The Chronicler has much to tell his readers in those first nine chapters, if only we stop to listen. The third section runs from 2 Chronicles 10 to 28, a study of the kings of Judah during the period of the divided kingdom, while the last part is 2 Chronicles 29–36, the history of Judah after the fall of the northern kingdom and up to its own downfall.

Of these four parts it is noticeable that the second one, covering the reigns of David and Solomon, comprises twenty-nine chapters out of the total of sixty-five. It is by far the longest section, almost half the book. If we ask why, the answer is that this is where the Chronicler's heart is. To understand Chronicles we must pay close attention to this focal point of the book, its living center. It is unfortunate that when Chronicles was translated into Greek it was roughly chopped into two halves, simply because the Greek language takes up more space than Hebrew and two scrolls were necessary. This split down the middle has unfortunately cut up the main section.

WHEN CHRONICLES WAS WRITTEN AND WHY

It is an essential part of the Christian doctrine of Scripture that divine revelation has been given in a particular historical setting. So it is important to try to reconstruct the period of the author, the circumstances in which he wrote, and the needs of the particular constituency he was consciously writing for. It is clear from 1 Chronicles 9:1–2 that he wrote in the post-exilic period and that the experiences of being displaced persons lay in recent history for his generation of the people of God. Survival had doubtless made them acutely appreciative of their past: in an insecure period when morale must often have been low, it gave them something firm to cling to. At what precise point after the Exile the Chronicler wrote is a less easy question to answer, especially as we know comparatively little about that period. Scholarship does not speak with a unanimous voice. A number of scholars put the date of composition about 515 B.C., a short while after the first wave of expatriates returned in 538

B.C. and about the time when the ruined temple was rebuilt. I prefer to side with others who claim that it was written later, sometime during the fourth century.

The important thing to grasp is that it is a post-exilic composition. The consecutive books of Samuel and Kings present a history of the monarchy primarily for exilic readers. They were designed to answer the burning question why the Exile had been the terrible lot of God's people. The Chronicler came to the same history with a different perspective. He retraced much of the same ground, but other, positive questions were at the forefront of his mind as he wrote. His selectivity and emphases suggest that he wanted the people of God in his day to understand who they were. To this end he gave a representation of their religious heritage, omitting certain material here and supplementing there. Who are we in relation to the world and to God? Where have we come from? Where are we going? These were the questions he was trying to answer. They are vital questions for any community and indeed for any individual. It is essential to establish one's identity and role if one is to live a satisfying and useful life.

THE KEYNOTES OF CHRONICLES

The message of this immense work may be reduced to a couple of verses, 1 Chronicles 17:12 and 2 Chronicles 7:14. Together they give a bird's eye view of most of its total agenda. Each is set in a context of divine revelation, to David and Solomon respectively. They sum up the Chronicler's theology to a considerable degree. The first verse, 'He [Solomon] shall build Me a house, and I will establish his throne forever,' announces through the prophet Nathan a new era of divine revelation, centered in the founding of the Davidic dynasty and the building of the Solomonic temple. For the Chronicler the era continued to his own day, as the qualifying "forever" implied. What preceded in Israel's history was the old dispensation of the law or Torah, established by Moses and Joshua, which regulated life in the land. The Chronicler throughout his work wrestled with the relation between the old era and the new, between the Law and the Prophets, and sought to show how the old Word from God still had relevance, even though partly superseded. The old Mosaic covenant had been subsumed into the new, royal covenant which God honored with His personal guarantee. Torah and temple were symbols of the complete revelation which God would have His people heed.

The span of the divine purpose stretched not only from the past to the present: it was to continue into the future. The Davidic monarchy had not survived the cataclysm of Exile. Yet the divine word "forever," echoed in 2 Chronicles 13:5 and 21:7, called for faith and hope that it would be restored. Accordingly David's genealogy in 1 Chronicles 3 is carefully traced down to the Chronicler's own time: the heirs to the ancient and future throne awaited God's summons. Meanwhile an important obligation for His people was to maintain temple worship faithfully. In this worship the Chronicler stressed the role of the Levites, who were "parapriests": one cannot help wondering whether he was not a Levite himself!

The second verse, 2 Chronicles 7:14, characterizes the new temple age as a dispensation of grace: "If My people who are called by My name will humble themselves, and pray and seek My face, and turn from their wicked ways, then I will hear from heaven, and will forgive their sin and heal their land." The temple constituted not only a place of worship but a place of answered prayer, especially the prayer of confession and repentance. It was a monument to God's grace, for His last word was not the Torah but a gracious promise. The conditionality of the Torah found a counterbalance in the temple-based promise of forgiveness to a remiss but repentant people. His first Word still stood as the divine standard for His people. When the Torah was broken by human sin, dire sanctions came into operation, the Chronicler is ever ready to insist—unless true repentance followed the breach of the Torah. In that case God's grace was at hand to repair the damage and ensure the survival of the believing community.

Who was this group called "My people"? The Chronicler gave an insistent answer throughout his work, devoting much space to defining its bounds. Many in post-exilic Judah would have stood staunchly for a narrow definition, claiming "We are the remnant, the elect people of God." The Chronicler challenges them to think again and to think bigger, in line with the ancient ideal of a twelve-tribed Israel. There were in the province of Samaria to the north many who claimed descent from Jacob. Were they to be written off, these prodigal sons and daughters? A favorite phrase of the Chronicler is "all Israel," which is his assertion that a partial fellowship falls feebly short of the divine ideal. Sadly, history paid no heed to his large-heartedness. Sometime between his own day and that of Jesus a permanent split developed between south and north, so that it could be said that "Jews have no dealings with Samaritans" (John 4:9).

PREACHING FROM CHRONICLES

It is not difficult to translate the Chronicler's concerns into contemporary, Christian ones: we stand so close to him in spirit. Like him and his own generation, we are far removed in time from the founding of God's new era, which for us is centered in Christ. We too have the difficult task of relating modern life to sacred history and gaining from it a self-understanding that satisfies as it challenges. The insistence on "all Israel" commends an ecumenical concern to a fragmented church. Temple and Torah speak to us of the balance of worship and way of life in Christian experience. The progression from Law to Prophets, from an old era to a new one which embraces the old even as in some respects it supersedes it, bids us consider the relevance of the Old Testament in relation to the New. The Chronicler's pastoral assurance that divine grace offered an answer to human guilt receives a resounding amen from the church, which has heard the New Testament's testimony that "where sin abounded, grace abounded much more" (Rom. 5:20) through the work of Jesus Christ, "who was born of the seed of David" (Rom. 1:3).

A number of the books in the Bible may not easily be transposed into the medium of preaching: they contain intransigent material with which the would-be preacher has to struggle. I am fortunate in my assignment, for the Chronicler was essentially a preacher of pastoral theology. The Greek sage Dionysius of Halicarnassus treated history as "philosophy teaching by examples." Similarly the Chronicler had a homiletic approach to history. He saw it as a source of spiritual models for his contemporaries to copy or shun. As we have observed, his basic theology accords with the agenda of a Christian pastor. Not only so: his material usually falls readily into sermon-sized pieces. I have found that my task was to spot the clues the Chronicler himself had placed in the text. Sometimes a key word runs through a section, such as the verb "rely" in 2 Chronicles 13:18; 14:11 (RSV); and 16:7–8. The repetition serves to isolate chapters 13–16 as a history-based sermon on faith in a time of crisis. The recurring stress on help from God and from friends in 1 Chronicles 11–12 reminds the believer that he or she need not be alone in pursuing the path of God's will. The portrayal of three successive kings in 2 Chronicles 24–26 as running well at first and then dropping out of the spiritual race was intended as a serious admonition to maintain the faith.

The heartbeat of Chronicles is a concern for spirituality. In this respect its key word is to "seek" God, a term which is continually contrasted with its polar opposites, to "forsake" God and to "be unfaithful" to Him. Pastors who are diligent in studying Chronicles will find that its exegesis flows smoothly into exposition and that its spiritual pulse beats in time with their own.

"No man is an island, entire of itself," especially in the task of commentary writing. The format of this volume does not lend itself to continual acknowledgment of insights into the text, not seldom gleaned from recondite journals. It must be owned, however, that a library of scholarship underlies my exposition. A major commentary which has been continually open on my desk is that written by my friend Hugh G. Williamson, *1 & 2 Chronicles* (New Century Bible Commentary, Grand Rapids: Wm. B. Eerdmans, 1982). Readers who want to delve further into exegesis—and I hope they will—are urged to seek it out: it has garnered and sifted recent exegetical work inaccessible to most readers. His long bibliography is a monument to his labors. Other names associated with work to which I am especially indebted are Peter R. Ackroyd, Roddy L. Braun, Raymond B. Dillard, John Goldingay, J. Gordon McConville, Rudolf Mosis, Jacob M. Myers, and Wilhelm Rudolph. (A short bibliography appears at the end of this volume.) I cannot conclude without tributes to my wife, Elizabeth, who pored over each chapter as it left my hands and improved its readability, and to David Sielaff who painstakingly transcribed the material onto the word processor of the School of Theology, Fuller Theological Seminary.

An Outline of Chronicles

CHAPTER ONE

Names Are People

1 Chronicles 1:1–5:26

Everybody knows the cautionary tale about the beginner in Bible study who decided to start with Genesis and read solidly through to Revelation—only to grind to a permanent halt over the 'begats" of Genesis 5. The moral of the tale is clear, to start with something easier and more digestible. But eventually we have to learn to cope with the genealogies. To leapfrog over the genealogical lists of 1 Chronicles 1–9 and begin our commentary with chapter 10 would be at the least a discourtesy to the Chronicler and at the worst a refusal to appreciate a particular mode God used in writing the Bible. A genealogy is one way to write history. It gives a panoramic view so nuanced in its selective range that the presenter tells us a lot about his understanding of history. Matthew picked up a cue from Chronicles by beginning his Gospel with a schematic genealogy (Matt. 1:1–17). It views Jesus as the climax of Jewish history, a worthy heir of Abraham and David (Matt. 1:1). Luke prefaced his account of the ministry of Jesus with a genealogy which traced His ancestry right back to Adam (Luke 3:23–38). In this way Luke conveyed at the outset a universal stress that introduced a keynote of his Gospel. Genealogies have something important to say.

Names are people: a genealogy is a technical way of condensing human experience. It has fallen out of favor in the study of history: we use other, comparable techniques such as statistical lists, graphs, and charts. Perhaps we think of genealogies as elitist, for people with blue blood in their veins, such as royalty. On the other hand, many Americans like to delve into their genealogies or, as they would call it, their family tree. I have a colleague who vacationed in England: the highlights of his vacation were a visit to Somerset House in London to look at old birth records relating to his family and an excursion to the Essex village from where his forebears migrated to the States. In a similar spirit Alex Haley wrote *Roots*, tracing his origins back to eighteenth-century West Africa. Both of these men were trying to uncover their past, and this is what 1 Chronicles 1–9 is doing.

Why should we linger over the Chronicler's genealogies? It is not our family tree that is in view, is it? Yes, in a way it is. Paul in Romans 11 spoke of the people of God over the ages as a gnarled old olive tree, now pruned of many (Jewish) branches and refurbished with fresh branches grafted into the trunk—meaning us Gentile believers. For him Israel was part of the family tree. He had a sense of theological history. If we stop to listen to Chronicles, we can come to share this perspective. It will help to confirm our spiritual bearings and tell us who we are by telling us about our roots.

GOD'S PEOPLE IN GOD'S WORLD

1:1 Adam, Seth, Enosh,
    2 Cainan, Mahalalel, Jared,
    3 Enoch, Methuselah, Lamech,
    4 Noah, Shem, Ham, and Japheth.
    5 The sons of Japheth *were* Gomer, Magog, Madai, Javan, Tubal, Meshech, and Tiras.
    6 The sons of Gomer *were* Ashkenaz, Diphath, and Togarmah.
    7 The sons of Javan *were* Elishah, Tarshishah, Kittim, and Rodanim.
    8 The sons of Ham *were* Cush, Mizraim, Put, and Canaan.
    9 The sons of Cush *were* Seba, Havilah, Sabta, Raama, and Sabtecha. The sons of Raama *were* Sheba and Dedan.
    10 Cush begot Nimrod; he began to be a mighty one on the earth.
    11 Mizraim begot Ludim, Anamim, Lehabim, Naphtuhim,
    12 Pathrusim, Casluhim (from whom came the Philistines and the Caphtorim).
    13 Canaan begot Sidon, his firstborn, and Heth;

28

14 the Jebusite, the Amorite, and the Girgashite;

15 the Hivite, the Arkite, and the Sinite;

16 the Arvadite, the Zemarite, and the Hamathite.

17 The sons of Shem *were* Elam, Asshur, Arphaxad, Lud, Aram, Uz, Hul, Gether, and Meshech.

18 Arphaxad begot Shelah, and Shelah begot Eber.

19 To Eber were born two sons: the name of one *was* Peleg, for in his days the earth was divided; and his brother's name *was* Joktan.

20 Joktan begot Almodad, Sheleph, Hazarmaveth, Jerah,

21 Hadoram, Uzal, Diklah,

22 Ebal, Abimael, Sheba,

23 Ophir, Havilah, and Jobab. All these *were* the sons of Joktan.

24 Shem, Arphaxad, Shelah,

25 Eber, Peleg, Reu,

26 Serug, Nahor, Terah,

27 and Abram, who *is* Abraham.

28 The sons of Abraham *were* Isaac and Ishmael.

29 These *are* their genealogies: The firstborn of Ishmael *was* Nebajoth; then Kedar, Adbeel, Mibsam,

30 Mishma, Dumah, Massa, Hadad, Tema,

31 Jetur, Naphish, and Kedemah. These *were* the sons of Ishmael.

32 Now the sons born to Keturah, Abraham's concubine, *were* Zimran, Jokshan, Medan, Midian, Ishbak, and Shuah. The sons of Jokshan *were* Sheba and Dedan.

33 The sons of Midian *were* Ephah, Epher, Hanoch, Abida, and Eldaah. All these were the children of Keturah.

34 And Abraham begot Isaac. The sons of Isaac *were* Esau and Israel.

35 The sons of Esau *were* Eliphaz, Reuel, Jeush, Jaalam, and Korah.

36 And the sons of Eliphaz *were* Teman, Omar, Zephi, Gatam, *and* Kenaz; and *by* Timna, Amalek.

37 The sons of Reuel *were* Nahath, Zerah, Shammah, and Mizzah.

38 The sons of Seir *were* Lotan, Shobal, Zibeon, Anah, Dishon, Ezer, and Dishan.

39 And the sons of Lotan *were* Hori and Homam; Lotan's sister was Timna.

40 The sons of Shobal *were* Alian, Manahath, Ebal, Shephi, and Onam. The sons of Zibeon *were* Ajah and Anah.

41 The son of Anah *was* Dishon. The sons of Dishon *were* Hamran, Eshban, Ithran, and Cheran.

42 The sons of Ezer *were* Bilhan, Zaavan, *and* Jaakan. The sons of Dishan *were* Uz and Aran.

43 Now these *were* the kings who reigned in the land of Edom before a king reigned over the children of Israel: Bela the son of Beor, and the name of his city was Dinhabah.

44 And when Bela died, Jobab the son of Zerah of Bozrah reigned in his place.

45 When Jobab died, Husham of the land of the Temanites reigned in his place.

46 And when Husham died, Hadad the son of Bedad, who attacked Midian in the field of Moab, reigned in his place. The name of his city *was* Avith.

47 When Hadad died, Samlah of Masrekah reigned in his place.

48 And when Samlah died, Saul of Rehoboth-by-the-River reigned in his place.

49 When Saul died, Baal-Hanan the son of Achbor reigned in his place.

50 And when Baal-Hanan died, Hadad reigned in his place; and the name of his city was Pai. His wife's name was Mehetabel the daughter of Matred, the daughter of Mezahab.

51 Hadad died also. And the chiefs of Edom were Chief Timnah, Chief Aliah, Chief Jetheth,

52 Chief Aholibamah, Chief Elah, Chief Pinon,

53 Chief Kenaz, Chief Teman, Chief Mibzar,

54 Chief Magdiel, and Chief Iram. These *were* the chiefs of Edom.

2:1 These *were* the sons of Israel: Reuben, Simeon, Levi, Judah, Issachar, Zebulun,

2 Dan, Joseph, Benjamin, Naphtali, Gad, and Asher.

1 Chron. 1:1–2:2

What we have here is the Book of Genesis in potted form. The Chronicler ransacked Genesis and copied out its genealogical lists. It was his way of affirming that Genesis is important as a book of beginnings. Genesis discloses a divine plan in world history. Its movement from primeval history to patriarchal history, from creation to covenant, from the universal to the particular, provided the Chronicler with a good introduction to the history of the Israelite monarchy, which is what his two books are. This movement in Genesis still had something to say to the generation of God's people among whom the Chronicler lived. One reason he liked it was because it raised with relish the issue of particularity. "How odd of God to choose the Jews!" No, corrected the Chronicler, how good of God. The church in turn has been criticized for its theological particularism and accused of arrogant presumption and blatant self-centeredness. It is a criticism that has grown louder in the modern world, where religious pluralism is rife. Ought not love of one's neighbor mean respect for his or her religion as an alternative way of reaching the one God, whatever name we give Him? If we interpret the second commandment in this way, how can we keep the first properly? What I mean is, how can we love and empathize with the God in whose Word Jesus is identified as exclusively "the way, the truth, and the life" (John 14:6)? It was no accident that an early name for the Christian faith was "the Way" (Acts 9:2, etc.).

1. *A significant milestone.* The Chronicler in his pre-Christian period of revelation is also speaking of the Way. Although the genealogy from Adam to the sons of Jacob or Israel is expressed in human terms, it is really communicating a message about God's purposes in the world. Human history is like an urban map with its intricate network of roads. Here the text is following one possible sequence in traveling from the beginning of human history to a significant stopping point. This selective choice of roads is regarded as the route of God's spiritual purpose. The stopping point is at the sons of Jacob. Chronologically it was a point in time centuries away from the Chronicler's own period, but it gave a vital self-understanding to the people of God then living: "We are the sons of Israel." They were God's "chosen ones" (16:13). Appreciated aright, it threw them to their knees in humility before God and then bid them stand and walk tall with a sense of God-given worth. We present-day Christians can

see here a parallel for ourselves in the importance attached to people who lived long before. The events of the Gospels and Acts all happened long ago, but we believe that they were a crucial stopping point in world history. Christmas, Easter, and Pentecost are red-letter days in the calendar, days for subsequent humanity to remember as decisive for its own destiny. Centuries later we have read the old, old story, and it has come alive for us. Here is history that refuses to stay in its own place but chases humanity down the corridors of time, demanding recognition and response.

For Luke in his genealogy the route of God's world purpose ran from Adam to Jesus. The Chronicler was saying something of comparable significance when he traced the earlier part of that route as running from Adam to Jacob and his sons. He preferred to use Jacob's "baptismal" name Israel because he saw a vital link between the person and the people, a link forged by God Himself. Israel stood at a midpoint of history as the culmination of what went before and the beginner of a new work of God. Of course, for us Christians Jesus is a no less significant figure.

Let us dig a little deeper into the passage and substantiate what we have been saying. It is worth pausing over the deliberate design of the text. There are two possible ways of selecting and presenting a genealogy. One is to give a linear genealogy, tracing a single line from grandfather to father to son. The other way is to provide a segmented or partially horizontal genealogy, which gives more than one line and fans out as it moves down, acknowledging that a person has more than one child, who in turn each have children of their own, and so on. The Chronicler might have presented his genealogy from Adam to Israel in a completely linear fashion, as he did partially in verses 1–4a (Adam–Noah) and 24–27 (Shem–Abraham). It would have made the chapter much shorter, because in genealogy, as in geometry, the shortest distance between two points is a straight line! The Chronicler preferred mainly to follow the pattern of Genesis in giving branches of the human family tree. The overall effect is to highlight the note of particularity. Each generation is a crossroads where God determines afresh the way forward.

The Chronicler might have gotten into a mess by opting to juggle with so much material. He chose "last and not least" as a controlling principle. Noah had three sons, Shem, Ham, and Japheth, verse 4 means to say. Japheth's and Ham's progeny are dealt with in verses

5–16 and then Shem's in verses 17–27. When Shem's descendants are enumerated, the final verses 24–27 pinpoint the line from Shem to Abraham. Of Abraham's sons, Ishmael and then his children by Keturah are given first in verses 29–33, while Isaac, the child of promise as Paul called him (Gal. 4:28), has his turn in verses 34–37. Esau, one of Isaac's two sons, has his family listed in verses 35–37, with its ramifications added in verses 38–54. Then Israel, Isaac's other son, has his twelve sons enumerated in 2:1–2. So the policy is to dispose of the subsidiary branches first and to concentrate on the line of promise by way of climax.

After 2:2 there is a break in the scheme, and a new policy of "first and foremost" comes into operation. Thus the tribe of Judah is analyzed in 2:3–4:23 before the other tribes. The change in policy stresses the climactic point reached in the sons of Israel. This is why we could say earlier that 2:2 is a significant stopping point. In the New Testament Paul pinpointed a son of Abraham as a prime figure of theological history: "Now we, brethren, as Isaac was, are children of promise" (Gal. 4:28). The Chronicler's perspective moves two generations down the line, but makes the same point to his Jewish readers: "Now we, brethren, as Israel's sons were, are children of promise."

2. *A lesser monarchy.* I have a niggling feeling that I have not done full justice to the Chronicler's purposes in this initial chapter. Why did he devote valuable space to the kings and chiefs of Edom in verses 43–54? It does flow on from the Esau material because Edom was another name for Esau (Gen. 36:1). Did he just want to keep faith with Genesis by cramming in all the material from Genesis 36 he could? I do not think that he suffered from the perfectionist streak which mars the lives of some of us. Obviously Edom was very much on his mind: he devoted twenty verses to its concerns, verses 35–54. Let us trace from Genesis 36 the fortunes of Esau's family, he seems to be saying, before we trace those of Israel's family. The focus of his history of Israel is going to be the Davidic monarchy with its capital at Jerusalem. He pauses to look at the parallel institution in Edom's history. Verse 43 is significant: *"Now these were the kings who reigned in the land of Edom before a king reigned over the children of Israel."* I suggest that this is more than a quotation from Genesis 36:31. One has to be alert in Chronicles for old material to take on new meaning—as in the New Testament when it quotes the Old. For

the Chronicler, in the light of his own concerns, it becomes a preface showing that he has Israel's monarchy at the back of his mind as a basis of comparison with the Edomite kings. By comparison, what a travesty the Edomite monarchy was! David's dynasty lasted from generation to generation by God's appointment: Edom had a chaotic series of unrelated kings. The house of David ruled from Jerusalem, the holy city: these kings had no less than three capitals (vv. 43, 46, 50). The Chronicler seems to have interpreted verses 51–54 as a sequel to the monarchy, a series of chieftains following on from the death of Hadad (v. 51). In other words, the monarchy petered out.

In the post-exilic period Judah and Edom had a cold-war relationship, and Judah had a strong sense of grievance against Edom for various reasons. That situation fits this interpretation of the text as a scoring over Edom and a promotion of Judah's interests at Edom's expense. We do it right in Judah, affirms the Chronicler, with our Davidic dynasty and capital. There is more than nationalism here: if it were only that, the contrast would have broken down, for the house of David was swept away by the Exile. But our author had a strong sense of the importance of the dynasty in God's purposes and believed that a Davidic king would yet rule over Israel. "God does it right!" is his message, which recital of Edom's royal experimentation in terms of blunders and bloopers serves to enhance. Here is a conviction that the world cannot do it right and that God's way, followed by His people in the pre-exilic past, is still to be the goal of His people in the post-exilic present. That word "goal" is important: the Chronicler was not expressing a lazy complacency but calling his fellows to understand their past history and to live their lives now, in the light of a conviction about God's ultimate purposes.

3. *A Davidic perspective.* If an implicit comparison with the house of David underlies verses 43–54, one's curiosity is aroused to look back over the preceding verses. We shall see as we go through the books of Chronicles that they are captivated not simply by the Davidic dynasty, but by its founders, David and Solomon. It is worth noting that no less than seventeen of the names in chapter 1 recur in the Chronicler's narratives of David and Solomon as subject to their control or influence. *"Tarshishah"* or Tarshish in verse 7 was the far-off place reached by Solomon's navy and from which exotic imports came, such as "ivory, apes, and monkeys" (2 Chron. 9:21). *"Sheba,"* mentioned three times, in verses 9, 22, and 32, reminds the careful

reader of the Arabian queen who brought tribute of gold, fabulous spices, and precious stones (2 Chron. 9:9). The *"Philistines"* of verse 12 were, of course, one of the most important of David's conquests (1 Chron. 14:8–17; 18:11; 20:4–8). *"Sidon"* in verse 13 was the place from where David ordered cedar for the temple (22:4). The *"Jebusite,"* *"Amorite,"* and *"Hivite"* in verses 14, 15 were all subjected to forced labor by King Solomon (2 Chron. 8:7). So one could go on. Anyone who prizes the reigns of David and Solomon as the Chronicles cannot fail to notice the parallels. In verse 10 the reference to Nimrod as an early example of greatness on a world scale (*"he began to be a mighty one on the earth"*) omits the references to hunting with which the text of Genesis explains the greatness (Gen. 10:8, 9) and leaves it general. I cannot help but think of David to whom God promised *"a name like the name of the great men who are on the earth"* (1 Chron. 17:8). For the Chronicler, I think, Nimrod's mantle fell eventually on David.

Here then is another agenda for our chapter. When the Chronicler looked at world history presented in the genealogies of Genesis, he saw the images of David and Solomon superimposed, like a photograph when the film has not been wound and the negative has captured two separate scenes together. Different ethnic groups all over the ancient world were to find a new focus in the subsequent history of Chronicles. David and Solomon reached out beyond Israel's frontiers: "The Lord brought the fear" of David "upon all nations" (1 Chron. 14:17). This first chapter is resonant with themes from Israel's early monarchy. Old Testament theology saw in the Davidic and Solomonic empire an earthly representation of theocracy, whereby David and Solomon ruled as regents for God. Since the God of Israel is the God of the whole world, there is a logic about their imperial rule which transcends human politics. It stood as a model for future expectation. The Davidic kings received as their heritage the divine promises, "I will give You/The nations for Your inheritance" (Ps. 2:8) and "The kings of Tarshish . . . /Will bring presents; /The kings of Sheba and Seba/Will offer gifts" (Ps. 72:10; compare these names with 1 Chron. 1:7, 9!). The prophets took up the cry and looked forward to the time when a Davidic king would again "be great to the ends of the earth" (Mic. 5:4). The Chronicler inherited this theology. For him Solomon sat "on the throne of the kingdom of the Lord" (1 Chron. 28:5). David and

Solomon were models for a future manifestation of this kingdom, for had not God promised to "establish" their "throne . . . forever" (1 Chron. 17:14)? So not unreasonably this conception which so colored Israel's past and future also reached back beyond its historical manifestation and colored the panorama of world history in 1 Chronicles 1. It became bright with promise of a new realization of God's kingdom.

If the Chronicler looked at the ancient world and saw there the subsequent empire of David and his son, what do we see when we look at the world? Paul regarded Jesus' title of Lord as "the name" to which "every knee" would one day "bow" and which "every tongue" would "confess" (Phil. 2:10, 11). Have we heard what this message of universal homage is saying and does it color our view of the world? If in the light of 1:43–54 we could describe the world in negative terms, now by contrast it is a scene of rich potential toward which the church is ever to push its frontiers, making "disciples of all the nations" (Matt. 28:19) in the service of the "Son of David" (Matt. 1:1). Names are more than names, they are people; as people they are potential subjects of the King of kings.

DAVID, KEY TO HISTORY

2:3 The sons of Judah *were* Er, Onan, and Shelah. *These* three were born to him by the daughter of Shua, the Canaanitess. Er, the firstborn of Judah, was wicked in the sight of the LORD; so He killed him.

4 And Tamar, his daughter-in-law, bore him Perez and Zerah. All the sons of Judah *were* five.

5 The sons of Perez *were* Hezron and Hamul.

6 The sons of Zerah *were* Zimri, Ethan, Heman, Calcol, and Dara—five of them in all.

7 The son of Carmi *was* Achar, the troubler of Israel, who transgressed in the accursed thing.

8 The son of Ethan *was* Azariah.

9 Also the sons of Hezron who were born to him *were* Jerahmeel, Ram, and Chelubai.

10 Ram begot Amminadab, and Amminadab begot Nahshon, leader of the children of Judah;

11 Nahshon begot Salma, and Salma begot Boaz;

12 Boaz begot Obed, and Obed begot Jesse;

13 Jesse begot Eliab his firstborn, Abinadab the second, Shimea the third,

14 Nethanel the fourth, Raddai the fifth,

15 Ozem the sixth, *and* David the seventh.

16 Now their sisters *were* Zeruiah and Abigail. And the sons of Zeruiah *were* Abishai, Joab, and Asahel—three.

17 Abigail bore Amasa; and the father of Amasa *was* Jether the Ishmaelite.

18 Caleb the son of Hezron had children by Azubah, *his* wife, and by Jerioth. Now these were her sons: Jesher, Shobab, and Ardon.

19 When Azubah died, Caleb took Ephrath as his wife, who bore him Hur.

20 And Hur begot Uri, and Uri begot Bezalel.

21 Now afterward Hezron went in to the daughter of Machir the father of Gilead, whom he married when he *was* sixty years old; and she bore him Segub.

22 Segub begot Jair, who had twenty-three cities in the land of Gilead.

23 (Geshur and Syria took from them the towns of Jair, with Kenath and its towns—sixty towns.) All these *belonged to* the sons of Machir the father of Gilead.

24 After Hezron died in Caleb Ephrathah, Hezron's wife Abijah bore him Ashhur the father of Tekoa.

25 The sons of Jerahmeel, the firstborn of Hezron, *were* Ram, the firstborn, and Bunah, Oren, Ozem, *and* Ahijah.

26 Jerahmeel had another wife, whose name was Atarah; she was the mother of Onam.

27 The sons of Ram, the firstborn of Jerahmeel, were Maaz, Jamin, and Eker.

28 The sons of Onam were Shammai and Jada. The sons of Shammai *were* Nadab and Abishur.

29 And the name of the wife of Abishur *was* Abihail, and she bore him Ahban and Molid.

30 The sons of Nadab *were* Seled and Appaim; Seled died without children.

31 The son of Appaim *was* Ishi, the son of Ishi *was* Sheshan, and Sheshan's son *was* Ahlai.

32 The sons of Jada, the brother of Shammai, *were* Jether and Jonathan; Jether died without children.

33 The sons of Jonathan *were* Peleth and Zaza. These were the sons of Jerahmeel.

34 Now Sheshan had no sons, only daughters. And Sheshan had an Egyptian servant whose name *was* Jarha.

35 Sheshan gave his daughter to Jarha his servant as wife, and she bore him Attai.

36 Attai begot Nathan, and Nathan begot Zabad;

37 Zabad begot Ephlal, and Ephlal begot Obed;

38 Obed begot Jehu, and Jehu begot Azariah;

39 Azariah begot Helez, and Helez begot Eleasah;

40 Eleasah begot Sismai, and Sismai begot Shallum;

41 Shallum begot Jekamiah, and Jekamiah begot Elishama.

42 The descendants of Caleb the brother of Jerahmeel *were* Mesha, his firstborn, who was the father of Ziph, and the sons of Mareshah the father of Hebron.

43 The sons of Hebron *were* Korah, Tappuah, Rekem, and Shema.

44 Shema begot Raham the father of Jorkoam, and Rekem begot Shammai.

45 And the son of Shammai *was* Maon, and Maon *was* the father of Beth Zur.

46 Ephah, Caleb's concubine, bore Haran, Moza, and Gazez; and Haran begot Gazez.

47 And the sons of Jahdai *were* Regem, Jotham, Geshan, Pelet, Ephah, and Shaaph.

48 Maachah, Caleb's concubine, bore Sheber and Tirhanah.

49 She also bore Shaaph the father of Madmannah, Sheva the father of Machbenah and the father of Gibea. And the daughter of Caleb *was* Achsah.

50 These were the descendants of Caleb: The sons of Hur, the firstborn of Ephrathah, *were* Shobal the father of Kirjath Jearim,

51 Salma the father of Bethlehem, *and* Hareph the father of Beth Gader.

52 And Shobal the father of Kirjath Jearim had descendants: Haroeh, *and* half of the families of Manuhoth.

53 The families of Kirjath Jearim *were* the Ithrites, the Puthites, the Shumathites, and the Mishraites. From these came the Zorathites and the Eshtaolites.

54 The sons of Salma *were* Bethlehem, the Netophathites, Atroth Beth Joab, half of the Manahethites, and the Zorites.

55 And the families of the scribes who dwelt at Jabez *were* the Tirathites, the Shimeathites, *and* the Suchathites. These *were* the Kenites who came from Hammath, the father of the house of Rechab.

3:1 Now these were the sons of David who were born to him in Hebron: The firstborn *was* Amnon, by Ahinoam the Jezreelitess; the second, Daniel, by Abigail the Carmelitess;

2 the third, Absalom the son of Maacah, the daughter of Talmai, king of Geshur; the fourth, Adonijah the son of Haggith;

3 the fifth, Shephatiah, by Abital; the sixth, Ithream, by his wife Eglah.

4 *These* six were born to him in Hebron. There he reigned seven years and six months, and in Jerusalem he reigned thirty-three years.

5 And these were born to him in Jerusalem: Shimea, Shobab, Nathan, and Solomon—four by Bathshua the daughter of Ammiel.

6 Also *there* were Ibhar, Elishama, Eliphelet,

7 Nogah, Nepheg, Japhia,

8 Elishama, Eliada, and Eliphelet—nine *in all*.

9 *These were* all the sons of David, besides the sons of the concubines, and Tamar their sister.

10 Solomon's son *was* Rehoboam; Abijah *was* his son, Asa his son, Jehoshaphat his son,

11 Joram his son, Ahaziah his son, Joash his son,

12 Amaziah his son, Azariah his son, Jotham his son,

13 Ahaz his son, Hezekiah his son, Manasseh his son,

14 Amon his son, *and* Josiah his son.

15 The sons of Josiah *were* Johanan the firstborn,

the second Jehoiakim, the third Zedekiah, and the fourth Shallum.

16 The sons of Jehoiakim *were* Jeconiah his son *and* Zedekiah his son.

17 And the sons of Jeconiah *were* Assir, Shealtiel his son,

18 *and* Malchiram, Pedaiah, Shenazzar, Jecamiah, Hoshama, and Nedabiah.

19 The sons of Pedaiah *were* Zerubbabel and Shimei. The sons of Zerubbabel *were* Meshullam, Hananiah, Shelomith their sister,

20 and Hashubah, Ohel, Berechiah, Hasadiah, and Jushab-Hesed—five *in all*.

21 The sons of Hananiah *were* Pelatiah and Jeshaiah, the sons of Rephaiah, the sons of Arnan, the sons of Obadiah, and the sons of Shechaniah.

22 The son of Shechaniah was Shemaiah. The sons of Shemaiah *were* Hattush, Igal, Bariah, Neariah, and Shaphat—six *in all*.

23 The sons of Neariah *were* Elioenai, Hezekiah, and Azrikam—three *in all*.

24 The sons of Elioenai *were* Hodaviah, Eliashib, Pelaiah, Akkub, Johanan, Delaiah, and Anani—seven *in all*.

4:1 The sons of Judah *were* Perez, Hezron, Carmi, Hur, and Shobal.

2 And Reaiah the son of Shobal begot Jahath, and Jahath begot Ahumai and Lahad. These *were* the families of the Zorathites.

3 These *were* the sons *of the father* of Etam: Jezreel, Ishma, and Idbash; and the name of their sister *was* Hazelelponi;

4 and Penuel *was* the father of Gedor, and Ezer *was the* father of Hushah. These *were* the sons of Hur, the firstborn of Ephrathah the father of Bethlehem.

5 And Ashhur the father of Tekoa had two wives, Helah and Naarah.

6 Naarah bore him Ahuzzam, Hepher, Temeni, and Haahashtari. These *were* the sons of Naarah.

7 The sons of Helah *were* Zereth, Zohar, and Ethnan;

40

8 and Koz begot Anub, Zobebah, and the families of Aharhel the son of Harum.

9 Now Jabez was more honorable than his brothers, and his mother called his name Jabez, saying, "Because I bore *him* in pain."

10 And Jabez called on the God of Israel saying, "Oh, that You would bless me indeed, and enlarge my territory, that Your hand would be with me, and that You would keep *me* from evil, that I may not cause pain!" So God granted him what he requested.

11 Chelub the brother of Shuhah begot Mehir, who *was* the father of Eshton.

12 And Eshton begot Beth-Rapha, Paseah, and Tehinnah the father of Ir-Nahash. These *were* the men of Rechah.

13 The sons of Kenaz *were* Othniel and Seraiah. The sons of Othniel *were* Hathath,

14 and Meonothai *who* begot Ophrah. Seraiah begot Joab the father of Ge Harashim, for they were craftsmen.

15 The sons of Caleb the son of Jephunneh *were* Iru, Elah, and Naam. The son of Elah *was* Kenaz.

16 The sons of Jehallelel *were* Ziph, Ziphah, Tiria, and Asarel.

17 The sons of Ezrah *were* Jether, Mered, Epher, and Jalon. And *Mered's wife bore* Miriam, Shammai, and Ishbah the father of Eshtemoa.

18 (His wife Jehudijah bore Jered the father of Gedor, Heber the father of Sochoh, and Jekuthiel the father of Zanoah.) And these were the sons of Bithiah the daughter of Pharaoh, whom Mered took.

19 The sons of Hodiah's wife, the sister of Naham, *were* the fathers of Keilah the Garmite and of Eshtemoa the Maachathite.

20 And the sons of Shimon *were* Amnon, Rinnah, Ben-Hanan, and Tilon. And the sons of Ishi *were* Zoheth and Ben-Zoheth.

21 The sons of Shelah the son of Judah *were* Er the father of Lecah, Laadah the father of Mareshah, and the families of the house of the linen workers of the house of Ashbea;

22 also Jokim, the men of Chozeba, and Joash;

41

Saraph, who ruled in Moab, and Jashubi-Lehem.
Now the records are ancient.
23 These *were* the potters and those who dwell at
Netaim and Gederah; there they dwelt with the king
for his work.

1 *Chron. 2:3–4:23*

The tribes descended from Israel's sons are now listed, a process
which continues until chapter 9. The Chronicler has his favorites
from among the tribes and does not give them all the same coverage.
Pride of place and space is given to Judah: it comes first, and one-
third of all the tribal material is devoted to it. Why? For one thing,
most of the post-exilic state of Judah belonged to this tribe. There is
much more than tribalism here, though. Judah had remained loyal to
the Davidic line of kings, when most tribes seceded and founded the
northern kingdom. The Chronicler consistently ignores those kings
and refuses to mention them unless his southern history demands it.
The best reason for the stress on Judah is that it gives an opportunity
to delve into David's family tree. David was Judah's most famous
son. In fact, most of this Judean genealogy is taken up with David's
clan! David is the key to Judean, and indeed Israelite, history and
hopes. He is the focus of God's promise, and it is by hanging on to
David's coattails, as it were, that Israel has meaning. We at once
think of the Lord Jesus as the counterpart in the Christian dispensation. He is the fulfiller of hopes which in the Chronicler's time were
vested in David and his line.

1. *The royal family.* This genealogy is a work of art. It is a good
example of the way in which Old Testament writers often expressed
meaning through literary artistry. Check what I am going to say
with the text. It is complicated but worth grasping. The center of
Judah's genealogy runs from 2:10 to 3:24. It is prefaced by 2:9,
where we are introduced to Hezron's three sons, *"Jerahmeel, Ram,
and Chelubai* (or Caleb)." Then the Chronicler tells us about some of
Ram's descendants (2:10–17), some of Caleb's (2:18–24), and some of
Jerahmeel's (2:25–33). At that point he backtracks and goes into re-
verse, presenting more of Jerahmeel's progeny (2:34–41), then more
of Caleb's (2:42–55), and finally more of Ram's (3:1–24). The overall
effect is to pinpoint Ram's family at the start and finish. Why? Because they were David's kinfolk! These three concentric circles have

two more around them: the genealogy begins with Judah's sons, including Shelah (2:3, 4) and ends it with information about Shelah's family (4:21–23). It gives second place to the family of Perez (and Zerah) in 2:5–8, and the penultimate place in 4:1–20. The overall effect is to let David's clan, Hezron, dominate the center of the composition and begin and end that center with mention of David's closer kin. A pattern of concentric bands is used to convey convictions about the role of David's family in God's purposes.

2:10–17 and 3:1–24 belong together as two halves of the lineage of Ram. In fact David is the dividing point: 2:10–17 lists David's ancestors and brothers and sisters, while 3:1–24 enumerates David's descendants. What was obviously once a single document has been split in two. Early in the genealogy of Judah one is encouraged to look back to David and his forbearers. Toward the end of the genealogy one looks back at David again, now tracing the line of royal descent on to the Chronicler's time. The division conveys a sense of the overarching importance of David as a figure of the past and as a character whose importance continues to the present.

The line does not stop at the exile, although the royal family lost its power then. In 3:17 the margin should be followed: *"Jeconiah"* the captive is King Jehoiachin who was taken into exile by Nebuchadnezzar: see 2 Chronicles 36:9, 10. Yet the list carries on! Humanly speaking, there was good reason for it to have stopped, for a Davidic king never again ruled the throne of Judah. One might consider that the exilic and post-exilic names represent just continuing human interest in a family respected for old times' sake—just as today in Jewish circles families called Cohen and the like are respected as of priestly stock and have synagogue privileges, although Judaism now has no priesthood. Whether this view is right or wrong depends on an assessment of all the Chronicles material dealing with David and his dynasty. The content of the Chronicler's future hope has been vigorously discussed, with arguments on both sides. The reader is invited to look carefully at the evidence as it occurs. My own conviction is that the Chronicler did include what we call messianic expectations in his vision of Israel's future under God.

2. *Readiness for the kingdom.* If the Chronicler did expect a return to Davidic kingship, he here presents a picture of each generation of the family being ready for duty. *"Anani"* (3:24) might have thought that he would not stand much of a chance of reigning, if the call

came in his generation. He could have consoled himself with the consideration that according to 2:15 David too was the seventh son! I like this picture of availability. It whispers something to me about the Christian's need to be ready for service, for which we would more obviously turn to Eli's advice to young Samuel to be alert to God's call (1 Sam. 3:9). The burden of the passage is Israel's readiness for the restoration of Davidic kingship. The Christian parallel is the hope of the return of our King, for which we are to stay spiritually awake, so as not to be caught off guard (see Luke 12:35–40; 1 Thess. 5:4–6). "Satan aims directly at the throat of the Church," warned John Calvin, "when he destroys faith in the coming of Christ." A spirit of readiness leaves room for the sovereignty of God, which obviously underlies these verses too. It does not selfishly and neurotically insist that the King must come in my generation, nor does it mean selling one's soul to a particular political scenario. It has an openness to the will of God as to when and how.

I remember traveling around Greece in the summer of 1956. Everywhere I went I saw the same sign painted in black letters on the white walls: *o vasilefs erchete,* "The King is coming." At first I thought they were Christian graffiti! On inquiry I found it was a political slogan in connection with a referendum as to whether the monarchy should be restored. The Chronicler and his generation were in no position to hold such a referendum, subjects as they were of the Persian Empire. Political agitation would have been quickly suppressed. But in spirit this is where the Chronicler stood, I believe, and this is where today's church must stand: "The King is coming!"

3. *Race and religion.* Let us notice a phenomenon which peeps out in each of these three chapters quite casually and is all the more impressive for that. At 2:17 mention is made of an Ishmaelite father and at 2:34 of a mother who was an Egyptian slave. At 3:2 one of David's wives was a Geshurite (Aramean) princess and at 4:18 a mother is mentioned who was an Egyptian princess. The Chronicler could easily have suppressed these foreign references in his sources, had he been so inclined: Samuel Butler's dictum that "God cannot alter the past, historians can" is unfortunately true. There is evidence of different attitudes toward non-Jews in the post-exilic period. Ezra and Nehemiah took a hard line, insisting on divorce of foreign spouses and disowning of the children of mixed race (see Ezra 10:3; Neh. 13:3, referring to "all those of foreign descent," RSV). Scholars

admit that under the circumstances such an attitude is not difficult to understand and that the survival of the Jewish faith was at stake. The Chronicler, living and writing a little later, I believe, in this and other respects wanted to stop a policy appropriate for a previous period from crystalizing into a permanent, "safe" attitude of xenophobia and apartheid. He was not disposed to "cook the books," rewriting history by excluding descendants of foreign marriages from the genealogy of Judah. Significantly he preserved from 1 Kings a portion of Solomon's prayer about foreigners at 2 Chronicles 6:32, 33, to the effect that any foreigner who adopted Israel's faith was welcome at the temple—religious faith, not race, was the criterion. There is an openness here which, one suspects, met with criticism from some religious quarters in Judah. The Chronicler refused to align himself with a hard attitude toward other people. There is a side of human nature which likes to add to the faith and in order to feel more secure withdraws snail-like into an exclusive shell. Every Christian, of whatever race, needs to look closely at his or her own attitude toward other racial groups, to pray for the Spirit's touch of release from racism, and to live in accord with that prayer.

LIGHTED WINDOWS

2:3 The sons of Judah *were* Er, Onan, and Shelah. *These* three were born to him by the daughter of Shua, the Canaanitess. Er, the firstborn of Judah, was wicked in the sight of the LORD; so He killed him.

4 And Tamar, his daughter-in-law, bore him Perez and Zerah. All the sons of Judah *were* five.

7 The son of Carmi *was* Achar, the troubler of Israel, who transgressed in the accursed thing.

4:9 Now Jabez was more honorable than his brothers, and his mother called his name Jabez, saying, "Because I bore *him* in pain."

10 And Jabez called on the God of Israel saying, "Oh, that You would bless me indeed, and enlarge my territory, that Your hand would be with me, and that You would keep *me* from evil, that I may not cause pain!" So God granted him what he requested.

1 Chron. 2:3–4, 7; 4:9–10

The train slowed down as it traveled through the suburbs of north London in the dusk of evening. I glanced up from my book and recognized the area: I was nearly home. Alongside the train, across the tracks, and beyond backyards, was a row of apartments above the first-floor stores. Every window in the apartments was an empty black mirror or a curtained glow, except for one where the drapes had not been drawn. Curious, I stared at two people sitting talking in a brightly lit room. All those apartments were homes where people lived; in this one instance I caught a glimpse of human life before it slipped past the moving train. In this section there are three such glimpses into individual lives, which break the pattern of listing simply by names.

1. *Escape from death.* The first lighted window occurs in 2:3, 4. It is a study in contrasts. On the one hand there is straightforward justice done in verse 3, which the Chronicler has copied from Genesis 38:7. In the case of Judah's eldest son, Er, wickedness received its just deserts. On the other hand, Judah himself was no saint. The Chronicler assumes that his readers know the pathetic story of Genesis 38:8–26, a tangled tale of human grievance and disappointment and of a willful attempt to get one's rights. Read it over before we go on. Judah reacts with righteous indignation to the report that his daughter-in-law Tamar has descended to prostitution: "Bring her out and let her be burned!" (Gen. 38:24). He changes his tune when he is shown proof that he himself had unwittingly been Tamar's client. He realizes that it had been Tamar's way of getting even with him. It was a family scandal, and the Chronicler does not mince matters: as a result of the sexual union *"Tamar, his daughter-in-law, bore him Perez and Zerah"* (2:4). In Hebrew law this was incest, for the relationship was within the forbidden degrees of Leviticus 18:15. The Chronicler and his readers knew the ruling of Leviticus 20:12, the death sentence for both parties. This makes his placing the cases of verses 3 and 4 together very striking: the wicked son lost his life, while the wicked father and wife not only had their lives spared but won a role in the line that led to David. Matthew picked up the message from the Chronicler's genealogy and passed it on in his own: Tamar (and Bathsheba too) was a link in the chain of human lives that led eventually to Jesus (Matt. 1:3). There is a mysterious grace at work here, which the Chronicler underlines by his dramatic contrast. Human failure is woven into the ongoing purpose of God. It is one illustration among so many of that

side of God's character revealed in the Old Testament as "abounding in mercy" (Ps. 103:8: read on to v. 14) and reaffirmed in the New in terms of "the riches of His grace" (Eph. 1:7; 2:7). I sense that the Chronicler passed this point in his genealogy with a sigh of relief and a prayerful murmur of gratitude to God.

2. *A threat from within.* The second of our lighted windows occurs a few verses later, at verse 7. Here again our author presupposes knowledge of the narrative, in Joshua 6 and 7. If you are not familiar with it, look it up. There *"Achar"* is called Achan; here his name is slightly changed to give clearer expression to the play on words in Joshua 7:24–26. There "the Valley of Achor" means Trouble Valley, commemorating Achan as the cause of trouble for Israel. Achan deliberately disobeyed a divine mandate relating to the occupation of Jericho and kept spoils for himself, some of which should have been destroyed and others handed over to the sacred coffers. The selfish and sinful act contaminated the entire community and laid it under a divine curse. It was a dire situation: the existence of the people was threatened—almost as soon as they had set foot inside the promised land. Achan would have brought total disaster on them, had not God accepted a way of decontaminating Israel. Their early life in the land was marred by this failure. It was a sad beginning, curiously like the story of Ananias and Sapphira's greed in Acts 5. Human nature soon raises its ugly head and radically disrupts a new work of God, if it is not dealt with quickly. If 2:3, 4 pointed to God's grace, this incident presents a serious warning.

3. *Liberation from a neurosis.* The third lighted window reveals a happier vignette, in 4:9, 10. Like the previous one it centers around a play on words, for which the Hebrew mind had an almost superstitious regard. Verse 9 is deliberately provocative to a Hebrew way of thinking: Jabez enjoys a position of greater honor and status in the community than his brothers did. What, with an ill-omened name like Jabez (it means "pain")! How did he do it? In popular thinking so negative a name, which commemorated the hard time his mother had in giving birth to him, made Jabez a born loser. Dogged with such an unlucky name, how could he ever succeed in life? But he did! The Chronicler gives away Jabez's secret with relish in verse 10. It was prayer that did it—or rather the God to whom Jabez had the sense to pray. Why did I say that the Chronicler wrote verse 10 with relish? Because it is a firm part of his spirituality to stress the power

of prayer, as we shall often observe. Here Jabez knew of resources in the communal faith which were available to him: he *called on the God of Israel"* (4:10). His prayer was for blessing and growth, which in his case involved keeping negative factors at bay, getting harm warded off by God's powerful hand, lest harm should "cause him pain," as the Hebrew may be better rendered. His name created an emotional hang-up, stopping him from leading a full life. Only God could deal with that negative image and flood his life with blessing. He had a psychological handicap, none the less real for being psychological. He was able to gain release from its grip and enjoy a social position of respect and honor which naturally he would never have attained, born loser as he was. Robert L. Stevenson contributed to this theme when he wrote: "Life does not consist of having a good hand at cards, but of learning how to play a poor hand well." The Chronicler would have agreed, adding that in the game of life an essential part of learning how to play is learning how to pray.

THE SECRET OF SURVIVAL

4:24 The sons of Simeon *were* Nemuel, Jamin, Jarib, Zerah, *and* Shaul,

25 Shallum his son, Mibsam his son, and Mishma his son.

26 And the sons of Mishma *were* Hamuel his son, Zacchur his son, and Shimei his son.

27 Shimei had sixteen sons and six daughters; but his brothers did not have many children, nor did any of their families multiply as much as the children of Judah.

28 They dwelt at Beersheba, Moladah, Hazar Shual,

29 Bilhah, Ezem, Tolad,

30 Bethuel, Hormah, Ziklag,

31 Beth Marcaboth, Hazar Susim, Beth Biri, and at Shaaraim. These *were* their cities until the reign of David.

32 And their villages *were* Etam, Ain, Rimmon, Tochen, and Ashan—five cities—

33 and all the villages that *were* around these cities as far as Baal. These *were* their dwelling places, and they maintained their genealogy:

34 Meshobab, Jamlech, and Joshah the son of Amaziah;

35 Joel, and Jehu the son of Joshibiah, the son of Seraiah, the son of Asiel;

36 Elioenai, Jaakobah, Jeshohaiah, Asaiah, Adiel, Jesimiel, and Benaiah;

37 Ziza the son of Shiphi, the son of Allon, the son of Jedaiah, the son of Shimri, the son of Shemaiah—

38 these mentioned by name *were* leaders in their families, and their father's house increased greatly.

39 So they went to the entrance of Gedor, as far as the east side of the valley, to seek pasture for their flocks.

40 And they found rich, good pasture, and the land *was* broad, quiet, and peaceful; for some Hamites formerly lived there.

41 These recorded by name came in the days of Hezekiah king of Judah; and they attacked their tents and the Meunites who were found there, and utterly destroyed them, as it is to this day. So they dwelt in their place, because *there was* pasture for their flocks there.

42 Now *some* of them, five hundred men of the sons of Simeon, went to Mount Seir, having as their captains Pelatiah, Neariah, Rephaiah, and Uzziel, the sons of Ishi.

43 And they defeated the rest of the Amalekites who had escaped. They have dwelt there to this day.

5:1 Now the sons of Reuben the firstborn of Israel—he *was* indeed the firstborn, but because he defiled his father's bed, his birthright was given to the sons of Joseph, the son of Israel, so that the genealogy is not listed according to the birthright;

2 yet Judah prevailed over his brothers, and from him *came* a ruler, although the birthright was Joseph's—

3 the sons of Reuben the firstborn of Israel were Hanoch, Pallu, Hezron, and Carmi.

4 The sons of Joel *were* Shemaiah his son, Gog his son, Shimei his son,

5 Micah his son, Reaiah his son, Baal his son,

6 and Beerah his son, whom Tiglath-Pileser king

49

of Assyria carried into captivity. He *was* leader of the Reubenites.

7 And his brethren by their families, when the genealogy of their generations was registered: the chief, Jeiel, and Zechariah,

8 and Bela the son of Azaz, the son of Shema, the son of Joel, who dwelt in Aroer, as far as Nebo and Baal Meon.

9 Eastward they settled as far as the entrance of the wilderness this side of the River Euphrates, because their cattle had multiplied in the land of Gilead.

10 Now in the days of Saul they made war with the Hagrites, who fell by their hand; and they dwelt in their tents throughout the entire *area* east of Gilead.

11 And the children of Gad dwelt next to them in the land of Bashan as far as Salcah:

12 Joel *was* the chief, Shapham the next, then Jaanai and Shaphat in Bashan,

13 and their brethren of their father's house: Michael, Meshullam, Sheba, Jorai, Jachan, Zia, and Heber—seven *in all.*

14 These *were* the children of Abihail the son of Huri, the son of Jaroah, the son of Gilead, the son of Michael, the son of Jeshishai, the son of Jahdo, the son of Buz;

15 Ahi the son of Abdiel, the son of Guni, *was* chief of their father's house.

16 And *the Gadites* dwelt in Gilead, in Bashan and in its villages, and in all the common-lands of Sharon within their borders.

17 All these were registered by genealogies in the days of Jotham king of Judah, and in the days of Jeroboam king of Israel.

18 The sons of Reuben, the Gadites, and half the tribe of Manasseh *had* forty-four thousand seven hundred and sixty valiant men, men able to bear shield and sword, to shoot with the bow, and skillful in war, who went to war.

19 They made war with the Hagrites, Jetur, Naphish, and Nodab.

20 And they were helped against them, and the

Hagrites were delivered into their hand, and all who *were* with them, for they cried out to God in the battle. He heeded their prayer, because they put their trust in Him.

21 Then they took away their livestock—fifty thousand of their camels, two hundred and fifty thousand of their sheep, and two thousand of their donkeys—also one hundred thousand of their men;

22 for many fell dead, because the war *was* God's. And they dwelt in their place until the captivity.

23 So the children of the half-tribe of Manasseh dwelt in the land. Their *numbers* increased from Bashan to Baal Hermon, that is, to Senir, or Mount Hermon.

24 These *were* the heads of their fathers' houses: Epher, Ishi, Eliel, Azriel, Jeremiah, Hodaviah, and Jahdiel. They were mighty men of valor, famous men, *and* heads of their fathers' houses.

25 And they were unfaithful to the God of their fathers, and played the harlot after the gods of the peoples of the land, whom God had destroyed before them.

26 So the God of Israel stirred up the spirit of Pul king of Assyria, that is, Tiglath-Pileser king of Assyria. He carried the Reubenites, the Gadites, and the half-tribe of Manasseh into captivity. He took them to Halah, Habor, Hara, and the river of Gozan to this day.

1 Chron. 4:24–5:26

Further tribal genealogies are now given, Simeon's in 4:27–43 and those of the two and a half tribes who lived east of the Jordan in 5:1–26. The Chronicler intended us to look at these together because they are polarized at the ends of the two passages. One group survived in the land *"to this day"* (4:43, compare v. 41), while the other was exiled from the land *"to this day"* (5:26). The polarization is provocative: it stimulates the reader to ask where the second group went wrong.

1. *The survivors.* The little tribe of Simeon, whose territory lay to the south of Judah, is put after Judah because it was absorbed into Judah for purposes of administration, as 4:31 hints. The Chronicler

admired little Simeon not just because it remained within the political orbit of Judah, but because it was a model of the blessing that resulted from staying with the Davidic dynasty, in line with God's will. The genealogy strays from its strict genre, which is represented in 4:24–27, and regales us with geography (vv. 28–33), leadership (vv. 34–38), and geographically oriented history (vv. 39–43). There is a stress on geography because in the Old Testament it is part of theology! The basic theology of the Old Testament is a triangle with three points: God, Israel, and the land. The theme of the land—promised, given, taken away, and given back—is a thread that weaves in and out of the providential history of God's people. From God's perspective the land is His gift of blessing; from Israel's standpoint it is a thermometer that registers their level of (dis)obedience to God. This theology of the land runs all through 4:24–5:26. The post-exilic community especially prized the land because they knew what it was to lose it. They relished return to the land, in accord with Solomon's prayer in 2 Chronicles 6:24–25, and they wanted to hold on to it. So the Chronicler's setting side by side stories of winning and losing the land was very relevant. In more general terms, the way of blessing and the way of backsliding are contrasted.

In 4:39–43 are two accounts of tribal expansion which have an "old world" ring and could have come straight out of the Book of Joshua. There is an assumption that Israel had a right to the land, not an inherent right, but a right in the sense of enjoying it when God gave it. By that right Simeon overcame resistance to their expansion. As we shall see in chapter 5, the right could be forfeited by disobedience—and in 2 Chronicles 6:24–25 and elsewhere repentance is the only human means whereby God would give it back.

2. *The losers.* The Transjordan tribes of Reuben (5:1–10), Gad (vv. 11–17), and the eastern half of Manasseh (vv. 23–24) are dealt with in a single narrative, as their common history in verses 18–22, 25, 26 indicates. Their story ends in tragedy. Yet they started well. Reuben's territorial experience (vv. 9–10) reads like a re-run of Simeon's, and that of the other groups (vv. 16, 23) is similar. They not only started well, they continued well for a time. A military campaign in which all three groups participated was successful. Why? For two reasons, because they prayed and, probing deeper, because their prayer was grounded in a true faith (v. 20). Unfortunately, they did not maintain their faith. They slipped into religious

infidelity, breaking the first of the Ten Commandments: "You shall have no other gods before Me" (Exod. 20:3). They suffered a crushing defeat at the hands of the Assyrian army, actually in 734 B.C., but their real enemy was God Himself. They lost the land and, attests the Chronicler, they have never come back.

The story is an uncomfortable one. Both the writer and his first readers would have winced over it, for Judah too had suffered loss of its land because of unfaithfulness to God (see 9:1). But the lesson must never be forgotten: the only way forward in the land and so in life was to stay with God, and they strayed from Him at their peril. "Stay—don't stray" is the message. Was not Paul thinking on these lines when he warned Gentile believers against gloating over their incorporation into God's people and the Jew's exclusion? "You stand by faith. Do not be haughty, but fear," he cautioned. Enjoyment of God's goodness would be theirs, "if you continue in His goodness. Otherwise you also will be cut off" (Rom. 11:20–22; compare Col. 1:23). The faith which is to be maintained is not a human virtue, but the humble commitment of oneself to God. As 5:20 indicated, it manifests itself in prayer to God for help. It is not a matter of our striving as feverishly as we can, but is allied with a dependent attitude of prayer, such as Psalm 119 exemplifies: "Incline my heart to Your testimonies" (v. 36) and "keep steady my steps" (v. 133, RSV). For the Chronicler and for us this is the secret of survival.

CHAPTER TWO

God's Relay Race

1 Chronicles 6:1–9:34

"History," said Thomas Carlisle, "is the essence of innumerable biographies." For the Chronicler it was both that and a single biography. The work of God and Israel's witness to God are both being traced tribe by tribe in the genealogies of chapters 1–9. Surveying so much history within a narrow span meant that eventful lives were mostly reduced to names. The overall message is not obscured, that God preserved a people as His witnesses down the centuries—and that the present generation of His people had received a living heritage which they were to promote and pass on. In spirit the Chronicler stands at the point of Hebrews 12:1, arguing a contemporary challenge from a past succession of believers: "Therefore we also . . . let us run with endurance the race that is set before us."

Be that as it may, do I see readers who are New Testament buffs fidgeting with impatience, and do I hear them muttering about "endless genealogies" being unprofitable, with reference to 1 Timothy 1:4? I am sure that it was not simply such genealogies as these that were being condemned, but fanciful interpretations. The Talmud has preserved a disapproving statement about rabbinic exposition of 1 Chronicles 8:38–9:44: "There are four hundred camel loads of exegetical interpretations of the material between the name Azel in 1 Chronicles 8:38 and the Azel in 1 Chronicles 9:44"! Even in reading the text there is a need not to be distracted by details but to stand back and grasp the organizing principles of the genealogies, lest we fail to see the wood for the trees.

1 Chronicles 2:3–9:34 really falls into five parts, although for convenience we have split the passage into two. Those five parts are a beginning, a middle, and an end, and two further portions sandwiched in between. The beginning is the genealogy of Judah, the

center is that of Levi, and the end that of Benjamin. Between the beginning and the middle are genealogies of half the northern tribes, and between the middle and the end are the genealogies of the other half. The three main sections represent the heritage of the dominant tribes in the state of Judah when the Chronicler lived, while the two intermediate sections are his insistence that the northern tribes still have a role in God's purposes. Through the Chronicler God was saying to the state of Judah, "Other sheep I have which are not of this fold; . . . and there will be one flock and one shepherd" (John 10:16).

PUTTING GOD AT THE CENTER

6:1 The sons of Levi *were* Gershon, Kohath, and Merari.

2 The sons of Kohath *were* Amram, Izhar, Hebron, and Uzziel.

3 The children of Amram *were* Aaron, Moses, and Miriam. And the sons of Aaron *were* Nadab, Abihu, Eleazar, and Ithamar.

4 Eleazar begot Phinehas, *and* Phinehas begot Abishua;

5 Abishua begot Bukki, and Bukki begot Uzzi;

6 Uzzi begot Zerahiah, and Zerahiah begot Meraioth;

7 Meraioth begot Amariah, and Amariah begot Ahitub;

8 Ahitub begot Zadok, and Zadok begot Ahimaaz;

9 Ahimaaz begot Azariah, and Azariah begot Johanan;

10 Johanan begot Azariah (it was he who ministered as priest in the temple that Solomon built in Jerusalem);

11 Azariah begot Amariah, and Amariah begot Ahitub;

12 Ahitub begot Zadok, and Zadok begot Shallum;

13 Shallum begot Hilkiah, and Hilkiah begot Azariah;

14 Azariah begot Seraiah, and Seraiah begot Jehozadak.

15 Jehozadak went *into captivity* when the LORD carried Judah and Jerusalem into captivity by the hand of Nebuchadnezzar.

16 The sons of Levi *were* Gershon, Kohath, and Merari.

17 These are the names of the sons of Gershon: Libni and Shimei.

18 The sons of Kohath *were* Amram, Izhar, Hebron, and Uzziel.

19 The sons of Merari *were* Mahli and Mushi. Now these *are* the families of the Levites according to their fathers:

20 Of Gershon *were* Libni his son, Jahath his son, Zimmah his son,

21 Joah his son, Iddo his son, Zerah his son, *and* Jeatherai his son.

22 The sons of Kohath *were* Amminadab his son, Korah his son, Assir his son,

23 Elkanah his son, Ebiasaph his son, Assir his son,

24 Tahath his son, Uriel his son, Uzziah his son, and Shaul his son.

25 The sons of Elkanah *were* Amasai and Ahimoth.

26 *As for* Elkanah, the sons of Elkanah *were* Zophai his son, Nahath his son,

27 Eliab his son, Jeroham his son, *and* Elkanah his son.

28 The sons of Samuel *were Joel* the firstborn, and Abijah the second.

29 The sons of Merari *were* Mahli, Libni his son, Shimei his son, Uzzah his son,

30 Shimea his son, Haggiah his son, *and* Asaiah his son.

31 Now these are the men whom David appointed over the service of song in the house of the LORD, after the ark came to rest.

32 They were ministering with music before the dwelling place of the tabernacle of meeting, until Solomon had built the house of the LORD in Jerusalem, and they served in their office according to their order.

33 And these *are* the ones who ministered with

their sons: Of the sons of the Kohathites *were* Heman the singer, the son of Joel, the son of Samuel,

34 the son of Elkanah, the son of Jeroham, the son of Eliel, the son of Toah,

35 the son of Zuph, the son of Elkanah, the son of Mahath, the son of Amasai,

36 the son of Elkanah, the son of Joel, the son of Azariah, the son of Zephaniah,

37 the son of Tahath, the son of Assir, the son of Ebiasaph, the son of Korah,

38 the son of Izhar, the son of Kohath, the son of Levi, the son of Israel.

39 And his brother Asaph, who stood at his right hand, *was* Asaph the son of Berachiah, the son of Shimea,

40 the son of Michael, the son of Baaseiah, the son of Malchijah,

41 the son of Ethni, the son of Zerah, the son of Adaiah,

42 the son of Ethan, the son of Zimmah, the son of Shimei,

43 the son of Jahath, the son of Gershon, the son of Levi.

44 Their brethren, the sons of Merari, on the left hand, *were* Ethan the son of Kishi, the son of Abdi, the son of Malluch,

45 the son of Hashabiah, the son of Amaziah, the son of Hilkiah,

46 the son of Amzi, the son of Bani, the son of Shamer,

47 the son of Mahli, the son of Mushi, the son of Merari, the son of Levi.

48 And their brethren, the Levites, *were* appointed to every kind of service of the tabernacle of the house of God.

49 But Aaron and his sons offered sacrifices on the altar of burnt offering and on the altar of incense, for all the work of the Most Holy *Place,* and to make atonement for Israel, according to all that Moses the servant of God had commanded.

50 Now these *are* the sons of Aaron: Eleazar his son, Phinehas his son, Abishua his son,

51 Bukki his son, Uzzi his son, Zerahiah his son,

52 Meraioth his son, Amariah his son, Ahitub his son,

53 Zadok his son, *and* Ahimaaz his son.

54 Now these *are* their dwelling places throughout their settlements in their territory, for they were *given* by lot to the sons of Aaron, of the family of the Kohathites:

55 They gave them Hebron in the land of Judah, with its surrounding common-lands.

56 But the fields of the city and its villages they gave to Caleb the son of Jephunneh.

57 And to the sons of Aaron they gave *one of* the cities of refuge, Hebron; also Libnah with its common-lands, Jattir, Eshtemoa with its common-lands,

58 Hilen with its common-lands, Debir with its common-lands,

59 Ashan with its common-lands, and Beth Shemesh with its common-lands.

60 And from the tribe of Benjamin: Geba with its common-lands, Alemeth with its common-lands, and Anathoth with its common-lands. All their cities among their families *were* thirteen.

61 To the rest of the family of the tribe of the Kohathites *they gave* by lot ten cities from half the tribe of Manasseh.

62 And to the sons of Gershon, throughout their families, *they gave* thirteen cities from the tribe of Issachar, from the tribe of Asher, from the tribe of Naphtali, and from the tribe of Manasseh in Bashan.

63 To the sons of Merari, throughout their families, *they gave* twelve cities from the tribe of Reuben, from the tribe of Gad, and from the tribe of Zebulun.

64 So the children of Israel gave *these* cities with their common-lands to the Levites.

65 And they gave by lot from the tribe of the children of Judah, from the tribe of the children of Simeon, and from the tribe of the children of Benjamin these cities which are called by *their* names.

66 Now some of the families of the sons of Kohath *were given* cities as their territory from the tribe of Ephraim.

67 And they gave them *one of* the cities of refuge, Shechem with its common-lands, in the mountains of Ephraim, also Gezer with its common-lands,

68 Jokmeam with its common-lands, Beth Horon with its common-lands,

69 Aijalon with its common-lands, and Gath Rimmon with its common-lands.

70 And from the half-tribe of Manasseh: Aner with its common-lands and Bileam with its common-lands, for the rest of the family of the sons of Kohath.

71 From the family of the half-tribe of Manasseh the sons of Gershon *were given* Golan in Bashan with its common-lands and Ashtaroth with its common-lands.

72 And from the tribe of Issachar: Kedesh with its common-lands, Daberath with its common-lands,

73 Ramoth with its common-lands, and Anem with its common-lands.

74 And from the tribe of Asher: Mashal with its common-lands, Abdon with its common-lands,

75 Hukok with its common-lands, and Rehob with its common-lands.

76 And from the tribe of Naphtali: Kedesh in Galilee with its common-lands, Hammon with its common-lands, and Kirjathaim with its common-lands.

77 From the tribe of Zebulun the rest of the children of Merari *were given* Rimmon with its common-lands and Tabor with its common-lands.

78 And on the other side of the Jordan, across from Jericho, on the east side of the Jordan, *they were given* from the tribe of Reuben: Bezer in the wilderness with its common-lands, Jahzah with its common-lands,

79 Kedemoth with its common-lands, and Mephaath with its common-lands.

80 And from the tribe of Gad: Ramoth in Gilead with its common-lands, Mahanaim with its common-lands,

81 Heshbon with its common-lands, and Jazer with its common-lands.

1 Chron. 6:1–81

The Chronicler prized the tribe of Levi. He devoted eighty-one verses to it, not much less than the hundred verses devoted to Judah.

The emphasis on Levi carried a theological message. The temple was of crucial importance for the post-exilic community of Judah, and the tribe of Levi had a divine commission to be its ministers. From a human perspective the size of the genealogy reflects the extensiveness of the records available in the Jerusalem archives. In order to officiate at the temple one had to prove hereditary legitimacy. Ezra 2:62–63 paint an unhappy picture of priests who could not verify their claims and were debarred from temple service. The Chronicler must have been glad to get his hands on the available records and to give full coverage to this tribe, because their existence was a witness to the temple and so to God.

One of the Chronicler's main aims in writing his history was to promote the interests of the temple. As the history continues, he leaves his readers in no doubt about his convictions that the temple merited the community's unstinting support and that worship should be conducted in a traditional and proper manner. This chapter is a foretaste of themes and emphases which will often recur. For the Chronicler the temple stood at the heart of Judah. Putting Levi in the very middle of his genealogical spectrum is a symbolic reflection of this belief. He seems to be following a cue from an earlier representation of God's people. Numbers 1:47–2:34 describes the arrangement of the tribes as they encamped in the wilderness. They camped in a square. On the east side were Judah, Issachar, and Zebulun; on the south Simeon, Reuben, and Gad; on the north Dan, Asher, and Naphtali; and on the west Ephraim, Manasseh, and Benjamin. And in the center—yes, you have guessed—the tribe of Levi. In fact they too formed four groups, Moses, Aaron, and the priests on the east side and the three clans of Levites, Merari, Gershon, and Kohath, on the other sides. In the absolute center stood the sacred tabernacle; its guardian, the tribe of Levi, surrounded it.

There is a beautiful spirituality about this ground plan which gave centrality to the tabernacle and its ministers. The Chronicler, who had a good eye for spirituality, appreciated it so much that he took it over as the design for his genealogical chapters, in which he seems to be following the layout of the wilderness camp as closely as he could. He also seems to be saying to his first readers that for "us" the temple corresponds to the tabernacle of olden times as a sort of dispensational counterpart. This latter fact was important since the

Torah or Law spoke much about the tabernacle as the holy focus of God's special presence, but for historical reasons had nothing to say about the temple. It is for this reason that in later chapters the Chronicler is going to stress that the ark, which the tabernacle housed, was brought to Jerusalem by David and that the temple was built for it by Solomon. The temple was the bonafide successor to the tabernacle and bore the same stamp of divine authority. "By what authority are You doing these things? And who gave you this authority?" (Matt. 21:23), Jesus was asked by the religious leaders of His day—a very important question. Religious claims are not necessarily true. There are many prophetic figures on the contemporary scene about whom one needs to take seriously John's advice to "test the spirits" (1 John 4:1).

The Chronicler's overall aim in his work was to establish that post-exilic temple worship was grounded in God's will, and he encouraged his readers to cherish it accordingly. The pre-exilic temple housed the ark, the symbol of God's presence with His people. The post-exilic community suffered the embarrassment of having no ark to put in it: evidently it was destroyed or mislaid when Jerusalem fell in 586 B.C. But the temple was still regarded as "the Lord's house" (Hag. 1:2), "the temple of the Lord" (Zech. 6:12–15), and "this house of God" (Ezra 6:16). The Chronicler too implies equivalent value for the pre-exilic and post-exilic temples, as the focal point of God's presence with His people and the prescribed meeting place for sacrifice and worship. The tribe of Levi had the function of maintaining this sacred place and its services. In their central position among the genealogies they reflected the role of the temple as the hub of the community.

Travelers through the English countryside often remark on a scene that greets them repeatedly, a village clustering around a dominant building, the parish church with its tall tower or steeple pointing up to heaven, a landmark for miles around. There is a representation of such a phenomenon in a painting by Lyonel Feininger, executed in the cubist tradition, called "The Church." I am proud to have a copy of it hanging in my home. It is a picture of houses surrounding a church. All the lines in the picture bring the eye down to this central feature; then the eye is taken up by the spire into heaven. It expresses the truth of the church as the heart of society, drawing the community to itself and then directing it to God.

One could conceive of a number of applications of the Chronicler's focus on the temple. Yet we would not represent his mind adequately if we simply spoke of putting God at the center of the individual's life. A truth faithful to his plain intent is the importance of institutional religion for the people of God. I am not claiming any such theological role for church buildings as the temple had, but the Christian faith necessarily has its institutional forms. From this perspective I can appreciate why Methodists refer to the main hall of a church as the sanctuary. There is a dimension of Christian experience which is lacking for those who worship solely in front of a television set or in private devotions. Over against such a solitary form of faith we may set the testimony of Psalm 42. Enforced deprivation of corporate worship was a source of deep anguish for the psalmist. He remembered with nostalgia the times when "I used to go with the multitude; I went with them to the house of God, with the voice of joy and praise, with a multitude that kept a pilgrim feast" (Ps. 42:4). The surrender of oneself to a worshiping group becomes a token of self-commitment to God. It is the opening of a door, which makes it possible for Him to enter one's life, enriching it and turning it in new directions. In a communal context self-centeredness is challenged and made aware of realities outside itself.

There is a healthy ring about a testimony such as Psalm 122:1, "I was glad when they said to me, 'Let us go into the house of the Lord!' Our feet have been standing within your gates, O Jerusalem!" This communal enthusiasm robustly defies the individualism rampant in our Western society, an individualism which is both the stepmother and stepchild of Protestantism. It refuses to acquiesce in that walling off of oneself from others, which so common a cultural object as the automobile serves to accentuate. For the Chronicler there was necessarily a communal side to putting God at the center of human affairs. Personal faith is essential, but it must find communal expression, if it is to be true to the Bible. "The New Testament knows nothing of a solitary religion," affirmed John Wesley. Nor does the Old Testament.

The details of the chapter introduce us to the various groups functioning in the temple, who are to find mention throughout Chronicles. The chapter falls into five sections.

1. *High priests.* Verses 1–15 present a list of the high priests, under God the leaders of the religious institution. The priests were a

branch line of the tribe of Levi, traced through Aaron, and the high priest belonged to this line. The list is carried down to the end of the monarchy, since the purpose of chapters 2-8 is to supply pre-exilic material, while chapter 9 takes the history on into the post-exilic age. There was an exception to this policy in the listing of the Davidic line down into pre-exilic times. The Chronicler could not resist leaping ahead in the case of David's family. That exception to the general rule is significant: it is a strong hint of a hope centering around the Davidic line. Strangely in this chapter the Chronicler has nothing to say about the priestly lines apart from that of the high priests. His heart is with the Levites.

2. *Levites.* In verses 16–30 he bids us meet for the first time, and by no means the last, the three clans of Levites, Gershon (elsewhere often Gershom), Kohath, and Merari. If the Chronicler has a love for the Levites, his special love is the three guilds of singers established by David, which he lists in verses 31–47. These are the guilds of Heman, Asaph, and Ethan (elsewhere in Chronicles often replaced by Jeduthun), who were descended from Kohath, Gershon, and Merari through their second sons. We certainly have not heard the last of these choirs. Here the Chronicler brings them on the stage and has them take an initial bow.

3. *What the priests and Levites did.* Verses 48 and 49 are a brief paragraph about the functions of the two groups, the priests being occupied with sacrifice and the innermost part of the temple, the Holy of Holies, and the Levites with responsibility for the rest of the work of the sanctuary.

4. *High priests again.* Verses 50–53 repeat the high priestly line down to David's time (compare vv. 4–9). Why was earlier material repeated? Surely it reflects a conception of the vital role which David had. The Chronicler thought of an old order, still largely valid, and a new order which vitally added to God's revelation as to how Israel should worship. The priesthood, established by *"Moses"* as *"the servant of God"* (v. 49), had a continuing authority. In David's time a dynamic new element emerged, the revelation of the temple as the focus of future worship, part of which was to be the system of Levitical choirs. In fact, the Chronicler stresses that when David brought the ark to Jerusalem and housed it temporarily in a tent, he then established these choirs to minister *"with music"* (v. 32).

In juggling with these conceptions of things old and new the

Chronicler reminds me of the Old and New Testaments with their respective eras. For us the counterpart to David as the new figure who revealed God's will is of course Jesus, the Son of David. Just as David's work did not cancel out the former revelation but vitally added to it, so it is the conviction of the church that the New Testament does not replace the Old, but is set alongside it to form God's complete revelation. I say that this is the church's conviction, but I speak theoretically. Sadly the actual testimony of the church falls far short of this ideal.

A survey was carried out in Victorian London in 1896. A significant number of churches were canvassed on a particular Sunday in March to find out the biblical texts of the sermons. The results showed that three-quarters of the texts were from the New Testament. A similar survey today anywhere in the Western world—I suspect that Africa might yield a different result—would most probably come up with an even higher percentage of New Testament texts. Latent in this phenomenon is a general assumption that the Christian Bible is the New Testament and perhaps, grudgingly, the Psalms. This is little other than heresy. My hope is that the Old Testament volumes of The Communicator's Commentary will help to filter to the modern church a conviction of the value of the Old Testament. As an Old Testament professor, I admit to some bias but venture to claim that it is a necessary bias! The time has come for positive discrimination in favor of the Old Testament, to compensate for long neglect.

5. *Levitical lands.* Verses 54–81 give details of the territories allotted to the tribe of Levi. This tribe had no mass holding of land comparable to those of its fellow tribes. It was maintained partly by the tithes and offerings given to God and partly by the allocation of land from within areas belonging to the other tribes, in recognition of its religious duties. The saying "The Lord is my portion" seems originally to have been used among the tribe of Levi in acknowledgment of this fact. In the psalms it has gained a far wider meaning as a beautiful expression of faith in God as the mainstay of the believer's life (see Pss. 16:5; 73:26). The land is catalogued by tribes (vv. 54–66) and by cities within tribal areas (vv. 67–81). The list had become a dead letter by the Chronicler's time, for the post-exilic state of Judah did not even occupy all the traditional area of the tribe of Judah, let alone other tribal areas. No matter, it had a message for his people, geographically shrunken though they were. Tra-

ditionally each of the tribes gave up part of its territory to God's religious representatives. It was like rent, for their surrender of part of their land spelled God's claim on the whole.

A firm part of Israel's understanding of the land was that it belonged to God. "The land is Mine," He proclaimed (Lev. 25:23). This factor was the theological basis of land tenure and economic theory in Israelite thinking, as the context of that verse reveals. Each tribe in turn gave partial expression to this truth by bestowing part of its territory on the tribe of Levi, to live in and to pasture their livestock. This shows a high regard for the temple as central to the life of Israel. It was evidenced not only in regular pilgrimage to Jerusalem but in allocating specific land in the home area to temple personnel.

This principle makes me think of God's claim on the Christian's life in all its aspects. It is not difficult to speak of surrendering one's life to God or to sing "All for Jesus." To be meaningful there must be practical expression in the allocation of time and resources to God and so to God's agencies in the world. Surrender of what a person has means not flinging it away, but placing it at the feet of the Lord and recognizing that to have possessions is to be the steward of the Master. One's financial resources, one's time, one's home—every aspect of human life—must have its quota of that which is used directly for God, for maintaining His work and spreading His love. This will be a sign that the whole of life belongs to God and is to be lived for Him.

OUR DENOMINATION AND GOD'S CHURCH

7:1 The sons of Issachar *were* Tola, Puah, Jashub, and Shimron—four *in all.*

2 The sons of Tola *were* Uzzi, Rephaiah, Jeriel, Jahmai, Jibsam, and Shemuel, heads of their father's house. *The sons* of Tola *were* mighty men of valor in their generations, their number in the days of David *was* twenty-two thousand six hundred.

3 The son of Uzzi *was* Izrahiah, and the sons of Izrahiah *were* Michael, Obadiah, Joel, and Ishiah. All five of them *were* chief men.

4 And with them, by their generations, according to their fathers' houses, *were* thirty-six thousand

troops ready for war; for they had many wives and sons.

5 Now their brethren among all the families of Issachar *were* mighty men of valor, listed by their genealogies, eighty-seven thousand in all.

6 *The sons* of Benjamin *were* Bela, Becher, and Jediael—three *in all*.

7 The sons of Bela were Ezbon, Uzzi, Uzziel, Jerimoth, and Iri—five *in all*. They *were* heads of *their* fathers' houses, and they were listed by their genealogies, twenty-two thousand and thirty-four mighty men of valor.

8 The sons of Becher *were* Zemirah, Joash, Eliezer, Elioenai, Omri, Jerimoth, Abijah, Anathoth, and Alemeth. All these *are* the sons of Becher.

9 And they were recorded by genealogy according to their generations, heads of their fathers' houses, twenty thousand two hundred mighty men of valor.

10 The son of Jediael *was* Bilhan, and the sons of Bilhan *were* Jeush, Benjamin, Ehud, Chenaanah, Zethan, Tharshish, and Ahishahar.

11 All these sons of Jediael *were* heads of their fathers' houses; *there were* seventeen thousand two hundred mighty men of valor fit to go out for war *and* battle.

12 Shuppim and Huppim *were* the sons of Ir, *and* Hushim *was* the son of Aher.

13 The sons of Naphtali *were* Jahziel, Guni, Jezer, and Shallum, the sons of Bilhah.

14 The descendants of Manasseh: his Syrian concubine bore him Machir the father of Gilead, the father of Asriel.

15 Machir took as his wife *the sister* of Huppim and Shuppim, whose name *was* Maachah. The name of *Gilead's* grandson *was* Zelophehad, but Zelophehad begot only daughters.

16 (Maachah the wife of Machir bore a son, and she called his name Peresh. The name of his brother *was* Sheresh, and his sons *were* Ulam and Rakem.

17 The son of Ulam *was* Bedan.) These *were* the descendants of Gilead the son of Machir, the son of Manasseh.

66

18 His sister Hammoleketh bore Ishhod, Abiezer, and Mahlah.

19 And the sons of Shemida were Ahian, Shechem, Likhi, and Aniam.

20 The sons of Ephraim *were* Shuthelah, Bered his son, Tahath his son, Eladah his son, Tahath his son,

21 Zabad his son, Shuthelah his son, and Ezer and Elead. The men of Gath who were born in *that* land killed *them* because they came down to take away their cattle.

22 Then Ephraim their father mourned many days, and his brethren came to comfort him.

23 And when he went in to his wife, she conceived and bore a son; and he called his name Beriah, because tragedy had come upon his house.

24 Now his daughter *was* Sheerah, who built Lower and Upper Beth Horon and Uzzen Sheerah;

25 and Rephah *was* his son, *as well* as Resheph, and Telah his son, Tahan his son,

26 Laadan his son, Ammihud his son, Elishama his son,

27 Nun his son, and Joshua his son.

28 Now their possessions and dwelling places *were* Bethel and its towns: to the east Naaran, to the west Gezer and its towns, and Shechem and its towns, as far as Ayyah and its towns;

29 and by the borders of the children of Manasseh *were* Beth Shean and its towns, Taanach and its towns, Megiddo and its towns, Dor and its towns. In these dwelt the children of Joseph, the son of Israel.

30 The sons of Asher *were* Imnah, Ishvah, Ishvi, Beriah, and their sister Serah.

31 The sons of Beriah *were* Heber and Malchiel, who was the father of Birzaith.

32 And Heber begot Japhlet, Shomer, Hotham, and their sister Shua.

33 The sons of Japhlet *were* Pasach, Bimhal, and Ashvath. These *were* the children of Japhlet.

34 The sons of Shemer *were* Ahi, Rohgah, Jehubbah, and Aram.

35 And the sons of his brother Helem *were* Zophah, Imna, Shelesh, and Amal.

36 The sons of Zophah *were* Suah, Harnepher, Shual, Beri, Imrah,

37 Bezer, Hod, Shamma, Shilshah, Jithran, and Beera.

38 The sons of Jether *were* Jephunneh, Pispah, and Ara.

39 The sons of Ulla *were* Arah, Haniel, and Rizia.

40 All these *were* the children of Asher, heads of *their* fathers' houses, choice men, mighty men of valor, chief leaders. And they were recorded by genealogies among the army fit for battle; their number *was* twenty-six thousand.

8:1 Now Benjamin begot Bela his firstborn, Ashbel the second, Aharah the third,

2 Nohah the fourth, and Rapha the fifth.

3 The sons of Bela *were* Addar, Gera, Abihud,

4 Abishua, Naaman, Ahoah,

5 Gera, Shephuphan, and Huram.

6 These *are* the sons of Ehud, who were the heads of the fathers' *houses* of the inhabitants of Geba, and who forced them to move to Manahath:

7 Naaman, Ahijah, and Gera who forced them to move. He begot Uzza and Ahihud.

8 Also Shaharaim had children in the country of Moab, after he had sent away Hushim and Baara his wives.

9 By Hodesh his wife he begot Jobab, Zibia, Mesha, Malcam,

10 Jeuz, Sachiah, and Mirmah. These *were* his sons, heads of their fathers' *houses*.

11 And by Hushim he begot Abitub and Elpaal.

12 The sons of Elpaal *were* Eber, Misham, and Shemed, who built Ono and Lod with its towns;

13 and Beriah and Shema, who *were* heads of their fathers' *houses* of the inhabitants of Aijalon, who drove out the inhabitants of Gath.

14 Ahio, Shashak, Jeremoth,

15 Zebadiah, Arad, Eder,

16 Michael, Ispah, and Joha *were* the sons of Beriah.

17 Zebadiah, Meshullam, Hizki, Heber,

18 Ishmerai, Jizliah, and Jobab *were* the sons of Elpaal.

19 Jakim, Zichri, Zabdi,

20 Elienai, Zillethai, Eliel,

21 Adaiah, Beraiah, and Shimrath *were* the sons of Shimei.

22 Ishpan, Eber, Eliel,

23 Abdon, Zichri, Hanan,

24 Hananiah, Elam, Antothijah,

25 Iphdeiah, and Penuel *were* the sons of Shashak.

26 Shamsherai, Shehariah, Athaliah,

27 Jaareshiah, Elijah, and Zichri *were* the sons of Jeroham.

28 These *were* heads of the fathers' *houses* by their generations, chief men. These dwelt in Jerusalem.

29 Now the father of Gibeon, whose wife's name *was* Maacah, dwelt at Gibeon.

30 And his firstborn son *was* Abdon, then Zur, Kish, Baal, Nadab,

31 Gedor, Ahio, Zecher,

32 and Mikloth, *who* begot Shimeah. They also dwelt alongside their relatives in Jerusalem, with their brethren.

33 Ner begot Kish, Kish begot Saul, and Saul begot Jonathan, Malchishua, Abinadab and Esh-Baal.

34 The son of Jonathan *was* Merib-Baal, and Merib-Baal begot Micah.

35 The sons of Micah *were* Pithon, Melech, Tarea, and Ahaz.

36 And Ahaz begot Jehoaddah; Jehoaddah begot Alemeth, Azmaveth, and Zimri; and Zimri begot Moza.

37 Moza begot Binea, Raphah his son, Eleasah his son, *and* Azel his son.

38 Azel had six sons whose names *were* these: Azrikam, Bocheru, Ishmael, Sheariah, Obadiah, and Hanan. All these *were* the sons of Azel.

39 And the sons of Eshek his brother *were* Ulam his firstborn, Jeush the second, and Eliphelet the third.

40 The sons of Ulam were mighty men of valor—

archers. *They* had many sons and grandsons, one hundred and fifty *in all*. They *were* all sons of Benjamin.

1 Chron. 7:1–8:40

We have commented on the overall framework of the genealogies, whereby Judah and Benjamin, the tribes of the post-exilic state of Judah, and Levi, the tribe devoted to the temple in Jerusalem, were given pride of place at the beginning, end, and middle. The framework is an inclusive one, for there is room in it for the northern tribes, some in chapter 5 and the others in chapter 7. The lists are scrappy: evidently the Chronicler retrieved what he could from contemporary Judean archives. There is nothing on Dan or Zebulun (contrast 2:1). Did they drop out of the list? More probably the lack reflects the Chronicler's difficulty in finding evidence. It was a matter of conviction for him to declare that God's people were not a minority of tribes but "all Israel," as he states in his summary at 9:1. This is to be a favorite phrase of his. It strikes out at an attitude which must have been prevalent in his time, that "we," and only "we," are the people of God. This attitude is present in the earlier books of Ezra and Nehemiah—read Ezra 4:1–3, for instance—and understandably so in a relatively new community. In the Chronicler's case sufficient time had elapsed to let traditional theology triumph over momentary needs, and he tried to stop a particular religious stress from hardening into a permanent attitude.

Each new work of God throws into focus a particular truth and creates champions for it. A new denomination builds a shrine to this truth and makes it a permanent tradition and the reason for its continued existence. Anthony Norris Groves, a nineteenth-century Christian who was for many years a missionary in Persia and India, after receiving adult baptism, was informed by a Baptist minister, "Of course, you must be a Baptist now that you are baptized." He replied, "No, I desire to follow all in those things in which they follow Christ; but I would not by joining one party cut myself off from others."[1] There is a certain idealism here, which in practice is hardly possible to attain. It is easier for me, as a professor in a multi-denominational seminary, to value and uphold the reality and recognition of all God's people than it is for the average member of a local church with a denominational flavor. The Chronicler's concern is, I believe, translatable into multidenominational awareness, whereby the Methodist makes opportunity—formal as well as informal—for fellowship with the Baptist, the Baptist with the Presbyterian, and the Presbyterian with the Pentecostalist. The Chronicler was aghast at the iron curtain which had fallen between members of God's people. Have we in turn built walls of partition to cut us off from our fellow-Christians?

The California poet Edwin Markham wrote in a short poem entitled "Outwitted":

> He drew a circle that shut me out—
> Heretic, rebel, a thing to flout.
> But Love and I had the wit to win:
> We drew a circle that took him in!

In like spirit the Chronicler drew his circle, with Levi at the center and Judah and Benjamin at the circumference. But there was room for others, for representatives of the northern tribes, whom others would reject as beyond the pale. The Chronicler had a wideness of heart which we do well to ponder and seek to emulate.

In 7:21–23 there is another of those lighted windows to which I drew attention in chapters 2 and 4. It discloses a sad series of events. My Americanized mind sees in verse 21 the flavor of the wild west. I catch a glimpse of cattle rustlers and a posse of cowboys who gallop after the rustlers and lynch them. Their bereaved father finds it impossible to shake off his grief, though his brothers rally round in sympathy. His next and now only son is given the name "Beriah," "In-tragedy," to commemorate the loss (v. 23). The perpetuation of mourning in a name is unusual. There are Hebrew names which attest the end of bereavement. The names Menachem and Manasseh are really cries of praise for the gift of a new child to the God who, respectively, "comforts" for the loss of an earlier child or children and "makes to forget" earlier calamity, often the loss of infants since the infant mortality rate was very high.

In this case there had been a loss not of an infant but of grown sons, and not one but two. It was a disaster the father never got over, and the new baby was made to bear the brunt of a perpetual bereavement by his hapless name. It was a means not of working it out of the father's system but of perpetuating it. The lad's presence ever reminded him of it. One sometimes encounters homes where metaphorically the drapes are kept closed for years and where children are made to wear a virtual ball and chain because of what happened years ago. There is something very human and yet very unhealthy about this vignette. I see in it a warning about human emotion which, changing from a natural force to a neurotic obsession, can suck others into its vortex and seek to drag down their lives in turn.

ANOTHER CHANCE

9:1 So all Israel was recorded by genealogies, and indeed, they *were* inscribed in the book of the kings of Israel. But Judah was carried away captive to Babylon because of their unfaithfulness.

2 And the first inhabitants who *dwelt* in their possessions in their cities *were* Israelites, priests, Levites, and the Nethinim.

3 Now in Jerusalem the children of Judah dwelt, and some of the children of Benjamin, and of the children of Ephraim and Manasseh:

4 Uthai the son of Ammihud, the son of Omri, the son of Imri, the son of Bani, of the descendants of Perez, the son of Judah.

5 Of the Shilonites: Asaiah the firstborn and his sons.

6 Of the sons of Zerah: Jeuel, and their brethren— six hundred and ninety.

7 Of the sons of Benjamin: Sallu the son of Meshullam, the son of Hodaviah, the son of Hassenuah;

8 Ibneiah the son of Jeroham; Elah the son of Uzzi, the son of Michri; Meshullam the son of Shephatiah, the son of Reuel, the son of Ibnijah;

9 and their brethren, according to their generations—nine hundred and fifty-six. All these men *were* heads of a father's *house* in their fathers' houses.

10 Of the priests: Jedaiah, Jehoiarib, and Jachin;

11 Azariah the son of Hilkiah, the son of Meshullam, the son of Zadok, the son of Meraioth, the son of Ahitub, the officer over the house of God;

12 Adaiah the son of Jeroham, the son of Pashur,

the son of Malchijah; Maasai the son of Adiel, the son of Jahzerah, the son of Meshullam, the son of Meshillemith, the son of Immer;

13 and their brethren, heads of their fathers' *houses*—one thousand seven hundred and sixty. *They were* very able men for the work of the service of the house of God.

14 Of the Levites: Shemaiah the son of Hasshub, the son of Azrikam, the son of Hashabiah, of the sons of Merari;

15 Bakbakkar, Heresh, Galal, and Mattaniah the son of Micah, the son of Zichri, the son of Asaph;

16 Obadiah the son of Shemaiah, the son of Galal, the son of Jeduthun; and Berechiah the son of Asa, the son of Elkanah, who lived in the villages of the Netophathites.

17 And the gatekeepers *were* Shallum, Akkub, Talmon, Ahiman, and their brethren. Shallum *was* the chief.

18 Until then *they had been* gatekeepers for the camps of the children of Levi at the King's Gate on the east.

19 Shallum the son of Kore, the son of Ebiasaph, the son of Korah, and his brethren, from his father's house, the Korahites, *were* in charge of the work of the service, gatekeepers of the tabernacle. Their fathers had been keepers of the entrance to the camp of the LORD.

20 And Phinehas the son of Eleazar had been the officer over them in time past; the LORD *was* with him.

21 Zechariah the son of Meshelemiah *was* keeper of the door of the tabernacle of meeting.

22 All those chosen as gatekeepers *were* two hundred and twelve. They were recorded by their genealogy, in their villages. David and Samuel the seer had appointed them to their trusted office.

23 So they and their children *were* in charge of the gates of the house of the LORD, the house of the tabernacle, by assignment.

24 The gatekeepers were assigned to the four directions: the east, west, north, and south.

25 And their brethren in their villages *had* to come with them from time to time for seven days.

26 For in this trusted office *were* four chief gatekeepers; they were Levites. And they had charge over the chambers and treasuries of the house of God.

27 And they lodged *all* around the house of God because they *had* the responsibility, and they *were* in charge of opening *it* every morning.

28 Now *some* of them were in charge of the serving vessels, for they brought them in and took them out by count.

29 *Some* of them *were* appointed over the furnishings and over all the implements of the sanctuary, and over the fine flour and the wine and the oil and the incense and the spices.

30 And *some* of the sons of the priests made the ointment of the spices.

31 Mattithiah of the Levites, the firstborn of Shallum the Korahite, had the trusted office over the things that were baked in the pans.

32 And some of their brethren of the sons of the Kohathites *were* in charge of preparing the showbread for every Sabbath.

33 These are the singers, heads of the fathers' *houses* of the Levites, *who lodged* in the chambers, *and were* free *from other duties;* for they were employed in *that* work day and night.

34 These heads of the fathers' *houses* of the Levites *were* heads throughout their generations. They dwelt at Jerusalem.

1 Chron. 9:1–34

There is an evangelical ring about this chapter. It has to begin with a sad testimony to sin and punishment (v. 1). Not only the northern tribes were deported to foreign parts (5:25, 26). The state of Judah, despite the presence of the temple in its midst as witness to God and to His claim on their lives, suffered the unthinkable: Judah *"was carried away captive to Babylon because of their unfaithfulness"* (compare 6:15). Theirs was the mental anguish of displaced persons, torn away from their roots, far from home—and from God. But their

God was such that He could take the failure of His people in stride. The passage 9:2–24 is the story of a restored people in a restored city and land. Israel is alive and well.

It is the only time in the Chronicler's history that he deals with the post-exilic period, for his overt concern is with the Davidic monarchy, from David to the final king, Zedekiah. Yet he is no antiquarian; his real concern is with the lessons which the period of the monarchy can teach his post-exilic contemporaries. Only here does he permit himself to speak directly of the return from Exile. He might have written in the enthusiastic tones of Psalm 126:1–3, ". . . The Lord has done great things for us, and we are glad." He wants to play down the return, not in order to minimize the grace of God but paradoxically in order to maximize it. If the clock has started ticking again for God's people, it is not the first time it has stopped nor the first time God has wound it up again. For the Chronicler the whole history of the people of God is the story of fresh starts by God's grace, and the return from Exile fits into a regular pattern. For the historian Edward Gibbon, history was "little more than the register of the crises, follies, and misfortunes of mankind." Human history is more than that, thank God. For the Chronicler it was a series of testimonies to the grace of a God who picks up the broken pieces and puts them together again.

There is ever a way back to God for the repentant, and so it proved in chapter 9, in the sixth century B.C., as new evidence of a perennial truth. The post-exilic age was for the Chronicler, unlike his contemporaries, not so much the beginning of a new era of latter-day saints as the continuation of God's purposes which stretched right back to David and Solomon. Post-exilic Israel was an extension of the monarchical Israel, sharing its ideals and religious institutions and trying to learn from its failures. There was a continuity in God's revelation which made the past meaningful for the present. Is there perhaps a hint here for Christians who set very great store by the Reformation? It is possible to let a great work of God eclipse His earlier work and blind one's eyes to the testimonies of believers in every generation of the church.

The list of 9:2b–17 also occurs substantially in Nehemiah 11:3–19 and was obviously taken from the same official archives. There is a significant addition at verse 3 because the Chronicler wants to set the record straight: the northern tribes of *"Ephraim and Manasseh"* were also represented among the citizens of the new state (compare Ezra 6:21). For him it was a matter of principle and a cause of joy that there was no exclusive restriction. Sinners though the northerners had been, the grace of God was a big enough umbrella to cover them as well as sinning Judeans and Benjaminites.

The list shows that laymen, priests, and Levites resumed the secular and religious tasks of a nation dedicated to God. It is glaringly obvious that the shortest listing and longest commentary relate to the Levitical section (vv. 14–34)! Ezra's memoirs attest that it was difficult to get together a quorum of Levites to return to Judah (Ezra 8:15–20). The three clans of Merari, Gershon (compare *"Asaph,"* v. 15, with 6:39–43), and Kohath (compare *"Korah,"* v. 19, with 6:22) are barely represented in these names, which represent heads of families. Much of the work the Levites had to do made it an unenviable job: it was the priests who enjoyed the limelight and the honor. The Chronicler wants to redress the balance throughout his history. He keeps shouting at his readers "Up with the Levite! God values him, and so should we."

There is a focus on the gatekeepers, the temple security guards. They have a marvellous genealogy, stretching back to the days of the tabernacle in the wilderness (v. 19). Moreover, their religious credentials were confirmed by *"David and Samuel the seer"* (v. 22). In a culture which valued genealogy and heritage, here indeed was an aristocracy! Let's not take them for granted, the Chronicler means to say, but appreciate the work they do for God and us, always on duty with watchful eyes, and behind the scenes doing such necessary work as looking after *"the furnishings"* (v. 29), and *"preparing the showbread for every Sabbath"* (v. 32). We can each of us make our own application of this concern in our particular ecclesiastical setting.

The Chronicler concludes with a reference to his favorite group, the Levitical singers (v. 33). It looks as though the source he was following was broken off at that point and he could not continue with details, but he wants to include the reference anyway. In view of his predilection it forms a fitting climax for the list. Here we are, the Chronicler seems to say, reconstituted under God. We have everything going for us as a society of laymen, priests, and Levites. "What manner of persons ought you to be in holy conduct and godliness?" (2 Pet. 3:11). In the next chapters the Chronicler will proceed to look back to David and Solomon as role models and pioneers of a new work which continued until his own day. Then he will turn to the subsequent fortunes of the dynasty, asking if and how later kings matched up to the earlier ideals. In like manner we Christians can look back to the Gospel, Acts, and Epistles to see how we are to live in the new dispensation established long ago and continuing still by God's grace. But let us not be too proud as Gentile Christians (see Rom. 11:17-20) to spend some time looking over the Chronicler's shoulder and to read how an older, Jewish saint urged his readers to extrapolate spirituality from history.

NOTE

1. G. H. Lang, *Anthony Norris Groves* (London: Paternoster Press, 1949), p. 279.

CHAPTER THREE

Israel at the Crossroads

1 Chronicles 9:35–12:40

The Bible is a book of decisive choices. It presents crucial alternatives, yet not impartially, as if urging one way or another would be a violation of a cosmic First Amendment. There is clear assertion that one way is right and another wrong, in order to help its readers toward a decision. "See, I have set before you today life and good, death and evil," declared Moses in Deuteronomy 30:15, 19; "therefore choose life." Jeremiah presented a choice for the citizens of Jerusalem to make, with the divine ultimatum, "Behold, I set before you the way of life and the way of death" (Jer. 21:8). The Sermon on the Mount closes with the challenge of alternatives, the narrow way leading to life or the broad way leading to destruction, and the choice of building one's life on a foundation of rock—the teaching of Jesus—or of sand (Matt. 7:13–14, 24–27). In the end there will be only two classes of people, those who have said to God "Your will be done" and those to whom God has regretfully to say "*Your* will be done." The message of these three chapters is the same decisive choice. The Chronicler intended these narratives about Saul and David to be read together as a contrast which, transcending time, confronted readers of his own day. In turn we have been brought within the circle of his readers and are meant to hear his implicit appeal to decide for God, for our own good.

The Way of Exile

9:35 Jeiel the father of Gibeon, whose wife's name *was* Maacah, dwelt at Gibeon.

36 His firstborn son *was* Abdon, then Zur, Kish, Baal, Ner, Nadab,

37 Gedor, Ahio, Zechariah, and Mikloth.

38 And Mikloth begot Shimeam. They also dwelt alongside their relatives in Jerusalem, with their brethren.

39 Ner begot Kish, Kish begot Saul, and Saul begot Jonathan, Malchishua, Abinadab, and Esh-Baal.

40 The son of Jonathan *was* Merib-Baal, and Merib-Baal begot Micah.

41 The sons of Micah *were* Pithon, Melech, Tahrea, *and Ahaz.*

42 And Ahaz begot Jarah; Jarah begot Alemeth, Azmaveth, and Zimri; and Zimri begot Moza;

43 Moza begot Binea, Rephaiah his son, Eleasah his son, and Azel his son.

44 And Azel had six sons whose names *were* these: Azrikam, Bocheru, Ishmael, Sheariah, Obadiah, and Hanan; these *were* the sons of Azel.

10:1 Now the Philistines fought against Israel; and the men of Israel fled from before the Philistines, and fell slain on Mount Gilboa.

2 Then the Philistines followed hard after Saul and his sons. And the Philistines killed Jonathan, Abinadab, and Malchishua, Saul's sons.

3 The battle became fierce against Saul. The archers hit him, and he was wounded by the archers.

4 Then Saul said to his armorbearer, "Draw your sword, and thrust me through with it, lest these uncircumcised men come and abuse me." But his armorbearer would not, for he was greatly afraid. Therefore Saul took a sword and fell on it.

5 And when his armorbearer saw that Saul was dead, he also fell on his sword and died.

6 So Saul and his three sons died, and all his house died together.

7 And when all the men of Israel who *were* in the valley saw that they had fled and that Saul and his sons were dead, they forsook their cities and fled; then the Philistines came and dwelt in them.

8 So it happened the next day, when the Philistines came to strip the slain, that they found Saul and his sons fallen on Mount Gilboa.

9 And they stripped him and took his head and

his armor, and sent word *throughout* the land of the Philistines to proclaim the news *in the temple* of their idols and among the people.

10 Then they put his armor in the temple of their gods, and fastened his head in the temple of Dagon.

11 And when all Jabesh Gilead heard all that the Philistines had done to Saul,

12 all the valiant men arose and took the body of Saul and the bodies of his sons; and they brought them to Jabesh, and buried their bones under the tamarisk tree at Jabesh, and fasted seven days.

13 So Saul died for his unfaithfulness which he had committed against the LORD, because he did not keep the word of the LORD, and also because he consulted a medium for guidance.

14 But *he* did not inquire of the LORD; therefore He killed him, and turned the kingdom over to David the son of Jesse.

1 Chron. 9:35–10:14

The genealogy of 9:35–44 is a re-run from the Benjaminite lists of chapter 8, intended to pave the way for the story of Saul in chapter 10. The text traces Saul's heritage back four generations and his posterity forward twelve generations down to late pre-exilic times, before narrating the tragedy that overtook Saul and three of his four sons. The rich potential of life turns into memories of catastrophe. Life went on, but not before the representative of one generation had done irreparable harm not only to himself and the next generation, but to his future line (see 1 Sam. 13:13) and to the people of God in his own day. The choice a person makes is made not only for oneself but for the weal or woe of others. The six sons of Azel in verse 44 invite comparison with the seven sons of Elioenai in 3:24. One group belonged to a family of tragic has-beens and the other to a family with a glorious past and an even more glorious future.

The Chronicler does not linger over Saul's reign in its own right, only on its lamentable outcome. Here was the grim harvest of wrong choices made previously, he wants to tell us. He concentrates on the narrative of 1 Samuel 31, Israel's last stand against the Philistines on Mount Gilboa. For the Chronicler the heart of the story is Saul's face-saving suicide in verses 4 and 6a. From this center the story ripples out to the fate of others which is bound up with his, in verses 2a and 6b: the death of his sons, which for all practical purposes meant the end of a dynasty. The horizons of the story in verses 1 and 7 are the flight of such Israelites as survived, first from their foes and eventually from their hometowns. The narrative continues in verses 8–10 with the humiliation, evaded in life, which overtook Saul in death. It is written in such a way as to remind its readers of two other Philistine narratives marked by happier content. Once the ark was taken as a prize of war to this very temple of Dagon—and the idol fell flat on its face in virtual homage (1 Sam. 5:1–4)! When David slew Goliath, the Philistines fled and Goliath's head was taken to Jerusalem (1 Sam. 17:50–54). Now the boot was very much on the other foot, and the allusions highlight by contrast the grimness of this situation. The only glimmer amid the gloom is the loyal bravery of the citizens of Jabesh Gilead, who had good cause to be grateful to Saul (see 1 Sam. 11:1–11). But even that serves to differentiate disparagingly between Saul's early promise and his tragic end.

The Chronicler wrote an obituary of Saul in verses 13–14, returning to the fatal center of the first episode and endeavoring to find meaning in this death. Saul's life could be summed up in one word, *"unfaithfulness."* The term is unpacked in two ways: disobeying God's commands and indulging in a substitute for true religious faith. The Chronicler is writing for biblically literate readers and assumes a knowledge of the narratives of 1 Samuel. In the first case he is referring to Saul's impatient refusal to wait for Samuel before sacrificing, and to his breaking the rules of holy war—both blatant acts of disobedience (1 Sam. 13:8–15). In the second case he recalls Saul's willful consultation of a spiritualist medium at Endor—after earlier outlawing all such magical practices (1 Sam. 28:3–14). Who killed Saul? In a grim sense his end was God's death sentence, and Saul acted as His executioner. The Chronicler remembers that both Saul's acts of disobedience triggered prophetic pronouncements that Saul had forfeited the kingship and God would give it to another (1 Sam. 13:13, 14; 15:20–28).

Is the Chronicler talking only about Saul? No, there is another agenda beneath the surface, of which there are three indications.

1. The first hint comes in the term *"unfaithfulness."* This is not the first time he has used it, but the third. It was the unfaithfulness of

the northern tribes that led to their exile (5:25, the two and a half tribes being typical of all the northern ones). And it was Judah's unfaithfulness that drove Judah into exile, as the Chronicler has stated (9:1) and will state again (2 Chron. 36:14 [read "were exceedingly unfaithful," RSV]). The exilic fate of God's people was prefigured in Saul and in the experience of Saul's subjects who fled and *"forsook their cities"* (10:7). Exile for the Chronicler was not a single event in Israel's history, but a recurring phenomenon. It ever loomed behind—and before—the people of God as a picture of the perils of unfaithfulness. Saul is a negative model for every generation to heed.

2. The second hint of this wider concern is that to *"keep the word of the Lord"* (10:13) not only has a prophetic reference in the Old Testament but relates also to general compliance with God's scriptural will (see Ps. 119:17, 67, 101).

3. The last hint concerns the Hebrew verb *dāraš,* used in verses 13 and 14 and better rendered "seek guidance" (RSV). It occurs here and four other times in Chronicles as a technical term for inquiry of God by special means. It is also a key part of the Chronicler's general vocabulary of spirituality: it is found no less than thirty-five times to indicate a turning to God in faith, for instance in 2 Chronicles 14:4. So the Chronicler is here suggesting a moral and spiritual lesson. Behind the specifics of the Saul obituary lies a message for the people of God in every generation.

This is the broad way that leads to destruction, and for every traveler on the highway of life Saul's experience is God's road sign "DO NOT ENTER." This is the house built on sand, and great was its fall. Sadly, Hegel's observation has usually been proved correct: "What experience and history teach is this: peoples and governments never have learned anything from history or acted on principles derived from it." The Chronicler had to admit as much in his record of the later exilic experiences of his people. Nevertheless, it was his hope that the trend would be halted by his readers' marking, learning, and inwardly digesting his story of Saul.

THE WAY OF RESTORATION

11:1 Then all Israel came together to David at Hebron, saying, "Indeed we *are* your bone and your flesh.

2 'Also, in time past, even when Saul was king, you *were* the one who led Israel out and brought them in; and the LORD your God said to you, 'You shall shepherd My people Israel, and be ruler over My people Israel.'"

3 Therefore all the elders of Israel came to the king at Hebron, and David made a covenant with them at Hebron before the LORD. And they anointed David king over Israel, according to the word of the LORD by Samuel.

4 And David and all Israel went to Jerusalem, which is Jebus, where the Jebusites *were*, the inhabitants of the land.

5 But the inhabitants of Jebus said to David, "You shall not come in here!" Nevertheless David took the stronghold of Zion (that is, the City of David).

6 Now David said, "Whoever attacks the Jebusites first shall be chief and captain." And Joab the son of Zeruiah went up first, and became chief.

7 Then David dwelt in the stronghold; therefore they called it the City of David.

8 And he built the city around it, from the Millo to the surrounding area. Joab repaired the rest of the city.

9 So David went on and became great, and the LORD of hosts *was* with him.

10 Now these *were* the heads of the mighty men whom David had, who strengthened themselves with him in his kingdom, with all Israel, to make him king, according to the word of the LORD concerning Israel.

11 And this *is* the number of the mighty men whom David had: Jashobeam the son of a Hachmonite, chief of the captains; he had lifted up his spear against three hundred, killed *by him* at one time.

12 After him *was* Eleazar the son of Dodo, the Ahohite, who *was one* of the three mighty men.

13 He was with David at Pasdammim. Now there the Philistines were gathered for battle, and there was a piece of ground full of barley. So the people fled from the Philistines.

14 But they stationed themselves in the middle of

that field, defended it, and killed the Philistines. So the LORD brought about a great victory.

15 Now three of the thirty chief men went down to the rock to David, into the cave of Adullam; and the army of the Philistines encamped in the Valley of Rephaim.

16 David *was* then in the stronghold, and the garrison of the Philistines *was* then in Bethlehem.

17 And David said with longing, "Oh, that someone would give me a drink of water from the well of Bethlehem, which is by the gate!"

18 So the three broke through the camp of the Philistines, drew water from the well of Bethlehem that *was* by the gate, and took *it* and brought *it* to David. Nevertheless David would not drink it, but poured it out to the LORD.

19 And he said, "Far be it from me, O my God, that I should do this! Shall I drink the blood of these men *who have put* their lives *in jeopardy?* For at the risk of their lives they brought it." Therefore he would not drink it. These things were done by the three mighty men.

20 Abishai the brother of Joab was chief of *another* three. He had lifted up his spear against three hundred *men,* killed *them,* and won a name among *these* three.

21 Of the three he was more honored than the other two men. Therefore he became their captain. However he did not attain to the *first* three.

22 Benaiah was the son of Jehoiada, the son of a valiant man from Kabzeel, who had done many deeds. He had killed two lion-like heroes of Moab. He also had gone down and killed a lion in the midst of a pit on a snowy day.

23 And he killed an Egyptian, a man of *great* height, five cubits tall. In the Egyptian's hand *there was* a spear like a weaver's beam; and he went down to him with a staff, wrested the spear out of the Egyptian's hand, and killed him with his own spear.

24 These *things* Benaiah the son of Jehoiada did, and won a name among three mighty men.

25 Indeed he was more honored than the thirty, but he did not attain to the *first* three. And David appointed him over his guard.

26 Also the mighty warriors *were* Asahel the brother of Joab, Elhanan the son of Dodo of Bethlehem,

27 Shammoth the Harorite, Helez the Pelonite,

28 Ira the son of Ikkesh the Tekoite, Abiezer the Anathothite,

29 Sibbechai the Hushathite, Ilai the Ahohite,

30 Maharai the Netophathite, Heled the son of Baanah the Netophathite,

31 Ithai the son of Ribai of Gibeah, of the sons of Benjamin, Benaiah the Pirathonite,

32 Hurai of the brooks of Gaash, Abiel the Arbathite,

33 Azmaveth the Baharumite, Eliahba the Shaalbonite,

34 the sons of Hashem the Gizonite, Jonathan the son of Shageh the Hararite,

35 Ahiam the son of Sacar the Hararite, Eliphal the son of Ur,

36 Hepher the Mecherathite, Ahijah the Pelonite,

37 Hezro the Carmelite, Naarai the son of Ezbai,

38 Joel the brother of Nathan, Mibhar the son of Hagri,

39 Zelek the Ammonite, Naharai the Berothite (the armorbearer of Joab the son of Zeruiah),

40 Ira the Ithrite, Gareb the Ithrite,

41 Uriah the Hittite, Zabad the son of Ahlai,

42 Adina the son of Shiza the Reubenite (a chief of the Reubenites) and thirty with him,

43 Hanan the son of Maachah, Joshaphat the Mithnite,

44 Uzzia the Ashterathite, Shama and Jeiel the sons of Hotham the Aroerite,

45 Jediael the son of Shimri, and Joha his brother, the Tizite,

46 Eliel the Mahavite, Jeribai and Joshaviah the sons of Elnaam, Ithmah the Moabite,

47 Eliel, Obed, and Jaasiel the Mezobaite.

12:1 Now these *were* the men who came to David at Ziklag while he was still a fugitive from Saul the son of Kish; and they *were* among the mighty men, helpers in the war,

2 armed with bows, using both the right hand and the left in *hurling* stones and *shooting* arrows with the bow. *They were* of Benjamin, Saul's brethren.

3 The chief *was* Ahiezer, then Joash, the sons of Shemaah the Gibeathite; Jeziel and Pelet the sons of Azmaveth; Berachah, and Jehu the Anathothite;

4 Ishmaiah the Gibeonite, a mighty man among the thirty, and over the thirty; Jeremiah, Jahaziel, Johanan, and Jozabad the Gederathite;

5 Eluzai, Jerimoth, Bealiah, Shemariah, and Shephatiah the Haruphite;

6 Elkanah, Jisshiah, Azarel, Joezer, and Jashobeam, the Korahites;

7 and Joelah and Zebadiah the sons of Jeroham of Gedor.

8 *Some* Gadites joined David at the stronghold in the wilderness, mighty men of valor, men trained for battle, who could handle shield and spear, whose faces *were like* the faces of lions, and *were* as swift as gazelles on the mountains:

9 Ezer the first, Obadiah the second, Eliab the third,

10 Mishmannah the fourth, Jeremiah the fifth,

11 Attai the sixth, Eliel the seventh,

12 Johanan the eighth, Elzabad the ninth,

13 Jeremiah the tenth, and Machbanai the eleventh.

14 These *were* from the sons of Gad, captains of the army; the least was over a hundred, and the greatest was over a thousand.

15 These *are* the ones who crossed the Jordan in the first month, when it had overflowed all its banks; and they put to flight all *those* in the valleys, to the east and to the west.

16 Then some of the sons of Benjamin and Judah came to David at the stronghold.

17 And David went out to meet them, and answered and said to them, "If you have come peaceably to me to help me, my heart will be united with you; but if to betray me to my enemies, since *there* is

no wrong in my hands, may the God of our fathers look and bring judgment."

18 Then the Spirit came upon Amasai, chief of the captains, *and he said:*

"We *are* yours, O David;
We *are* on your side, O son of Jesse!
Peace, peace to you,
And peace to your helpers!
For your God helps you."

So David received them, and made them captains of the troop.

19 And *some* from Manasseh defected to David when he was going with the Philistines to battle against Saul; but they did not help them, for the lords of the Philistines sent him away by agreement, saying, "He may defect to his master Saul *and endanger* our heads."

20 When he went to Ziklag, those of Manasseh who defected to him were Adnah, Jozabad, Jediael, Michael, Jozabad, Elihu, and Zillethai, captains of the thousands who *were* from Manasseh.

21 And they helped David against the bands *of raiders,* for they *were* all mighty men of valor, and they were captains in the army.

22 For at *that* time they came to David day by day to help him, until *it was* a great army, like the army of God.

23 Now these *were* the numbers of the divisions *that were* equipped for *the* war, *and* came to David at Hebron to turn *over* the kingdom of Saul to him, according to the word of the LORD:

24 of the sons of Judah bearing shield and spear, six thousand eight hundred armed for war;

25 of the sons of Simeon, mighty men of valor fit for war, seven thousand one hundred;

26 of the sons of Levi four thousand six hundred;

27 Jehoiada, the leader of the Aaronites, and with him three thousand seven hundred;

28 Zadok, a young man, a valiant warrior, and from his father's house twenty-two captains;

29 of the sons of Benjamin, relatives of Saul, three

thousand (until then the greatest part of them had remained loyal to the house of Saul);

30 of the sons of Ephraim twenty thousand eight hundred, mighty men of valor, famous men throughout their father's house;

31 of the half-tribe of Manasseh eighteen thousand, who were designated by name to come and make David king;

32 of the sons of Issachar who had understanding of the times, to know what Israel ought to do, their chiefs were two hundred; and all their brethren were at their command;

33 of Zebulun there were fifty thousand who went out to battle, expert in war with all weapons of war, stouthearted men who could keep ranks;

34 of Naphtali one thousand captains, and with them thirty-seven thousand with shield and spear;

35 of the Danites who could keep battle formation, twenty-eight thousand six hundred;

36 of Asher, those who could go out to war, able to keep battle formation, forty thousand;

37 of the Reubenites and the Gadites and the half-tribe of Manasseh, from the other side of the Jordan, one hundred and twenty thousand armed for battle with every *kind* of weapon of war.

38 All these men of war, who could keep ranks, came to Hebron with a loyal heart, to make David king over all Israel; and all the rest of Israel *were* of one mind to make David king.

39 And they were there with David three days, eating and drinking, for their brethren had prepared for them.

40 Moreover those who were near to them, from as far away as Issachar and Zebulun and Naphtali, were bringing food on donkeys and camels, on mules and oxen—provisions of flour and cakes of figs and cakes of raisins, wine and oil and oxen and sheep abundantly, for *there was* joy in Israel.

1 Chron. 11:1–12:40

The Chronicler highlighted the reigns of David and Solomon as a special manifestation of the goodness of God and a revelation of guidelines for His people thereafter. He set the period within its own literary frame, which served to isolate its special theological nature from the comparative mundaneness of history before and after. The frame occurs in 10:14, "He turned . . . the kingdom over to David," and in 2 Chronicles 10:15, the "turn of events" arranged by God for Rehoboam. These two turning points in sacred history, at the end of Saul's reign and the beginning of Rehoboam's, have the effect of drawing attention to the intervening reigns of David and Solomon as a period when God's will was supremely realized. Here above all, history was His story. What this means is that 1 Chronicles (10 or) 11 through 2 Chronicles 9 is a single section and, since it covers no less than twenty-nine of the total of sixty-five chapters, is the main part of the Chronicler's work. Accordingly one has to listen very carefully to his presentation of the double reign, if one wants to catch his message.

Let us pick up the threads of chapter 10. Saul's death has been a graphic illustration from history of the way of exile from God. Yet it does not spell the death of God's purposes. From the ashes of failure raises a new flame of achievement. God raises up a new king for his people. John Bunyan in *Pilgrim's Progress* saw in a dream that there was a way to hell even from the gates of heaven. The Chronicler wants virtually to say the opposite, and in his history he loves to illustrate it, that there is a way to heaven even from the gates of hell. God's redeeming grace shines out in the darkest state of spiritual decline. He stoops to re-enter human experience at its lowest point of failure and, bending the downward trend into a U-curve, lifts its victims to new life.

The Chronicler rushes on in his story from the death of King Saul to the crowning of his successor as king of Israel at Hebron. Life is not like that, and in his biblical source four traumatic chapters had to elapse between 1 Samuel 31 and 2 Samuel 5, on which latter chapter 1 Chronicles 11:1–9 is relying. He feels no need to go over all the ground of 2 Samuel—it is there for any to read—and instead leaps to the eventual outcome. He riffles the pages until David is at the mountaintop. But afterward he goes back to portray in his own way the hard climb to the top and the grasping of outstretched hands without which David would never have gotten there. So the text is not so triumphalist as it appears at the start. First our historian wants to draw an impressionistic contrast between the defeated, leaderless-nation and a united, virile people under a God-given leader. It serves to accentuate the triumph of divine grace. It also functions as a vision for the people of his own day. In a similar vein the writer to the Hebrews endeavored to put new heart into his demoralized, doubt-ridden readers by bidding them lift their weary eyes to "Mount Zion and to the city of the living God, the heavenly Jerusalem . . . to Jesus the Mediator of the new covenant" (Heb. 12:22, 24; compare v. 12).

Both 11:1–3 and 11:4–9 begin with the Chronicler's favorite phrase, "all Israel." To many in post-exilic Judah the spiritual heirs of God's pre-exilic people were the tribes of Judah and Benjamin: it was they who constituted latter-day Israel (see Ezra 4:1, 3). The Chronicler emerges as representative of a broader view, as we saw in 9:1, 3. He is going to unpack the phrase in 12:23–37 as essentially composed of members of all the ancestral tribes. It is his blow against denominationalism and certainly against sectarianism. I was brought up among—and humanly speaking owe my spiritual life to—a godly group whose attitude toward other Christians could in many cases be not unjustly summed up in this story, which I often heard told about them. Peter, showing some new arrivals round heaven and coming to a walled area from which hymns and prayers could be heard, cautioned his questioners with the words "Sh! They think they are the only ones here!"

If the Chronicler could have read John's Gospel, I suggest that his favorite text would have been the prayer of Jesus, "that they all may be one . . . , that the world may believe that You sent Me" (John 17:21). For him the way forward was not via the holy huddle which nervously finds security in its own traditions of the faith and perhaps pays lip-service to some hidden, mystical unity. There was need of intrepid visionaries open to the potential of rich fellowship with others of God's flock outside their own particular fold. If the Gospel of John was originally composed for the Christians to whom the First Epistle of John was written—a dispirited group who had been victims of dissension and schism (see 1 John 2:18, 19)—I suspect that one of the aims of the evangelist was to encourage them not to be so embittered by the experience as to withdraw into their shells but to maintain a broad perspective. If so, it was tragically ironic that by the time the Third Epistle was written one of the church's leaders, Diotrephes, had arrogantly broken off fellowship with John and other Christians (3 John 9, 10). For the Chronicler such an attitude would have been an antitype of the disunited fleeing which marks the road away from God into spiritual exile (10:7).

Earlier in the book we observed a theological triangle with Israel, God, and the land as its three points. In chapters 11–12 there is another triad of references: David, God, and Israel. Its first appearance is in 11:1–3. God's prophetic promise (11:2, 3: compare 1 Sam. 16:1) initiated the process whereby representatives of *"all Israel"* *"anointed David king over Israel."* This coronation promoted the covenant between God and his *"people"* (v. 2). For the Chronicler this was the beginning of a new era for God's people, which by faith he saw persisting to his own day and beyond. In the words of Psalm 78, an older composition which shares this viewpoint, in this new work God *"chose David His servant . . . to shepherd Jacob His people, and Israel His inheritance"* (Ps. 78:70, 71). Here was theological history being made; here was the divine word being fulfilled. I suppose that the nearest New Testament approximation to this passage would be Romans 1:1–6. There Paul celebrated the gospel of God as the keeping of His prophetic promises; it centers around His Son who was descended from David, and it has created a community of those who are called to belong to Jesus Christ.

The same triad of Israel, David, and God cooperating in beautiful harmony reappears in 11:4–9. The Chronicler cannot resist rushing on for a moment from Hebron to Jerusalem. He wants to paint a perfect picture of people, king, and royal capital as an ideal which he hoped would be realized afresh. The triad of three parties frames 11:4–9. The capture of Jerusalem was a joint effort of *"David and all Israel"* (v. 4) and a preliminary to David's ever increasing greatness, the secret of which was the fact that *"the Lord of Hosts was with him"* (v. 9). There was a divine power behind the human throne, as well as an undergirding from popular support.

I said that the Chronicler rushes on to encompass Jerusalem in his theological vision, because essentially the coronation at Hebron is the scene which dominates not only 11:1–3 but also verses 10–47, as verse 10 with its reference to king-making indicates. Verse 10 brings his readers back to the same triad as verses 1 and 3, and telescopes them to make sure that the penny has dropped! Notice the repeated stress on *"all Israel"* and the observation that the prophetic word was not only about David but promised a new deal for *"Israel."* In principle

God's people—not a fragmented caricature of that people—had received in the person of David a divine economy of grace.

The plan of chapters 11–12 is an interesting one. After the coronation at Hebron (11:1–3), if we ignore for the moment the impetuous jump to Jerusalem, the material lingers at Hebron to survey who David's supporters were (vv. 10–47). Then there is a flashback to David's experience at Ziklag near the end of Saul's life and a description of the support he received even then (12:1–7). There follows a flashback further to David's stay at *the stronghold* in his Robin Hood days (12:8–15). Then the literary clock, having been twice put back, is correspondingly moved forward. Before it is, there is a lingering at *the stronghold* to record further support (12:16–18). Next Ziklag is revisited to see how fresh followers were added (12:19–22); then the text brings us to Hebron again and recounts the support of Israel tribe by tribe (12:23–37). Finally the story of the coronation at Hebron, begun at 11:1–3, is rounded off at 12:38–40. This intricate structure is a double pattern of four elements, in an A B C D / D' C' B' A' arrangement. The impressions which this literary tapestry wants to convey are the gradual growth of support for David and his transformation from the nervous victim of harassment (12:1, 17) to the secure recipient of greatness (11:9; 12:22).

Alongside this structural concern is another, in part independent, scheme: a roll call of David's army, from its commander-in-chief Joab (11:6) and the Three and the Thirty (11:10–47) to the *mighty men* (12:1–21) and finally the rank and file of this *great army* which the Chronicler enthusiastically compared to the *army of God* (12:22–37). It must be remembered that the end of chapter 10 had left the people of God defenseless, at the mercy of their enemies and bereft of both their liberty and their land. Now they are pictured as militarily strong; over against the fleeing of chapter 10 there is a portrayal of strength that comes from unity. The Old Testament concept of God's people as an army becomes in the New an image of the church militant, for instance in Ephesians 6:10–18. The church has cosmic foes to fight, who have chosen the planet earth as the battleground for their sinister aims. The call rings out to *be strong in the lord and in the power of His might* (Eph. 6:10). Bishop Reginald Heber testified to this truth in a challenging hymn, "The Son of God Goes Forth to War," which bridges the Chronicles narrative and the imagery of Ephesians:

> The Son of God goes forth to war,
> A kingly crown to gain;
> His blood-red banner streams afar;
> Who follows in His train?

By the end of 1 Chronicles 12 king and people stand together, ready to take on their foes and win their freedom under God. For the Chronicler it was also a vision of the future when, united under a restored monarchy, Israel was to win back the land in which they lived by grace of the Persian emperor and to realize their promised heritage in the manifestation of the kingdom of God. The unity of the people of God was an element for which Judah could begin training now! The example of Israel in David's days is intended to be inspirational. Unity was a process achieved in 11:1–9 and 12:23–40, but only gradually realized, as one group after another pledged its allegiance to the new king, who had a divine claim on their support. This representation of growing unity corresponds to the broad canvas which in its own way Ephesians 3:14–4:16 unrolls before its Christian readers. It portrays a panorama of the universal church in which "all the saints" find themselves represented (Eph. 3:18). It challenges to endeavor "to keep the unity of the Spirit in the bond of peace" as "one body" (Eph. 4:3, 4), made up of members who each have their unique contribution to make to its health and growth (Eph. 4:7–16).

The Chronicler says something similar when he not only surveys the army en masse and enumerates its tribal divisions but gives examples of the exploits of individuals, largely using material from 2 Samuel 23. There was plenty of room to have *"won a name"* by the manifestation of personality and particular flair (11:20, 24), provided that it was subordinated to the leader and was the outworking of allegiance to him. No personality cults were established! Joab's single-handed initiative led to the capture of a city for his master (11:4–8). David had giant-killers in his entourage (11:23) and commandos who braved the flood waters swollen by winter rains (12:15), "the least" of whom was "a match for a hundred, the greatest a match for a thousand" (12:14, NEB). There are many such acts of personal courage enumerated in 11:11–25 and 12:15, and much listing of names in the intervening material. Individuals counted in this venture. I am reminded of the listing in Hebrews 11:32–38 and indeed of the whole honors board of Old Testament believers in that chapter. The Epistle to the Hebrews throughout sets store by the insight that individuals still count and are never lost in the Christian crowd (see Heb. 3:12, 13; 4:11; 5:11; 10:24, 25; 12:15).

There is a structural intent to highlight the concerted unity of Israel and David under a God who has kept His promise. It appears not only in 11:1–4 but at two significant joints in his composition, 11:10 and 12:23. Another related thread running through this prose tapestry is the motif of help. David does not stand alone. He becomes what he is because, as he was told in a prophetic pronouncement, *"your God helps you"* (12:18). The assurance picks up the initial statement, relating to a point later in time, that *"the Lord of hosts was with him* [David]*"* (11:9). The setting of 12:18 is the period when David was at the stronghold, out in the wilds. Superficially it has a Robin Hood glamor, but the reality was far different. David was psychologically low, forced to flee from the court and hounded by a psychotic Saul. He did not know whom to trust and which of his new-found friends might be traitors, awaiting an opportunity to hand him over to the king. In this crisis of confidence he greets some new arrivals at his camp with suspicion, especially since some of them belong to the royal tribe of Benjamin. He challenges them: *"Friend or foe?"* (12:17). In his inability to discern, he reinforces his query with an appeal to God: should they be secret foes, *"may the God of our fathers look and bring judgment."* The appeal, spoken out of human helplessness, receives a gracious answer from God. Amasai, prophetically endowed, gives a reassuring pledge of support from the arrivals and from God Himself. The triple greeting woven into his reply, *šālôm, šālôm, šālôm,* is meant to bring emotional encouragement to David. He is surrounded by *"helpers"* on every side, and not least aided by God as patron of his cause.

Later on at Ziklag, when David was unable to "move about freely because of Saul" (12:1, RSV) and chafing at this loss of freedom, there was encouragement to be gained from those who identified themselves with him and *"helped"* him. There is also mention of those who *"helped"* David at Ziklag when Amalekite raiders attacked the town in his absence (12:21; see 1 Sam. 30). At this period too there was increasing support from those who *"came to David day by day to help him"* (12:22). The Chronicler underlines this motif by his use of names. In the stronghold period, David's prime supporter in a Gadite contingent was *"Ezer,"* which means help (12:9). Likewise, in the Zik-lag phase *"the chief"* of his Benjamite allies was *"Ahiezer,"* a name compounded by the Hebrew for help (12:3), while *"Joezer"* also fea-tures in a list (12:6). The motif of help overflows into the Hebron material, first by the names *"Eleazar"* (11:12) and *"Abiezer"* (11:28), and then by a plain statement about members of Zebulun who came to David "to help" (12:33, RSV). When I think of this motif of dual help, human and divine, I recall that the Epistle to the Romans not only celebrates the Spirit who "helps in our weaknesses" (Rom. 8:26) but also honors Phoebe as "a helper of many and of myself also" (Rom. 16:1, 2).

In these two chapters there is a beautiful expression of a triple unity, of God, David, and Israel joining hands in a common ven-ture. At the outset it is affirmed that *"with"* David were both God (11:9) and his followers who "gave him strong support" (11:10, RSV). David speaks of his *"heart"* being *"united with"* his allies (12:17), while they in turn had singleness of purpose, were "of a single mind" (12:38, RSV), and had "a loyal heart," literally "a whole heart." The Christian reader recalls the challenge of his Lord, that "no one can serve two masters" (Matt. 6:24). In David's political situation there was a rival cause, the house of Saul, which enjoyed the support especially of his own tribe Benjamin for a long period (12:29). It was an act of religious and political faith to throw in one's lot with David: such allegiance was underwritten by God's explicit word (11:2, 3). Until that cause triumphed, it meant swim-ming against the public tide and anticipating the "tribulation of the world" which Jesus promised His own followers but countered with the encouragement that in principle He had already "overcome the world" (John 16:33).

One episode in particular encapsulates the devotion of David's supporters and his own devotion to God. In 11:17–19, which the Chronicler took over from 2 Samuel 23:13–17, David with a soldier's nostalgia for home wishes he could have a drink from the well of enemy-occupied Bethlehem. For three of his followers his wish was their command. They take it upon themselves to break through the enemy lines and fetch some water from the well. Overcome, David cannot bring himself to drink it but pours it out on the ground as a libation to God. He counts it as the equivalent of the blood of those who risked their lives for him. By this dramatic gesture David both acknowledges his appreciation of their self-sacrificial loyalty and gives God the glory.

The section ends with 12:38–40. It resumes the covenant of king-making between Israel and David in God's presence (11:1–3; there was a sanctuary at Hebron) and caps it with the account of a covenant meal in celebration (compare Gen. 26:26–30; Josh. 9:11–15). It is an expression of solidarity and fellowship. The Chronicler cannot resist including a reference to three northern tribes among those who brought supplies for the potluck festivities. They too have a contribution to make, he insists! Just as we are told that there is joy in heaven over repenting sinners (Luke 15:7), so there was *"joy in Israel"* at this reunion when north and south celebrated their shared king. For the Chronicler the event broke the bounds of history and constituted an ideal for which he was waiting. This covenant meal rings bells in Christians ears. The young church in Jerusalem partook of fellowship meals which were marked by "gladness" (Acts 2:46). Down the ages the church has known a sacred meal not unlike the one described here. It too bears witness to a covenant. As a meal of communion, it too is a perpetual testimony—and challenge—to the unity of God's people: "We, though many, are one bread and one body; for we all partake of that one bread" (1 Cor. 10:17).

We entitled this chapter of the commentary "Israel at the Crossroads." For the Chronicler the generation of his day stood at crossroads and had to decide for or against God. Saul still lurked in contemporary hearts, seeking to drag them down the path that led to exile from God. But David beckoned, challenging to a largeness of spirit, exemplifying a commitment to God and people, and calling to a hope that God would again work in such a fashion. In like manner the letters to the churches in Revelation 2–3 appear to function as positive and negative models. Repeatedly the challenge rings out: "He who has an ear, let him hear what the Spirit says to the churches" (Rev. 2:7, etc.). The Chronicler too was saying to his generation and to the generations of believers down to our own: "He who has an ear, let him hear."

CHAPTER FOUR

Giving God Pride of Place

1 Chronicles 13:1–16:43

Here is the process by which the city of David (11:7) becomes the city of God. Jerusalem has been captured and become the royal, political capital of Israel. But there is something missing. The triad of entities that ran through chapters 11 and 12, David, Israel, and God, has yet to be fully represented. Jerusalem must become the religious center of Israel. There is a spiritual logic about the movement of the ark to Jerusalem, which is accomplished in these chapters.

The ark was a chest of precious wood that symbolized God's presence with His people. The Chronicler takes over from his source in 2 Samuel 6:2 a pair of complementary truths. First, it functioned as the footstool of God (see 1 Chron. 28:2), above which was the invisible throne of the Lord who "sits enthroned above the cherubim" (13:6, RSV). Secondly, one must not conceive of this presence in any crude fashion. Later on, Solomon in his prayer of dedication will marvel at the mystery of the special presence of God in relation to His transcendence. The temple does not contain God as a cage contains a bird! God has been neither trapped nor tamed. Rather, God's true home is beyond this created world, and His name is set upon the temple as a spiritual representation of Him (2 Chron. 6:18, 20). The same theological point is evidently being made in the description of the ark as a place "where His name is proclaimed" (13:7). Both truths are affirmed, each one qualifying the other, lest too great or too little significance be attached to this dynamic representation of God.

For the Chronicler the ark was supremely "the ark of the covenant" (15:29). Sometimes he adapts thus his source's description of the ark (see 15:25–29 in comparison with 2 Sam. 6:12–16) or so describes it in his own passages (see 16:6, 37), in order to bring out this significance. It stood as a symbol of the covenant relationship between

97

God and Israel. When the Chronicler thought of the ark, he was reminded that Israel was God's people, the object of His claim and care. We shall have occasion to develop this thought when we reach 2 Chronicles 5.

For a generation the ark had languished at a place some eight miles away from Jerusalem, for reasons the Chronicler can assume his readers know from 1 Samuel 4:1–7:2. Now that a new era had dawned with David, this situation could be tolerated no longer. The restoration of the ark was necessary. It was a symbol of putting God at the heart of the community's life. For the Chronicler and his first readers, as for us, the story needed mental re-interpretation; he assumes that they can grasp the message behind it. By their lifetime the ark no longer rested in the Holy of Holies. Although the ark had gone, what it stood for had not gone. Along with the missing ark there was not removed a conviction of the vital presence of God with His people nor the need to acknowledge Him as the King of kings nor the privilege and responsibility of the covenant relationship.

GOOD INTENTIONS

13:1 Then David consulted with the captains of thousands and hundreds, *and* with every leader.

2 And David said to all the assembly of Israel, "If *it seems* good to you, and if it is of the LORD our God, let us send out to our brethren everywhere *who are* left in all the land of Israel, and with them to the priests and Levites *who are* in their cities *and* their common-lands, that they may gather together to us;

3 "and let us bring the ark of our God back to us, for we have not inquired at it since the days of Saul."

4 Then all the assembly said that they would do so, for the thing was right in the eyes of all the people.

5 So David gathered all Israel together, from Shihor in Egypt to as far as the entrance of Hamath, to bring the ark of God from Kirjath Jearim.

6 And David and all Israel went up to Baalah, to Kirjath Jearim, which belonged to Judah, to bring up from there the ark of God the LORD, who dwells *between* the cherubim, where *His* name is proclaimed.

7 So they carried the ark of God on a new cart from the house of Abinadab, and Uzza and Ahio drove the cart.

8 Then David and all Israel played *music* before God with all *their* might, with singing, on harps, on stringed instruments, on tambourines, on cymbals, and with trumpets.

9 And when they came to Chidon's threshing floor, Uzza put out his hand to hold the ark, for the oxen stumbled.

10 Then the anger of the LORD was aroused against Uzza, and He struck him because he put his hand to the ark; and he died there before God.

11 And David became angry because of the LORD'S outbreak against Uzza; therefore that place is called Perez Uzza to this day.

12 David was afraid of God that day, saying, "How can I bring the ark of God to me?"

13 So David would not move the ark with him into the City of David, but took it aside into the house of Obed-Edom the Gittite.

14 The ark of God remained with the family of Obed-Edom in his house three months. And the LORD blessed the house of Obed-Edom and all that he had.

1 Chron. 13:1-14

The road to hell is paved with good intentions, runs the proverb. But the intentions of this chapter are not mere mental aspirations that die before seeing the light of day. Rather, they are matched with an energetic endeavor to realize them. They are the sincere outworking of integrity, and it is this fact which makes subsequent failure hard to handle. Life is like that for all of us. Who has not known the consternation of a serious setback, when all seemed to be going well in a life committed, one thought, to the will of God? Joy vanished, and one was left in spiritual limbo. It is at this realistic midpoint that the chapter is to end, tantalizingly leaving loose ends dangling. Since the previous chapters portrayed David's reign as the way of restoration, in contrast to the way of exile, it might have been expected that David would go from strength to strength, living happily ever after. There is a human realism about this chapter which teaches otherwise. The river of steady progress suddenly and unexpectedly turns into dangerous rapids, and David is overwhelmed.

It started so well. There was unanimity at the meeting convened to discuss what should be done about the ark, such unanimity as echoes the harmony of chapters 11 and 12. Seemingly the beginning of chapter 13 continues the end of chapter 12 in spirit as well as in letter. After consultation with the military leaders present at Hebron for the coronation (12:38), the main body of Israelites, also present, are assembled to come to an epoch-making decision about moving the ark to Jerusalem. The deliberations are marked by submission to the will of God. There is planning for a national venture which will merit even more total representation than David's coronation, as God is greater than any human being however exalted.

The meeting of 13:1–4 serves to fill the gap suggested by *again* in the Chronicler's source, 2 Samuel 6:1. It also reflects other concerns of his. The proposal to invite *our brethren everywhere who are left in all the land of Israel* (v. 2) on the surface refers to those Israelites who had not already come to Hebron. But the Chronicler's Jewish readers could hardly fail to catch an exilic reference and would think both of the exile-like ravages of the Philistines in 10:7 and of the inhabitants of the northern kingdom who escaped the Assyrian exile (compare 2 Chron. 34:9, 21). The Chronicler is brilliant at double entendre, at wearing the hats of the historian and the preacher at the same time. One of the words the Chronicler uses to refer to the inclusiveness of Israel is *brethren* (look up 2 Chron. 11:4; 28:11). Here is part of the Chronicler's unremitting campaign to stress the unity of the people of God, which his following references to *all Israel,* no less than three times in verses 5–8, serve to reinforce. God could not be fully honored till *brethren . . . dwell together in unity,* worshiping together in the presence of God (Ps. 133:1). The Chronicler never tires of repeating this ecumenical aim.

Another of his concerns emerges at the end of verse 3. There had been no inquiry at the ark during *the days of Saul.* The verbal phrase means literally *we did not seek it.* The reader's mind is meant to travel back to 10:13, 14 to the failure to seek God which is mentioned twice, using the Hebrew verb *dāraš,* which recurs here. To neglect the ark, and so God Himself, was symptomatic of the way of exile chosen by Saul. The message is that the way of restoration calls for a lively concern for God and for the discharge of religious duties which serve to express it. Jesus reaffirmed this truth in principle when He taught "Seek first the kingdom of God and His righteousness" (Matt. 6:33)—even when one's life is filled with questions about basic necessities such as food and clothing. In the context of the Sermon on the Mount God's "righteousness" is His practical claim on human life, which is more radical than the scribes and Pharisees interpreted it to be.

It is to the religious and institutional dimension of such claim that the Chronicler is drawing his readers' attention. To whatever denomination we belong, we all have religious rites and forms which are part and parcel of that denominational tradition, whether high or low, old or recent. There is a false spirituality which would characterize all such phenomena as of the flesh. Certainly any means of grace, great or small, can degenerate into "a commandment of men, learned by rote," when the "hearts" of those who perform it are "far from me [God]" (Isa. 29:13, RSV). There is an opposite danger when religious habits are disdained. As the Jewish scholar Israel Abrahams shrewdly observed, "What can be done at any time and in any manner is liable to be done at no time and in no manner."[1]

The Chronicler mainly uses the narrative of 2 Samuel 6 to tell the story of the procession—and its sudden halt. Uzza *put out his hand to hold the ark*" (v. 9). Here is another good intention, but it has devastating results. The underlying ancient concept is that the ark shared in the holiness of God, His transcendent power, which could be a force for good or ill. Holiness here has a physical quality: it takes the form of an electrical or radioactive force into whose strong field Uzza strayed to his destruction. The jolt the story gives the modern reader at this point can serve as a measure of the rude shock David receives. What is happening here? Why has this occurred?

At this point I could interject, like some precocious child putting up a hand in class, that the answer lies in chapter 15. But the expositor knows nothing yet of chapter 15. He has to linger by David's side, sharing his gamut of emotions. One must respect the narrator's sequence: there is a time to explain, but it is not yet. A rule of exposition is not to go beyond the spirit of the text. Such biblical and other parallels as are furnished must stay within its bounds. The skill of the hermeneutical task is to honor this principle while applying the text to readers with a different cultural and religious orientation.

David is *"angry"* (v. 11). It is the anger of frustration, hammering impotently at a locked door, shaking prison bars in fury. It often occurs as a natural response in the laments of the psalms, to express the disappointment and resentment which are the human reactions to trauma. After the emotion is worked through, another emotion rushes in to fill the vacuum of David's disturbed mind—fear. He is *"afraid"* of God (v. 12), scared by what has happened. He realizes that he is in the presence of a mysterious power which he can neither control nor comprehend. One might regard this fear as a spiritually more appropriate response than anger, but the human frame is too weak to attain to spirituality at a single leap. There has to be an unfolding of human emotions in reaction to crisis. The narrative closes on the unsatisfying note of unfinished business. The failure of the venture reflects the disintegration of spiritual hopes. The only positive ray is the blessing received by the family of Obed-Edom with whom the ark is left, but that can bring little personal consolation to David. The dominant impression is of a fiasco. "Unless the Lord builds the house, they labor in vain who build it" (Ps. 127:1)—but how can one be sure that the Lord is behind the project? There's the rub. The Chronicler leaves the problem unresolved longer than his source in 2 Samuel 6, partly perhaps to lay greater stress on the solution, when it emerges in chapter 15. Until then there is a period of waiting. Even while other matters are spoken of, the reader's mind is preoccupied with the problem of chapter 13, disturbed and uneasy. Life can be like that. At such times one has to live through a range of emotions and cling to such redeeming features as can bolster faith and hope.

. . . HONORED BY GOD

14:1 Now Hiram king of Tyre sent messengers to David, and cedar trees, with masons and carpenters, to build him a house.

2 So David knew that the LORD had established him as king over Israel, for his kingdom was highly exalted for the sake of His people Israel.

3 Then David took more wives in Jerusalem, and David begot more sons and daughters.

4 And these are the names of his children whom he had in Jerusalem: Shammua, Shobab, Nathan, Solomon,

5 Ibhar, Elishua, Elpelet,

6 Nogah, Nepheg, Japhia,

7 Elishama, Beeliada, and Eliphelet.

8 Now when the Philistines heard that David had been anointed king over all Israel, all the Philistines went up to search for David. And David heard *of it* and went out against them.

9 Then the Philistines went and made a raid on the Valley of Rephaim.

10 And David inquired of God, saying, "Shall I go up against the Philistines? Will You deliver them into my hand?" The LORD said to him, "Go up, for I will deliver them into your hand."

11 So they went up to Baal Perazim, and David defeated them there. Then David said, "God has broken through my enemies by my hand like a breakthrough of water." Therefore they called the name of that place Baal Perazim.

12 And when they left their gods there, David gave a commandment, and they were burned with fire.

13 Then the Philistines once again made a raid on the valley.

14 Therefore David inquired again of God, and God said to him, "You shall not go up after them; circle around them, and come upon them in front of the mulberry trees.

15 "And it shall be, when you hear a sound of marching in the tops of the mulberry trees, then you shall go out to battle, for God has gone out before you to strike the camp of the Philistines."

16 So David did as God commanded him, and they drove back the army of the Philistines from Gibeon as far as Gezer.

17 Then the fame of David went out into all lands, and the LORD brought the fear of him upon all nations.

1 Chron. 14:1-17

Yes, good intentions are honored by God. At least, David's were—but not poor Uzza's. Did the ancient reader too experience a sense of unfairness? If so, life is like that. One person, too close to the catastrophe, is engulfed by it; another survives, shocked and bruised, and has to make the best of the longer lease on life, even as he or she wonders at the randomness of providence. There is a wordplay that dominates chapters 13–15 and binds them together. The English reader is made aware of two of the instances by the transliterations "Perez Uzza" or "outbreak against Uzza" at 13:11 and *"Baal Perazim"* or "Lord of breakthroughs" at 14:11. Both are place-names accompanied by use of the verb *pāraṣ*, rendered respectively "outbreak" and "(God) *has broken through."* Both instances are taken over from the source in 2 Samuel 5–6, but the Chronicler adds two more, one in 13:2, rendered together with a second verb as "let us send out . . . everywhere," and another in 15:13, which picks up 13:11. The fourfold wordplay is complex, but it is not too difficult to grasp the Chronicler's intent. The first two cases are associated with a problematic black and white contrast, of good intentions in seeking God and the damning of another's good intentions. The third, at 14:11, relieves the discord by focusing on the first and showing how David's good intentions are honored by God in military victory. The fourth, at 15:13, will relieve the discord further by showing how a lesson is learned from the disaster and how God's will is eventually discerned: there is again a seeking of God ("consult"), at a deeper level.

Chapter 14 serves to fill the three-month gap between the two attempts to bring the ark to Jerusalem. It is a literary device that conveys a sense of waiting. More importantly, it preaches the message that God honors good intentions. The seeking after God signified by the new seeking out of the ark after its neglect in Saul's reign (13:3) was good. God measures spiritual progress by endeavors, not by results. So the verb in David's statement at 14:11 acts as a counterpoint to its use in his speech of 13:2–3. The framing of 14:11 with the double use of *"Baal Perazim"* serves to drive home the message, which the whole chapter intends to reinforce, that God is here respecting David's good intentions. His seeking of God has not gone unnoticed. It is the way of blessing. The Chronicler wants his readers to find in it a message for themselves, a message which Jesus also gave in His exhortation: "Seek first the kingdom of God and His righteousness, and all these things shall be added to you" (Matt. 6:33). David's heart was in the right place and, although this basic fact could not guarantee the automatic success of his venture, in other respects he experiences the blessing of God. That the Chronicler is tracing the blessed outcome of seeking God can be illustrated from another passage, 2 Chronicles 30:19. There Hezekiah prays that Israelites who had not undergone proper ritual purification may yet enjoy participation in the Passover with impunity, since they belong to the category of him who "prepares his heart to seek God . . . , even though not according to the sanctuary's rules of cleanness" (RSV). In this case David, although he made a ritual mistake, had certainly prepared his heart to seek God; accordingly he won blessing. The measure in which he gave to God was the measure in which he received blessing, pressed down, shaken together, and running over.

The blessing is traced in several dimensions: foreign tribute, the gift of sons and daughters with hint of a dynasty in the inclusion of Solomon's name, and conquest of the Philistines, who had been the human assailants in the way of exile traveled by Saul and the nation. There is a pervading concern to exemplify the way of restoration. While Saul consulted a medium, which was definitely not a means of seeking God (10:13), David twice *inquired of God*" (14:10, 14; cf. 13:3), relying on God in these enterprises. Accordingly, while in Saul's case the sequel was defeat, which resulted in the attribution of power to the gods of Philistia (10:10), in David's case the sequel was victory which included the Philistines' abandonment of their gods in the battlefield and so spelled the glorification of the true God (14:12). Another such contrast is to appear in 15:29. Saul's daughter Michal, unable to recognize the true meaning of events, despises her husband David as he honors the ark in worshiping God. It is an instance of "like father, like daughter." Saul is typical of those who do not seek the things of God and are blind to such endeavors.

By these means the Chronicler is posing a warning: along which road are you traveling, dear reader, a road of backsliding and exile or a road of restoration and blessing? The crossroads are ever there, confronting us. Constant choosing and diligent self-examination are needed so that we identify with the things of God and live accordingly.

The chapter begins and ends with two reflections, one that of David, taken over from 2 Samuel 6 (v. 2), and the other the Chronicler's own (v. 17). The first reflection reminds us of the triangle of good relations so dominant in chapters 11–12, the beautiful phenomenon of God, Israel, and David working together in harmony. David in his royal prosperity gives pride of place to God, as the power behind the throne and the source of his success. The people of God come a close second: the prospering of his royal cause was *for the sake of His people Israel"* (v. 2). The king belongs in the third place as minister of both God and Israel. His role in the theocracy is to serve the interests of the God so signally backing him and to serve the interests of the people. There is a lovely sensitivity here which must find reflection among all believers who are in a position of responsibility. It is a natural corollary of seeking God. The child in Sunday school is taught this truth simply by the spiritual acronym of J.O.Y.: Jesus, others, yourself.

David's perception was a healthy one, and all the more creditable because human nature finds it a hard lesson to learn. Naturally speaking, we are all inclined to see ourselves as the movie star, with our associates playing supporting roles, and the rest of the world milling around as mere extras. We are each the center of our little universe, the sun around which the constellations and planets move in constant homage. David is able to break away from this self-centered fantasy. Nor does his perception unite him only to God; there is a human dimension of concern. He may not rule as a tyrant whose divine right enables him to ride roughshod over subjects in his power. His rise to power has not swept away the basic rights and duties of the people under God: the royal covenant is characterized as an outworking of the earlier covenant between God and Israel. In any sphere power may easily be abused. As a Victorian political historian perceived, "power tends to corrupt and absolute power corrupts absolutely." Here is a contrary perception: as David's star reaches its zenith it is God who is honored and the people who profit.

The Chronicler probably saw a deeper significance in verse 2 than social harmony, in the light of his own observation in verse 17. This monarchy was God's means of realizing His will for Israel itself. In this respect the mention of Solomon's name in verse 4 is significant. The purposes of God for His people were to go beyond David and in their ongoing progression were to embrace Solomon. There is a hint of a continuing dynasty. For the Chronicler the future of Israel was bound up with a descendant of David. The establishment of the dynasty created a hope still dear to his heart and shaped his understanding of Israel's future under God. In like manner the New Testament gives an interpretation of Jesus as "made" by God "the head over all things for the church" and enjoying a heavenly position "far above . . . every name that is named, not only in this age but also in that which is to come" (Eph. 1:21, 22, RSV). This latter Christological reference finds a parallel in the present chapter at verse 17: *"the fame* (literally "name") *of David went out into all lands."* This *"fame"* and the *"fear"* with which *"all nations"* react to David invite comparison with chapter 1, where it was suggested that the world is viewed as David's realm. Here again there is an implicit typical and predictive note. For the Davidic king in his role as representative of the sole and universal God, worldwide rule was a logical culmination. Accordingly the royal Psalm 2 promises to the king of David's line universal submission from "the nations" and "the ends of the earth" (Ps. 2:8, 9). Revelation 19:11–16 does not hesitate to apply the psalm's language to the conquering Messiah whose name is "King of kings and Lord of lords." For the Chronicler and for the Christian there is a divine arc drawn between past revelation and future hope: both stand in the present gap between these two points looking forward with a hope which has been shaped by that past.

DOING IT RIGHT

15:1 *David* built houses for himself in the City of David; and he prepared a place for the ark of God, and pitched a tent for it.

2 Then David said, "No one may carry the ark of God but the Levites, for the LORD has chosen them to carry the ark of God and to minister before Him forever."

3 And David gathered all Israel together at Jerusalem, to bring up the ark of the LORD to its place, which he had prepared for it.

4 Then David assembled the children of Aaron and the Levites:

5 of the sons of Kohath, Uriel the chief, and one hundred and twenty of his brethren;

6 of the sons of Merari, Asaiah the chief, and two hundred and twenty of his brethren;

7 of the sons of Gershom, Joel the chief, and one hundred and thirty of his brethren;

8 of the sons of Elizaphan, Shemaiah the chief, and two hundred of his brethren;

9 of the sons of Hebron, Eliel the chief, and eighty of his brethren;

10 of the sons of Uzziel, Amminadab the chief, and one hundred and twelve of his brethren.

11 And David called for Zadok and Abiathar the priests, and for the Levites: for Uriel, Asaiah, Joel, Shemaiah, Eliel, and Amminadab.

12 He said to them, "You *are* the heads of the fathers' *houses* of the Levites; sanctify yourselves, you and your brethren, that you may bring up the ark of the LORD God of Israel to *the place* I have prepared for it.

13 "For because you *did* not *do it* the first *time,* the LORD our God broke out against us, because we did not consult Him about the proper order."

14 So the priests and the Levites sanctified themselves to bring up the ark of the LORD God of Israel.

15 And the children of the Levites bore the ark of God on their shoulders, by its poles, as Moses had commanded according to the word of the LORD.

16 Then David spoke to the leaders of the Levites to appoint their brethren *to be* the singers accompanied by instruments of music, stringed instruments, harps, and cymbals, by raising the voice with resounding joy.

17 So the Levites appointed Heman the son of Joel; and of his brethren, Asaph the son of Berechiah; and of their brethren, the sons of Merari, Ethan the son of Kushaiah;

18 and with them their brethren of the second *rank:* Zechariah, Ben, Jaaziel, Shemiramoth, Jehiel, Unni, Eliab, Benaiah, Maaseiah, Mattithiah, Elipheleh, Mikneiah, Obed-Edom, and Jeiel, the gatekeepers;

19 the singers, Heman, Asaph, and Ethan, *were* to sound the cymbals of bronze;

20 Zechariah, Aziel, Shemiramoth, Jehiel, Unni, Eliab, Maaseiah, and Benaiah, with strings according to Alamoth;

21 Mattithiah, Elipheleh, Mikneiah, Obed-Edom, Jeiel, and Azaziah, to direct with harps on the Sheminith;

22 Chenaniah, leader of the Levites, was instructor *in charge of* the music, because he *was* skillful;

23 Berechiah and Elkanah *were* doorkeepers for the ark;

24 Shebaniah, Joshaphat, Nethanel, Amasai, Zechariah, Benaiah, and Eliezer, the priests, were to blow the trumpets before the ark of God; and Obed-Edom and Jehiah, doorkeepers for the ark.

25 So David, the elders of Israel, and the captains over thousands went to bring up the ark of the covenant of the LORD from the house of Obed-Edom with joy.

26 And so it was, when God helped the Levites who bore the ark of the covenant of the LORD, that they offered seven bulls and seven rams.

27 David was clothed with a robe of fine linen, as were all the Levites who bore the ark, the singers, and Chenaniah the music master *with* the singers. David also wore a linen ephod.

28 Thus all Israel brought up the ark of the covenant of the LORD with shouting and with the sound of the horn, with trumpets and with cymbals, making music with stringed instruments and harps.

29 And it happened, *as* the ark of the covenant of the LORD came to the City of David, that Michal, Saul's daughter, looked through a window and saw King David whirling and playing music; and she despised him in her heart.

16:1 So they brought the ark of God, and set it in the midst of the tabernacle that David had erected for it. Then they offered burnt offerings and peace offerings before God.

2 And when David had finished offering the burnt offerings and the peace offerings, he blessed the people in the name of the LORD.

3 Then he distributed to everyone of Israel, both man and woman, to everyone a loaf of bread, a piece *of meat,* and a cake of raisins.

4 And he appointed some of the Levites to minister

before the ark of the LORD, to commemorate, to thank, and to praise the LORD God of Israel:

5 Asaph the chief, and next to him Zechariah, *then* Jeiel, Shemiramoth, Jehiel, Mattithiah, Eliab, Benaiah, and Obed-Edom: Jeiel with stringed instruments and harps, but Asaph made music with cymbals;

6 Benaiah and Jahaziel the priests regularly *blew* the trumpets before the ark of the covenant of God.

37 So he left Asaph and his brothers there before the ark of the covenant of the LORD to minister before the ark regularly, as every day's work required;

38 and Obed-Edom with his sixty-eight brethren, including Obed-Edom the son of Jeduthun, and Hosah, *to be* gatekeepers;

39 and Zadok the priest and his brethren the priests, before the tabernacle of the LORD at the high place that *was* at Gibeon,

40 to offer burnt offerings to the LORD on the altar of burnt offering regularly morning and evening, and *to do* according to all that is written in the Law of the LORD which He commanded Israel;

41 and with them Heman and Jeduthun and the rest who were chosen, who were designated by name, to give thanks to the LORD, because His mercy *endures* forever;

42 and with them Heman and Jeduthun, to sound aloud with trumpets and cymbals and the musical instruments of God. Now the sons of Jeduthun *were* gatekeepers.

43 Then all the people departed, every man to his house; and David returned to bless his house.

1 Chron. 15:1–16:6, 37–43

Chapter 14 has left unresolved the issue of bringing the ark to Jerusalem. Now the narrative reaches a climax, picking up the *pāraṣ* wordplay in 15:13 with an explanation which can dictate a contrary and successful course. The ark is duly installed, worship is offered, and new staffing arrangements are made in the light of the ark's new home. Each of these phases is for the Chronicler pregnant with meaning for his own age: he is very much aware that his text has significance beyond the historical period of David.

15:1–2 convey the gist of 15:1–24: the preparation of a place for the ark in Jerusalem and the preparation of a Levitical entourage for the transportation of the ark. The preparation of a place, in the form of a tent and presumably a suitably sanctified site, is a dominant concern of 15:1–15, finding mention in verses 1, 3 and 12. It is a development of 2 Samuel 6:17. The reader of the New Testament is reminded of the assurance of Jesus that He went to His Father—to the heavenly Jerusalem!—to "prepare a place" for His followers before coming again and taking them to join Him at that place (John 14:2, 3; cf. Heb. 9:24, 28). Both concerns are marked by a theme of unfinished business and by determination to complete an enterprise undertaken for God.

The major thrust of the passage is the preparing of personnel for the procession and its aftermath. The kernel of the Chronicler's material lies in the disclosure of 2 Samuel 6:13 that the second attempt, unlike the first, involved "those bearing the ark." For the Chronicler this is a clue that David had to pursue his seeking of God at a deeper level. The preparation of both the place and the personnel reveals David's seeking via his care of and concern for the ark. Now this seeking is more enlightened, although his less exact understanding earlier had by no means debarred him from divine blessing. In 15:13 there is an admission that "we did not consult"—literally "seek," using the significant Hebrew verb dāraš—"Him about the proper order." This meant for the Chronicler that there had to be a searching of Scripture to find the divine prescription. It is found in Deuteronomy 10:8, which is echoed in 15:2, and in Numbers 7:9 and Exodus 25:13–15, to which allusion is made in 15:15. According to these prescriptions in the Torah, God's law, it was Levites who were to carry the ark on their shoulders by means of poles, at a discreet distance from the ark itself. For the Chronicler "the word of the Lord" was paramount. In 11:3 and 12:23 it had been a prophetic word. Now it was the word of the law, "as Moses had commanded." The Law and the Prophets were the divine word to Israel and in them was to be sought expression of His will for each generation.

This emphasis on the Scriptures is an essential trait of the Chronicler. They were the source of divine authority and were to be the basis of Judah's self-understanding and ongoing comportment. In like manner the church too was later to learn that "all Scripture is given by inspiration of God, and is profitable for doctrine, for reproof, for correction, for instruction in righteousness" (2 Tim. 3:16). In other words, they are profitable for both doctrinal and ethical purposes, teaching positive and negative lessons concerning what to believe and how to behave. For the Chronicler the niceties of ritual detail could be established by reference to the Torah. However, the Christian has not been furnished with such detailed information about the institutional side of his faith. As R. W. Dale pertinently observed about church order, "if every church must be built on the exact model of the church at Corinth, at Ephesus or at Antioch, we are in hopeless difficulties. The plans have been lost and the specifications destroyed."[2] The Old Testament and the New do not prescribe in the same way about institutional order. In the New Testament there are a few basic church observances, such as baptism and the communion meal, and general principles like unity, faith, love, and the need that "all things be done decently and in order" (see 1 Cor. 10–14). Denominational traditions have variously clothed with flesh and blood the skeletons of these practices and principles. What really matters is to stay true to the institutional basics.

In accord with his scriptural model, the Chronicler envisages a restructuring of the procession of 13:7–8. The Levites carry the ark, while other Levites engage in music and song, and priests blow trumpet blasts. In addition there is a suitable entourage of priests and Levites to accompany the ark and make visible its holy status. There also had to be adequate security arrangements at the ark's destination, and so Levitical gatekeepers are appointed. There is a beautiful little touch at 15:26. There has been much focus on the Levites as the right people for the task. They come into their own in the second procession, and all eyes are on them. Certainly they do a necessary and successful job of work, but the Chronicler bids his readers lift their eyes to God and give Him the glory: *"God helped the Levites."* The reference is to their transportation of the ark without mishap—in contrast to 13:9–10!—which was taken as proof of God's favor and so cause for sacrifices of grateful worship. The Chronicler envisaged God not as the inspirer of the Torah who left His people to obey His ancient commands as best they could, but as also providentially present with them and promoting His will in their lives.

The note of *"joy"* which closed the previous section (12:40) also comes to the fore in this second procession at 15:16 and 15:25.

Comparison of the two verses shows that there had to be a measure of institutionalism in the expression of joy. To say this is to appear to sound the death knell for joy! This is not so. Every church has to translate the spirit of worship into appropriate religious forms. It is true; there is always a danger that forms turn into formalities, and new Christian groups ever appear with fresh and "informal" forms for the edification of the Church in general. Forms there must be and their character should be a constant challenge. Existing forms have to be re-evaluated regularly as to whether they are still adequate vehicles for the worship of God. In time wineskins wear out and are inadequate for the ever new wine of worship and faith. Worship must ever be a living thing, ascending to God from hearts and minds in appropriate language and modes.

A prominent feature of the Chronicler's account is that in between the two halves of 2 Samuel 6:19 is inserted, in 16:4–42, a long account of the musical and related arrangements David makes for the functioning of religion in his day. This was to be an interim period. Until the temple was built there still existed the central sanctuary at Gibeon as the main place of sacrifice and the continuing scene of worship (cf. 2 Chron. 1:3). So priestly personnel are appointed for the sacrificial system faithfully operated there on the lines laid down in the Torah (16:40), while two of the Levitical guilds, those of Heman and Jeduthun, are commissioned to discharge a musical ministry. Correspondingly, at the new altarless location of the ark, the guild of Asaph, along with priestly trumpeters, engaged in song and music and in caring for the ark. The role of the three musical guilds was to give expression to Israel's praise (16:4, 41). This role is described in three ways:

1. To praise is *"to commemorate"* (16:4) the Lord or more literally to "make mention" of His name in praise. It is no accident that all three of the psalm selections of 16:8–36 refer to God's "name," in verses 8, 10, 29, and 35 (look too at 17:21, 24). The name of God, and so the unpacking of what He has revealed Himself to be and do, is the theme of praise.

2. To praise is *"to thank"* (16:4). In other Old Testament contexts this is often a precise word, as in the psalms of thanksgiving, such as Psalms 18 and 116, in response to a specific and recent act of divine deliverance. Here it is a wider term in reaction to all God's manifestations of grace—because His "steadfast love endures for ever" (RSV),

as 16:41 expands. Israel's God is celebrated as a gracious God to whom they owe not only their coming into being as God's people but also their preservation and prospects.

3. The third term, *"to praise"* (16:4), is a general one that encompasses all of Israel's hymns, of which a large number are preserved in the Psalter. Truly God was "enthroned on the praises of Israel" (Ps. 22:3, RSV).

It was a prime function of Israel to praise God. The church has inherited this role. A key activity of Christian meetings according to the New Testament was "speaking to one another in psalms and hymns and spiritual songs, singing and making melody in your hearts to the Lord" (Eph. 5:19). There was an ongoing need to "offer the sacrifice of praise . . . , giving thanks to His name" (Heb. 13:15). The purpose of the church as a chosen community corresponding to Israel is to "proclaim the praises" of God (1 Pet. 2:9). We praise what we prize. The ardor of our praising is the measure of how much we prize God's revelation in Christ.

DOXOLOGY—ANTIDOTE TO DESPAIR

16:7 On that day David first delivered *this psalm* into the hand of Asaph and his brethren, to thank the LORD:
  8 Oh, give thanks to the LORD!
    Call upon His name;
    Make known His deeds among the peoples!
  9 Sing to Him, sing psalms to Him;
    Talk of all His wondrous works!
  10 Glory in His holy name;
    Let the hearts of those rejoice who seek the
       LORD!
  11 Seek the LORD and His strength;
    Seek His face evermore!
  12 Remember His marvelous works which He has
       done,
    His wonders, and the judgments of His mouth,
  13 O seed of Israel His servant,
    You children of Jacob, His chosen ones!
  14 He *is* the LORD our God;
    His judgments *are* in all the earth.

15 Remember His covenant forever,
   The word which He commanded, for a thou-
      sand generations,
16 *The covenant which* He made with Abraham,
   And His oath to Isaac,
17 And confirmed it to Jacob for a statute,
   To Israel *for* an everlasting covenant,
18 Saying, "To you I will give the land of Canaan
   As the allotment of your inheritance,"
19 When you were few in number,
   Indeed very few, and strangers in it.
20 When they went from one nation to another,
   And from *one* kingdom to another people,
21 He permitted no man to do them wrong;
   Yes, He rebuked kings for their sakes,
22 *Saying,* "Do not touch My anointed ones,
   And do My prophets no harm."
23 Sing to the LORD, all the earth;
   Proclaim the good news of His salvation from
      day to day.
24 Declare His glory among the nations,
   His wonders among all peoples.
25 For the LORD *is* great and greatly to be praised;
   He *is* also to be feared above all gods.
26 For all the gods of the peoples *are* idols,
   But the LORD made the heavens.
27 Honor and majesty *are* before Him;
   Strength and gladness are in His place.
28 Give to the LORD, O families of the peoples,
   Give to the LORD glory and strength.
29 Give to the LORD the glory *due* His name;
   Bring an offering, and come before Him.
   Oh, worship the LORD in the beauty of holiness!
30 Tremble before Him, all the earth.
   The world also is firmly established,
   It shall not be moved.
31 Let the heavens rejoice, and let the earth be
      glad;
   And let them say among the nations, "The LORD
      reigns."
32 Let the sea roar, and all its fullness;
   Let the field rejoice, and all that *is* in it.

33 Then the trees of the woods shall rejoice before
    the LORD,
    For He is coming to judge the earth.
34 Oh, give thanks to the LORD, for *He is* good!
    For His mercy *endures* forever.
35 And say, "Save us, O God of our salvation;
    Gather us together, and deliver us from the
    Gentiles,
    To give thanks to Your holy name,
    To triumph in Your praise."
36 Blessed *be* the LORD God of Israel
    From everlasting to everlasting!
And all the people said, "Amen!" and praised the
    LORD.

1 Chron. 16:7–36

In verses 8–36 the Chronicler gives three samples of praise in an anthology derived from the Book of Psalms, Psalms 105:1–15; 96:1–13, and 106:1, 47, 48. He adduces them as appropriate expressions of praise at this juncture in Israel's history. In so doing, he has to adapt his material slightly, removing the references to the temple as an existing institution in verses 27 and 29 (compare Ps. 96:6, 8). The chief merit of these particular extracts for the Chronicler is that they served to reflect, as in a mirror, his dominant concerns in this overall section and bridged the gap between ancient history and contemporary worship in the Chronicler's day. Verses 23–33, derived from Psalm 96, function as the main part of the anthology. This center is bordered by material from Psalm 105 and from Psalm 106 by way of an introduction and a conclusion. The whole anthology is resonant with themes to which the New Testament is no stranger.

1. *A vision of greatness.* In verse 23 to *"proclaim the good news of"* God's *"salvation"*—a remarkably Christian-sounding phrase—is a mark of the new age established by David. It replaces the defeat of the way of exile, which encouraged the impression that other gods had triumphed: see 10:9 where "proclaim the news" renders the same Hebrew verb. *"The nations"* and *"all peoples"* in verses 24 and 31 have figured in 14:17 as awed witnesses of David's God-given victories, which pointed forward to God's future kingdom. The Lord's greatness (v. 25a) has already been the implicit theme of 11:9 and 12:22, underlying David's greatness. The impotence of the

"gods" has been demonstrated in 14:12. The sacred *"place"* of verse 27 relates to the place provided by David for the ark. The kingship of God (v. 31) had already been manifested through David's reign and indeed was part of the theology of the ark (13:6, RSV). Israel's hope was that it would one day be manifested afresh in a world kingdom.

Psalm 96 reflects the theology of post-exilic Judah in giving God a universal role and in confidently hoping that this role, grounded in His work as Creator, would be vindicated in a future intervention, when He would claim the world as His own and set it aright. In the Chronicler's thought there had already been a significant manifestation of God in the period of David. To the post-exilic community, living in a *"day of small things"* (Zech. 4:10), he offered the greatness of the past associated with David and Solomon as an encouraging image of future greatness under God.

2. *A veiled hope.* This message is reinforced in the introductory verses 8–22. *"Let the hearts of those rejoice who seek the Lord!"* (v. 10) is an apt commentary on the preceding chapters. Seeking God had been David's overall concern and had borne fruit in the successful transportation of the ark to Jerusalem, while the accompanying and consequent expressions of joy were a fitting response of worship. For the Chronicler to seek God was a perpetual mandate, as verse 11 seems to say. The community of faith in the Chronicler's time, as in David's, was still the *"seed of Israel"* and God's *"chosen ones"* (v. 13). *"Abraham"* in the original Psalm 105:6 is significantly changed to *"Israel,"* in whom patriarchal history comes to a head, as we noticed in 2:2. We are the chosen people, affirms the Chronicler not in any spirit of wrongful pride but to convey a necessary sense of continuity and destiny. When pride is the opposite of humility, it is bad; when it is the opposite of shame, it is good. At a time when so much in the environment of post-exilic Judah shouted "No!" at Judah's claims, faith dared to shout "Yes!" The *"covenant"* dominates verses 15–18, appropriately enough, for was not the ark *"the ark of the covenant"* (v. 6)? These verses serve as a commentary on the concept of the covenant, stressing its everlasting nature and so its relevance to the Chronicler's age. The picture painted in verses 19–22 of the patriarchs as bearers of the noble promise of the land, yet *"few in number,"* insignificant, and *"strangers"* in their own land, is also an eloquent description of the Jewish community after the Exile. Yet they could derive comfort from the truth that like the patriarchs they

stood under the protection of God (vv. 21, 22). Promise, privation, protection: such was the checkered pattern of light and shade that dappled the Jewish community in its faith and fortunes.

3. *Invocation of God's grace.* The closing verses 34–36 quoted from Psalm 106 accentuate the contrasts of the introduction. On the one hand, God's people are the recipients of His goodness and "steadfast love" (RSV), not only yesterday and today but *"forever."* On the other hand, they pray to God for deliverance from *"the nations."* Their inferior status is not one befitting the people of the universal God. God's *"salvation,"* experienced in the past, is invoked afresh.

The Chronicler is recalling his contemporaries to their great traditions. He helps this small and struggling community to appropriate these truths as their own, to live in the good of them, and to make them the basis of a sure hope in a God who is preserving them for a purpose. God is the focus of praise stretching from the remote past to the remote future (v. 36). This God is the God of Israel, and His praises match His dealings with them since the days of Abraham, Jacob, and David, until now and on into the unseen future!

What shall we say to these things? Here is theology set to music. In the midst of praise divine truths are taking firmer root in the hearts of God's people. Theology functions as encouragement, giving new strength to the weary and fresh hope to the disheartened. Hold on, runs the message: *"the Lord is great"* and *"the Lord . . . is coming"* (vv. 25, 33). I cannot help thinking of the pastoral theology of Romans 5:1–11 and 8:18–39. The church is represented as externally weak, suffering, and persecuted. The church is also a community marked by joy, not because its members are blind to the facts but because they look beyond bare facts to see God at work, preparing for them a glorious destiny. They feel the rain, but see the rainbow. God's electing love lies around them, embracing them in its strong grip. It is as strong as death and many waters cannot quench it, nor can the floods drown it. That love brings an assurance of victory, even now enjoyed in spirit. Come wind, come weather, they are to remain valiant in the faith, conscious of God's preserving grace. Soon the tide will turn, and then Christians will be revealed in their true colors as sons and daughters of God. This hope is a vital ingredient of their initial salvation and means that future salvation will be theirs. The work of God through the Lord Jesus is the guarantee of their own destiny.

There is a remarkable affinity between the message of Chronicles and what Paul is saying. Both inspired authors have reached into the heart of biblical faith and hope. For both their roots lie in the past, but the focus of their life is in the future. The aims of both will be realized if their pastoral theology evokes from their present readers an *"Amen"* and a hallelujah (v. 36). J. S. Whale once wrote of the danger of reducing theology to an intellectual exercise: "Instead of putting off our shoes from our feet because the place whereon we stand is holy ground, we are taking nice photographs of the burning bush from suitable angles. We are chatting about theories of the atonement with our feet on the mantelpiece, instead of kneeling down before the wounds of Christ."[3] In Chronicles and Romans such theology is conspicuous by its absence.

NOTES

1. Cited from *Studies in Pharisaism and the Gospels,* Second Series, p. 84, by E. W. Heaton, *Daniel* (London: SCM Press, 1956), p. 164.

2. Cited from *Essays and Addresses,* p. 33, by H. Cook, *What Baptists Stand For* (London: Carey Kingsgate Press, third edition, 1958), p. 83.

3. John S. Whale, *Christian Doctrine* (New York: Macmillan Company, 1941), p. 152.

CHAPTER FIVE

Thy Kingdom Come!

1 Chronicles 17:1–20:8

The rest of the account of David's reign, in chapters 17–29, is taken up with the temple, directly or indirectly. In these chapters the theme of the temple is tightly interwoven with David's role as king. David's son is to build the temple—and to be his successor in a permanent dynasty. David's own role is to pave the way by creating a stable, prosperous society in which his son may carry out his own task. Father and son have each a vital and different part to play in establishing what is regarded as the kingdom of God (17:14).

The house of God, the house of David, the kingdom of God—what glorious images these conjured up for the Chronicler! The first spoke to him of a heritage of worship still enjoyed in his own day. The second was a matter of spiritual hope, that it would be restored. The third was both a present reality and a future hope. Asaph's choir had just sung "The Lord reigns" (16:31), but yet to materialize was the perfect establishment of His kingdom on earth (16:33). For the Chronicler there was a glorious prefiguring of that coming kingdom in the reigns of David and Solomon. Their work revolved around ideals which, six centuries later, still engrossed the Chronicler. Through them God had revealed His will in a unique and once-for-all way, which meant that the future could be understood only in terms of that particular period of history.

The Christian too knows of a sacred moment in humanity's experience. Though in the middle of the sweep of history, it is also its theological climax, the "last days" in which God "has spoken to us by His Son" (Heb. 1:2). Proclaimed then were the restoration of the house of David (Luke 1:32), the coming of God's kingdom (Mark 1:15), and the building of a spiritual temple (Eph. 2:20–22).

A glorious beginning was made then, but still awaited is an even more glorious consummation. We Christians stand in a position remarkably parallel to that of the Chronicler. It helps us not only to understand his double perspective but also to learn from his faith and from the way he expressed it.

GOD'S PROMISES ARE FOREVER

17:1 Now it came to pass, when David was dwelling in his house, that David said to Nathan the prophet, "See now, I dwell in a house of cedar, but the ark of the covenant of the LORD *is* under tent curtains."

2 Then Nathan said to David, "Do all that *is* in your heart, for God *is* with you."

3 But it happened that night that the word of God came to Nathan, saying,

4 "Go and tell My servant David, 'Thus says the LORD: "You shall not build Me a house to dwell in.

5 "For I have not dwelt in a house since the time that I brought up Israel, even to this day, but have gone from tent to tent, and from *one* tabernacle *to another.*

6 "Wherever I have moved about with all Israel, have I ever spoken a word to any of the judges of Israel, whom I commanded to shepherd My people, saying, 'Why have you not built Me a house of cedar?' " '

7 "Now therefore, thus shall you say to My servant David, 'Thus says the LORD of hosts: "I took you from the sheepfold, from following the sheep, to be ruler over My people Israel.

8 "And I have been with you wherever you have gone, and have cut off all your enemies from before you, and have made you a name like the name of the great men who *are* on the earth.

9 "Moreover I will appoint a place for My people Israel, and will plant them, that they may dwell in a place of their own and move no more; nor shall the sons of wickedness oppress them anymore, as previously,

10 "since the time that I commanded judges *to be* over My people Israel. Also I will subdue all your enemies. Furthermore I tell you that the LORD will build you a house.

11 "And it shall be, when your days are fulfilled, when you must go *to be* with your fathers, that I will set up your seed after you, who will be of your sons; and I will establish his kingdom.

12 "He shall build Me a house, and I will establish his throne forever.

13 "I will be his Father, and he shall be My son; and I will not take My mercy away from him, as I took *it* from *him* who was before you.

14 "And I will establish him in My house and in My kingdom forever; and his throne shall be established forever." ' "

15 According to all these words and according to all this vision, so Nathan spoke to David.

1 Chron. 17:1–15

In this narrative, which reflects 2 Samuel 7:1–17 fairly closely, David is concerned by an inconsistency which he wants to see resolved. Why should he be better housed than the ark, the symbol of God's presence as Lord of the covenant? The Chronicler has been building up to this point in his narration, for at structurally significant points he has mentioned David's palace, at 14:1 and 15:1; indeed, the mention of "cedar" recalls 14:1. The king broaches his concern to the court prophet Nathan, hoping for a seal of approval. Nathan, evidently not conscious of divine disapproval, gives the promise his blessing and assures him of God's support. The prophet's hazy apprehension of God's will receives subsequent clarification in a precise and complex oracle. We are reminded of the situation in 13:1–4 and the unanimous perception that the ark should be moved to Jerusalem, without the vital consideration of how it should be moved. We dare not be too hard on Nathan here nor on David and the assembly there. It is reassuring to us lesser mortals that even a prophet apprehended God's will in stages. Nathan's general apprehension that the temple should be built was correct, but the how and when had yet to be revealed. Nathan jumped to a natural but wrong conclusion. There is a maturing gradualness in the discovery of the divine will. God's servants in every age have known this experience of moving slowly forward in the direction of God's will, as they understand it, and the necessity to push hard on this door and that as they come to them, to see which will open, and sometimes mistaking His will before they eventually see it fulfilled in their lives. Such is the path of faith toward spiritual maturity.

Even Nathan did not get it right the first time. I am reminded of the apostle Paul's difficulties in discovering where to go on his first missionary journey in Turkey (Acts 16:6–10). After fruitful work Paul wanted to go west to the Roman province of Asia but found his way blocked by the Holy Spirit; whether via human opposition, physical sickness, or a direct supernatural communication we are not told. He turned north to Bithynia, but the result was the same. He traveled west to the port of Troas and at last received clear guidance through a vision to catch a boat to Macedonia. I once had a colleague who at a crucial point in her life was definitely pointed in a certain direction by encountering particular Scriptures. Through them she received remarkable messages which exactly matched her situation and moved her unerringly forward. I do not doubt that she was guided in that way. For many of us, however, there is a slower and more experimental route, not necessarily illumined by vision, voice, or verse. The main things to note in the cases of guidance here in Chronicles and also in Acts 16 are a sincere desire to be guided by God and a moving forward in the general direction of God's will, as it is apprehended. In spite of our best intentions we can be mistaken in our perception of what God really wants us to do. If we sit around waiting until we are 100 percent sure, we will not do anything: there will usually be some degree of uncertainty and a call for faith. We have boldly to act in accord with what we believe to be His will, putting that belief to the test even as we await confirmation.

Nathan's clearer perception about the project is not "no" but "not yet." Not the project but the timing and the person were inappropriate. Structurally verse 4 links with verse 12: "you shall not build," but David's son "shall build" the temple. The need was there, but it did not constitute a call for David, eager volunteer though he was! God was in no such hurry. He could wait a little longer (vv. 5, 6). Yet there was a preparatory role for David, which had to be performed before his son could build. Verses 8b–10a present a pre-temple program for him, and in fact the function of chapters 18–20 will be to record the implementation of that program. One is reminded of the condition laid down in Deuteronomy 12:10, 11: only after God had given His people rest from all their enemies could they offer worship at the place of His choosing. David was to be God's agent in procuring this territorial security. Verse 9 would have had post-exilic reverberations for the Chronicler's first readers. How God's people longed for *"a place of their own,"* unharassed and serenely secure! The implicit promise is that if they follow the way of restoration associated with David and seek God's will as he did, it would one day be theirs.

The term *"house"* acts as a structural marker in this chapter. We have noted already how verses 4 and 12 are polarized. Shooting off at a tangent from these verses is verse 10b: *"the Lord will build you a house."* There is a play on a different meaning of the word *"house,"* family or dynasty. Verse 10b is eventually to find a remarkable counterpoint in verse 14: David's dynasty would constitute a manifestation of God's kingdom. These verses, 4 and 12, 10b, and 14, are the four focal points of the prophetic message. There is obviously significant development in this complex revelation. According to verses 10b–11 God was going to do His own architectural work, in the course of which He would provide a son—Solomon, as it turned out—who would carry out the task David had wanted to do. Look very carefully at verse 12: *"He shall build Me a house, and I will establish his throne forever."* It is a focal point not only of the oracle but of the whole work of the Chronicler. In its importance it has a counterpart in 2 Chronicles 7:14. The two verses are Chronicles in a nutshell. Their two divine statements present the heart of the Chronicler's message in prescribing God's role for Himself and His role for Israel. If these two verses are understood, the whole of Chronicles falls into place around them. In this verse temple and dynasty are inextricably intertwined as a dual purpose of God. The house of God was bound up with the house of David in the sense that a representative of the latter would build it. Not only so, but the building of the temple constituted a guarantee of the perpetuity of the Davidic dynasty. For the Chronicler the two halves of verse 12 were related as cause and effect, as root and fruit. The construction of the temple marked a new era for Israel's royalty. The old era of Saul had seen a temporary manifestation of God's "steadfast love"

(v. 13, RSV), but now an unqualified, permanent relationship is promised. Solomon—and by implication his successors—would be forever supported by God as his patron. His function would be to represent God like a son sent on a mission by his father. The kingdom would thus be not merely Solomon's. God was to be the real king of Israel. The house of David was to transcend human history, for through it was to shine the kingdom of God. The Chronicler here adapts his source in 2 Samuel 7:16 to bring out this truth. That which is eternal had stooped down to enter the dimension of time: the kingdom of God had descended to earth. Henceforth the truth that "the Lord reigns" (16:31) would take on new meaning. God would rule in Israel and so in the world not only through the temple but through the Davidic throne. In this light the term *"servant,"* used of David in verses 4 and 7, leaps into new significance as a vassal king subordinate to his royal Overlord.

This portrayal of a new era founded on the temple and the Davidic dynasty finds a parallel in Psalm 78. Its review of the twists and turns of Israelite history culminates in the opening of a new age marked by God's building "His sanctuary" as secure as heaven and earth and by His choosing "David His servant" as the shepherd of His people (Ps. 78:69, 70). Israelite history was to witness many more twists and turns after that psalm and the basic 2 Samuel 7 were recorded. The temple was to be wrecked, as Psalm 79 was to attest, and the house of David with it, as Psalm 89 was to bemoan. Yet from the ruins the temple had been rebuilt, and the Chronicler rejoiced in the privilege of living in the new era of God's grace that continued still. One element was missing: a restored house of David. Spiritual logic demanded that it was only a matter of time before that too occurred. Verse 12 was God's pledge.

This event in divine revelation was a shining moment in the spiritual history of the people of God. It dealt with themes which in a more advanced form are precious to God's present people. It represented a milestone in God's revelation of His will. From a New Testament perspective it pointed forward to Jesus, Son of David, and in nature as well as in function Son of God, and to His fresh establishment of the kingdom of God in fact and in hope. He has provided a temple for us, giving us access to God, so that we may "come boldly to the throne of grace" with our prayers and "by Him offer the sacrifice of praise" to God (Heb. 4:16; 13:15). Despite all the ups and downs of human experience we are in the process of receiving "a kingdom which cannot be shaken" (Heb. 12:28).

DAVID'S AMEN TO GOD'S WILL

17:16 Then King David went in and sat before the LORD; and he said: "Who *am* I, O LORD God? And what is my house, that You have brought me this far?

17 "And *yet* this was a small thing in Your sight, O God; and You have *also* spoken of Your servant's house for a great while to come, and have regarded me according to the rank of a man of high degree, O LORD God.

18 "What more can David *say* to You for the honor of Your servant? For You know Your servant.

19 "O LORD, for Your servant's sake, and according to Your own heart, You have done all this greatness, in making known all these great things.

20 "O LORD, *there is* none like You, nor *is there any* God besides You, according to all that we have heard with our ears.

21 "And who *is* like Your people Israel, the one nation on the earth whom God went to redeem for Himself *as* a people—to make for Yourself a name by great and awesome deeds, by driving out nations from before Your people whom You redeemed from Egypt?

22 "For You have made Your people Israel Your very own people forever; and You, LORD, have become their God.

23 "And now, O LORD, the word which You have spoken concerning Your servant and concerning his house, *let it* be established forever, and do as You have said.

24 "So let it be established, that Your name may be magnified forever, saying, 'The LORD of hosts, the God of Israel, *is* Israel's God. And let the house of Your servant David be established before You.

25 "For You, O my God, have revealed to Your servant that You will build him a house. Therefore Your servant has found it *in his heart* to pray before You.

26 "And now, LORD, You are God, and have promised this goodness to Your servant.

27 "Now You have been pleased to bless the house
of Your servant, that it may continue before You
forever; for You have blessed it, O LORD, and *it shall
be* blessed forever."

1 Chron. 17:16-27

David might have been resentful that his son was to do the work
that he himself wanted to do. (I once knew a father who in a fit of
envy smashed the completed woodwork project his eldest son
proudly brought home from high school, to the lasting detriment of
that boy.) Unlike 13:11, there is here no outburst of anger after the
overruling of his wishes. Rather, David was glad to have a by no
means insignificant preparatory role to play in God's plans and is
proud of a son who is to build the temple. He has the generous spirit
of 1 Corinthians 3:6: "I planted, Apollos watered, but God gave the
increase." The Chronicler presents David's prayer of thanksgiving in
a form which closely reflects his source, 2 Samuel 7:18-29. There is
a convention in the Old Testament that a person endowed with a
divine revelation and mission responds in self-disparaging tones.
Moses did so in Exodus 3:11 ("Who am I . . . ?"). So did Gideon in
Judges 6:11. David continues this healthy tradition—indeed, in a
human setting he had displayed the same humble attitude when
given the opportunity of marrying into the royal family of Saul (1
Sam. 8:18). Here the prayer strikes a note of amazement at the gracious initiative of God. It reminds the Christian of such snatches of
hymns as John Ireland's "O who am I that for my sake . . . ?" and
Thomas Campbell's "Amazing Love! How can it be that Thou . . . ?"

The king is overwhelmed. His heart is too full for words, but God
can read his grateful heart (v. 18). He turns the themes of God's
revelation into thankful praise.

1. *"Servant."* The double use of the term *"servant"* in the divine
oracle is a cue for David's repetition of it. It appears in his prayer no
less than ten times. He affirms his servant role under God, speaking like a loyal courtier in the presence of his king (compare 2 Sam.
9:6, 8).

2. *"Your people Israel."* God's people, who featured four times in
Nathan's message from God, are now mentioned an equal number of
times. There is the amazement as in 14:2 that David's "kingdom was
highly exalted for the sake of his people Israel." David is no tyrant

who exploits his subjects for his own ends, as Samuel warned could be Israel's experience under a king (1 Sam. 8:11–17). They are the Lord's people entrusted to his conscientious care. What a privilege to belong to the people whose very creation is a testimony to the unique, saving power of God (v. 21)! The perpetuity of David's dynasty has implications for the people of God. They are caught up in God's royal purposes. Its *"forever"* extends to the covenant relationship which bound God to His people and them to Him (v. 22). This is a leap forward in Israel's experience of God. Indeed, verse 21 is virtually the last time that Exodus is highlighted in Chronicles. Hereafter Israel looks back to the Davidic covenant as the charter of a new era which gathers the old into its broader and deeper scope. God's people enjoy the benefits of a new dispensation.

3. *"Name."* God had promised David a "name" among the great (v. 8). He twice returns the compliment, as it were. He deflects the glory back to God, speaking of the *"name"* won by God in the *"great . . . deeds"* of the Exodus (v. 21) and urging God to keep His promises concerning David's house so that His *"name may be magnified"*—or acknowledged as great—*"forever"* (v. 24). God's *"forever"* to David means everlasting glory for God Himself.

4. *"Forever."* Verses 21 and 24 have already been considered. In verse 23 David prays that God's promise may come true *"forever."* Verse 23b is the counterpart of verse 2. Nathan had said "Do all that is in your heart" (v. 2), and David would have been glad to do so. Now he bows to God's better will: *"do as You have said."* The close of the prayer in verse 27 has a more definite ring to it than the basic 2 Samuel 7:29. The Chronicler rejoices in the validity of God's *"forever."* His hope is founded on the rock of His divine promise. The purpose of God that David's house would *"continue before"* Him *"forever"* is a vital element in the Chronicler's theology. The genealogy of 3:19–24 had been his testimony that in a veiled way the prayer had been answered thus far in the post-exilic period of Israel. Better things lay ahead.

FITTING INTO GOD'S PLANS

18:1 After this it came to pass that David attacked
the Philistines, subdued them, and took Gath and its
towns from the hand of the Philistines.

2 Then he defeated Moab, and the Moabites became David's servants, *and* brought tribute.

3 And David defeated Hadadezer king of Zobah *as far as* Hamath, as he went to establish his power by the River Euphrates.

4 David took from him one thousand chariots, seven thousand horsemen, and twenty thousand foot soldiers. Also David hamstrung all the chariot *horses,* except that he spared enough of them for one hundred chariots.

5 When the Syrians of Damascus came to help Hadadezer king of Zobah, David killed twenty-two thousand of the Syrians.

6 Then David put *garrisons* in Syria of Damascus; and the Syrians became David's servants, *and* brought tribute. So the LORD preserved David wherever he went.

7 And David took the shields of gold that were on the servants of Hadadezer, and brought them to Jerusalem.

8 Also from Tibhath and from Chun, cities of Hadadezer, David brought a large amount of bronze, with which Solomon made the bronze Sea, the pillars, and the articles of bronze.

9 Now when Tou king of Hamath heard that David had defeated all the army of Hadadezer king of Zobah,

10 he sent Hadoram his son to King David, to greet him and bless him, because he had fought against Hadadezer and defeated him (for Hadadezer had been at war with Tou); and *Hadoram brought with him* all kinds of articles of gold, silver, and bronze.

11 King David also dedicated these to the LORD, along with the silver and gold that he had brought from all *these* nations—from Edom, from Moab, from the people of Ammon, from the Philistines, and from Amalek.

12 Moreover Abishai the son of Zeruiah killed eighteen thousand Edomites in the Valley of Salt.

13 He also put garrisons in Edom, and all the Edomites became David's servants. And the LORD preserved David wherever he went.

14 So David reigned over all Israel, and administered judgment and justice to all his people.

15 Joab the son of Zeruiah *was* over the army; Jehoshaphat the son of Ahilud *was* recorder;

16 Zadok the son of Ahitub and Abimelech the son of Abiathar *were* the priests; Shavsha *was* the scribe;

17 Benaiah the son of Jehoiada *was* over the Cherethites and the Pelethites; and David's sons *were* chief ministers at the king's side.

19:1 It happened after this that Nahash the king of the people of Ammon died, and his son reigned in his place.

2 Then David said, "I will show kindness to Hanun the son of Nahash, because his father showed kindness to me." So David sent messengers to comfort him concerning his father. And David's servants came to Hanun in the land of the people of Ammon to comfort him.

3 And the princes of the people of Ammon said to Hanun, "Do you think that David really honors your father because he has sent comforters to you? Did his servants not come to you to search and to overthrow and to spy out the land?"

4 Therefore Hanun took David's servants, shaved them, and cut off their garments in the middle, at their buttocks, and sent them away.

5 Then *some* went and told David about the men; and he sent to meet them, because the men were greatly ashamed. And the king said, "Wait at Jericho until your beards have grown, and *then* return."

6 When the people of Ammon saw that they had made themselves repulsive to David, Hanun and the people of Ammon sent a thousand talents of silver to hire for themselves chariots and horsemen from Mesopotamia, from Syrian Maacah, and from Zobah.

7 So they hired for themselves thirty-two thousand chariots, with the king of Maacah and his people, who came and encamped before Medeba. Also the people of Ammon gathered together from their cities, and came to battle.

8 Now when David heard *of it,* he sent Joab and all the army of the mighty men.

9 Then the people of Ammon came out and put themselves in battle array before the gate of the city, and the kings who had come *were* by themselves in the field.

10 When Joab saw that the battle line was against him before and behind, he chose some of Israel's best and put *them* in battle array against the Syrians.

11 And the rest of the people he put under the command of Abishai his brother, and they set *themselves* in battle array against the people of Ammon.

12 Then he said, "If the Syrians are too strong for me, then you shall help me; but if the people of Ammon are too strong for you, then I will help you.

13 "Be of good courage, and let us be strong for our people and for the cities of our God. And may the LORD do *what* is good in His sight."

14 So Joab and the people who *were* with him drew near for the battle against the Syrians, and they fled before him.

15 When the people of Ammon saw that the Syrians were fleeing, they also fled before Abishai his brother, and entered the city. So Joab went to Jerusalem.

16 Now when the Syrians saw that they had been defeated by Israel, they sent messengers and brought the Syrians who were beyond the River, and Shophach the commander of Hadadezer's army *went* before them.

17 When it was told David, he gathered all Israel, crossed over the Jordan and came upon them, and set up in battle array against them. So when David had set up in *battle* array against the Syrians, they fought with him.

18 Then the Syrians fled before Israel; and David killed seven thousand charioteers and forty thousand foot soldiers of the Syrians, and killed Shophach the commander of the army.

19 And when the servants of Hadadezer saw that they were defeated by Israel, they made peace with David and became his servants. So the Syrians were not willing to help the people of Ammon anymore.

20:1 It happened in the spring of the year, at the time

kings go out *to battle*, that Joab led out the armed
forces and ravaged the country of the people of Ammon, and came and besieged Rabbah. But David
stayed at Jerusalem. And Joab defeated Rabbah and
overthrew it.

2 Then David took their king's crown from his
head, and found it to weigh a talent of gold, and
there were precious stones in it. And it was set on
David's head. Also he brought out the spoil of the
city in great abundance.

3 And he brought out the people who *were* in it,
and put *them* to work with saws, with iron picks, and
with axes. So David did to all the cities of the people
of Ammon. Then David and all the people returned
to Jerusalem.

4 Now it happened afterward that war broke out at
Gezer with the Philistines, at which time Sibbechai
the Hushathite killed Sippai, *who was one* of the sons
of the giant. And they were subdued.

5 Again there was war with the Philistines, and
Elhanan the son of Jair killed Lahmi the brother of
Goliath the Gittite, the shaft of whose spear *was* like
a weaver's beam.

6 Yet again there was war at Gath, where there
was a man of *great* stature, with twenty-four fingers
and toes, six on *each hand* and six *on each foot*; and he
also was born to the giant.

7 So when he defied Israel, Jonathan the son of
Shimea, David's brother, killed him.

8 These were born to the giant in Gath, and they
fell by the hand of David and by the hand of his
servants.

1 Chron. 18:1–20:8

The function of these two chapters is to show how David fulfilled
the mission entrusted to him in 17:8b–10a as a preliminary to the
great project of building the temple. The Chronicler uses a selection
of material: from 2 Samuel 8 in chapter 18, from 2 Samuel 10–12 in
19:1–20:3, and from 2 Samuel 21 in 20:4–8. The reference in 18:1
to the conquest of the Philistines (*"David . . . subdued them"* = 2
Samuel 8:1) is transformed by the Chronicler into a structural

marker. He imports it into the final narrative, at 20:4, *"and they were subdued."* He also projects it back into Nathan's oracle at 17:10, "I will subdue all your enemies," replacing the clause used in 2 Samuel 7. It is his literary way of telling the reader what the role of these chapters is. In the light of 17:10, all David's victories are God-given victories, a note not lacking in the biblical source which the Chronicler used. Verses 6 and 13 (= 2 Sam. 8:6, 14) function as a refrain: "And the Lord gave victory to David wherever he went" (RSV). There is a concern, as there was in David's prayer, to give God the credit for his exploits.

In the same vein Paul, returning from his third missionary journey, gave the church leaders in Jerusalem a report of "those things which God had done . . . through his ministry"—and the response was that "they glorified the Lord" (Acts 21:19, 20). In their different ways both David and Paul were God's agents. One hesitates to call them instruments of God or channels of His power. Such terms have an impersonal ring which is unbecoming. There is a type of theology which makes God big by making humans small and urges them to be nothing that God may be everything. This is an exaggerated way of speaking which can do more harm than good in the development of the human personality under God. These were no clones but individual personalities with their own identities which they used in God's service, even as God was using them.

Chapter 18 reviews a series of victories on Israel's every side: the Philistines to the west, Moab to the east, the Aramean states of Zobah and Damascus to the north, and Edom to the south. Moreover, an alliance is granted to Hamath in the far north. There is an interest in the spoils which David took and the tribute he received. David *"dedicated these to the Lord"* (18:11) in personal acknowledgment that, as the theological refrain affirms, God has given the victory. Eventually they were to be transferred to the temple coffers (26:26; 2 Chron. 5:1). The Chronicler adds his own observation in verse 8b that from this campaigning resources were gained for eventual use in building the temple. Here the theme of preparation for the temple which underlies chapters 18–20 in general finds a specific expression. There is an undercurrent of anticipation, of living for and working toward what is yet to come.

The Chronicler finds in his biblical text grist for his own mill at 18:11 and 14: *"all these nations"* and *"all Israel."* He looked forward to the time when every nation would submit to God's sovereign rule; he was ever urging his readers to take seriously their destiny as members of the larger people of God. The role of verse 14 is to show how internally as well as externally security was achieved for the people, in accord with 17:9. Indeed, *"Israel"* and *"people"* serve as links with that verse. 18:14–17 is taken over from 2 Samuel 8. However, 18:15–17 does not merely come along for the ride, as it were. These verses introduce the reader to *"Joab,"* who is to feature in the next three chapters. And in speaking of *"Zadok"* and *"Ahimelech"* (RSV) they look forward to David's organization of temple personnel with their aid (24:3, 6, 31).

The Ammonite campaign of 19:1–20:3 is a long footnote to the mention of the Ammonites in 18:11. It affirms in a different way that God is the giver of victory, in 19:13. Joab's battle speech polarizes human factors (19:12–13a) and the divine factor (v. 13b). Both have their place, in accord with the famous cry "Put your trust in God and keep your powder dry!" The human factors through which God works are proven ability—here in the sphere of shrewd military tactics—sheer courage, and a loyal love for those for whose good one is laboring (*"our people,"* *"the cities"*) and for God (*"our God"*). In the expression of the divine factor a keen sense of God's sovereignty is manifested. The commitment of the venture to Him releases from crippling anxiety and enables one to do his or her best in His service.

The account is rounded off by ending with the national foes with whom it began. The Philistines function as the A and Z of opposition to God's people. They are the object of such a focus because back in chapter 10 they were the arch-enemies of Israel and the agents of defeat. There is an implicit contrast with Saul: where Saul lost, David won, and won again. Power once possessed by Israel's enemies now passes to David and his forces: *"from the hand of the Philistines"* (18:1) into *"the hand of David and . . . the hand of his servants"* (20:8). God's cause has victory associated with it. Doubtless the Chronicler, living in a far less glorious age, sensed and wished his readers to sense that to be on God's side and to identify with His cause culminates in victory, even though that victory may appear remote. The Christian affirmation "we are more than conquerors" was spoken in defiance of current tribulation and persecution (Rom. 8:35, 37).

CHAPTER SIX

Saved to Serve

1 Chronicles 21:1–22:19

Chapters 17–29 are all temple-oriented. The purpose of chapter 21 is to designate the site of the temple, and of chapter 22 to delineate which of David's sons was to be the builder—Solomon's name is to be mentioned in this connection for the first time. In human terms one might expect to find in these chapters a thorough survey of Jerusalem and its environs, analyzing the merits and demerits of this piece of land and that, and an invitation of bids from various contractors with careful appraisal of their previous projects. God's Word is full of surprises: His ways are not our ways. In fact David discovers the site in quite a different connection, as part of a divine answer to his own moral failure—he stumbles on the site, one might say. As for Solomon, his very inexperience seems almost to be a qualification for the job: his eventual success will thereby be a tribute to God's enabling. These two chapters turn out to be a study of divine rescue from sin's consequences and of divine resources for service.

A GRACIOUS DISCOVERY

21:1 Now Satan stood up against Israel and moved David to number Israel.

2 So David said to Joab and to the leaders of the people, "Go, number Israel from Beersheba to Dan, and bring the number of them to me that I may know it."

3 And Joab answered, "May the LORD make His people a hundred times more than they are. But, my lord the king, *are* they not all my lord's servants?

135

Why then does my lord require this thing? Why should he be a cause of guilt in Israel?"

4 Nevertheless the king's word prevailed against Joab. Therefore Joab departed and went throughout all Israel and came to Jerusalem.

5 Then Joab gave the sum of the number of the people to David. All Israel *had* one million one hundred thousand men who drew the sword, and Judah *had* four hundred and seventy thousand men who drew the sword.

6 But he did not count Levi and Benjamin among them, for the king's word was abominable to Joab.

7 And God was displeased with this thing; therefore He struck Israel.

8 So David said to God, "I have sinned greatly, because I have done this thing; but now, I pray, take away the iniquity of Your servant, for I have done very foolishly."

9 Then the LORD spoke to Gad, David's seer, saying,

10 "Go and tell David, saying, 'Thus says the LORD: "I offer you three *things*; choose one of them for yourself, that I may do *it* to you."'"

11 So Gad came to David and said to him, "Thus says the LORD: 'Choose for yourself,

12 'either three years of famine, or three months to be defeated by your foes with the sword of your enemies overtaking *you,* or else for three days the sword of the LORD—the plague in the land, with the angel of the LORD destroying throughout all the territory of Israel.' Now consider what answer I should take back to Him who sent me."

13 And David said to Gad, "I am in great distress. Please let me fall into the hand of the LORD, for His mercies *are* very great; but do not let me fall into the hand of man."

14 So the LORD sent a plague upon Israel, and seventy thousand men of Israel fell.

15 And God sent an angel to Jerusalem to destroy it. As he was destroying, the LORD looked and relented of the disaster, and said to the angel who was destroying, "It is enough; now restrain your hand."

And the angel of the LORD stood by the threshing floor of Ornan the Jebusite.

16 Then David lifted his eyes and saw the angel of the LORD standing between earth and heaven, having in his hand a drawn sword stretched out over Jerusalem. So David and the elders, clothed in sackcloth, fell on their faces.

17 And David said to God, "Was it not I who commanded the people to be numbered? I am the one who has sinned and done evil indeed; but these sheep, what have they done? Let Your hand, I pray, O LORD my God, be against me and my father's house, but not against Your people that they should be plagued."

18 Therefore, the angel of the LORD commanded Gad to say to David that David should go and erect an altar to the LORD on the threshing floor of Ornan the Jebusite.

19 So David went up at the word of Gad, which he had spoken in the name of the LORD.

20 Now Ornan turned and saw the angel; and his four sons *who were* with him hid themselves, but Ornan continued threshing wheat.

21 So David came to Ornan, and Ornan looked and saw David. And he went out from the threshing floor, and bowed before David with *his* face to the ground.

22 Then David said to Ornan, "Grant me the place of *this* threshing floor, that I may build an altar on it to the LORD. You shall grant it to me at the full price, that the plague may be withdrawn from the people."

23 But Ornan said to David, "Take *it* to yourself, and let my lord the king do *what is* good in his eyes. Look, I *also* give *you* the oxen for burnt offerings, the threshing implements for wood, and the wheat for the grain offering; I give *it* all."

24 Then King David said to Ornan, "No, but I will surely buy *it* for the full price, for I will not take what is yours for the LORD, nor offer burnt offerings with *that which* costs *me* nothing."

25 So David gave Ornan six hundred shekels of gold by weight for the place.

26 And David built there an altar to the LORD, and offered burnt offerings and peace offerings, and called on the LORD; and He answered him from heaven by fire on the altar of burnt offering.

27 So the LORD commanded the angel, and he returned his sword to its sheath.

28 At that time, when David saw that the LORD had answered him on the threshing floor of Ornan the Jebusite, he sacrificed there.

29 For the tabernacle of the LORD and the altar of the burnt offering, which Moses had made in the wilderness, *were* at that time at the high place in Gibeon.

30 But David could not go before it to inquire of God, for he was afraid of the sword of the angel of the LORD.

22:1 Then David said, "This *is* the house of the LORD God, and this *is* the altar of burnt offering for Israel."

1 Chron. 21:1–22:1

Chapter divisions in the Bible are a useful human addition to the text, but they are not infallible. In this case 22:1 is the climax of the story and its whole point: "Here shall be the house of the Lord God" (RSV). The discovery was the result of a traumatic personal experience, told in chapter 21. The Chronicler is sometimes accused of triumphalism in his depiction of David. He passes over the Bathsheba affair and the Uriah cover-up narrated in 2 Samuel 11–12, which in Chronicles is telescoped to a single blame-free verse (20:1). On reflection that criticism is hardly fair. Those chapters in Samuel belong to narrative about the royal succession and were designed to show that the Davidic dynasty was founded on divine grace which overcame human sin. As for the succession, the Chronicler's interests in the dynasty were better served by concentrating on the outcome, the passing of the crown to Solomon by divine choice. His own message was that the origins of the dynasty were God's cradle for the temple. Yet grace cannot be shut out of any divine-human enterprise. God's workmanship ever depends on a "But God . . ." that redirects misused human energies into new and wholesome channels (Eph. 2:1–10). In particular the temple project was grounded in grace. The Chronicler uses 1 Samuel 24 as the basis

for this teaching, making explicit the probable implicit intention of
that chapter.

The sad story is presented in verses 2–6. It is set in a supernatural
framework of cause and effect in verses 1 and 7: Satan tempts,
David succumbs, and God punishes. Comparison with 2 Samuel
24:1 discloses a striking change the Chronicler has made. His source,
working with a theology which was at once simpler and more profound, spoke of a God who first incites to sin and then punishes.
The Chronicler evidently found theological difficulty in this sequence. Without wanting to deny his source, he unpacked its content
with the help of God-given insights afforded by other Scriptures. In
Job 1–2 and Zechariah 3:1–5 "the Satan" or "the Accuser" is the mali-
cious prosecutor in the celestial lawcourt, gloating over human
weakness and exploiting it. He is like a vicious watchdog, alert for
moral trespassing but kept on a leash and prevented from going too
far. He has a mysterious role in the purposes of God, but the harm
he is permitted to do is limited by His sovereign control and by His
eventual overruling. The entrapment techniques which he practices
permit no denial of human responsibility for human actions. There
is no suggestion that the buck can be passed back with the excuse
"He made me do it." The problem of evil is not solved by these explanations in terms of this perverted angelic figure. But both biblical
passages do reassuringly affirm that evil is enclosed within a framework of divine providence and is ultimately eclipsed by the triumph
of good and, in the case of Zechariah 3, by grace. Christian readers
will recall a parallel in the New Testament where Judas's incitement
by the Devil (= the Satan, translated into Greek) to betray Jesus is
circumscribed by two overarching factors, His purpose to redeem
His own and His knowledge that ultimate authority belongs to Him
(John 13:1–3). The Chronicler finds the explanations in the Books of
Job and Zechariah helpful for the David narrative. He develops the
theme by using for the first time *"Satan"* as a name instead of a
descriptive noun. He creatively re-uses Scripture, deriving *"stood
up"* from the provocative stance of Zechariah 3:1 and the notion of
inciting (*"moved,"* using the same Hebrew verb) from Job 2:3 (RSV).
Also taken over from Job is the concept of a challenge or test.

David fails the test. In irony that is true to life; the area in which
he has been so successful proves to be the place of his falling. Chapters 18–20 have described David's military victories as part of the

overall divine plan for building the temple. His role had been a dangerous one, not least spiritually. Yet thus far David has shown wisdom in sailing the good ship Victory on the high seas, giving God the glory and acknowledging that his success was just a reflection of God's success (compare 17:8 with 17:24). Now his ship is wrecked on the reefs of pride. He listens to Satan's whisper that he is great in his own right. His decision to take a census of his military battalions is a desire to bask in his own glory. It betrays a trust in human resources rather than in God as their giver and user. In verse 3 Joab has the spiritual insight to see that this is trespassing on God's prerogatives and objects that it is unnecessary and inviting trouble. *"Nevertheless the king's word prevailed against Joab"* (v. 4). Satan had found a chink in David's armor.

I remember once reading a story—I hope that it was not a true one—featuring a gifted evangelist. He was to conduct a crusade in the town where an old friend lived and wrote ahead inviting him to come to the hall one evening. The friend duly came and listened appreciatively to the fine message and its appropriate backing with music and song and prayer. He watched a stream of people touched by the Lord surge forward. Afterward he joined a line to shake hands with the evangelist. When he arrived at the head of the line, the evangelist leaned forward and with a grin said quietly in his ear, "I didn't do badly, did I?" His friend murmured something and hurriedly walked out, a disillusioned man. Satan had found a chink in the shining armor of this man of God. Success had turned into an ego trip.

Pride goes before a fall. Deuteronomy 8:11–17 warns of the temptation in the midst of material success to take selfish credit for it: "My power and the might of my hand have gained me this wealth" (Deut. 8:17). In Luke 12:16–21 Jesus wove the warning into a parable of self-centered engrossment with "my crops," "my goods"—and "my soul." This claim to be in control of one's own life is the last straw, and it triggers a nemesis whereby it is taken away in death. In David's case God *"struck Israel,"* the object of his selfish pride (v. 7). That triangle of beautiful harmony featuring God, David, and Israel in earlier chapters is broken into pieces because of David's folly. David had cut off the lifeline between himself and God, and now God followed his cue by snapping the lifeline of blessing that linked Him to Israel.

"Israel" features at the beginning and end of the episode, the real object of Satan's challenge and the victim of God's displeasure with David (vv. 1, 7). David does not function simply as an individual. In his relationship with both God and Israel he is Israel's representative before God and the agent of its destiny. The triangle of blessing is transformed by his action into a triangle of doom. Later he was magnanimously to plead that he should bear the punishment alone and that his people should not suffer (v. 17). It was a noble offer and an appropriate gesture of remorse, but quite irrational. The fate of king and country were inextricably bound together. In his distinctive role as Israel's representative he could not protect his people by the notion that he was a private individual and by the cry *"mea culpa."* His failure set in motion a wide-reaching series of consequences. David was trying to act as an individualist, forgetting that self-centered willfulness begins with oneself, yet does not end there but drags down others with oneself. "No man is an island, entire of itself," warned John Donne, and his warning may be applied in the area of social consequences of private acts. Personal infidelity can break up a home and damage children for life. Too much to drink can cause an accident which maims or even kills other users of the road. For David also it was too late to say that he did not want others to be involved as victims of his folly.

The literary role of verses 8–14 is to function as a flashback which eventually brings the reader to the point of verse 7 and defines its divine blow. 2 Samuel 24:10 discloses that before punishment was executed David's conscience smote him. Joab's challenge had a belated effect. The king realized that his action had created a conflict of interests. He had set his own interests before those of God and would have to answer for it. He admits his mistake and prays to God to forgive his sin. David was asking for restoration to fellowship with God. Was he also requesting release from all punishment? Probably not. The flow of the narrative and comparison with Numbers 14:19–23 suggest that what was sought was mitigation of punishment, escape from the crushing weight of total annihilation which his sin had created. If so, somber realism is manifested here. Christians sometimes bandy about the notion of forgiveness as if it were an easy way of getting off the hook. In the New Testament a profound sense of gut relief and of submission to a sovereign God belongs with forgiveness (see, for instance, Eph. 2:1–4). There is no such thing as cheap grace. In the Old Testament the grace of God is often displayed *after* an experience of judgment, in the mitigation of punishment and the renewal of fellowship and blessing. It is salutary for the Christian to be reminded that sinning tends to unleash natural consequences of suffering that cannot be held in check. To recall the instances given above, repentance cannot mend the consequences of drunken driving nor necessarily of marital infidelity. There is a natural providence in human life which may not be averted. Confession of sin and recognition of accountability to God do not put the clock back. It is in this sobering sense that Christians can accept the words of Fitzgerald's *Omar Khayyâm:*

> The Moving Finger writes; and, having writ,
> Moves on: nor all thy Piety nor Wit
> Shall lure it back to cancel half a Line,
> Nor all thy Tears wash out a Word of it.[1]

David is given an ironic choice, not whether Israel should suffer or not, but in what way Israel should suffer. He opts for direct punishment from God as a judge who has the quality of mercy, rather than for punishment mediated through human agents who could by contrast cruelly overstep the divine mandate (see Isa. 10:5–12; 37:26–29). His shuddering choice to *"fall into the hand of the Lord, for His mercies are very great"* (21:13) superficially reminds the New Testament-oriented readers of the grim words and grimmer context of Hebrews 10:31, "It is a fearful thing to fall into the hands of the living God." The contrast is significant. There is an unfortunate tendency to disparage the Old Testament as full of God's wrath and to prefer the New as full of God's love. The reversal of negative and positive factors in this pair of cases is a warning against such generalizations. Here *"distress"* (v. 13) due to *"greatly"* sinning (v. 8), would find mitigation, *"for His mercies are very great"* (v. 13). Sin was serious and devastating in its consequences but was succeeded and surpassed by God's grace. Where sin abounded, grace was to super-abound, to paraphrase Romans 5:20. Indeed, this is to be the message of the whole chapter. The temple, whose site is discovered, is to be a monument to divine grace.

The next paragraph, verses 15–27, works out this consequence in detail. Throughout, the *"drawn sword"* of the destroying *"angel"* is brandished over Jerusalem (v. 16), with the possibility of total destruction being an ever-present threat, until the sword is sheathed in verse 27. The factor that turns the scales emerges in verse 18, the angel's directing that David should *"erect an altar . . . on the threshing floor of Ornan the Jebusite."* The motif of the angel, agent of both threat and promise, is accompanied by another motif, the threshing floor, which similarly features at the beginning and middle (vv. 15, 18) and then dominates the narrative. The place of threat becomes the place of atonement. In terms of the relationship between God and David, the paragraph falls into three parts, David's prayer of repentance to God (v. 17), the arranging of the means of atonement (vv. 18–25), and God's acceptance of this means (v. 26).

By his prayer David does not prevail upon an unwilling God to grudgingly forgive. God had already determined a course of action beyond judgment in verse 15. When he prays, God listens not to the logic but to the spirit of David's prayer of repentance, rather like the father in the parable of the prodigal son (Luke 15:18, 21–24). In both cases it was a good sign that the sinner asked to be treated severely rather than presuming upon forgiveness. Do the two prayers of verses 8 and 17 reveal an advance in David's spiritual awareness?

Forgiveness has its proper channels, which are sacrifices and an altar. The Chronicler told us as much in 6:49, where he spoke of the priests offering "sacrifices on the altar of burnt offering and on the altar of incense . . . to make atonement for Israel." The writer to the Hebrews took these elements seriously, even as he transmuted them in terms of the atoning work of Jesus: "we have an altar" (Heb. 13:10) and "one sacrifice for sins" (Heb. 10:12). It is through His sacrificial death and His exaltation to the heavenly sanctuary in a priestly role that God now forgives. In the Old Testament there were material—but no less spiritual—counterparts. One might have expected David to visit the sanctuary at Gibeon to offer sacrifice at the altar there (v. 29; compare 16:39, 40), but instead he is given a plain prophetic mandate to erect a fresh altar (vv. 18, 19) on a site to be purchased. Arrangements are duly made with the owner of the site. Ornan's offer to donate the land, including materials for a sacrifice, is declined. It is to be David's sacrifice, and so he must bear the cost if it is to have personal value. Otherwise it could hardly function as a symbol of his repentance. Malachi was making a not dissimilar

point when he complained that some of the sacrificial animals which
the people were bringing had been stolen, while others were blind
or lame (Mal. 1:8, 13–14)! Sacrifice had to reflect spirituality. For
integrity's sake there had to be equivalence between the offering
and its value; to proceed otherwise would be an act of disrespect to
God. This is a principle worth pondering by the Christian in offering to God the spiritual sacrifices of praise and good turns and
shared resources (Heb. 13:15, 16). The ostensible price tags do not
necessarily represent the value, which often only God and the giver
know. As Jesus graphically illustrated, drawing attention to the respective donations of the widow and of the wealthy (Luke 21:1–4),
the same act done by different persons can be of utterly different
worth in God's eyes. David's sacrifices, duly offered in a right spirit
on the altar built on the designated site, are graciously accepted, and
the threat to Jerusalem is withdrawn.

There is an agenda in this narrative other than the plain one of
David's sin and its immediate and negative consequences. The last
paragraph, 21:28–22:1, draws out what it is. Technically David
might have been judged to be in the wrong for not using the official
sacrificial resource of Gibeon. However, the vision of the drawn
sword and the threat to Jerusalem have kept David glued to the spot.
Indeed, the narrative has made clear that it was by prophetic and so
by divine warrant (22:1) that David built the new altar. His action
was grounded in explicit revelation. The religious site had been
found by following God's leading. In verse 26 the Chronicler has
added the last clause. He is drawing a parallel with 1 Kings 18:38,
whose context is the contest between Elijah and the prophets of Baal
on Mount Carmel. It is not insignificant that Elijah first built an altar
and then prayed to the God of Israel that He would prove that he
had "done all these things at Your word." In response "the fire of the
Lord fell." So here there is an endorsement of David's religious actions. The Chronicler recapitulates verse 26 at verse 28, stressing the
divine endorsement of David's sacrificing. His sacrifice was a trial
offer, one might say, that, once accepted by God, proved that the
altar had a far wider-reaching significance. Good enough for God
and the king, it would be good enough for Israel. The national dimensions of the affair have been hinted at in verse 22 and implicitly
in verse 24. David's insistence on paying *the full price*" is a touch
added by the Chronicler reminiscent of Genesis 23:9. He wants his

readers to think of Abraham's purchase of the cave at Machpelah to be a burial place for his dead wife Sarah. It was a landmark in Israel's history, for it was the first piece of real estate owned in the promised land. For the Chronicler this was a comparable landmark, the purchase of the site for Israel's sanctuary.

The atmosphere of the whole passage is electric with the sense of a new dispensation dawning. We trace our spiritual heritage back to this point in time, the Chronicler is saying, for the temple is dedicated to bringing repentant sinners back to God. For the Chronicler the divinely nominated place and this theology of grace are interwoven, as he will later expound in 2 Chronicles 7:14–16. David serves as a model for every backslider. There is always a way back to God, and He has graciously provided the means whereby generations thereafter might return to Him. David was the pioneer in treading this temple way. We Christians, every one of us prodigal sons and daughters, know what the Chronicler meant. From our own perspective we can share his hallelujah.

RESOURCES FOR THE TASK

22:2 So David commanded to gather the aliens who *were* in the land of Israel; and he appointed masons to cut hewn stones to build the house of God.

3 And David prepared iron in abundance for the nails of the doors of the gates and for the joints, and bronze in abundance beyond measure,

4 and cedar trees in abundance; for the Sidonians and those from Tyre brought much cedar wood to David.

5 Now David said, "Solomon my son *is* young and inexperienced, and the house to be built for the LORD *must be* exceedingly magnificent, famous and glorious throughout all countries. I will now make preparation for it." So David made abundant preparations before his death.

6 Then he called for his son Solomon, and charged him to build a house for the LORD God of Israel.

7 And David said to Solomon: "My son, as for me, it was in my mind to build a house to the name of the LORD my God;

8 "but the word of the LORD came to me, saying, 'You have shed much blood and have made great wars; you shall not build a house for My name, because you have shed much blood on the earth in My sight.

9 'Behold, a son shall be born to you, who shall be a man of rest; and I will give him rest from all his enemies all around. His name shall be Solomon, for I will give peace and quietness to Israel in his days.

10 'He shall build a house for My name, and he shall be My son, and I *will be* his Father; and I will establish the throne of his kingdom over Israel forever.'

11 "Now, my son, may the LORD be with you; and may you prosper, and build the house of the LORD your God, as He has said to you.

12 "Only may the LORD give you wisdom and understanding, and give you charge concerning Israel, that you may keep the law of the LORD your God.

13 "Then you will prosper, if you take care to fulfill the statutes and judgments with which the LORD charged Moses concerning Israel. Be strong and of good courage; do not fear nor be dismayed.

14 "Indeed I have taken much trouble to prepare for the house of the LORD one hundred thousand talents of gold and one million talents of silver, and bronze and iron beyond measure, for it is so abundant. I have prepared timber and stone also, and you may add to them.

15 "Moreover *there are* workmen with you in abundance: woodsmen and stonecutters, and all types of skillful men for every kind of work.

16 "Of gold and silver and bronze and iron *there is* no limit. Arise and begin working, and the LORD be with you."

17 David also commanded all the leaders of Israel to help Solomon his son, *saying,*

18 "*Is* not the LORD your God with you? And has He *not* given you rest on every side? For He has given the inhabitants of the land into my hand, and the land is subdued before the LORD and before His people.

19 "Now set your heart and your soul to seek the
LORD your God. Therefore arise and build the sanctuary of the LORD God, to bring the ark of the
covenant of the LORD and the holy articles of God
into the house that is to be built for the name of the
LORD."

1 Chron. 22:2-19

That one of David's sons was to build the temple had been revealed in 17:11, 12. Now the narrative identifies Solomon as the son
in question. The heart of the chapter lies in verses 6–16, David's
commissioning of Solomon. It is introduced by verses 2–5, which
narrate David's own material preparations, to which his speech
makes reference in verse 14. The speech is rounded off in verses
17–19 by a supplementary speech to Israel's leaders, encouraging
them to back Solomon in his temple-building venture.

The identification of the temple site made it possible to proceed
with plans for its construction. A threefold series of instructions toward this end binds the passage together (vv. 2, 6, 17). David is
excluded from building: he does everything but that. If a thing is
worth doing, it is worth preparing well—this is the principle behind
what in verse 14 David calls taking *"much trouble."* His mental reflection in verse 5 reveals the complementary nature of the work of
David and Solomon. Solomon was not able to discharge the whole
task unaided; nor was David. Their reigns represent a joint venture
in completing the institution which thereafter in Israel's experience
was to be the channel of divine grace and human worship. Each had
a complementary role, bringing to the joint task such personal qualities, resources, and opportunities as were individually available.
Paul's First Epistle to the Corinthians is a testimony to this principle
of complementarity in Christian service. "I planted, Apollos watered,
but God gave the increase," he affirmed, "and each one will receive
his own reward according to his own labor" (1 Cor. 3:6, 8). While
Paul "laid the foundation," others had the opportunity to build on it
with such resources as he or she was able to contribute, "gold, silver,
precious stones" (1 Cor. 3:10–12). "There are diversities of gifts, but
the same Spirit" (1 Cor. 12:4; cf. vv. 6–30). Timid Timothy needed
encouragement to carry out his own ministry, "for he does the work
of the Lord, as I also do" (1 Cor. 16:10).

147

The overall criterion in building the temple was that the end product should be worthy of God. It was to be a showpiece, reflecting the universality of God and commanding the admiration of all. One of the Songs of Zion with the temple in mind similarly celebrates Mount Zion as "beautiful in elevation, the joy of the whole earth" (Ps. 48:2), while another psalm calls Zion "the perfection of beauty" (Ps. 50:2). Here are principles for Christians to take seriously as to the visible and tangible qualities of their output in working for God.

Chapter 28 will contain the public charge to Solomon to build the temple; here there is a preliminary, private commissioning. David's speech, like many a good sermon, falls into three parts, 22:7–10, 11–13, and 14–16, which express respectively God's predestinating word to David, David's pastoral advice to Solomon, and the practical impetus David gave to Solomon.

1. *God's predestinating word.* In this section the Chronicler is alluding to Solomon's message of Hiram in 1 Kings 5:3–5, and both are based on Deuteronomy 12:9–11.

> There is a tide in the affairs of men,
> Which, taken at the flood, leads on to fortune.[2]

In Israel's affairs that tide had come in the period and person of Solomon, the Chronicler argues. Deuteronomy 12 had laid down a two-part program for the establishment of God's chosen sanctuary: it was to follow God's gift of rest. In this respect David had to bow to Solomon. Great as his role was to God, it was branded with a "not yet" in the matter of the temple. His was the preliminary role of being "a man of war" (28:3), while Solomon was *a man of rest* (v. 9). By Solomon's reign the necessary condition was met. The argument is supported by a play on Solomon's name in Hebrew: *"peace"* or šālôm had come in the *"days"* of šelōmōh. Next there is a reiteration of the crucial 17:13, 14: the blessing of a permanent dynasty would follow on the heels of the building of the temple. Verses 7–10 contain crucial theology. A new era had dawned with David and Solomon, in which David had the role of the forerunner and Solomon the fulfiller. For the Chronicler this was a new day of grace which, though old in time, was still operating. He rejoices at living in this new temple age and clutches to his heart the *"forever"* of the promise to David. The

Christian feels at home with this way of thinking, for in the New Testament there is a comparable ring about the advent of Jesus. "When the fullness of the time had come, God sent forth His Son" (Gal. 4:4). He is the One who has secured peace, a vertical peace with God (Rom. 5:1) and a horizontal peace for Gentiles who have the privilege of sharing with Jewish believers the Jewish heritage and the Jewish Messiah (Eph. 2:11–18). In fact, "He Himself is our peace" (Eph. 2:14), and the very claim seems to be an echo of the royal prophecy of Micah 5:5: "this One shall be peace." The New Testament is in these places moving in an orbit of thought similar to the Chronicler's. Each is of help in understanding the viewpoint of the other.

2. *David's pastoral advice.* Verses 11–15 are the heart of the king's speech. They represent the actual commissioning of Solomon and apply the message of 1 Kings 2:2, 3 to the temple task. God's helping presence is invoked for Solomon in a prayerful wish (v. 13b). The final element, *"Be strong and of good courage; do not fear nor be dismayed,"* will ring a bell for Old Testament buffs. Was not Joshua described in this way? The parallel is no accident: there seems to be a deliberate reminiscence of the Joshua material. The three elements in David's charge of verses 11–13 are a repetition of those in Moses' commissioning of Joshua in Deuteronomy 31:7, 8 and recur in the divine words to him in Joshua 1:6, 9. Moreover, the verb *"prosper"* (vv. 11, 13) is found in Joshua 1:8. A deliberate parallel is being drawn here between Moses and Joshua on the one hand and David and Solomon on the other. As not Moses but Joshua crossed the Jordan in the role of Israel's human leader to win the land (Deut. 31:2, 3), so not David but Solomon was to build the temple. There is a dispensational relationship of type and antitype between the old pair of God's servants and this new pair. Here then is further argumentation concerning a temple age in succession to the era of Moses and Joshua. God was doing a comparable new work, and resetting the stopwatch of theological history. The Christian is reminded of the way in which temple language is reapplied to Jesus and the church in similar argumentation that now God has moved on yet further (see John 2:19–22; 1 Cor. 3:16; 6:19; Eph. 2:21), and parallels are also drawn with the Mosaic era (e.g., Heb. 3:1–6).

The New Testament's concern to establish God's new way by reference to the old may sound irrelevant to the modern Christian, who paradoxically takes the authority of the New Testament message for granted and looks askance at the Old. This is an understandable but superficial attitude. I once had a sincere theological student who, when I asked her why she believed what she did as a Christian, replied simply "Because I feel in my heart that it is true." She had not entered into the truth of C. S. Lewis's dictum that "Christ wants a child's heart, but a grown-up's head. . . . He has room for people with very little sense, but He wants everyone to use what sense they have."[3] The Bible urges us to understand that there is continuity and development in God's purposes over the centuries of human history. Elements old and new are intermingled in the New Testament, and their significance cannot be understood until the Old Testament is taken seriously as an anticipatory milestone rather than slighted as an antiquarian millstone.

Verses 11–13 have an obvious value for the commissioning of any servant of God to a new work. Natural fears are brought out into the open and faced, and God's enabling presence is offered as an antidote. Positive psychological build-up is interwoven with necessary negative cautions. Of importance is the truth that a special task does not exempt us from the general standards of God's will. Indeed, this is another element taken over from Joshua's case (Josh. 1:7, 8). In this respect as well Solomon was to be a latter-day Joshua. None of God's servants is ever placed in a privileged position above His law, despite the fact that the campfollower of prestige and authority is a temptation to consider oneself untrammeled by the ordinary conventions that govern lesser mortals. The shores of secular history are littered with the wrecks of persons who have abused their position and been dismissed with ignominy. Sadly the church too has had its quota of scandals in high places. No denomination and few churches need look hard to find such skeletons in their closets. Here then is a wise and relevant word from David in verse 13: however special the task is, it grants no immunity from ordinary standards laid by God on all His people.

For the Chronicler temple and Torah went together. Certainly the new temple-oriented age was not exempt from the moral claims of the old. The life-giving river of Torah was to flow down from the new mountain spring of temple worship into the valley of daily living. The Christian, rejoicing over the grace of God in the Lord Jesus, dares not dispense with the New Testament's assertion that to love God still involves keeping His commandments (1 John 5:3; cf. Exod. 20:6).

Living in the Spirit means fulfilling "the righteous requirement of the law" (Rom. 8:4). Life's train runs along the railtrack of Mosaic morality, fueled by the dynamics of Christian love (Rom. 13:8–10).

3. *David's practical impetus.* An ounce of practical help is worth a pound of good advice. David's speech is not a pat on the back and a conventional murmur "go in peace," such as James sarcastically condemned (James 2:15, 16). He had a practical stake in the project and felt himself closely involved. If he cannot build, he will do the most that opportunity permits. In a Christian context there are men and women who are highly conscious of the needs of the mission field and deeply wish they had the opportunity to serve in this particular way, but life's constraints have bidden them follow God along other paths. They do not feel themselves excluded from a wider concern for mission. Theirs is the task of loyal support in encouragement and prayer and also in such practical ways as their hands find to do.

David had been unstinting in his amassing of resources to give Solomon a head start in his personal assignment. His vision of the temple as a magnificent showpiece for God (v. 5) was no idle dream but an incentive to live up to. The colossal number of talents of gold and silver in verse 14 takes the thoughtful reader aback. They are considerably larger than those of 29:4 (and 7), while Solomon's import of 420 talents of gold from Ophir in 1 Kings 9:28 was obviously intended to be a breathtaking amount. These factors call into question the literal interpretation of the numbers. Such numbers as have been supplied hitherto in Chronicles all seem to have had a rational basis in relation to their literary source or context. Later in Chronicles, however, sometimes mammoth numbers are mentioned that set the mind reeling. These considerations suggest that the Chronicler at times resorted to his own branch of mathematics, rhetorical mathematics, which must be respected for its intention. Indeed, it is idiomatic in English to reuse precise mathematical language to convey hyperbole, as when we say "Thanks a million!" or "A thousand pardons!" Rhetoric is a valid use of language; the prosaically minded reader needs to be aware of linguistic dimensions beyond what he or she may personally be accustomed to. In this case the intent is to convey that no expense was spared in David's generous provision of raw materials. The huge numbers are meant to have the same rhetorical effect as the accompanying phrases *"beyond measure"* and *"no limit"* (vv. 14, 16), and the juxtaposition of these phrases is not insignificant. David's generosity was probably mentioned not simply for its own sake, but as a model for his own generation. David was generous—hint, hint! It behooved them in turn to be generous in financial support of the temple.

Solomon needed the backing of Israel's national and tribal leaders, and David encourages them to support him in verses 17–19. The powerful presence of God had been manifested in the momentous achievements of David's reign. As they contemplated the daunting task laid on the future king and on them, they needed the assurance that He would be with them still. Sometimes a feeling of impotence paralyzes the Christian worker. One looks back at what God has done through one's ministry as if it were a high jump one somehow managed to achieve before but now feels inadequate to reach. The impending task is viewed with pessimism: "I was just fortunate before, helped by a variety of factors which aren't necessarily going to be there this time." Psychologists speak of a pre-performance worrying ritual that imagines failure.[4] To all such obsessive fears David had the answer, a morale-building question which alerts to a power beyond oneself: *"Is not the Lord your God with you?"* (v. 18). This factor is the first of three elements which David repeats from his charge to Solomon: divine aid as the basis of assurance, personal encouragement (v. 19a), and a description of the task (v. 19b). A precise, factual job description can be useful in allaying imaginary, irrational fears and promoting realism. The exhortation to *"set your heart and your soul to seek the Lord your God"* includes the Chronicler's key term for spirituality, already encountered negatively in 10:13, 14; 13:3; and positively in 15:13. It is a summons to total commitment to God. Any venture to which we in turn hear God's call warrants nothing less from us.

NOTES

1. Edward Fitzgerald, *The Rubáiyát of Omar Khayyám*, 51.
2. William Shakespeare, *Julius Caesar*, act 4, sc. 3, lines 205–6.
3. C. S. Lewis, *Mere Christianity* (New York: Macmillan, 1952), p. 61.
4. See, for example, J. C. Harvey and C. Katz, *If I'm Successful, Why Do I Feel Like a Fake?* (New York: St. Martin's Press, 1981), ch. 2.

CHAPTER SEVEN

Varieties of Ministry

1 Chronicles 23:1–26:32

Here is a series of dry lists about temple administration. They are perhaps the most difficult part of Chronicles for the Christian reader to empathize with. They remind me of some equally difficult material, Leviticus 1–7, a technical manual of sacrifice, which at first glance is as much use as the manual for one's previous automobile! Let us first relate these chapters to their context. 23:1 functions as the heading for the rest of 1 Chronicles. David's convocation of the national assembly in 23:1–2 is evidently resumed in 28:1. It relates to the public presentation of Solomon as temple builder and successor to David, which is unfolded in chapters 28 and 29. The narrative is interrupted by 23:3–27:34 as an extended footnote or excursus. The reader will remember that, when the ark was brought to Jerusalem, lists of religious personnel and their roles were presented in 15:4–24; 16:4–6, 37–42. Now sacred history has moved on a stage. The temple is in view, and so David's administration of religious affairs in earlier chapters needs supplementing with a more extensive organization. Just as he prepared materials for building the temple, so according to these chapters he also prepared a suitable system for administering it. In this respect the chapters represent the outworking of a principle affirmed in the New Testament: "Let all things be done decently and in order" (1 Cor. 14:40). From this perspective the details themselves do not matter, but the principle they embody does.

Let us look at this section from a cultural angle and examine basic differences from our own age. When Tevye, the dairyman in *Fiddler on the Roof,* sang his song "Tradition" and sadly came to realize that in the face of modernity the old order was on its way out and much had to change, he was referring to a development which has left its mark not only on modern Judaism but also on modern Christianity. People today have a chronological snobbery, which is impatient with the past and ever wants to start all over again and give everything a new look. Tradition has become a dirty word, while "history is bunk" according to that saint of the cult of technology, Henry Ford. The New Testament knows a crisis for religious tradition—see for instance Mark 7:1–23 and Acts 15:1–29—but it also claims continuity with its Jewish past and even speaks of apostolic "traditions" which were to be maintained (2 Thess. 2:15). As the French politician Jean Jaurès observed in a different context, "Take from the altars of the past the fire—not the ashes."

Where did the Chronicler stand? He belonged to a struggling little community, politically insignificant, and low down in the Third World category of nations. It was searching for an identity in a modern world of political giants. The Chronicler directed his readers to heroes of the past, David and Solomon, as role models for the present and future. Supremely they were religious models, in whose light the contemporary temple was honored as the center of the community's existence. This ideology brought meaning into life and the assurance that to do it David's way and Solomon's way was to do it right. So the thread of Davidic organization which runs through these chapters is important. It gave the satisfaction of knowing that post-exilic religion rested on divine foundations. A generation that is aware of its own bankruptcy in possessing inner resources for putting its world right is forced to look back into the past to rediscover secrets which earlier and wiser folk possessed.

The Christian living in the modern world has to juggle with cultural pressures and biblical roots and, as a citizen of two worlds, try to discover what he or she should stand for. Perhaps modern Christians find these chapters uninteresting because in response, partially at least, to cultural pressures they have become weary of organization and highly developed structures. We hanker after a free, pioneering spirit in the face of a computer-ridden bureaucracy which reduces us to a series of numbers, a social security number, a driver's license number, and a credit card number. There is an urge to start again with smaller groups which can relate heart to heart and shrug off the burden of large religious structures with all their organizational appendages. I am speaking sociologically and do not wish to deny a real movement of the Spirit of God. I also speak as a religious conservative—like the Chronicler!—who does not want to see the baby thrown out with the bathwater. I recall sitting as a boy in a little independent chapel and often hearing the adage "The Church is not an organization; it is an organism." I think I know what the preacher meant, but I also remember the noticeboard at the back of the chapel being full of rotas and lists for preachers and flowers and cleaning and prayer-meeting leaders and drivers for the aged, and so on. The Christian who visits a church on vacation and enjoys a Sunday service knows nothing about the labors of love that lie behind it. Yet one should be able to guess and, when one thanks the preacher, should mentally throw in thanks to the host of others who have contributed behind the scenes. Commitment to the Lord means, whether it is a welcome truth or not, commitment to a mass of details. Viewed aright, they become windows through which the face of the Lord may be glimpsed. This is the Chronicler's attitude as he takes us into a hive of religious industry.

"WHO SWEEPS A ROOM . . ."

23:1 So when David was old and full of days, he made his son Solomon king over Israel.

2 And he gathered together all the leaders of Israel, with the priests and the Levites.

3 Now the Levites were numbered from the age of thirty years and above; and the number of individual males was thirty-eight thousand.

4 Of these, twenty-four thousand *were* to look after the work of the house of the LORD, six thousand *were* officers and judges,

5 four thousand *were* gatekeepers, and four thousand praised the LORD with *musical* instruments, "which I made," *said David,* "for giving praise."

6 Also David separated them into divisions among the sons of Levi: Gershon, Kohath, and Merari.

7 Of the Gershonites: Laadan and Shimei.

8 The sons of Laadan: the first Jehiel, then Zetham and Joel—three *in all.*

9 The sons of Shimei: Shelomith, Haziel, and

Haran—three *in all.* These were the heads of the fathers' *houses* of Laadan.

10 And the sons of Shimei: Jahath, Zina, Jeush, and Beriah. These *were* the four sons of Shimei.

11 Jahath was the first and Zizah the second. But Jeush and Beriah did not have many sons; therefore they were assigned as one father's house.

12 The sons of Kohath: Amram, Izhar, Hebron, and Uzziel—four *in all.*

14 Now the sons of Moses the man of God were reckoned to the tribe of Levi.

15 The sons of Moses *were* Gershon and Eliezer.

16 Of the sons of Gershon, Shebuel *was* the first.

17 Of the descendants of Eliezer, Rehabiah was the first. And Eliezer had no other sons, but the sons of Rehabiah were very many.

18 Of the sons of Izhar, Shelomith *was* the first.

19 Of the sons of Hebron, Jeriah *was* the first, Amariah the second, Jahaziel the third, and Jekameam the fourth.

20 Of the sons of Uzziel, Michah *was* the first and Jesshiah the second.

21 The sons of Merari *were* Mahli and Mushi. The sons of Mahli *were* Eleazar and Kish.

22 And Eleazar died, and had no sons, but only daughters; and their brethren, the sons of Kish, took them *as wives.*

23 The sons of Mushi *were* Mahli, Eder, and Jeremoth—three *in all.*

24 These *were* the sons of Levi by their fathers' houses—the heads of the fathers' *houses* as they were counted individually by the number of their names, who did the work for the service of the house of the LORD, from the age of twenty years and above.

25 For David said, "The LORD God of Israel has given rest to His people, that they may dwell in Jerusalem forever";

26 and also to the Levites, "They shall no longer carry the tabernacle, or any of the articles for its service."

27 For by the last words of David the Levites *were* numbered from twenty years old and above;

28 because their duty *was* to help the sons of Aaron in the service of the house of the LORD, in the courts and in the chambers, in the purifying of all holy things and the work of the service of the house of God,

29 both with the showbread and the fine flour for the grain offering, with the unleavened cakes and *what is baked in* the pan, with what is mixed and with all kinds of measures and sizes;

30 to stand every morning to thank and praise the LORD, and likewise at evening;

31 and at every presentation of a burnt offering to the LORD on the Sabbaths and on the New Moons and on the set feasts, by number according to the ordinance governing them, regularly before the LORD;

32 and that they should attend to the needs of the tabernacle of meeting, the needs of the holy *place,* and the needs of the sons of Aaron their brethren in the work of the house of the LORD.

24:20 And the rest of the sons of Levi: of the sons of Amram, Shubael; of the sons of Shubael, Jehdeiah.

21 Concerning Rehabiah, of the sons of Rehabiah, the first *was* Isshiah.

22 Of the Izharites, Shelomoth; of the sons of Shelomoth, Jahath.

23 Of the sons *of Hebron,* Jeriah *was the first,* Amariah the second, Jahaziel the third, *and* Jekameam the fourth.

24 *Of* the sons of Uzziel, Michah; of the sons of Michah, Shamir.

25 The brother of Michah, Isshiah; of the sons of Isshiah, Zechariah.

26 The sons of Merari *were* Mahli and Mushi; the son of Jaaziah, Beno.

27 The sons of Merari by Jaaziah *were* Beno, Shoham, Zaccur, and Ibri.

28 Of Mahli: Eleazar, who had no sons.

29 Of Kish: the son of Kish, Jerahmeel.

30 Also the sons of Mushi *were* Mahli, Eder, and Jerimoth. These *were* the sons of the Levites according to their fathers' houses.

31 These also cast lots just as their brothers the

sons of Aaron did, in the presence of King David,
Zadok, Ahimelech, and the heads of the fathers'
houses of the priests and Levites. The chief fathers *did*
just as their younger brethren.

1 Chron. 23:1-12, 14-32; 24:20-31

The general structure of these chapters is indicated in the introductory verses 23:4-5. Each of these groups will feature the
maintenance staff, the musicians, singers, the *"gatekeepers,"* and a
heterogeneous group here lumped together as *"officers and judges."* A
Levitical genealogy related to the three clans of Gershon, Kohath,
and Merari is given in 23:7-23, probably from a source independent
of the one used in chapter 6. It supplies the names of family heads
alive at the time of its composition. Similar ground is covered in the
genealogy of 24:20-31, an updated version that moves forward a
generation. Probably the first of the genealogies was understood to
refer to the maintenance staff: so 23:24 suggests. If so, it is significant that they were given priority and pride of place in the Chronicler's listing.

However, the description of Levitical duties that follows in 23:28-
32 is a more general one: it includes the singers in verse 30. It specifies more menial tasks than the context mentions. Scholars think that
23:28-32 continue 23:13 and that both passages are a supplement
written from a priestly perspective. Certainly the subordinate role of
the Levites is stressed at 23:28 and 32. In 9:2, which relates to the
early post-exilic period, there was a threefold list of "priests, Levites,
and Nethinim," the last group being temple slaves, the lowest grade
of religious staff. There is no trace of them here, which suggests that
they and their duties were incorporated into the Levitical order as
the lower of a two-tier system. In practice this must have meant a
pecking order. I well remember in my student days working as a
ward orderly in a hospital and being made to feel in that exalted
world of doctors and nurses that I was of very little account. I suspect that the Levites had the same experience. Part of the Chronicler's overall purpose was to call for a round of applause for their
labors. The cleaning they did (23:28) had to be up to hospital standards for reasons not of hygiene but of holiness. They did menial
work for their more exalted colleagues, the priests. The Chronicler
would have liked George Herbert's poem, "Employment":

> A servant with this clause ['for Thy sake"]
> Makes drudgery divine;
> Who sweeps a room as for Thy laws
> Makes that and th' action fine.

PRIESTLY DUTIES

23:13 The sons of Amram: Aaron and Moses; and Aaron was set apart, he and his sons forever, that he should sanctify the most holy things, to burn incense before the LORD, to minister to Him, and to give the blessing in His name forever.

24:1 Now *these are* the divisions of the sons of Aaron. The sons of Aaron *were* Nadab, Abihu, Eleazar, and Ithamar.

2 And Nadab and Abihu died before their father, and had no children; therefore Eleazar and Ithamar ministered as priests.

3 Then David with Zadok of the sons of Eleazar, and Ahimelech of the sons of Ithamar, divided them according to the schedule of their service.

4 There were more leaders found of the sons of Eleazar than of the sons of Ithamar, and *thus* they were divided. Among the sons of Eleazar *were* sixteen heads of *their* fathers' houses, and eight heads of their fathers' houses among the sons of Ithamar.

5 Thus they were divided by lot, one group as another, for there were officials of the sanctuary and officials *of the house* of God, from the sons of Eleazar and from the sons of Ithamar.

6 And the scribe, Shemaiah the son of Nethanel, *one of* the Levites, wrote them down before the king, the leaders, Zadok the priest, Ahimelech the son of Abiathar, and the heads of the fathers' *houses* of the priests and Levites, one father's house taken for Eleazar and *one* for Ithamar.

7 Now the first lot fell to Jehoiarib, the second to Jedaiah,

8 the third to Harim, the fourth to Seorim,

9 the fifth to Malchijah, the sixth to Mijamin,

10 the seventh to Hakkoz, the eighth to Abijah,

11 the ninth to Jeshua, the tenth to Shecaniah,

12 the eleventh to Eliashib, the twelfth to Jakim,

13 the thirteenth to Huppah, the fourteenth to Jeshebeab,

14 the fifteenth to Bilgah, the sixteenth to Immer,

15 the seventeenth to Hezir, the eighteenth to Happizzez,

16 the nineteenth to Pethahiah, the twentieth to Jehezekel,

17 the twenty-first to Jachin, the twenty-second to Gamul,

18 the twenty-third to Delaiah, the twenty-fourth to Maaziah.

19 This *was* the schedule of their service for coming into the house of the LORD according to their ordinance by the hand of Aaron their father, as the LORD God of Israel had commanded him.

1 Chron. 23:13; 24:1–19

The priest, who belonged to a subgroup of the tribe of Levi as a descendant of Aaron, had a variety of specialist duties of which only some are listed here. In the new era of the temple their old roles carried over unchanged, unlike the Levites, who were assigned new tasks (23:26). One of the priest's roles was the pronouncement of divine *"blessing"* (23:13). This role is elaborated in Numbers 6:22–27, which is well worth looking up if you are not familiar with the passage. The beautiful formula of benediction which they used has been taken over in Christian circles as a parting prayer. The priest's words, expressed as a prayerful wish with third-person references to God, were underwritten by God's warranty: "I will bless them" (Num. 6:27). Divine blessing would enter the lives of the members of the congregation as a result of the priestly benediction. The benediction was associated with the end of a service (cf. Lev. 9:22, 23) or festival. It comes alive in a personal setting in the story of Hannah, who received new hope from the benediction of blundering old Eli (1 Sam. 1:1–18). In the Book of Psalms such lovely specimens as Psalms 91 and 121 functioned originally within the sphere of a priestly benediction to individual believers. It is noticeable that Psalm 121, with its keyword "keep," echoes Numbers 6:24. The benediction formed a bridge between temple worship and mundane life back home, promising fulfillment and satisfaction to those who had met with God at the sanctuary.

The priests were organized into twenty-four divisions (24:1–19). They were to minister in the temple on a rota system and were free to engage in other work the rest of the time. Interestingly 24:10 with its mention of *"Abijah"* spans the Testaments. The father of John the Baptist, Zechariah, belonged to this division (Luke 1:5). He was on duty in the temple burning incense when he received an angelic vision and message about the birth of John and his role under God. Struck dumb, he was unable to deliver the benediction in the temple court (Luke 1:5–23). 1 Chronicles 23:13 and 24:10 serve as a commentary on that New Testament passage.

SACRED MUSIC AND SONG

25:1 Moreover David and the captains of the army separated for the service *some* of the sons of Asaph, of Heman, and of Jeduthun, who *should* prophesy with harps, stringed instruments, and cymbals. And the number of the skilled men performing their service was:

2 Of the sons of Asaph: Zaccur, Joseph, Nethaniah, and Asharelah; the sons of Asaph *were* under the direction of Asaph, who prophesied according to the order of the king.

3 Of Jeduthun, the sons of Jeduthun: Gedaliah, Zeri, Jeshaiah, Shimei, Hashabiah, and Mattithiah, six, under the direction of their father Jeduthun, who prophesied with a harp to give thanks and to praise the LORD.

4 Of Heman, the sons of Heman: Bukkiah, Mattaniah, Uzziel, Shebuel, Jerimoth, Hananiah, Hanani, Eliathah, Giddalti, Romamti-Ezer, Joshbekashah, Mallothi, Hothir, *and* Mahazioth.

5 All these *were* the sons of Heman the king's seer in the words of God, to exalt his horn. For God gave Heman fourteen sons and three daughters.

6 All these *were* under the direction of their father for the music *in* the house of the LORD, with

cymbals, stringed instruments, and harps, for the service of the house of God. Asaph, Jeduthun, and Heman *were* under the authority of the king.

7 So the number of them, with their brethren who were instructed in the songs of the LORD, all who were skillful, *was* two hundred and eighty-eight.

8 And they cast lots for their duty, the small as well as the great, the teacher with the student.

9 Now the first lot for Asaph came out for Joseph; the second for Gedaliah, him with his brethren and sons, twelve;

10 the third for Zaccur, his sons and his brethren, twelve;

11 the fourth for Jizri, his sons and his brethren, twelve;

12 the fifth for Nethaniah, his sons and his brethren, twelve;

13 the sixth for Bukkiah, his sons and his brethren, twelve;

14 the seventh for Jesharelah, his sons and his brethren, twelve;

15 the eighth for Jeshaiah, his sons and his brethren, twelve;

16 the ninth for Mattaniah, his sons and his brethren, twelve;

17 the tenth for Shimei, his sons and his brethren, twelve;

18 the eleventh for Azarel, his sons and his brethren, twelve;

19 the twelfth for Hashabiah, his sons and his brethren, twelve;

20 the thirteenth for Shubael, his sons and his brethren, twelve;

21 the fourteenth for Mattithiah, his sons and his brethren, twelve;

22 the fifteenth for Jeremoth, his sons and his brethren, twelve;

23 the sixteenth for Hananiah, his sons and his brethren, twelve;

24 the seventeenth for Joshbekashah, his sons and his brethren, twelve;

25 the eighteenth for Hanani, his sons and his brethren, twelve;
26 the nineteenth for Mallothi, his sons and his brethren, twelve;
27 the twentieth for Eliathah, his sons and his brethren, twelve;
28 the twenty-first for Hothir, his sons and his brethren, twelve;
29 the twenty-second for Giddalti, his sons and his brethren, twelve;
30 the twenty-third for Mahazioth, his sons and his brethren, twelve;
31 the twenty-fourth for Romamti-Ezer, his sons and his brethren, twelve.

1 Chron. 25:1-31

This aspect of Levitical duties was especially dear to the Chronicler's heart. We have encountered earlier the three Levitical guilds of Asaph, Heman, and Jeduthun. Verses 7–31 enumerate a rota of attendance, like that of the priests. An interesting phenomenon is that the work of these guilds is described in terms of prophesying (vv. 1, 3, 5). In pre-exilic times there were temple prophets who had an important role alongside the priests, especially in transmitting divine answers to prayers of lament brought in times of national or personal crisis. Their ministry underlies the "Do not fear!" of Lamentations 3:57. In Psalm 85:8–13 such a prophet delivers God's one-word answer "peace" and proceeds sensitively to expound its meaning to a distressed people. In two of the psalms we hear him taking part in a service of worship, challenging the worshipers to believe in their hearts what they have said with their lips and to do in their lives what they have heard with their ears (Pss. 81:5b–16; 95:7b–11). This dynamic role was woven into their ministry of sacred song. In post-exilic times this prophetic role seems gradually to have disappeared from the Levitical ranks, but the guilds were regarded as the legitimate heirs of the earlier temple prophets. In a similar vein preaching is often called the counterpart of the New Testament prophesying. (The New Testament prophet was actually the descendant of the temple prophet rather than of the classical prophet associated with the prophetic books of the Old Testament.) The link of the later

Levitical singer with the earlier prophecy was presumably that a soloist would now sing the individual prophetic portions of such prophecies as are contained in Psalms 81 and 95, which were used long after a prophet was initially inspired to participate in them. In more general terms these choirs had the role of being spokespersons for God even as they brought to God the praises of His people (v. 3; 23:30). The songs they sang expressed high theology, of which examples are given in chapter 16. They lifted the hearts and minds of the congregation up to God and stimulated them to a loftier spirituality than probably they came with. They led the worship and voiced the praises and prayers to which the congregation added their "Amen" and from which they found inspiration for their own praises (16:36).

There is mention of the high standards associated with their ministry of music and song in verses 7, 8. Evidently there was a general training scheme to test and improve professional competence (v. 7) and rehearsals designed to teach accomplished renderings of the traditional songs. According to the Jewish Talmud, in later times the temple choristers underwent five years' training. These references, tantalizingly brief though they are, speak volumes to the Christian church. There is a Philistine streak in some extreme quarters of Protestantism that austerely relegates instrumental music to a pre-Christian era. (This phenomenon corresponds to the practice in the traditional Jewish synagogue, where a musical instrument was and is never heard, because that form of worship belongs exclusively to temple worship and is not to be revived until the temple is rebuilt.) Instead, the references in Ephesians 5:19 to "psalms and hymns and spiritual songs" (cf. Col. 3:16; 1 Cor. 14:26) is regarded as the only New Testament basis of worship. On the principle that all in the Bible remains permissible unless the New Testament rules otherwise, I find in these verses in Chronicles insights into the aesthetic role of musicians and singers in contemporary church services. Indeed, the hymns in Revelation were significantly sung to the music of the harp (Rev. 5:8; 15:2): in the second instance there is mention of "harps of God," which seem to mean harps used in the worship of God.

Music appeals more to the emotions and accompanying words more to the mind, so that the whole person is brought nearer to God. Of course, music and song, instead of being a divine window, may function simply as art for art's sake. As George Herbert wrote in his poem, "The Elixir":

> A man that looks on glass
> On it may stay his eye;
> Or, if he pleaseth, through it pass,
> And then the heaven espy.

The same objection might be leveled at the sermon, in the light of Ezekiel 33:30–32! Good servants always make bad masters. John Wesley's general principle is applicable here: "Let the abuse be removed and the use remain." There is a fine heritage of ecclesiastical music at the disposal of the local church; in turn it sets standards for the selection of contemporary music. A choir may sing pieces impracticable for congregational use, which turn the listeners' hearts to God. Martin Luther well testified: "With all my heart I would extol the precious gift of God in the noble art of music. . . . Music is to be praised as second only to the Word of God because by it are all the emotions swayed. Nothing on earth is more mighty . . . to hearken the downcast, mellow the overweening, temper the exuberant or mollify the vengeful. . . . When natural music is sharpened and polished by art, then one begins to see with amazement the great and perfect wisdom of God."[1]

"WHO MAY ASCEND TO THE HILL OF THE LORD?"

26:1 Concerning the divisions of the gatekeepers: of the Korahites, Meshelemiah the son of Kore, of the sons of Asaph.

2 And the sons of Meshelemiah *were* Zechariah the firstborn, Jediael the second, Zebadiah the third, Jathniel the fourth,

3 Elam the fifth, Jehohanan the sixth, Eliehoenai the seventh.

4 Moreover the sons of Obed-Edom *were* Shemaiah the firstborn, Jehozabad the second, Joah the third, Sacar the fourth, Nethanel the fifth,

5 Ammiel the sixth, Issachar the seventh, Peulthai the eighth; for God blessed him.

6 Also to Shemaiah his son were sons born who governed their fathers' houses, because they *were* men of great ability.

7 The sons of Shemaiah *were* Othni, Rephael, Obed, and Elzabad, whose brothers Elihu and Semachiah *were* able men.

8 All these *were* the sons of Obed-Edom, they and their sons and their brethren, able men with strength for the work: sixty-two of Obed-Edom.

9 And Meshelemiah had sons and brethren, eighteen able men.

10 Also Hosah, of the children of Merari, had sons: Shimri the first (for *though* he was not the first-born, his father made him the first),

11 Hilkiah the second, Tebaliah the third, Zechariah the fourth; all the sons and brethren of Hosah *were* thirteen.

12 Among these *were* the divisions of the gatekeepers, among the chief men, *having* duties just like their brethren, to serve in the house of the LORD.

13 And they cast lots for each gate, the small as well as the great, according to their father's house.

14 The lot for the East *Gate* fell to Shelemiah. Then they cast lots *for* his son Zechariah, a wise counselor, and his lot came out for the North Gate;

15 to Obed-Edom the South Gate, and to his sons the storehouse.

16 To Shuppim and Hosah *the lot came out* for the West Gate, with the Shallecheth Gate on the ascending highway—watchman opposite watchman.

17 On the east were *six* Levites, on the north four each day, on the south four each day, and for the storehouse two by two.

18 As for the Parbar on the west, *there were* four on the highway *and* two at the Parbar.

19 These were the divisions of the gatekeepers among the sons of Korah and among the sons of Merari.

1 Chron. 26:1–19

The Levitical group of gatekeepers is considered next. Their divisions are not chronologically arranged, but topographically, assigning them to four gates of the temple and other areas where security was deemed to be necessary. The *"Parbar"* of verse 18 was probably a "colonnade" (NEB). Their role as security police did not concern only theft from the temple area, although the reference to *"the storehouse"* (vv. 15, 17) indicates that this concern was not irrelevant. According to 2 Chronicles 23:19 the purpose of their work was "that no one who was in any way unclean should enter." There is evidence in the Old Testament that the temple gates were spiritual checkpoints. Psalm 15 is the main evidence. It represents an interchange between a pilgrim and evidently a gatekeeper as to God's standards for the would-be worshiper. There is listed a series of moral and social requirements and then a promise of blessing. The privileges of worship and blessing depend on a prior commitment to good neighborliness. This interchange attested in Psalm 15 occurs in a shorter form at Psalm 24:3–6 and shorter still at Psalm 118:19–20, while Isaiah 33:14–16 echoes this convention in a prophetic message. Moreover, the religious condemnation of Isaiah 1:10–17 seems to imply that in Isaiah's day this moral security check was a perfunctory one, if it was done at all. People were being let into the temple courts who had no moral right to be there. A blind eye was being turned to low social standards. In God's name the prophet thunders: "I cannot endure [a combination of] iniquity and the sacred meeting" (Isa. 1:13). He challenges to "cease to do evil, learn to do good" (vv. 16, 17).

In the Sermon on the Mount Jesus made use of this custom, I suggest, at Matthew 5:23–24. To any who brought an offering in worship He counseled self-examination as to how that person had been treating others. If the answer was a negative one, the offering was not to be completed until the matter had been put right. A striking word picture is painted of an empty altar and an offering lying beside it, with the worshiper conspicuous by his absence. "First be reconciled to your brother, and then come and offer your gift," was Jesus' directive. Here was the Lord doing the work of a gatekeeper and commending His standards to His disciples. The principle is widened in 1 John 4:20: "He who does not love his brother . . . , how can he love God?"

FINANCE

26:20 Of the Levites, Ahijah *was* over the treasuries of the house of God and over the treasuries of the dedicated things.

21 The sons of Laadan, the descendants of the Gershonites of Laadan, heads of their fathers' *houses,* of Laadan the Gershonite: Jehieli.

22 The sons of Jehieli, Zetham and Joel his brother, *were* over the treasuries of the house of the LORD.

23 Of the Amramites, the Izharites, the Hebronites, and the Uzzielites:

24 Shebuel the son of Gershom, the son of Moses, *was* overseer of the treasuries.

25 And his brethren by Eliezer *were* Rehabiah his son, Jeshaiah his son, Joram his son, Zichri his son, and Shelomith his son.

26 This Shelomith and his brethren *were* over all the treasuries of the dedicated things which King David and the heads of fathers' *houses,* the captains over thousands and hundreds, and the captains of the army, had dedicated.

27 Some of the spoils won in battles they dedicated to maintain the house of the LORD.

28 And all that Samuel the seer, Saul the son of Kish, Abner the son of Ner, and Joab the son of Zeruiah had dedicated, every dedicated *thing,* was under the hand of Shelomith and his brethren.

1 Chron. 26:20–28

A miscellaneous group of Levites was mentioned in 23:4, "officers and judges." This term is now unpacked in verses 20–32, and its first ingredient is the treasurers. There were two types of treasury; one was *"the treasuries of the dedicated things"* (vv. 20, 26–28). This was a sort of combined bank and museum. Ancient temples regularly contained valuable objects accumulated over the centuries, and the temple in Jerusalem was no exception. A tour of these treasuries would have provided a history lesson. They contained spoils of war *"dedicated to maintain the house of the Lord"* (v. 27). David, we remember, contributed to such a treasury in 18:11. There was an understandable tendency not to sell these spoils but to preserve them as trophies of God's grace. The other treasuries, those *of the house of God*￼ (vv. 20, 22, 24), were the busy, bustling ones of everyday usage. In Ezra 8:34 we get a glimpse of activity there on a special day when Ezra arrived from Babylonia with a consignment of money and vessels. It is noticeable that a tight security system was in force before and during the journey (Ezra 8:25–30) and at its end. Good care had to be taken of God's property, not least so as to keep faith with the donors. One sometimes reads stories in the newspaper of a church treasurer running off with the church's funds or the discovery that he or she had been steadily milking them. How amazing is the misplaced faith in human nature which underlies these thefts! A door of temptation has been left wide open instead of instituting a foolproof system of precautions to protect not only the funds from misappropriation but their steward from temptation.

A WIDER MINISTRY

26:29 Of the Izharites, Chenaniah and his sons *performed* duties as officials and judges over Israel outside Jerusalem.
30 Of the Hebronites, Hashabiah and his brethren, one thousand seven hundred able men, had the oversight of Israel on the west side of the Jordan for all the business of the LORD, and in the service of the king.
31 Among the Hebronites, Jerijah *was* head of the Hebronites according to his genealogy of the fathers. In the fortieth year of the reign of David they were sought, and they were found among them capable men at Jazer of Gilead.
32 And his brethren *were* two thousand seven hundred able men, heads of fathers' *houses,* whom King David made officials over the Reubenites, the Gadites, and the half-tribe of Manasseh, for every matter pertaining to God and the affairs of the king.
1 Chron. 26:29–32

Here are the *"officials and judges"* proper. Certain Levites were evidently seconded for judicial work in Israel as magistrates and legal executives. This work may have been an extension of the administration of Levitical cities, since "Jazer" (v. 31) was one such city. Certainly it made use of an expertise not mentioned here but referred to in 2 Chronicles 17:7–9 (and Neh. 8:7), an expert knowledge of the Torah. This group is put last as furthest away from a temple ministry, but it was a legitimate and valuable work. It reminds me of the Anglican archbishops and bishops who sit as "lords spiritual" in the British House of Lords. This civil appointment is a traditional part of their overall duties as men of God. On a less grandiose level, I think of ordained ministers who sit on social committees concerned with welfare work, such as the needs of minority groups. A minister whose labors my wife and I came to appreciate was the general secretary of a Christian adoption society in England. He had a fruitful ministry on behalf of childless couples and unmarried mothers, for which his Christian love was perhaps an even better qualification than his civil training as a probation officer. Later his society amalgamated with another one, which had responsibility over residential homes for children. His love was given an even wider ministry in caring for the interests of battered children and the unfortunate victims of broken homes. I would like to take the opportunity of saluting the Rev. R. H. Johnson for his work as a Christian minister, far from a church but near to the Lord.

NOTE

1. R. H. Bainton, *Here I Stand* (Nashville: Abingdon Press, 1950), p. 343.

CHAPTER EIGHT

Transition

1 Chronicles 27:1–29:30

Chapter 28 opens with David assembling "all the leaders" and "mighty men" at Jerusalem (v. 1), and chapter 29 virtually closes with "all the leaders and the mighty men" acknowledging Solomon's kingly rank (v. 24). It is the story of a transfer of power, of one leader preparing to step down in order that another may take over. Most of the intervening material is concerned not with privilege and rank but with responsibility, Solomon's responsibility to take over the temple project from David and bring it to completion. So it ever is in God's work. In a game of word associations "Solomon" would probably suggest "glory," but the impression of him which the Chronicler wants to leave us with is of a man with a mission: to use his status as a means of forwarding the work of God, especially in the building of the temple. "Everyone to whom much is given, from him much will be required" (Luke 12:48).

GOD'S STEWARDS

27:1 And the children of Israel, according to their number, the heads of fathers' *houses,* the captains of thousands and hundreds and their officers, served the king in every matter of the *military* divisions. *These divisions* came in and went out month by month throughout all the months of the year, each division *having* twenty-four thousand.

2 Over the first division for the first month *was* Jashobeam the son of Zabdiel, and in his division *were* twenty-four thousand;

3 *he was* of the children of Perez, and the chief of all the captains of the army for the first month.

4 Over the division of the second month *was* Dodai an Ahohite, and of his division Mikloth also *was* the leader; in his division *were* twenty-four thousand.

5 The third captain of the army for the third month *was* Benaiah, the son of Jehoiada the priest, who was chief; in his division *were* twenty-four thousand.

6 This was the Benaiah *who was* mighty *among* the thirty, and was over the thirty; in his division *was* Ammizabad his son.

7 The fourth *captain* for the fourth month *was* Asahel the brother of Joab, and Zebadiah his son after him; in his division *were* twenty-four thousand.

8 The fifth *captain* for the fifth month *was* Shamhuth the Izrahite; in his division were twenty-four thousand.

9 The sixth *captain* for the sixth month *was* Ira the son of Ikkesh the Tekoite; in his division *were* twenty-four thousand.

10 The seventh *captain* for the seventh month *was* Helez the Pelonite, of the children of Ephraim; in his division *were* twenty-four thousand.

11 The eighth *captain* for the eighth month *was* Sibbechai the Hushathite, of the Zarhites; in his division *were* twenty-four thousand.

12 The ninth *captain* for the ninth month *was* Abiezer the Anathothite, of the Benjamites; in his division *were* twenty-four thousand.

13 The tenth *captain* for the tenth month *was* Maharai the Netophathite, of the Zarhites; in his division *were* twenty-four thousand.

14 The eleventh *captain* for the eleventh month *was* Benaiah the Pirathonite, of the children of Ephraim; in his division *were* twenty-four thousand.

15 The twelfth *captain* for the twelfth month *was* Heldai the Netophathite, of Othniel; in his division *were* twenty-four thousand.

16 Furthermore, over the tribes of Israel: the officer over the Reubenites *was* Eliezer the son of Zichri; over the Simeonites, Shephatiah the son of Maachah;

17 *over* the Levites, Hashabiah the son of Kemuel; over the Aaronites, Zadok;

18 *over* Judah, Elihu, *one* of David's brothers; *over* Issachar, Omri the son of Michael;

19 *over* Zebulun, Ishmaiah the son of Obadiah; *over* Naphtali, Jerimoth the son of Azriel;

20 *over* the children of Ephraim, Hoshea the son of Azaziah; *over* the half-tribe of Manasseh, Joel the son of Pedaiah;

21 *over* the half-*tribe* of Manasseh in Gilead, Iddo the son of Zechariah; *over* Benjamin, Jaasiel the son of Abner;

22 *over* Dan, Azarel the son of Jeroham. These *were* the leaders of the tribes of Israel.

23 But David did not take the number of those twenty years old and under, because the LORD had said He would multiply Israel like the stars of the heavens.

24 Joab the son of Zeruiah began a census, but he did not finish, for wrath came upon Israel because of this census; nor was the number recorded in the account of the chronicles of King David.

25 And Azmaveth the son of Adiel *was* over the king's treasuries; and Jehonathan the son of Uzziah was over the storehouses in the field, in the cities, in the villages, and in the fortresses.

26 Ezri the son of Chelub was over those who did the work of the field for tilling the ground.

27 And Shimei the Ramathite *was* over the vineyards, and Zabdi the Shiphmite was over the produce of the vineyards for the supply of wine.

28 Baal-Hanan the Gederite was over the olive trees and the sycamore trees that *were* in the lowlands, and Joash *was* over the store of oil.

29 And Shitrai the Sharonite *was* over the herds that fed in Sharon, and Shaphat the son of Adlai was over the herds *that were* in the valleys.

30 Obil the Ishmaelite *was* over the camels, Jehdeiah the Meronothite *was* over the donkeys,

31 and Jaziz the Hagrite *was* over the flocks. All these *were* the officials over King David's property.

32 Also Jehonathan, David's uncle, *was* a counselor,

a wise man, and a scribe; and Jehiel the son of Hachmoni *was* with the king's sons.

33 Ahithophel *was* the king's counselor, and Hushai the Archite *was* the king's companion.

34 After Ahithophel *was* Jehoiada the son of Benaiah, then Abiathar. And the general of the king's army *was* Joab.

28:1 Now David assembled at Jerusalem all the leaders of Israel: the officers of the tribes and the captains of the divisions who served the king, the captains over thousands and captains over hundreds, and the stewards over all the substance and possessions of the king and of his sons, with the officials, the valiant men, and all the mighty men of valor.

2 Then King David rose to his feet and said, "Hear me, my brethren and my people. I *had* it in my heart to build a house of rest for the ark of the covenant of the LORD, and for the footstool of our God, and had made preparations to build it.

3 "But God said to me, 'You shall not build a house for My name, because you *have been* a man of war and have shed blood.'

4 "However the LORD God of Israel chose me above all the house of my father to be king over Israel forever, for He has chosen Judah *to be* the ruler. And of the house of Judah, the house of my father, and among the sons of my father, He was pleased with me to make *me* king over all Israel.

5 "And of all my sons (for the LORD has given me many sons) He has chosen my son Solomon to sit on the throne of the kingdom of the LORD over Israel.

6 "Now He said to me, 'It is your son Solomon *who* shall build My house and My courts; for I have chosen him *to be* My son, and I will be his Father.

7 'Moreover I will establish his kingdom forever, if he is steadfast to observe My commandments and My judgments, as it is this day.'

8 "Now therefore, in the sight of all Israel, the assembly of the LORD, and in the hearing of our God, be careful to seek out all the commandments of the LORD your God, that you may possess this good land,

174

and leave *it* as an inheritance for your children after you forever.

9 "As for you, my son Solomon, know the God of your father, and serve Him with a loyal heart and with a willing mind; for the LORD searches all hearts and understands all the intent of the thoughts. If you seek Him, He will be found by you; but if you forsake Him, He will cast you off forever.

10 "Consider now, for the LORD has chosen you to build a house for the sanctuary; be strong, and do it."

11 Then David gave his son Solomon the plans for the vestibule, its houses, its treasuries, its upper chambers, its inner chambers, and the place of the mercy seat;

12 and the plans for all that he had by the Spirit, of the courts of the house of the LORD, of all the chambers all around, of the treasuries of the house of God, and of the treasuries for the dedicated things;

13 also for the division of the priests and the Levites, for all the work of the service of the house of the LORD, and for all the articles of service in the house of the LORD.

14 *He gave* gold by weight for *things* of gold, for all articles used in every kind of service; also *silver* for all articles of silver by weight, for all articles used in every kind of service;

15 the weight for the lampstands of gold, and their lamps of gold, by weight for each lampstand and its lamps; for the lampstands of silver by weight, for the lampstand and its lamps, according to the use of each lampstand.

16 And by weight *he gave* gold for the tables of the showbread, for each table, and silver for the tables of silver;

17 also pure gold for the forks, the basins, the pitchers of pure gold, and the golden bowls—*he gave gold* by weight for every bowl; and for the silver bowls, *silver* by weight for every bowl;

18 and refined gold by weight for the altar of incense, and for the construction of the chariot, that is, the gold cherubim that spread *their wings* and overshadowed the ark of the covenant of the LORD.

19 "All *this,*" said David, "the LORD made me understand in writing, by *His* hand upon me, all the works of these plans."

20 And David said to his son Solomon, "Be strong and of good courage, and do *it;* do not fear nor be dismayed, for the LORD God—my God—*will be* with you. He will not leave you nor forsake you, until you have finished all the work for the service of the house of the LORD.

21 "*Here are* the divisions of the priests and the Levites for all the service of the house of God; and every willing craftsman *will be* with you for all manner of workmanship, for every kind of service; also the leaders and all the people *will be* completely at your command."

1 Chron. 27:1–28:21

1. *Order—virtue and vice.* Chapter 27 looks both forward and backward. The list of civil officials in chapter 27 is followed in chapter 28 by David's public commissioning of Solomon and handing over of the plans he had drawn up for the temple. In this connection the former chapter supplies the vocabulary for the summary of Israel's leaders who are assembled in 28:1. It also rounds off David's organization of religious and state affairs: 23:3–27:34 supply a breakdown of "the leaders of Israel, with the priests and the Levites," as they were constituted when assembled by the King (23:2; cf. 28:1). There is an impression of harmony and order in each aspect of the nation's life, secular and religious, which in principle was to serve as a model for the Chronicler's community. Order is not merely a human convenience but also a means of honoring God. "Order," suggested Alexander Pope, "is Heaven's first law."

In detail chapter 27 presents first an account of a systematic division of the people into twelve groups of monthly conscripts under particular leaders (vv. 1–15), then a list of tribal chiefs connected with David's census of chapter 21 (vv. 16–24), a list of officials responsible for administering the royal estates (vv. 25–31), and finally names of the members of what might be called David's privy council (vv. 32–34). There are two features of interest in 27:16–24. The first is that the Chronicler does not miss a further opportunity to emphasize the full scope of God's people. His slogan "all Israel" here takes the form of a listing of the tribes one by one as equal citizens of the kingdom. It stirs in him, and he trusts in his readers, a response of hope and endeavor to realize the larger dimensions of the people of God. The second point of interest is a redeeming feature in the ill-fated census. The younger generations were not included, so that the full number of God's people would not be known (27:23). In this way a balance was to be struck between human practicality and divine promise. God's promise to *multiply Israel like the stars* echoes His words to Abraham in Genesis 15:5. There is always a tension between divine sovereignty and human ordering. A desire for mere efficiency kills spirituality and puts cold sterility in its place. A new movement of the Spirit sometimes has to leave its ecclesiastical mausoleum, in order to do justice to the principle of the untamed wind (John 3:8). A service may be organized down to the last detail, but without dependence on God in a spirit of trust and prayer, it can hardly be a medium of true worship. A systematic theology that seeks to dot every "i" and cross every "t" of the divine nature is doomed to misrepresent a God whose work and character are ultimately mysterious and ineffable, as Jewish theology has stressed. The alternative is not to try to dispense with theology, but to let God be God, as Tennyson's lines counseled:

> Let knowledge grow from more to more,
> But more of reverence in us dwell;
> That mind and soul, according well,
> May make one music . . .[1]

2. *Constraining grace.* David has given Solomon a private charge in chapter 22. Now that the time is ripe for Solomon to become king, David assembles the people (23:1; 28:1) and delivers a public charge. It is a double address, to the people (28:2–8) and to the crown prince (28:9, 10). The Chronicler's own hand in these addresses appears in the fact that they follow the pattern of what scholars call "the Levitical sermon." There are other examples of these sermons in 2 Chronicles. Each has a threefold basic structure, an initial specification of the hearer(s), the citation of a biblical text, and a concluding challenge. These parts are here doubly represented in verses 2a/9a, 6–7a/9b and 8/10. The first text is 2 Samuel 7:13, 14a (= 1 Chron. 17:13a, 14b), while the second appears to be Jeremiah 29:13, 14a.

When we expounded 1 Chronicles 17, we observed that 17:12 and 2 Chronicles 7:14 are the two pillars of divine revelation in the Chronicler's literary edifice. It is no accident that here we have a human response of affirmation to both those propositions. (2 Chronicles 7:14 with its mention of praying and seeking and God's hearing matches Jeremiah 29:12–13a.) The institutions of temple and dynasty and the spirituality of seeking God are placed side by side in an expression of the Chronicler's dominant concerns. Their presence here is fitting, for the institutional and spiritual revolve around the person of Solomon, who is being commissioned as royal builder of the temple. While in 2 Chronicles 7:14 it is the people who are to seek God, in the context of a divine response to Solomon's prayer, here it is Solomon who is to seek Him in obedience. This obedience is crucial, for it will secure the permanence of the Davidic dynasty (28:7). Moreover, Solomon as seeker after God is the intended model for the people to follow.

28:2b–5 is a recapitulation from chapters 17 and 22 of David's disqualification from building the temple. These verses introduce us to a motif we have not encountered before, that of election: David was God's chosen king within a chosen tribe. The double claim is reminiscent of Psalm 78:68, 70 in the context of a celebration of a new ark- and temple-centered era: God "chose the tribe of Judah. . . . He also chose David His servant." David goes on to apply the motif to Solomon: he in turn is God's chosen king—and, as 28:6 and in resumption verse 10 are to affirm, the chosen builder of the temple. God's word through Nathan was a revelation of Solomon's election, from among David's *many sons* (28:5). The extension of the concept of election to Solomon, which recurs in 29:1, is striking. Nowhere else in the Old Testament is this terminology used of any king after David. In royal rank Solomon stood beside David as jointly elect. As for building the temple, Solomon stood alone as God's elect servant. The effect is to pinpoint David and Solomon as joint key figures of sacred history and twin foci of God's purposes. Here was the foundation of a new era under God, an era which from the Chronicler was still current. God's will was to be seen henceforth by looking back to this dual human fountainhead. It is no wonder that Solomon is said to *sit on the throne of the kingdom of the Lord* (28:5) for here is a key manifestation of the kingdom of God in earth.

As Christians we are not unfamiliar with this line of theological reasoning. Matthew and Luke both claim for Jesus the fulfillment of the prophecy of Isaiah 42:1 concerning God's "chosen" Servant (Matt. 12:18; Luke 9:35, RSV), in the latter case by direct divine endorsement. Similarly, in Ephesians 1:4 God's election of the church is grounded in that of Christ: "He chose us in Him." He initially is God's elect; Christians are God's elect through Him. Karl Barth well observed that "as elected man, He is the Lord and Head of all the elect, the revelation and reflection of their election and the organ and instrument of all divine electing."[2] For us He is the focal point of history and the personal embodiment of the divine will. "Listen to Him," was God's bidding, and it is His bidding still.

A similar role of permanence is attached to the figures of David and Solomon. David was the founder of the dynasty which was to last *"forever"* (28:4), and Solomon shared in this inauguratory role (vv. 5–7). In the latter verse a question mark hangs over the role. In the basic verses 7–12 the establishment of the Davidic dynasty is conditional on Solomon's building the temple: once that is done the other automatically follows. Here a wider condition emerges, Solomon's overall obedience. The dynastic promise calls for moral responsibility to God, a responsibility so serious that it can put the promise at risk. Notice the two instances of *"forever"* in verses 7 and 9! Obedience of God is here envisaged not as impossible, but within the human grasp, as it is in Deuteronomy 30:11–14 ("not too hard for you," v. 11, RSV). Indeed, Solomon has complied thus far (28:7). The Chronicler in his account of Solomon's reign never contradicts this assessment and ends the account on the laudatory notes of wisdom and wealth as implicit signs of God's blessing for obedience (2 Chron. 9). He is insisting that Solomon's adherence to God's moral requirements was sufficient not to disqualify him from being a channel of the divine promise.

The permanent dynastic succession is founded on the promise to David and the twofold positive response of Solomon as obedient in the spheres of temple and Torah. Grace and active conformity, revelation and a living response: these are the twin foundations of this era created by God. I cannot help being reminded that both aspects were combined in the work of Jesus. In Him were focused not only a revelation of divine grace but a response of righteousness and obedience (see Rom. 5:19; Heb. 5:8). God's purpose was that through Him "grace might reign through righteousness to eternal life" (Rom. 5:21).

In view of Solomon's crucial role it is not surprising that the need to obey is rammed home with a variety of exhortations, repeatedly using the conditional "*if*" and reinforcing with a dire warning of the possibility of God's sovereign power turning election into rejection. These imperatives stress the human side of the matter: in 29:19 they are to be balanced by David's committal of Solomon to God, that He might undergird his endeavors with His enabling. In 28:8 the verbs and second person pronouns are all plural in the Hebrew: David turns to Solomon, but includes Israel in his challenge. Not only is Solomon to "*observe*" God's "*commandments*" (28:7), but he is to be a model for the people in that both he and they are to "*be careful to seek out all the commandments*" (28:8). An incentive is thrown in, enjoyment of God's gift of the land. Verse 8 is meant to transcend its historical context. Every reader's mind leaps on to the disappointing fact that the people failed in this trust and lost the land. However, the Chronicler and his Jewish readers rejoiced in the gracious renewal of the gift. For him the verse is intended as a challenge to his own and succeeding generations to stay within the bounds of God's will. The bounds of God's will turn out to be the bounds of His blessing. Are there somber parallels for Christian readers in the "if" of Romans 11:22 and the "if indeed" of Colossians 1:23? Each generation of God's people in turn is confronted by that challenge to live out their faith with ever-renewed commitment to God.

It is this note of commitment that comes to the fore in 28:9, which begins a direct address to Solomon. This exhortation is surely one that every Christian parent would wish to give to his or to her child. It would be difficult to find in Scripture a more emphatic call to commitment. A "whole heart" (RSV) is a phrase which in general the Chronicler has taken over from the Books of Kings and made part of his own spiritual vocabulary. The entire clause evokes in more sophisticated form the call in Deuteronomy 10:12 and 11:13 to "serve the Lord your God with all your heart and with all your soul." The "*willing mind*" (28:9) (or "soul") reminds me of Tennyson's line, "Our wills are ours, to make them Thine." In a play called *The Passion Drama* by Hugh Bishop a character is made to pray, "Dear Lord, I want whatever You want for me. I want it because You want it. I want it whatever way You want it. I want it as long as You want it."

In citing this reference another author has spoken for most of us when he commented, "I often have to say, 'I *want* to want it because You want it.'"[3]

David adds a reference to the omniscience of God. Every motive is under His scrutiny. Sometimes we hoodwink ourselves, and try to hoodwink God, that our service is wholehearted, when in reality it is obviously less than that. Of course, so complex is our psychological make-up and so pervasive is our fallen nature that lesser motives tag along with our noblest endeavors. The best one can do is never quite good enough. What God asks of us in this situation, I suggest, is that our main intent be Godward. At times we are too hard on ourselves, and God's greater insight as the master psychologist can be a consolation, for He knows our frame (see 1 John 3:19, 20). More often perhaps we need to hear the message of God's insight as a challenge. A dire example is the attempt of Ananias and Sapphira to deceive the church and God (Acts 5:1–11).

"Seek, and you will find," taught Jesus (Matt. 7:7; Luke 11:9). The biblical background to His teaching here was 28:9 and Jeremiah 29:13 and Deuteronomy 4:29. There is seemingly a stress on human initiative unusual for Scripture, but on second thought this impression is misleading. Divine resources are already there waiting to be discovered and tapped:

> I sought the Lord, and afterward I knew
> He made my soul to seek Him, seeking me . . .
> I find, I walk, I love, but O the whole
> Of Love is but my answer, Lord, to Thee!
> For Thou wert long beforehand with my soul,
> Always Thou lovedst me. (Anonymous)

Here again, then, we are in the sphere of human response. Opportunity knocks in the person and provision of the Lord (see Rev. 3:20), but if it and He go unheeded, great will be our loss. *"Be strong, and do it"* (28:10).

3. *God's plans.* If David could not build the temple, he made sure that he did everything but. According to the Chronicler part of the preparations he made was drawing up detailed plans. He functioned as the architect of the temple and its furnishings. There is a stress, however, that the plans he drew up were the product of

divine inspiration (28:19; in 28:12 the more natural rendering of the Hebrew is "all that he had in mind," RSV). The Lord's *"hand upon me"* is a prophetic phrase: compare 2 Kings 3:15 and Ezekiel 1:3. The intent is to show the inbuilt authority of the temple as the product of divine revelation. David and later Solomon were necessarily involved as stewards of God's work, but essentially it was the work of God. A parallel intent comes to the fore in the New Testament. The church is "a holy temple in the Lord," "built on the foundation of the apostles and prophets, Jesus Christ Himself being the chief cornerstone" (Eph. 2:19–21). If the church were a society for the study and preservation of religious antiquities, a very limited group would throw their eccentric energies into it. What kept Paul going was the conviction that "we are God's fellow workers . . . you are God's building" and that his labors were the consequence of a divine commission (1 Cor. 3:9, 10).

The Chronicler, living many centuries after the advent of the temple, rejoiced that he was able to participate in God's revealed will for His people. Time has caused certain ravages. The ark with its cherubim, given a position of climax in 28:18 as well as a foremost place in verse 11, was no more; nor was Solomon's temple still standing in all its glory (see Ezra 3:10–13; Hag. 2:3). No matter, the second temple was its adequate successor in spiritual, if not natural, terms. The traditional *"division of the priests and the Levites"* (28:13) was still in operation. Above all, the temple "vessels" (28:13, 14, RSV) provided continuity between the old and new temples. Many were doubtless missing, but post-exilic Judah rejoiced in its repossession of the sacred vessels looted by Nebuchadnezzar from the first temple and returned by Cyrus (Ezra 1:7–11), and newly donated vessels (Ezra 1:6) soon took on the aura of the old. It is true that yesterday's means of grace can become tomorrow's superstition (see 2 Kings 18:4); nevertheless, there is a spiritual beauty attached to objects associated with sacred usage. A silver chalice and plate long used at Holy Communion have sacred associations that help to convey the thrill of participating in the Supper instituted by the Lord. A communion table given pride of place at the front of the church similarly has attached to it the aura of the sacred in the most radically Protestant of churches. We can empathize with the Chronicler as he listed the objects that spoke to him of God and mostly still functioned for him as means of grace centuries later.

The Chronicler hints at a factor that confirms the authority of the temple. In Exodus 25:9–40 Moses was given a revelation of "the pattern of the tabernacle and the pattern of all its furnishings." There is a list very similar to the one supplied here. The message is that David is a second Moses, doing for the temple what Moses did for the tabernacle. Moreover, the temple ranked as a divine replacement for the tabernacle. There is a felt need to verify that here is a new era of worship which corresponds to the old one laid down in the Torah but which carries it further along the path of God's will. In a similar vein the writer to the Hebrews felt it necessary to give careful arguments for his contention that what the tabernacle meant in the Torah, now the heavenly sanctuary signified, into which the ascended Christ had entered (Heb. 5–10; The Hebrews writer was writing for Hellenistic Jews who were more Torah-oriented than temple-oriented.) For us the New Testament has gained a venerable authority of its own, but in the days of the early church it was obligatory to trace the consistency and consecutiveness of the work of God, balancing things old with things new. Woe betide the church if it naïvely replaces the old revelation with the new, without a qualm or query. The Old and New Testaments together represent the total Word of God, and their mutual relationship deserves careful evaluation. The Chronicler had a similar task in his day, valuing the Torah but aware that the Law had been supplemented—not supplanted— by the Prophets. If we glance ahead to 29:29–30, we may note that the Chronicler's sources for David's reign are given in prophetic terms, as invested with the authority of "Samuel the seer," "Nathan the prophet," and "Gad the seer." Scholars are now agreed that the reference is only to 1 and 2 Samuel. Only! As in the later Jewish canon of Scripture these books belonged to the Former Prophets and carried prophetic authority, so already in the Chronicler's day they seem to have had a prophetic role. The Law and the Prophets stood for him as joint bearers of the revelation of God's will for his own age. Diligent study and careful discrimination were necessary to show their complex unity and the contemporary value of each part of God's Word. Let us, as heirs of the Testaments Old and New, listen to the Chronicler and seek to emulate him.

4. *Affirming strokes.* David has formally handed over the documents of temple specifications. What else is there for him to do? There is something important he can yet do: give encouragement.

Has he not discharged that duty already in 22:11–13, 16 and in 28:10? There is always room for more encouragement. I recall that a couple of years ago a friend of mine acted as worship leader for a month at the Sunday morning services of her church. After the period of duty she approached the minister, asking if he had been in any way unhappy with her contributions since he had passed not a comment. His surprised reply was that he had thought she was too mature to need a pat on the back. In fact, appreciation and encouragement are regular channels of God's grace, to bolster these feeble frames of ours. Individualistic as we are by culture, we are still tied to others in this respect. We need this communal support and wither without it. "Treated with respect and appreciation, [people] expand like a magnolia flower in the morning sun. . . . Human beings are so constructed that it is impossible for them to give themselves, physically and spiritually, a pat on the back. If we were really mature, we might not need this, but who is? We all need our egos massaged, or our spinal cords will shrivel up."[4] We become better and more useful persons as we receive affirming strokes from our peers or superiors.

David wisely reiterates his encouragement of 22:11–13, 16. He is aware of the intimidating aspect of the task for his "young and inexperienced" son (29:1) and of the natural fear that lurks behind the confident mask he is wearing on this state occasion. He overwhelms Solomon with assurances of various kinds. In his task of building "the house" (29:2) he will enjoy the powerful presence of God. David adds "my God" (29:2), a little phrase that speaks volumes. He is virtually giving his personal testimony that he gives on two other occasions, that the Lord has seen him through every problem: He "redeemed my life from every distress" (1 Kings 1:29; cf. 2 Sam. 4:9). As long as there was work for God to be done, He would be there, supplying resources for the task. (The Christian will think of Philippians 1:6; 4:13.) *"He will not leave you nor forsake you"* (28:20), David continues. Here was motivation indeed for human stickability. *"Leave"* is literally "drop." Research workers have known the bitter experience of being dropped by the agencies that funded them. Artists have been dropped by the patrons who supported them and gave them opportunity to develop their gifts. Here is a Patron who supports unstintingly to the end.

Another motive for Solomon's persisting is the cooperation of suitably qualified personnel. The work of God is never a one-man show, and those who try to treat it thus do so to their loss. In the account of the building of the temple in 2 Chronicles 3–4, there will be much attention paid to what "Solomon made." When we come to that passage, it will be necessary to remind ourselves that these statements are in the nature of shorthand. The *"willing craftsman"* (28:21) was the one who in each case "made" the various objects. Solomon's responsibility was the ultimate one of supervision, ensuring that work was done and done well. Solomon had the support of others, equipped to advise and assist, and the goodwill of *"all the people"* (28:21), for whom Solomon's word was their command. When David was struggling toward kingship in chapters 11–12, it was underlined that he reached the top only with the assistance of God and of his fellows. Help, vertical and horizontal, was forthcoming. So it would be in this great work (29:1): there would be teamwork. Such are the strokes of affirmation with which David bolsters Solomon. If today you are a Solomon, weighed down with a task for which you feel inadequate, take seriously what David has to say. If you are a David, an observer of another's task, whether or not you think that he or she can cope, take a leaf out of David's book and make it your job to apply these affirming strokes.

There is another agenda being pursued in verses 20, 21. We saw it in chapter 22 and it appears here, capping the inspirational message of 28:11–19. The passage is resonant with themes associated with Moses' handing over the reins of power to Joshua. Indeed, the double pattern of a private and public commissioning of Solomon (22:6–16; 28:20, 21) is matched in the former case: the private charge of Deuteronomy 31:23 follows the public one of 31:7, 8 "in the sight of all Israel" (= 1 Chron. 28:8). The encouragement of God's continual support, not leaving nor forsaking but present with the novice, is repeated from Deuteronomy 31 and Joshua 1. Similarly, the bidding of fear to take its leave and the psychological strengthening of the exhortation *"Be strong"* (28:20) have first appeared there. The transition of leadership from Moses to Joshua is a model for the presentation of a counterpart in Chronicles. It suggests that this pair belongs together, as the former pair of saints did, Solomon taking over from David and completing the unfinished business he left. It suggests too that here is a comparable great work of God. The God who had revealed Himself through Moses and Joshua had something new to say and do, for which David and Solomon were His comparable agents. The work of God continued, developing further what He had done earlier. The old was a model of the new, and the new was an updated, revised version of the old. The Chronicler is here using the principle of typology. Properly understood, typology is not a weird and wonderful allegorizing treatment which disparages the historical value of the earlier material and reduces the Scriptures to the level of Aesop's fables. Rather, it traces between the historical phases of God's revelations correspondences which serve to endorse them as the ongoing work of the same God. The New Testament in turn makes much use of this principle. Like the Old Testament, the New knows of a covenant ratified by blood. It knows of a last Adam, a heavenly Jerusalem, a sacrifice for sins, a temple. God's work goes on, unfolding more of His will as time continues. The badge of authenticity which the new development must wear is an underlying consistency, whereby the old is not simply repeated but transmuted into the new. The Chronicler is flourishing this badge in these chapters, just as the New Testament was to brandish it at a later time.

WILLING GIFTS AND WORSHIPING GOD

29:1 Furthermore King David said to all the assembly: "My son Solomon, whom alone God has chosen, *is* young and inexperienced; and the work *is* great, because the temple *is* not for man but for the LORD God.

2 "Now for the house of my God I have prepared with all my might: gold for *things to be made of* gold, silver for *things of* silver, bronze for *things of* bronze, iron for *things of* iron, wood for *things of* wood, onyx stones, *stones* to be set, glistening stones of various colors, all kinds of precious stones, and marble slabs in abundance.

3 "Moreover, because I have set my affection on the house of my God, I have given to the house of my God, over and above all that I have prepared for the holy house, my own special treasure of gold and silver:

4 "three thousand talents of gold, of the gold of Ophir, and seven thousand talents of refined silver, to overlay the walls of the houses;

5 *the gold for *things of* gold and the silver for *things of* silver, and for all kinds of work *to be done* by the hands of craftsmen. Who *then* is willing to consecrate himself this day to the LORD?*

6 Then the leaders of the fathers' *houses,* leaders of the tribes of Israel, the captains of thousands and of hundreds, with the officers over the king's work, offered willingly.

7 They gave for the work of the house of God five thousand talents and ten thousand darics of gold, ten thousand talents of silver, eighteen thousand talents of bronze, and one hundred thousand talents of iron.

8 And whoever had *precious* stones gave *them* to the treasury of the house of the LORD, into the hand of Jehiel the Gershonite.

9 Then the people rejoiced, for they had offered willingly, because with a loyal heart they had offered willingly to the LORD; and King David also rejoiced greatly.

10 Therefore David blessed the LORD before all the
assembly; and David said:
"Blessed are You, LORD God of Israel, our Father,
forever and ever.

11 Yours, O LORD, *is* the greatness,
The power and the glory,
The victory and the majesty;
For all *that is* in heaven and in earth *is Yours;*
Yours *is* the kingdom, O LORD,
And You are exalted as head over all.

12 Both riches and honor *come* from You,
And You reign over all.
In Your hand *is* power and might;
In Your hand *it is* to make great
And to give strength to all.

13 *Now therefore, our God,
We thank You
And praise Your glorious name.

14 But who *am* I, and who *are* my people,
That we should be able to offer so willingly as
this?
For all things *come* from You,
And of Your own we have given You.

15 For we *are* aliens and pilgrims before You,
   As *were* all our fathers;
   Our days on earth *are* as a shadow,
   And without hope.
16 "O LORD our God, all this abundance that we
have prepared to build You a house for Your holy
name is from Your hand, and *is* all Your own.
17 "I know also, my God, that You test the heart
and have pleasure in uprightness. As for me, in the
uprightness of my heart I have willingly offered all
these *things;* and now with joy I have seen Your people, who are present here to offer willingly to You.
18 "O LORD God of Abraham, Isaac, and Israel, our
fathers, keep this forever in the intent of the thoughts
of the heart of Your people, and fix their heart toward
You.
19 "And give my son Solomon a loyal heart to keep
Your commandments and Your testimonies and Your
statutes, to do all *these things,* and to build the temple
for which I have made provision."

1 Chron. 29:1–19

David solicits contributions to defray the cost of building the temple. Then he lifts up his heart to God in praise. The key word of
verses 1–19 is *"prepared"* (vv. 2, 3, 16, 19 [NKJV varies its translation
with *"made provision"*]), which appropriately sums up David's role.
He is the human author of the temple project, while Solomon is to be
its finisher.

1. *"God loves a cheerful giver."* When one listens to a speech or
reads an editorial, sometimes one has to wait until the end to appreciate its real point. So it is here with verses 1–5. Verse 5 discloses
that David is making an appeal for financial support, an appeal
which he buttresses with persuasive arguments. The flow of the
passage from 28:21 to 29:1–5 suggests that here was one practical
way in which the people could help the temple project. Just as in
22:5 the formidable nature of the task confronting Solomon caused
David to prepare in advance, so here it motivates not only David's
preparations but contributions from the people. God's work is worth
the investment of His people's resources. No leader should ask his
followers to do what he or she is not ready to do personally. Here

David leads with his pocket, giving not public money but his own (29:3) and thus setting an example of generosity.

In 29:5 the phrase *"consecrate himself"* is an interesting one. It is a special term used, for instance in Exodus 28:41, of a priest when he offered his first sacrifice. The act had symbolic value, acknowledging his admission to the priesthood. Here the phrase is employed as a spiritualizing metaphor. It is not simply the gift that is consecrated to God but the giver. As one bids the gift farewell, one takes on a new role before God, a role of consecration to the service of God. We are accustomed to speaking of the ordination of the minister who puts his or her hand to God's service. In the light of 29:5 we might speak of the ordination of those who give financial sponsorship, for they declare themselves radically involved in the work of the ministry and committed to its success.

Inspired by David's example and moved by his appeal, the people give unstintingly. At 22:14 we mentioned the principle of rhetorical mathematics in which the Chronicler sometimes indulges. It appears to be present in the fabulous sums of 29:7. Strangely the reference to *"ten thousand darics,"* where the Chronicler uses a contemporary, Persian unit of currency to convey meaning, is the exception to the pattern of the verse. The sum accentuates by contrast the magnitude of the rest: it amounts to 84 kilograms, whereas one talent alone weighs 34 kilograms. The overall intent of the verse is to give an impression of overwhelming generosity. 29:9 presents the joy of giving. A consumer experiences self-gratification in his spending, and so does a miser in his saving; but a contributor knows a deeper joy and a greater gain. On the grave of an early Earl of Devonshire in Tiverton (Devon, England) there was engraved the following epitaph:

> What we gave, we have;
> What we spent, we had;
> What we kept, we lost.

As Jesus said, in a saying recorded not in the Gospels but in one of Paul's speeches in Acts, "It is more blessed to give than to receive" (Acts 20:35).

The "whole heart" (RSV) in 29:9 is the measure of unreserved giving. A virtue praised by the Chronicler, it appeared earlier at 28:9 as a quality of spiritual service. Here it is a practical outworking of serving God. David does not levy a tax to finance the work. This contribution was of a special, one-off nature and was not intended to displace the support of the sanctuary and its personnel by means of tithes and offerings. It was a giving over and above regular commitments. A keynote of 29:5–9 is willingness or, to use a more contemporary term, volunteering. In a similar context Exodus 35:21 speaks of the heart stirring, or moving, the person to give. Understandably the idea of willingness features also in the New Testament equivalent of this passage, 2 Corinthians 8–9. For both Paul and the Chronicler, willing giving was a measure of spirituality and fellowship. While in Chronicles David is the model, significantly in 2 Corinthians "the grace of our Lord Jesus Christ" is the example (8:9).

The reader who is an Old Testament connoisseur will recognize in the language of 29:1–9 overtones from Exodus concerning the occasion when in the wilderness the people gave for the construction of the tabernacle and its contents (Exod. 25:1–7; 35:4–9, 20–29). Again the temple is being put on a par with the tabernacle, and there are echoes of old events in the context of a new work of God. Here, declares the Chronicler, is a comparable milestone further along the road of divine revelation and human response, a road which we Christians believe led to Jesus and His church.

2. *"Great is the Lord and greatly to be praised."* David's reign consisted of two great religious phases according to the Chronicler, his movement of the ark to Jerusalem (chapters 13–15) and his preparations for the temple (chapter 17 onward). It is significant that both of these phases end in praise, in chapter 16 and here. Praise is the climax of service for God. In the context of the human workplace retirement is marked by an expression of appreciation for the worker. The clock, or whatever, is the warm response of others to the work the retiring person has completed. In this case, at the end of each of David's religious tasks, appreciation of the God for whom the work has been done is expressed by the worker. It is David's recognition that God has been at work through him. In a similar manner Paul and Silas, after the success of their first missionary tour, "reported all things that God had done with them" at Jerusalem (Acts 15:4). If the work was God's, it was proper for them to give the glory to Him.

This magnificent prayer is probably the best known passage in the

Books of Chronicles. It has an exuberant tone, which can be measured in part by its expression of totality in the term *"all"*: it occurs no less than ten times. The prayer falls into three parts, each introduced by a fresh address of God which uses liturgical language, in 29:10b, 13, and 18a. There is a standard acronym for prayer, A.C.T.S., which I remember being taught as a youngster in Sunday school. It stands for adoration, confession, thanksgiving, and supplication. The three parts of this prayer correspond to the first, third, and fourth of these elements respectively.

The first part, verses 10b–12, belongs in a liturgical tradition which also finds expression in the ecclesiastical supplement to the Lord's Prayer (Matt. 6:13b: see the footnote). The doxology of 29:11 ransacks the theological dictionary, piling up terms for God's sovereign power. Comparable are the doxologies in honor of God and the Lamb in Revelation 4:11; 5:13. Four elaborations of God's greatness are given here: (a) God as Creator owns the world; (b) as its King He is supreme over the world; (c) He is the source of all human wealth; and (d) He is the providential supplier of human power.

In ancient letters a crucial point was signaled by an introductory *"and now"* (29:13, RSV). The custom was carried over into speeches and, as here, into prayers. This middle section of the prayer, 29:13–17, is its heart. It translates into the direct language of thanksgiving the joy of king and people in 29:9. Thanks are given for the wholehearted response to the claims of God's work: evidently He is regarded as its inspirer (cf. 29:18). The praise of 29:10b–12 has created a logical stumbling block for the giver, which must be overcome. Is not the very notion of giving to God, the giver of all, an absurdity? C. S. Lewis verbalized this problem well: "It is like a small child going to its father and saying, 'Daddy, give me sixpence to buy you a birthday present.' Of course, the father does and is pleased with the child's present. It is all very nice and proper, but only an idiot would think that the father is sixpence to the good in the transaction."[5] We cannot give God anything that is not in a sense His already. Paul asked a humbling question in 1 Corinthians 4:7: "What do you have that you did not receive?"

The end of 29:14 says more literally *"and (what is) from Your hand we have given You."* This thought is to be resumed in 29:16 (*". . . from Your hand"*). First, in 29:15 Israel's role as the child without sixpence to call his own, to use Lewis's illustration, is considered. There can be no self-congratulation on the human side, as if we were self-made, David is saying. On the contrary we share the patriarchs' position as aliens in the promised land (cf. 16:19, 20). Even in occupying the land Israel acquired no intrinsic rights. "The land is Mine," declared God, "for you are strangers and sojourners with Me" (Lev. 25:23) or *"aliens and pilgrims"* since the same Hebrew words occur in that passage and in 29:15 here. Human life is marked by transitoriness. At the end of verse 15 *"hope"* is in the context better rendered "abiding" with KJV and RSV or "abiding place" with NEB. The ancient Greek and Latin versions recognized that the Hebrew word can bear this meaning.

All this signifies a natural emptiness. The picture is at first sight contradicted by the factor of *"all this abundance"* given to God. The paradox is resolved by the consideration that it is God-given, down to the last penny, and returned to God for the building of His temple. George Matheson presented an expansion of this thought in the hymn lines from "O Love That Wilt Not Let Me Go":

> I give Thee back the life I owe,
> That in Thine ocean depths its flow
> May richer, fuller be.

In the end the only offering being made was not a material one, for its substance belonged to God anyway. No, the real offerings were spiritual, a right motivation to honor God in sincerity and a devoted willingness to give. These are the offerings which king and people gladly bring to God (29:17).

The prayer closes with petitions, in recognition that God's enabling, graciously contributed hitherto, must continue into the future. The old triangular points of God, people, and king reappear. There were lifelines stretching from God to the people and from Him to the king. Unless He took responsibility for maintaining these lines, they would disintegrate. So David's prayer is that in both cases God would undertake, and keep fresh and sweet the people's devotion and Solomon's obedience, in both his specific and general duties before God. In the former case (29:18) there is an open-endedness which the Chronicler surely wants his own generation to heed. Unstinting giving to God in support of the temple was still necessary as one manifestation among others of spiritual devotion (cf. Mal. 3:8–10). In the Christian era too, of course, this need has not gone away.

As for Solomon, he had a heavy burden to bear: we have seen that the weight of the survival of the Davidic dynasty rested on his obedience to God. How could he maintain that *"loyal* (or whole) *heart"* (29:9)? God never gives burdens for us to bear alone: "underneath are the everlasting arms" (Deut. 33:27). There is a beautiful prayer in the Jewish *bar mitzvah* service, when a thirteen-year-old boy takes on himself the yoke of the Torah. It speaks, rightly, of duty and resolve, but it manifests throughout a sense of utter dependence on God's help, as in this extract: "I pray humbly and hopefully before Thee to grant me Thy gracious help, so that I have the will and understanding to walk firmly in Thy ways all the days of my life. Implant [literally "create"] in me a spirit of sincere devotion to Thy service." The Christian too is called to trust and obey, in the sense of trusting in God's enabling even as he obeys. "God works in you both to will and to do for His good pleasure": this is the premise of the call to "work out your own salvation with fear and trembling" (Phil. 2:12, 13).

Finally David gives an opportunity for the people to participate in praise. If Solomon's building of the temple was not to be a one-man show, neither was David's expression of praise. It must ever be the concern of the worship leader to ensure that the congregation does not lag behind as silent observers but keeps pace with the leader as sincere participants. We noted earlier that David's praising is a structural counterpart to the psalmodic praise of chapter 16. The themes of both are very similar. There is a polarized stress on God as the great King and the people as insignificant of themselves but caught up in His great purposes. The tension is brought to a focus in the patriarchs firstly as recipients of God's revelation of promise, to whom the people proudly traced their roots (vv. 10 [read "Israel our father," RSV], 18), and secondly as relative nobodies without rights (29:15). In both these ascriptions of praise the Chronicler was presenting a theology on which the people of his own day might base their lives. Significantly both passages end in prayer, for personal commitment is the corollary of theology. In chapter 16 it was an eschatological prayer. Here it is an existential prayer for God's help in the duties of life assigned by Him. The people of God need to pray both types of prayer.

GOD'S EARTHLY THRONE

29:20 Then David said to all the assembly, "Now bless the LORD your God." So all the assembly blessed the LORD God of their fathers, and bowed their heads and prostrated themselves before the LORD and the king.

21 And they made sacrifices to the LORD and offered burnt offerings to the LORD on the next day: a thousand bulls, a thousand rams, a thousand lambs, with their drink offerings, and sacrifices in abundance for all Israel.

22 So they ate and drank before the LORD with great gladness on that day. And they made Solomon the son of David king the second time, and anointed *him* before the LORD *to be* the leader, and Zadok *to be* priest.

23 Then Solomon sat on the throne of the LORD as king instead of David his father, and prospered; and all Israel obeyed him.

24 All the leaders and the mighty men, and also all the sons of King David, submitted themselves to King Solomon.

25 So the LORD exalted Solomon exceedingly in the sight of all Israel, and bestowed on him *such* royal majesty as had not been on any king before him in Israel.

26 Thus David the son of Jesse reigned over all Israel.

27 And the period that he reigned over Israel *was* forty years; seven years he reigned in Hebron, and thirty-three *years* he reigned in Jerusalem.

28 So he died in a good old age, full of days and riches and honor; and Solomon his son reigned in his place.

29 Now the acts of King David, first and last, indeed they *are* written in the book of Samuel the seer, in the book of Nathan the prophet, and in the book of Gad the seer,

30 with all his reign and his might, and the events that happened to him, to Israel, and to all the kingdoms of the lands.

1 Chron. 29:20–30

The celebrations extend to a second day, on which Solomon is finally crowned king. He wears two hats, that of temple builder and the royal crown. The first hat is for the Chronicler the crucial role, and the second is the means to its end. David does not abdicate to make way for the new king, but there is a co-regency, a phenomenon borrowed from Egyptian royal practice. This twin royalty symbolized a truth important for the historian. David's and Solomon's total reigns were a unity, a single manifestation of God at work among His people in a new and decisive way. The intertwining of the two reigns, the start of Solomon's preceding the end of his father's, is a hook and eye link that binds the reigns together as a single whole. King-making functions as an outer framework for David's reign. It started with Israel making David king (chapters 11–12), and it finishes with David making Solomon king.

The new king wins the unanimous support of Israel's leaders, including *"all the sons of King David"* (v. 24). Thereby hangs a long tale which is told in the Succession Narrative of 2 Samuel 9–20 and 1 Kings 1–2. As in the case of David's accession, the Chronicler is not concerned with the tangled process, but passes to the outcome. *"All Israel obeyed him"* (v. 23): there is a stress on the unity of Israel under Solomon. In fact this is for the Chronicler a significant feature which characterizes and unifies the reigns of David and Solomon. They ruled over a united kingdom, an ideal which also constituted a promise. The statement is a quotation of what earlier appertained to Joshua: see Deuteronomy 34:9. Again, Solomon is a second Joshua, as David was a second Moses. The particular point here is that the unity of God's people was not only a vital factor in the former era, but remained so in the present one.

A striking ingredient of this passage is that Solomon in his royal role reflects the kingship of God. Solomon's *"majesty"* is a manifestation of that of God (vv. 11, 25). His God-given greatness—*"exalted"* in verse 25 is literally "made great"—is a participation in God's own greatness (v. 11; cf. the same verb in v. 12). Solomon *"sat on the throne of the Lord"* (v. 23)! As in 28:5, the message is that here was a revelation of God's kingdom on earth. "Thy kingdom come!" was the future hope of Israel. "The Lord reigns" (16:31) was their understanding of the present. For the Chronicler the past too contained a crucial witness to God's kingdom in the phenomenon of Solomon's reign. In the greatness of its domain and in its unity of the people of

God under a Davidic king, it was a picture of what was yet to be. It was also an ideal to be partially realized in present experience: it revealed a basis for worship and for life, fidelity to temple and Torah. The overall purposes of God, set out earlier in the work of Joshua whom also God *exalted . . . exceedingly in the sight of all Israel"* (v. 25; see Josh. 4:14), came to a clearer focus in Solomon.

For the Christian reader the purposes of God have found an even sharper focus in the Lord Jesus Christ as the inaugurator of a final era of revelation. "A greater than Solomon is" now "here" (Luke 11:31). If Solomon was great David's greater son (v. 25), He is the greatest. So precisely is He regarded as the mirror image of the Father that a prophetic promise of God's world sovereignty (Isa. 45:23) is freely applied to Him in Philippians 2:11. The principles of His kingdom were declared in His earthly teaching and affirm the Gospels. His right to the kingdom was established in His life, death, resurrection, and ascension. The One who has gone "to receive . . . a kingdom" is also "to return" to reign (Luke 19:12).

David's reign is drawn to a close with a suitable epilogue which gives pride of place to a united people ("*all Israel"*), characterizes him as the object of God's abundant blessing, and concludes with David's impact not only on Israel but on the ancient world at large. Here was a figure of world history. For the Chronicler his history had something to say too about the world's future. For the Christian in turn the eternal purposes of God are hidden in the person and work of Christ, the Son of David.

NOTES

1. Alfred Lord Tennyson, *In Memoriam*, prologue.

2. Karl Barth, *Church Dogmatics*, vol. 2, part 2 (Edinburgh: T. & T. Clark, 1957), p. 117.

3. "Pilgrim," *Country Parson's Evensong* (London: Skeffington Press, 1961), p. 126.

4. D. Le Vay, *Scenes from Surgical Life* (London: Peter Owen, 1976), p. 29.

5. C. S. Lewis, *Mere Christianity* (New York: MacMillan, 1952), pp. 110f.

CHAPTER NINE

A Great Work for a Great God

2 Chronicles 1:1–5:1

It is unfortunate that in the Christian canon of Scripture, Chronicles has been divided into two books. In the Jewish canon it was originally a single book. The division came about when the Hebrew work was translated into Greek. Greek takes up one and three-fourths more space than vowelless Hebrew, and so one scroll's worth of Hebrew writing had to be spread over two Greek scrolls. The break was made on the basis of quantity. It had the insensitive effect of splitting David's and Solomon's reigns, since these first two reigns comprise a literary and theological unity. After 1 Chronicles 9 the next major break does not come until 2 Chronicles 10, if we want to be true to the author's intent.

Solomon's role was complementary to that of David, to finish what David had begun under God. According to the Chronicler David's religious work was twofold, to bring the ark to Jerusalem and to prepare for building the temple in which it would eventually be housed. Solomon's task was to build the temple. This task occupies nearly three-fourths of the Chronicles material devoted to Solomon, much more than in its source, 1 Kings 1–11, although even there it is regarded as important. David and Solomon were men with a mission, a mission which was still crucial for the Chronicler living some six centuries later. The temple constituted a focal point for faith and worship. What is God like? How does He reveal Himself? How may we approach Him? These are vital questions which receive fresh or refined answers in this material. It is worthwhile to look over the Chronicler's shoulder as he writes and to reflect on the answers he gives. Moreover, we recall that for him the building of the temple was the prime condition for the establishment of an everlasting Davidic dynasty (1 Chron. 17:12). Once that was achieved, a vista of royal promise opened up, for which the Chronicler still had eyes bright with hope. Like every Christian, he was a spiritual royalist.

QUALIFICATIONS

1:1 Now Solomon the son of David was strengthened in his kingdom, and the LORD his God *was* with him and exalted him exceedingly.

2 And Solomon spoke to all Israel, to the captains of thousands and of hundreds, to the judges, and to every leader in all Israel, the heads of the fathers' *houses*.

3 Then Solomon, and all the assembly with him, went to the high place that *was* at Gibeon; for the tabernacle of meeting with God was there, which Moses the servant of the LORD had made in the wilderness.

4 But David had brought up the ark of God from Kirjath Jearim to *the place* David had prepared for it, for he had pitched a tent for it at Jerusalem.

5 Now the bronze altar that Bezalel the son of Uri, the son of Hur, had made, he put before the tabernacle of the LORD; Solomon and the assembly sought Him *there*.

6 And Solomon went up there to the bronze altar before the LORD, which *was* at the tabernacle of meeting, and offered a thousand burnt offerings on it.

7 On that night God appeared to Solomon, and said to him, "Ask! What shall I give you?"

8 And Solomon said to God: "You have shown great mercy to David my father, and have made me king in his place.

9 "Now, O LORD God, let Your promise to David my father be established, for You have made me king over a people like the dust of the earth in multitude.

10 "Now give me wisdom and knowledge, that I may go out and come in before this people; for who can judge this great people of Yours?"

11 Then God said to Solomon: "Because this was in your heart, and you have not asked riches or wealth or honor or the life of your enemies, nor have you

asked long life—but have asked wisdom and knowledge for yourself, that you may judge My people
over whom I have made you king—

12 "wisdom and knowledge *are* granted to you;
and I will give you riches and wealth and honor,
such as none of the kings have had who *were* before
you, nor shall any after you have the like."

13 So Solomon came to Jerusalem from the high
place that *was* at Gibeon, from before the tabernacle
of meeting, and reigned over Israel.

14 And Solomon gathered chariots and horsemen;
he had one thousand four hundred chariots and
twelve thousand horsemen, whom he stationed in
the chariot cities and with the king in Jerusalem.

15 Also the king made silver and gold as common
in Jerusalem as stones, and he made cedars as abundant as the sycamores which *are* in the lowland.

16 And Solomon had horses imported from Egypt
and Keveh; the king's merchants bought them in
Keveh at the *current* price.

17 They also acquired and imported from Egypt a
chariot for six hundred *shekels* of silver, and a horse
for one hundred and fifty; thus, through their agents,
they exported them to all the kings of the Hittites
and the kings of Syria.

2 Chron. 1:1-17

The account of Solomon's reign opens with a general statement
about his consolidation of power. He "established himself" (RSV): the
Hebrew verb is reflexive rather than passive. There is a suggestion
of opposition, of finding his feet in a new role amid contrary pressures. 1 Kings 2 probes these underlying currents, which the Chronicler sweepingly sums up in a sentence. New ventures call for human
effort and maneuvering. Solomon won though, but only because he
had divine backing. His "sufficiency is from God" (2 Cor. 3:5). It is 1
Chronicles 11:9 all over again: "David became greater and greater,
for *the Lord . . . was with him*" (RSV). The parallelism means that
Solomon was going along a track parallel to David's at this stage.

Solomon's royal power was a means to an end, a secular foundation for a religious edifice—the building of the temple. It is very
much in the Chronicler's mind even this early in his narrative. The

rest of the chapter is made up of three paragraphs which present Solomon's qualifications for the task. These qualifications are worship, wisdom, and wealth. In 1:2–2:18, although there are side glances at Solomon's kingly role with mention of his ruling and his need for a palace, the major key of the composition is the theme of the temple. In 3:1–7:22 the actual building of the temple and its dedication will be in view. Then in 8:1–9:31 the initial motifs of Solomon's worship, wisdom, and wealth will be repeated, with the major key now being his royal rule, while the temple theme persists as a minor key.

1. *Worship.* According to the Chronicler the first thing that David did after he became king was to "seek" the ark (1 Chron. 13:3; cf. 15:13) with a national pilgrimage to its location ("David and all Israel," 1 Chron. 13:6). It was a case of like father, like son. *"Solomon, and all the assembly"* correspondingly *"sought"* another traditional object associated with worship of God, the bronze altar of burnt offering at Gibeon (vv. 3–6). In verse 5 a preferable translation is "sought . . . it" with KJV, which followed the way the ancient Greek and Latin versions understood the ambiguous Hebrew. The parallelism with 1 Chronicles 13:3 so suggests. The use of the Chronicler's characteristic word for spirituality is significant. Although it is used in a precise religious sense, it is of course a means of seeking God Himself. "Seek first . . ." is the Chronicler's message, like that of the Master in the Sermon on the Mount (Matt. 6:33). Here in verses 3 and 5 is a beautiful picture of a united people worshiping together under God's chosen king. It sent reverberations of challenge and hope down the centuries to the Chronicler's own day and beyond. Solomon's own act of worship gives expression to his faithfulness to God. Here is a prime qualification for engaging in God's work. It marks Solomon out as a fitting bearer of the responsibility for building the temple.

The corresponding passage in 1 Kings conveys a hint of impropriety (1 Kings 3:3–4). In defense of Solomon the Chronicler is at pains to point out that Gibeon was a legitimate place of worship. Moreover, he regards Solomon's visit not as a private one but as part of a public pilgrimage which marked the phasing out of the old, Torah-based *"tabernacle"* era and the launching of a new temple age. This was to be the last recorded act of worship at the old sanctuary; soon it was to be superseded. Under God the old order was to change and a new focus of worship was to appear. The Chronicler takes trouble to perceive and pass on the historical purposes of God and His unfolding revelation. This means for him a proper understanding of Scripture, namely the Law and the Prophets, as the basis of the life of God's people, where his generation is concerned. In principle such diligence is by no means redundant in our own day.

2. *Wisdom.* Solomon's spirituality was an essential basic qualification, but it would need supplementing with specific qualities, if he was to fulfill his role acceptably. To this end verses 7–10 recount how he had an experience of God and engaged in prayer to Him. The passage is an abbreviation and adaptation of 1 Kings 3:5–15. The divine invitation *"Ask! What shall I give you?"* has a flavor associated with the Davidic dynasty. In the royal Psalm 2 it occurs in the context of universal rule: "Ask of Me, and I will give You . . ." (v. 8). The invitation sets some value on human initiative. Divine resources are there to be tapped, there for the asking. For the Christian, if verses 3–6 serve to illustrate "Seek, and you will find," these verses exemplify "Ask, and it will be given to you" (Matt. 7:7). The fabled senior citizen who lived a poverty-stricken existence and was found after his death to have had assets sufficient to wallpaper the house with hundred-dollar bills has not a few spiritual counterparts in the Christian church.

Solomon's prayer begins with praise. He does not blurt out his "I want," but pauses respectfully to review the grace that underlay his royal position. His prime request is for the fulfillment of 1 Chronicles 17:23, 24, David's prayer for a dynasty descended for him. According to the revelatory first half of 1 Chronicles 17 that prayer depended for its fulfillment on Solomon's building the temple, which was to be his vocation under God (1 Chron. 17:12). So in praying for that dynastic end, Solomon implicitly includes the religious means. When in verse 10 he goes on to pray for wisdom, it is primarily wisdom in building the temple, and the mention of the governmental side or aspect of wisdom is a secondary concern. Wisdom, once given, will essentially be used for the temple, as 2:12 will state. It will take the form of creative mental abilities, such as organizational and management skills and appropriate architectural acumen.

3. *Wealth.* Solomon has unselfishly asked for that which will equip him for his particular work for God. In return he has *"riches and*

wealth and honor" thrown in (v. 12). Here indeed is an extravagant example of the Master's principle "Seek first . . . and all these things shall be added to you" (Matt. 6:33). For the Chronicler the main purpose of this wealth was to provide resources for the temple. To this end he has moved here a passage which in his source stood much later (vv. 14–17 = 1 Kings 10:26–29). In its new setting it sends out feelers to what follows. *"Silver and gold"* and *"cedars"* (v. 15) point forward to 2:7, 8, where they feature as materials for the temple. Verse 12 glances at another aspect of Solomon's wealth, to bolster his royal role, an aspect which is to be amplified in chapter 9. Nevertheless, God has first claim on the wealth, in that it provides funding for His work. This principle of giving, which was dear to the Chronicler's heart and which earlier he extended democratically to all of God's people (1 Chron. 29:9, 17), is by no means irrelevant today.

Solomon, the chosen temple builder, has shown appropriate qualifications for the task, in the forms of a basic attitude of seeking God and endowment with wisdom and wealth. Vocation, spirituality, and appropriate gifts are all united in Solomon, and so his fitness to serve in this particular capacity is indicated. I recall that for over twenty years part of my responsibilities in ministering at a theological college was to serve on a committee responsible for interviewing prospective students. We were looking for latter-day Solomons, in the sense that we wanted to perceive a sense of God's calling and evidence of qualities that matched such aspects of the vocation as had been made clear to the applicant.

PREPARATIONS

2:1 Then Solomon determined to build a temple for the name of the LORD, and a royal house for himself.

2 Solomon selected seventy thousand men to bear burdens, eighty thousand to quarry *stone* in the mountains, and three thousand six hundred to oversee them.

3 Then Solomon sent to Hiram king of Tyre, saying: As you have dealt with David my father, and sent him cedars to build himself a house to dwell in, *so deal with me.*

4 Behold, I am building a temple for the name of the LORD my God, to dedicate *it* to Him, to burn before Him sweet incense, for the continual showbread, for the burnt offerings morning and evening, on the Sabbaths, on the New Moons, and on the set feasts of the LORD our God. This *is an ordinance* forever to Israel.

5 And the temple which I build *will be* great, for our God is greater than all gods.

6 But who is able to build Him a temple, since heaven and the heaven of heavens cannot contain Him? Who *am* I then, that I should build Him a temple, except to burn sacrifice before Him?

7 Therefore send me at once a man skillful to work in gold and silver, in bronze and iron, in purple and crimson and blue, who has skill to engrave with the skillful men who are with me in Judah and Jerusalem, whom David my father provided.

8 Also send me cedar and cypress and algum logs from Lebanon, for I know that your servants have skill to cut timber in Lebanon; and indeed my servants *will be* with your servants,

9 to prepare timber for me in abundance, for the temple which I am about to build *shall be* great and wonderful.

10 And indeed I will give to your servants, the woodsmen who cut timber, twenty thousand kors of ground wheat, twenty thousand kors of barley, twenty thousand baths of wine, and twenty thousand baths of oil.

11 Then Hiram king of Tyre answered in writing, which he sent to Solomon:

Because the LORD loves His people, He has made you king over them.

12 Hiram also said:

Blessed *be* the LORD God of Israel, who made heaven and earth, for He has given King David a wise son, endowed with prudence and understanding, who will build a temple for the LORD and a royal house for himself!

13 And now I have sent a skillful man, endowed with understanding, Huram my master *craftsman*

14 (the son of a woman of the daughters of Dan, and his father was a man of Tyre), skilled to work in gold and silver, bronze and iron, stone and wood, purple and blue, fine linen and crimson, and to make any engraving and to accomplish any plan which may be given to him, with your skillful men and with the skillful men of my lord David your father.

15 Now therefore, the wheat, the barley, the oil, and the wine which my lord has spoken of, let him send to his servants.

16 And we will cut wood from Lebanon, as much as you need; we will bring it to you in rafts by sea to Joppa, and you will carry it up to Jerusalem.

17 Then Solomon numbered all the aliens who *were* in the land of Israel, after the census in which David his father had numbered them; and there were found to be one hundred and fifty-three thousand six hundred.

18 And he made seventy thousand of them bearers of burdens, eighty thousand stonecutters in the mountain, and three thousand six hundred overseers to make the people work.

2 Chron. 2:1–18

Now Solomon can make necessary arrangements for the practicalities of carrying out his God-appointed task. Verse 1 is a headline for the chapter, stressing the temple project and giving a side glance at matters of royalty. Two factors are necessary, personnel and materials. The first requirement provides a literary framework for the chapter, being summarily mentioned in verse 2 and given fuller treatment at the end (vv. 17, 18). In an individual sense it is also a central concern, at verses 7 and 13–14. In ancient times, with the comparative absence of machinery, building projects were labor-intensive. The mind boggles at the building of the Egyptian pyramids! In Solomon's case an adequate labor force had to be prepared. Moreover, Solomon needed an expert to supervise the artistic aspects of the work and to provide quality control. Apart from manpower, the question of materials was pertinent. Although David had provided materials in abundance, such was to be the splendor of Solomon's project that more were necessary, verse 9 implies.

His negotiations with the Phoenician king Hiram open with a communication that falls into two parts, an introduction in verses 3–6 and its substance in verses 7–10. The introduction contains a threefold presentation of the theology of the temple.

1. *The temple was to accord with God's written Word.* Although the temple was a religious innovation, the functions were to be the traditional ones associated with God's prior revelation (v. 4). For the Chronicler Israel had a once-and-for-all religious mandate in the Torah. Its provisions, specifically in Exodus, Numbers, and Leviticus, were to be followed with care. The Chronicler was sensitive to the blend of old and new. One covets for the Christian a similar sense of honoring the Old Testament as God's Word and carefully tracing the relation of the New to it.

2. *The temple building was to accord with God's nature.* If Israel's *"God is greater than all gods"* (v. 5; cf. 1 Chron. 16:25), it follows that an edifice in His honor should be *"great"* (vv. 5, 9). It may have been an application of this principle that the traditional synagogue had to be the highest building in town. In both Christian and Muslim communities this policy naturally ran into opposition and there was insistence that the church steeple or mosque minaret should soar higher than the synagogue. The Jewish response was shrewdly characteristic: either to erect a pole on the synagogue roof, so as to give it greater nominal height, or to excavate the ground beneath and lower the floor, so that the building was lofty on the inside!

Solomon's principle of a great building for a great God was that of the medieval church, which channeled immense profits, made by its members from trading, into magnificent cathedrals which were showpieces of artistic beauty. The modern church, with eyes opened up to human needs, both local and worldwide, can hardly emulate such architectural masterpieces. It should never be forgotten, however, that church buildings are a silent witness to the faith of its worshipers and that outsiders receive from them an impression of the God who is worshiped there. The role of the building committee and the fabric committee is to communicate theology.

3. *Temple worship was to accord with God's nature.* There is in these

verses a particular theological agenda relating to worship. Both Kings and Chronicles are careful not to claim too much for the temple. Exodus 25:8 had baldly spoken of the tabernacle as a place where God was to *"dwell among"* His people. However, here in verse 4 it is *"a temple for"* His *"name"*: it will not *"contain Him"* (v. 6). Rather, the role of the temple is for worship, of which three media are listed in verse 4. The presence of God in the temple is not denied, but it is a partial presence. He is by no means limited to the temple, this cosmic God. There is a wrestling here with the paradox of the transcendence of God and His immanence, seeking to do justice to each without doing despite to the other. God is near—yet He is also enthroned beyond the stars and is no mere element within His own universe. There is a kind of Christian who thinks he has God in his pocket, so sure is he of his version of the Christian faith and of God's predictability. Here by contrast is a high conception which reacts with awe to the mystery of God's being. He is no tame God to be manipulated. The majestic Aslan is not the sort of lion that fits into any cage! The awesomeness of God is manifested in the positive role of the temple. *"Incense," "showbread," "burnt offerings"*—these were to be fitting expressions of worship from a people aware of His majesty and committed to His will.

The substance of Solomon's communication makes two points: it broaches his need of a master craftsman (v. 7) and of lumber (vv. 8–10). Hiram's letter is to reply to both requests, in verses 13–14 and 15–16 respectively. There are interesting differences between the description of the craftsman in 1 Kings 7:13, 14 and here. In Kings he is called simply Hiram and he is a bronzesmith, while ethnically he is a Phoenician with an Israelite mother from the tribe of Naphtali. Here he has a long appellation ("Huramabi," RSV; cf. *"Huram my master craftsman,"* NKJV) and skills in a whole range of materials, while his mother's tribe is Dan. As elsewhere, the Chronicler is writing with one eye on his historical source and the other on the phenomenon of the tabernacle, in this case its construction described in Exodus 35. There the chief craftsman was Bezalel, a Judahite. Mention of him slipped out in 2 Chronicles 1:5, while earlier he featured in a genealogy at 1 Chronicles 2:20, and so he has been on the Chronicler's mind. Bezalel had an assistant Aholiab from the tribe of Dan, and between them they had such multiple skills as verses 7 and 14 indicate (see Exod. 35:30–35). The Chronicler wants his readers to regard Solomon typologically as a second Judahite Bezalel and Huramabi as a second Danite Aholiab. In the latter case the longer appellation is a clue to the typologizing. In chapters 3–4 we shall read repeatedly "and he made" about Solomon's work on the temple. It is based on the same refrain concerning Bezalel in Exodus 36–39. In all these respects the Chronicler is making a theological affirmation, that the temple is a second tabernacle.

Typological comparison is his way of describing the new era which was comparable with the old and succeeded it. What the tabernacle meant in the Torah and to Israel hitherto, henceforth the temple would mean. The old was a model for the new, and the new replaced it. This sense of newness which reuses language relevant to the old even as it supersedes it, reappears in the New Testament. An instance is the description of Christ as "the last Adam" (1 Cor. 15:45), the head of a new humanity corresponding to and yet surpassing the first Adam. In the New Testament there is the same painstaking concern as here in Chronicles, to trace continuity between the old and new revelations. Human history never repeats itself, but it often resembles itself, it has been said. Theological history is a series of decisive interventions, with each new intervention marked by features comparable with earlier revelation. Only thus is its authenticity proved.

Hiram's letter of reply corresponds closely to Solomon's communication, both in its structure of introduction and main part (vv. 11–12, 13–16) and in its content. The introduction, which echoes Solomon's, is noteworthy. In verse 11 King Solomon is described as God's love-gift to His people. In the light of the Chronicler's theological agenda, this means that Solomon as royal temple builder functioned as God's agent of a new era of grace. God so loved His people that He gave them Solomon—one's mind irresistibly leaps ahead to another era of grace, which could be described in similar terms: "God so loved the world that He gave His Son." At first sight one might think that the universal dimension of the latter is missing in the former. That is not quite true, if verse 12 is taken into account. King Hiram is presented as the model of a Gentile who adds his amen to Israel's testimony. Solomon's witness to God's cosmic greatness (vv. 5–6) is here capped with praise of His creatorial power. For the careful reader of Chronicles here is the theological program of 1 Chronicles 16:25–30 being realized. The Phoenician king represents the "kindreds of the peoples" who are urged to "give to the Lord the glory due to His name." From the Chronicler's perspective this new temple era, announced by David, inaugurated by Solomon, and awaiting consummation at a coming time was marked by non-Jewish worship of Judah's God. Indeed, there was a political side to this religious submission, for Hiram is portrayed as a vassal king subject to Solomon as his "lord" (v. 15). Solomon, sitting on God's throne (1 Chron 29:23), was His viceroy and received foreign homage on God's behalf. This is an aspect of Solomon's reign which is to be developed in chapter 9. It has a prospective aspect. Would not God's future king be "great to the ends of the earth" (Mic. 5:4)? History and hope are interwoven in the Chronicler's theology of the new era. So they are in the New Testament, where the past work of Christ who "appeared at the end of the ages" is the pledge of a future appearing to consummate His work (Heb. 9:26, 28).

IMPLEMENTATION

3:1 Now Solomon began to build the house of the LORD at Jerusalem on Mount Moriah, where *the* LORD had appeared to his father David, at the place that David had prepared on the threshing floor of Ornan the Jebusite.

2 And he began to build on the second *day* of the second month in the fourth year of his reign.

3 This is the foundation which Solomon laid for building the house of God: The length *was* sixty cubits (by cubits according to the former measure) and the width twenty cubits.

4 And the vestibule that *was* in front *of the sanctuary* was twenty cubits long across the width of the house, and the height *was* one hundred and twenty. He overlaid the inside with pure gold.

5 The larger room he paneled with cypress which he overlaid with fine gold, and he carved palm trees and chainwork on it.

6 And he decorated the house with precious stones for beauty, and the gold *was* gold from Parvaim.

7 He also overlaid the house—the beams and

doorposts, its walls and doors—with gold; and he carved cherubim on the walls.

8 And he made the Most Holy Place. Its length was according to the width of the house, twenty cubits, and its width twenty cubits. He overlaid it with six hundred talents of fine gold.

9 The weight of the nails *was* fifty shekels of gold; and he overlaid the upper area with gold.

10 In the Most Holy Place he made two cherubim, fashioned by carving, and overlaid them with gold.

11 The wings of the cherubim *were* twenty cubits in *overall* length: one wing *of the one cherub was* five cubits, touching the wall of the room, and the other wing *was* five cubits, touching the wing of the other cherub;

12 *one* wing of the other cherub *was* five cubits, touching the wall of the room, and the other wing *also was* five cubits, touching the wing of the other cherub.

13 The wings of these cherubim spanned twenty cubits overall. They stood on their feet, and they faced inward.

14 And he made the veil of blue, purple, crimson, and fine linen, and wove cherubim into it.

15 Also he made in front of the temple two pillars thirty-five cubits high, and the capital that *was* on the top of each of *them* was five cubits.

16 He made wreaths of chainwork, as in the inner sanctuary, and put *them* on top of the pillars; and he made one hundred pomegranates, and put *them* on the wreaths of chainwork.

17 Then he set up the pillars before the temple, one on the right hand and the other on the left; he called the name of the one on the right hand Jachin, and the name of the one on the left Boaz.

4:1 Moreover he made a bronze altar: twenty cubits was its length, twenty cubits its width, and ten cubits its height.

2 Then he made the Sea of cast *bronze*, ten cubits from one brim to the other; *it was* completely round. Its height *was* five cubits, and a line of thirty cubits measured its circumference.

3 And under it *was* the likeness of oxen encircling it all around, ten to a cubit, all the way around the Sea. The oxen *were* cast in two rows, when it was cast.

4 It stood on twelve oxen: three looking toward the north, three looking toward the west, three looking toward the south, and three looking toward the east; the Sea *was set* upon them, and all their back parts *pointed* inward.

5 It *was* a handbreadth thick; and its brim was shaped like the brim of a cup, *like* a lily blossom. It contained three thousand baths.

6 He also made ten lavers, and put five on the right side and five on the left, to wash in them; such things as they offered for the burnt offering they would wash in them, but the Sea *was* for the priests to wash in.

7 And he made ten lampstands of gold according to their design, and set *them* in the temple, five on the right side and five on the left.

8 He also made ten tables, and placed *them* in the temple, five on the right side and five on the left. And he made one hundred bowls of gold.

9 Furthermore he made the court of the priests, and the great court and doors for the court; and he overlaid these doors with bronze.

10 He set the Sea on the right side, toward the southeast.

11 Then Huram made the pots and the shovels and the bowls. So Huram finished doing the work that he was to do for King Solomon for the house of God:

12 the two pillars and the bowl-shaped capitals *that were* on top of the two pillars; the two networks covering the two bowl-shaped capitals which *were* on top of the pillars;

13 four hundred pomegranates for the two networks (two rows of pomegranates for each network, to cover the two bowl-shaped capitals that *were* on the pillars);

14 he also made carts and the lavers on the carts;

15 one Sea and twelve oxen under it;

16 also the pots, the shovels, the forks—and all their articles Huram his master *craftsman* made of

burnished bronze for King Solomon for the house of the LORD.

17 In the plain of Jordan the king had them cast in clay molds, between Succoth and Zeredah.

18 And Solomon had all these articles made in such great abundance that the weight of the bronze was not determined.

19 Thus Solomon had all the furnishings made for the house of God: the altar of gold and the tables on which *was* the showbread;

20 the lampstands with their lamps of pure gold, to burn in the prescribed manner in front of the inner sanctuary,

21 with the flowers and the lamps and the wick-trimmers of gold, of purest gold;

22 the trimmers, the bowls, the ladles, and the censers of pure gold. As for the entry of the sanctuary, its inner doors to the Most Holy *Place,* and the doors of the main hall of the temple, *were* gold.

5:1 So all the work that Solomon had done for the house of the LORD was finished; and Solomon brought in the things which his father David had dedicated: the silver and the gold and all the furnishings. And he put *them* in the treasuries of the house of God.

2 Chron. 3:1–5:1

These two chapters follow a clearly marked track defined by Solomon's beginning (3:1) and finishing (5:1) of the building of the temple and by over a dozen milestones along the way, the repeated *"and he made"* (3:8 onward). It is at first sight unexpected that the Chronicler has considerably shortened his source, 1 Kings 6–7, to about half its length. Fuller details were evidently available to his readers, and he does not feel obliged to copy it all out again. For him the details were a means to a more important end, the worship of God. They were spiritually meaningful as the necessary grounding of worship and as means of grace for generations of believers. Obviously, however, he did not attach precise and differentiating significance to each detail. The theology of the temple will be expounded in chapters 5–7: here it finds little expression. The Christian allegorist who lingers over the minutest detail of the tabernacle and finds mysterious significance in its every nook and cranny will not find a kindred spirit in the Chronicler.

1. *A promise kept.* Mention of the location of the temple in verse 1 provides opportunity for further evidence of its divine authenticity. A not surprising reminder is given of David's preparatory work in finding—or rather being led to—*"the threshing floor of Ornan"* (3:1; 1 Chron. 21). It is associated with divine revelation. The Hebrew verb is probably what is called an impersonal passive, meaning "revelation was made" (NKJV *"the Lord had appeared"*). The Chronicler has yet another card in his theological hand. He appeals to an ancient tradition that associated the place where Abraham almost sacrificed Isaac with a future religious revelation. In Genesis 22:14 there is a wordplay linking God's provision of an alternative sacrifice with the establishment of a sanctuary. The Hebrew verb "see" or "reveal" also means "see to" or "provide." So the statement of the future significance of this site in Genesis 22:14, playing on the two meanings of the one verb, according to the most likely rendering reads "In the mount of the Lord revelation shall be made." The form seems to be an impersonal passive, relating to the future. The Chronicler's claim is that this omen associated with a patriarchal experience of God has now come true. This is the *"Mount Moriah"* or "Mount Revelation" of Genesis 22:2, 14! It was David who received the promised revelation. The effect is to reinforce David's passing over of the sanctuary at Gibeon in 1 Chronicles 21:28–22:1. In the Torah there was warrant for worship more ancient than the tabernacle, and it pointed beyond the tabernacle to the temple.

The argumentation is strongly reminiscent of that used in Hebrews 7. How may Jesus, a member of the non-priestly tribe of Judah, be high priest of the heavenly tabernacle? The answer lies in Genesis 14:18–20 and Psalm 110:4. Jesus is heir to the Davidic throne and so to this royal psalm. Thereby He has inherited the role of the priest-king Melchizedek, of whom Genesis 14 speaks. In both Hebrews and Chronicles there is the same unashamedly intellectual concern to establish authenticity by appeal to the Torah. A member of an adult Sunday school class which I was recently teaching made the insightful comment that the contemporary church by ignoring the Old Testament makes an improper appeal to faith. Its call to believe in Christ, valid in itself, is quite wrongfully applied wholesale to the work of Christ. In the New Testament, on the other hand, there is constant appeal to the mind, with careful argumentation to support and verify claims that are being made. In the world of the New Testament it was only Jews and Gentile proselytes—who knew and accepted the Old Testament—who, under God, could be argued into the kingdom (cf. Acts 17:2, 11). Nevertheless, Old Testament back-up formed a considerable part of Christian teaching in the days of the early church. Is it not important for today's members, if faith is to be illuminated by understanding? Just as the Torah was the Chronicler's theological dictionary to which he often turned for clarification, so the Old Testament once had, and should surely have again, no less a role for the church. If the explicit purpose of the Fourth Gospel was that its readers should "believe . . . and . . . have life" (John 20:31), the concern of the Third was that its recipients should "know the certainty" of what they had been taught (Luke 1:4). Faith must find corroboration, if it is to satisfy and to survive.

2. *An overall description.* Verses 3–7 are concerned with the main structure of the temple, giving its overall size and appearance. Verse 3 presents a ground plan, and so probably did verse 4 originally. There are scholarly reasons for thinking that *"and the height was one hundred and twenty"* was initially *"and the width . . . extended ten cubits,"* as in 1 Kings 6:3. The temple was a long building, about ninety feet long in relation to its width of thirty feet. At the top of a flight of steps was an open porch with the entrance to the building flanked by free-standing pillars. Beyond the entrance was a narthex, then a main hall, and beyond that a rear room, *"the Most Holy Place"* of verse 8. The impression one receives from these verses is of opulence and artistic ornamentation. The layperson never entered the temple but worshiped only in its courts. Yet here was splendor and beauty as worthy of God as consecrated giving and dedicated craftsmanship could make them. Only the best—always a relative best— that particular human hands can give and do is good enough for God. He never asks for less, nor for more. It is this human best that God will graciously fill with His glory (5:14).

3. *"And he made."* The individual components of the temple are now listed, from verse 8 onward. The repeated formula *"and he made,"* which marks the various sections of the passage, has been taken over from the description of the tabernacle's furnishings in Exodus 36–39. The Chronicler is teaching his Torah-versed readers that here was a further counterpart in this next stage of divine revelation.

What Solomon made corresponded to what Bezalel made at the previous stage.

In fact this refrain means that Solomon *"had"* them *"made,"* as NKJV paraphrases in 4:18 after a paragraph that specifies certain work as Huram's (4:11–17). The paraphrase could stand as well in any of the places. The language is that of direction and ultimate responsibility. It indicates where the buck landed rather than whose hands labored and whose brow sweated. The minions of 2:2, 18, the craftsmen of 2:14, and the master craftsman of 2:13 were Solomon's executives. They were the seven-eighths of the productive iceberg that lies beneath the surface of these chapters. So it always is in God's service. As I write, the desk and floor in my office are cluttered with literature relating to Chronicles, texts, commentaries, books, and articles. A scholar could dissect this particular volume and cry "Here is Ackroyd and here is Mosis and here is Williamson and here . . ." He would be right. My name appears at the front almost by courtesy! I recall once seeing a commentary advertised as having been written in prison without recourse to other commentaries and by reliance on the Holy Spirit alone. I doubt whether those last two phrases are complementary. If God has set teachers in the church (1 Cor. 12:28; Eph. 4:11) and many have written books, can good come out of ignoring them, let alone parading that ignorance as glorifying God? God's work is never a one-man show. The one who represents the visible part of the iceberg must ever acknowledge his or her debt to others. I like to remember that the First Epistle to the Corinthians was from Paul *and* Sosthenes (1 Cor. 1:1) and that the Epistle to the Colossians was from Paul *and* Timothy. Do you know the *three* people credited with writing the Epistles to the Thessalonians? Paul was a fine role model of large-hearted fellowship in the service of God.

Pride of place is deliberately given to the Holy of Holies, mention of which in the Kings account is reserved for a later place. This pushing forward of the material represents the importance of the ark which was to be installed there (5:7). The very name of this inner chamber indicates the ultimate in gradation of holiness. It symbolized the sovereign mystery of God, whose gracious fellowship with Israel was never to be interpreted as familiarity. The Chronicler draws attention to the impressive pillars in front of the temple (vv. 15–17), to the bronze altar of burnt offering (4:1), and to the bronze *"Sea"*

214

and the ten smaller *"lavers"* used for ritual purification and cleansing (4:2–6). Special attention is drawn to the *"ten lampstands"* by twice categorizing them "as prescribed" (vv. 7, 20, RSV). The tabernacle, like the second temple built after the Exile, had only one lampstand, so that the prescription must be that of David (1 Chron. 28:15). For the Chronicler their light was the traditional fourth medium of worship that belonged with the other three listed in 2:4: he enumerates all four in 13:11 (cf. 29:7). Worship is essentially grounded in particular traditional sacred acts which transcend the present time and the personal concerns of worshipers and remind us that we belong to an entity much greater than ourselves. They unite us with worshipers of past generations. They link us with symbols that stir deep within us a sense of the mystery and grace of God.

4. *A finished task.* Have you noticed that the account of the building of the temple begins and ends with a reference to David (3:1; 5:1)? In 5:1 there is also a finishing touch whereby Solomon acknowledges all that David did toward the project: David's victory trophies are duly installed in the temple. It is a fine tribute to his father's labors. It is like actors who, receiving an ovation from the audience at the end of the play, call for the director standing in the wings to come onto the stage and share the applause. The Chronicler is affirming that David and Solomon had been involved in a joint work.

In 1 Chronicles we noted a wordplay in the Hebrew on Solomon's name (*šelōmōh*) and "peace" (*šālôm*). It has been suggested that there is another play on his name here, with the verbal phrase *"and . . . was finished"* (*wattišlam*). Solomon has fulfilled his function as temple builder, and so he is fittingly characterized as the finisher. It reminds us of Another who was to cry "It is finished" (John 19:30). It was evidently this cry that triggered the tearing of the veil of the Holy of Holies from top to bottom, if one examines Matthew 27:50, 51 and Mark 15:37, 38 and compares Luke 23:45, 46. The Evangelists were making a theological point. The temple era, inaugurated with its exclusive veil (3:14), had indeed lasted until the period of Jesus. Then God did a new work. It was symbolized by His tearing the veil and giving fuller access to His presence. This theology implied by the Gospels is spelled out with reference not to the temple but to the tabernacle in Hebrews 9:1–14; 10:19–22.

On one occasion a Christian missionary was reading 2 Chronicles 3–4 in Hebrew and he proceeded to reflect on its relevance to his own ministry. He was due to write an important letter to a church he had recently planted, where certain problems had since developed. He decided to incorporate his meditation as a useful lesson for them. The missionary was the apostle Paul. He was staying at Ephesus and preparing to write to the church at Corinth. You can find his meditation in 1 Corinthians 3:10–17. That the account of building the temple was on his mind is clear from his references to the Corinthian church as an antitype of the temple. How do I know that he had been reading the Chronicles account of the temple building rather than the Kings one? Because only the Chronicler has references to founding and precious stones. And why in Hebrew? Because the Greek version does not represent the reference to founding. In the new Christian era Paul envisages himself as another Solomon, the temple builder who laid the foundation (3:3). He may have fused this image with that of Huram the "skillful . . . master craftsman" (2:13). Paul's foundation work had been done, the initial work of church planting involving evangelism and basic teaching, both of which centered around Jesus Christ. Now each member of the recently formed group had the individual responsibility of building on this work and making his or her own contribution to the fellowship as it grew in love and grace. The apostle was thinking of the craftsmen at work on the temple site. What was their contribution? A golden bowl or a silver goblet or jeweled ornamentation—all lovingly wrought with skill and effort commensurate with the durable material they handled. Here was work that would last for their lifetime and far beyond.

Would any bring less durable materials to work on—say, hay or straw? In the setting of a building metaphor the suggestion is ludicrous, and is intended to be. It is made to bring out the sacred significance of the Christian group as no less than a spiritual replica of the temple. It expresses the solemn responsibility of each of its members to make contributions of lasting worth. Paul envisages the local congregation as involved in a continual building program of a spiritual nature. As they met together in worship, fellowship, and service, what each was becoming and contributing was an influence for good or ill on his or her fellow-Christians. The apostle is working with a typological equation of temple and church, and thinking in terms of a new era that supersedes the earlier one. On the basis of this theological typologizing he creates an illustration relevant to the needs of the Corinthian church. A Christian expositor, glancing at 2 Chronicles 3–4, might not find it very fruitful material, especially its lists of materials and articles. I am glad that we have the example of Paul's exposition. He did not disdain such apparently unpromising material but studied it and with hermeneutical creativity applied it to a particular Christian context.

CHAPTER TEN

God's House, People, and King

2 Chronicles 5:2–9:31

The temple has been built and finished, but it remains an empty shell until the ark, which it was built to house, is moved into it. This is to be the culmination of Solomon's great religious task. The text runs on lines parallel with David's transfer of the ark to Jerusalem (1 Chron. 13–16), but at a later stage. There is first a consultation with Israel's leaders and then a convening of the people for a national procession (5:2, 3), as in David's day (1 Chron. 13:1–5). David—eventually at least—transported the ark with correct religious procedure (1 Chron. 15:1–16:3), and now so does Solomon in transferring it to the temple (5:2–10). On arrival there was a celebration of praise in David's case (1 Chron 16:7–36), and now there is in Solomon's (5:11–14). David and Solomon both look forward to the future by organizing a system of regular worship (1 Chron. 16:4–6, 37–42; 2 Chron. 8:12–16). Most important of all, a divine revelation is associated with each event (1 Chron. 17:1–15; 2 Chron. 7:12–22), in David's case followed by a prayer of thanksgiving (1 Chron. 17:16–27), and in Solomon's preceded by a prayer of petition (6:12–22). Both of these messages from God are pivotal for the Chronicler's theology. The parallelism between the work of David and that of Solomon expresses its joint nature: they functioned under God as fellow-founders of a new era of grace. Solomon had two roles, temple builder and God's viceroy. As to the latter, his reign was a preliminary manifestation of the kingdom of God for the Chronicler. This aspect of Solomon's work will be explored in 8:1–9:28. God's house and God's king are two of the three main topics of chapters 5–9. Both are shown to be the means of forwarding God's plans for His people.

THE GLORY OF THE LORD

5:2 Now Solomon assembled the elders of Israel and all the heads of the tribes, the chief fathers of the children of Israel, in Jerusalem, that they might bring the ark of the covenant of the LORD up from the City of David, which *is* Zion.

3 Therefore all the men of Israel assembled with the king at the feast, which *was* in the seventh month.

4 So all the elders of Israel came, and the Levites took up the ark.

5 Then they brought up the ark, the tabernacle of meeting, and all the holy furnishings that *were* in the tabernacle. The priests and the Levites brought them up.

6 Also King Solomon, and all the congregation of Israel who were assembled with him before the ark, were sacrificing sheep and oxen that could not be counted or numbered for multitude.

7 Then the priests brought in the ark of the covenant of the LORD to its place, into the inner sanctuary of the temple, to the Most Holy *Place,* under the wings of the cherubim.

8 For the cherubim spread *their* wings over the place of the ark, and the cherubim overshadowed the ark and its poles.

9 The poles extended so that the ends of the poles of the ark could be seen from *the holy place,* in front of the inner sanctuary; but they could not be seen from outside. And they are there to this day.

10 Nothing was in the ark except the two tablets which Moses put *there* at Horeb, when the LORD made *a covenant* with the children of Israel, when they had come out of Egypt.

11 And it came to pass when the priests came out of the *Most* Holy *Place* (for all the priests who *were* present had sanctified themselves, without keeping to their divisions),

12 and the Levites *who were* the singers, all those of Asaph and Heman and Jeduthun, with their sons and their brethren, stood at the east end of the altar,

clothed in white linen, having cymbals, stringed instruments and harps, and with them one hundred
and twenty priests sounding with trumpets—

13 indeed it came to pass, when the trumpeters
and singers *were* as one, to make one sound to be
heard in praising and thanking the LORD, and when
they lifted up their voice with the trumpets and cymbals and instruments of music, and praised the LORD,
saying:

For He *is* good,

For His mercy *endures* forever,"
that the house, the house of the LORD, was filled
with a cloud,

14 so that the priests could not continue ministering because of the cloud; for the glory of the LORD
filled the house of God.

6:1 Then Solomon spoke:

"The LORD said

He would dwell in the dark cloud.

2 I have surely built You an exalted house,

And a place for You to dwell in forever."

3 Then the king turned around and blessed the
whole assembly of Israel, while all the assembly of
Israel was standing.

4 And he said: "Blessed *be* the LORD God of Israel,
who has fulfilled with His hands *what* He spoke
with His mouth to my father David, saying,

5 'Since the day that I brought My people out of
the land of Egypt, I have chosen no city from any
tribe of Israel *in which* to build a house, that My
name might be there, nor did I choose any man to be
a ruler over My people Israel.

6 'Yet I have chosen Jerusalem, that My name
may be there, and I have chosen David to be over My
people Israel.'

7 "Now it was in the heart of my father David
to build a temple for the name of the LORD God of
Israel.

8 "But the LORD said to my father David, 'Whereas it was in your heart to build a temple for My name,
you did well in that it was in your heart.

9 'Nevertheless you shall not build the temple,

220

but your son who will come from your body, he shall
build the temple for My name.

10 "So the LORD has fulfilled His word which He
spoke, and I have filled the position of my father
David, and sit on the throne of Israel, as the LORD
promised; and I have built the temple for the name of
the LORD God of Israel.

11 "And there I have put the ark, in which is the
covenant of the LORD which He made with the children of Israel."

2 Chron. 5:2–6:11

1. *Installing the ark in the temple.* Here in 5:2–10 is the climax
of the religious work started by David. There is a grand procession
from *"the City of David,"* where the ark had been temporarily
housed, to the temple a few hundred yards to the north. The Chronicler mainly follows the account in 1 Kings 8:1–9, except to stress the
traditional role of the Levites in carrying the ark, now evidently for
the last time. The occasion is the Feast of Tabernacles. It was a festival associated with Israel's wanderings in the wilderness, as Leviticus 23 explains. Now the ark which had journeyed with them was to
find a resting place, even as Israel under God's grace had found
theirs. At the temple the Levites handed their sacred charge over to
the priests to install in the Holy of Holies, for only the priests were
permitted so to do (see Num. 4:4–15). The account virtually closes
with a glimpse of the ark poles from the main hall of the temple. The
Chronicler retains the phrase of his source, *"to this day"* (5:9), but for
him and his readers it was an antiquarian reference. The second
temple in whose courts they worshiped had no ark. They did possess, however, ."the holy vessels" (5:5, RSV) which provided a link
of continuity and confirmed that their own religious building was
the legitimate temple. All this narrative about Solomon's work under
God is resonant with new beginnings. The Chronicler looks back
over the centuries to a sacred moment in history. In the same vein
Mark the Evangelist was to look back to "the beginning of the"
Christian "gospel" (Mark 1:1) and lovingly recount its details.

The final note of the account, as in Kings, concerns the contents of
the ark, the stone "tables" (5:10, RSV) of the Ten Commandments. The
ark was indeed the *"ark of the covenant"* (5:2, 7), a title the Chronicler
bestows on it even when he is writing independently of his literary

source. It was a symbol of the covenant relationship that linked God and Israel. The bond was essentially one of mutual commitment, to which the Ten Commandments bore witness. God's commitment was grounded in the event of the Exodus, an act of redeeming love: "I am the Lord your God, who brought you out of the land of Egypt" (Exod. 20:2). Equally Israel was committed to God, with an obligation that involved a particular lifestyle, spelled out in Exodus 20:3–17. This emphasis on Torah is to re-emerge a little later as a continuing mandate for king and people, laid on them by the God of the temple (7:17–22; see also 6:11). The worship-centered new revelation did not eclipse the broader obligations of the old. This continuity between the revelation of Torah and the revelation of temple teaches a necessary truth. In eighteenth-century Jewish history the charismatic Hasidim emerged in Poland, with a stress on joy and feeling God's presence in the heart every waking moment. It was a dynamic reaction against Jewish scholarship which had buried the Torah in a cemetery of academic learning. It was left to the second generation of the Hasidim to restore the balance and learn again that the Torah comprised God-given guidelines for living. In the early church there were those who identified the new wine of Christianity with antinomianism and made divine grace an argument for human licentiousness (Jude 4, RSV). Indeed, Paul was accused of so doing (Rom. 3:8; compare 6:1, 2). He firmly rebutted the charge, insisting on obedience "from the heart to the standard of teaching to which" Christians have been "committed" (Rom. 6:17, RSV) and even on the fulfilling of "the righteous requirement of the law" in the power of the Spirit (Rom. 8:4).

2. *Temple worship and revelation.* The Chronicler envisages a beautiful service of worship after the installation of the ark. In 5:11–12 he hands us a snapshot of the scene, as it were. Here is the massed presence of the priests, just leaving the temple. And over here are the Levitical choristers and musicians in their white robes, accompanied by the priestly trumpeters, arranged in front of the massive altar of burnt offering in the court outside the temple. The Levites are exulting in their comparatively new role as God's singers instead of carrying the ark (compare 1 Chron. 6:31, 32). They sing what was in fact the favorite chorus of the post-exilic people of God: "He is good, for His steadfast love endures for ever" (5:13, RSV). God's steadfast love is His supreme attribute as Lord of the covenant,

so that its celebration is fitting in this service of thanksgiving and praise to mark the installing of the ark of the covenant. The same chorus had been included in David's ark service according to 1 Chronicles 16:34. In chapters 6 and 7 Solomon's prayer and God's answer are both to be marked by this theme of divine grace—it is no wonder that the chorus is joyfully sung again in 7:3. God's steadfast love is a love that makes the future bright with hope. A new era was dawning for God's people and its keynote was to be His "steadfast love for David" (6:42, RSV), a love that met His people's repentance with forgiveness and blessing (7:14).

All this reminds me of what I like to think of as a little psalm in the Epistle to the Romans, 5:1–11. It too celebrates the beginning of a new era ("in due time," Rom. 5:6), when the love of God was demonstrated toward sinners in the death of Christ (Rom. 5:8), so that they were transformed from foes to friends and blessed with lasting salvation (Rom. 5:9–11). No wonder that joy is the response that frames this Christian celebration of God's love (Rom. 5:2, 11). Nor is that note missing from the Chronicler's account. Later in the narrative there is to be mention of the people returning home "joyful and glad of heart for the good that the Lord had done for David, for Solomon, and for His people Israel" (7:10). The statement reverberates with a sense of God's breaking into His people's history with a new epoch marked by His goodness and grace.

Worship is followed by God's revelation of Himself, as it was in 1:3–7. In general terms the sequence is not an uncommon one. Those who bow their hearts before God in worship are in an attitude which is ready to receive new insights from God, insights which will enrich their subsequent lives. Here, just as in 1 Kings 8:10–11, the divine revelation takes a material form. The temple is *filled with a cloud* (5:13), which symbolizes God's *glory.* At a similar point in the Exodus dispensation, when the tabernacle was completed, the same phenomenon had occurred (Exod. 40:34–35). It was God's seal of approval on the venture. Now the resting place of the ark is authenticated as in accord with the will of God. The narrative deliberately harks back to the parallel in the old age: God is affirming the new sanctuary in the same way, and the repetition is corroborative. Interestingly, there is a similar appeal to the glory that enveloped the tabernacle in a description of the beginning of the Christian era: "The Word became flesh and dwelt"—one might

223

say "tabernacled" to bring out John's thought—"among us, and we beheld His glory" (John 1:14). In Jesus there was a new manifestation of divine presence. The Fourth Gospel develops that imagery by giving to Jesus the value of the temple (John 2:19–22). What the temple was, now He is: the new dispensation is described in the language of the old. At an earlier stage of divine revelation Kings and Chronicles were doing the same thing.

3. *Solomon's temple sermon.* In 6:1–11 the king takes stock of the situation and analyzes its theological meaning. Here the Chronicler is following 1 Kings 8:13–21. First, in 6:1–2 the cloud which conceals even as it reveals is implicitly compared with the Holy of Holies in which the ark has been placed out of sight. Although the New Testament rejoices in the rending of the veil, literally and figuratively, and in the fuller access to God afforded by the work of Christ, there must ever be a sense of mystery associated with God. It is a feature of traditional Jewish theology to stress that from an intellectual standpoint—but not from a spiritual one—God is unknowable. Perhaps it was provoked by the claims of Christian systematic theologians and the impression they gave of dissecting anatomically the being of God. Behind that Jewish denial lies a sense of the inadequacy of human language to describe one whom Oliver Wendell Holmes characterized in his hymn as "Lord of all being, throned afar," whose "glory flames from sun and star." Was not Paul saying as much when he stated that "we know in part" (1 Cor. 13:9)? He was attacking an attitude of cocksureness he detected among the Christians at Corinth (compare 1 Cor. 8:1, 2). Isaac Newton's assessment of his great scientific discoveries shows a commendable humility which the Christian may well adopt in his or her attitude to the things of God: "To myself I seem to have been only a boy playing on the seashore and diverting myself in now and then finding a smoother pebble or a prettier shell than ordinary, whilst the great ocean of truth lay all undiscovered before me."

There follows a statement of thanksgiving addressed to the people for what God had done. The Exodus age had been overshadowed by a new revelation of God in the election of David as king and of Jerusalem as the place of God's special presence. Yet God's nominee for building the temple had been not David but Solomon. Accordingly, Solomon had built it, duly installing the ark. The event engenders a sense not of human achievement but of divine sovereignty.

God had kept His promise. This is another way of affirming the divine authenticity of the temple. It was prophecy come true, and this history-in-advance shows that present history was indeed His story. In 6:10 the NKJV endeavors to convey a Hebrew play on words that expresses this truth: Solomon's filling his father's place was part of the fulfilling of God's promise. The New Testament is no stranger to this type of endorsement, in respect of its own new era. Just as the note of fulfillment begins and ends Solomon's speech (6:4, 10), so in Luke's Gospel the oral ministry of Jesus begins and ends on the note of Scripture fulfilled (Luke 4:21; 24:44). It is a note which those whose ears are not attuned to the Old Testament find difficult to hear.

ANSWERED PRAYER

6:12 Then *Solomon* stood before the altar of the LORD in the presence of all the assembly of Israel, and spread out his hands

13 (for Solomon had made a bronze platform five cubits long, five cubits wide, and three cubits high, and had set it in the midst of the court; and he stood on it, knelt down on his knees before all the assembly of Israel, and spread out his hands toward heaven);

14 and he said: "LORD God of Israel, *there is* no God in heaven or on earth like You, who keep *Your* covenant and mercy with Your servants who walk before You with all their hearts.

15 "You have kept what You promised Your servant David my father; You have both spoken with Your mouth and fulfilled *it* with Your hand, as *it is* this day.

16 "Therefore, LORD God of Israel, now keep what You promised Your servant David my father, saying, 'You shall not fail to have a man sit before Me on the throne of Israel, only if your sons take heed to their way, that they walk in My law as you have walked before Me.'

17 "And now, O LORD God of Israel, let Your word come true, which You have spoken to Your servant David.

225

18 "But will God indeed dwell with men on the earth? Behold, heaven and the heaven of heavens cannot contain You. How much less this temple which I have built!

19 "Yet regard the prayer of Your servant and his supplication, O LORD my God, and listen to the cry and the prayer which Your servant is praying before You:

20 "that Your eyes may be open toward this temple day and night, toward the place where *You* said *You would* put Your name, that You may hear the prayer which Your servant makes toward this place.

21 "And may You hear the supplications of Your servant and of Your people Israel, when they pray toward this place. Hear from heaven Your dwelling place, and when You hear, forgive.

22 "If anyone sins against his neighbor, and is forced to take an oath, and comes *and* takes an oath before Your altar in this temple,

23 "then hear from heaven, and act, and judge Your servants, bringing retribution on the wicked by bringing his way on his own head, and justifying the righteous by giving him according to his righteousness.

24 "Or if Your people Israel are defeated before an enemy because they have sinned against You, and return and confess Your name, and pray and make supplication before You in this temple,

25 "then hear from heaven and forgive the sin of Your people Israel, and bring them back to the land which You gave to them and their fathers.

26 "When the heavens are shut up and there is no rain because they have sinned against You, when they pray toward this place and confess Your name, and turn from their sin because You afflict them,

27 "then hear *in* heaven, and forgive the sin of Your servants, Your people Israel, that You may teach them the good way in which they should walk; and send rain on Your land which You have given to Your people as an inheritance.

28 "When there is famine in the land, pestilence or blight or mildew, locusts or grasshoppers; when

their enemies besiege them in the land of their cities;
whatever plague or whatever sickness *there is;*

29 *"*whatever prayer, whatever supplication is *made*
by anyone, or by all Your people Israel, when each
one knows his own burden and his own grief, and
spreads out his hands to this temple:

30 *"*then hear from heaven Your dwelling place,
and forgive, and give to everyone according to all his
ways, whose heart You know (for You alone know
the hearts of the sons of men),

31 *"*that they may fear You, to walk in Your ways
as long as they live in the land which You gave to our
fathers.

32 *"*Moreover, concerning a foreigner, who is not
of Your people Israel, but has come from a far country for the sake of Your great name and Your mighty
hand and Your outstretched arm, when they come
and pray in this temple;

33 *"*then hear from heaven Your dwelling place,
and do according to all for which the foreigner calls
to You, that all peoples of the earth may know Your
name and fear You, as *do* Your people Israel, and that
they may know that this temple which I have built is
called by Your name.

34 *"*When Your people go out to battle against
their enemies, wherever You send them, and when
they pray to You toward this city which You have
chosen and the temple which I have built for Your
name,

35 *"*then hear from heaven their prayer and their
supplication, and maintain their cause.

36 *"*When they sin against You (for *there is* no one
who does not sin), and You become angry with them
and deliver them to the enemy, and they take them
captive to a land far or near;

37 *"yet* when they come to themselves in the land
where they were carried captive, and repent, and
make supplication to You in the land of their captivity, saying, 'We have sinned, we have done wrong,
and have committed wickedness';

38 *"*and *when* they return to You with all their heart
and with all their soul in the land of their captivity,

where they have been carried captive, and pray toward their land which You gave to their fathers, the city which You have chosen, and toward the temple which I have built for Your name:

39 "then hear from heaven Your dwelling place their prayer and their supplications, and maintain their cause, and forgive Your people who have sinned against You.

40 "Now, my God, I pray, let Your eyes be open and *let* Your ears *be* attentive to the prayer *made* in this place.

41 "Now therefore,

Arise, O LORD God, to Your resting place,
You and the ark of Your strength.
Let Your priests, O LORD God, be clothed with salvation,
And let Your saints rejoice in goodness.

42 "O LORD God, do not turn away the face of Your Anointed;
Remember the mercies of Your servant David."

7:1 When Solomon had finished praying, fire came down from heaven and consumed the burnt offering and the sacrifices; and the glory of the LORD filled the temple.

2 And the priests could not enter the house of the LORD, because the glory of the LORD had filled the LORD's house.

3 When all the children of Israel saw how the fire came down, and the glory of the LORD on the temple, they bowed their faces to the ground on the pavement, and worshiped and praised the LORD, *saying:*

"For *He is* good,
For His mercy *endures* forever."

4 Then the king and all the people offered sacrifices before the LORD.

5 King Solomon offered a sacrifice of twenty-two thousand bulls and one hundred and twenty thousand sheep. So the king and all the people dedicated the house of God.

6 And the priests attended to their services; the Levites also with instruments of the music of

the LORD, which King David had made to praise the LORD, saying, "For His mercy *endures* forever," whenever David offered praise by their ministry. The priests sounded trumpets opposite them, while all Israel stood.

7 Furthermore Solomon consecrated the middle of the court that *was* in front of the house of the LORD; for there he offered burnt offerings and the fat of the peace offerings, because the bronze altar which Solomon had made was not able to receive the burnt offerings, the grain offerings, and the fat.

8 At that time Solomon kept the feast seven days, and all Israel with him, a very great assembly from the entrance of Hamath to the Brook of Egypt.

9 And on the eighth day they held a sacred assembly, for they observed the dedication of the altar seven days, and the feast seven days.

10 On the twenty-third day of the seventh month he sent the people away to their tents, joyful and glad of heart for the good that the LORD had done for David, for Solomon, and for His people Israel.

11 Thus Solomon finished the house of the LORD and the king's house; and Solomon successfully accomplished all that came into his heart to make in the house of the LORD and in his own house.

12 Then the LORD appeared to Solomon by night, and said to him: "I have heard your prayer, and have chosen this place for Myself as a house of sacrifice.

13 "When I shut up heaven and there is no rain, or command the locusts to devour the land, or send pestilence among My people,

14 "if My people who are called by My name will humble themselves, and pray and seek My face, and turn from their wicked ways, then I will hear from heaven, and will forgive their sin and heal their land.

15 "Now My eyes will be open and My ears attentive to prayer *made* in this place.

16 "For now I have chosen and sanctified this house, that My name may be there forever; and My eyes and My heart will be there perpetually.

17 "As for you, if you walk before Me as your father David walked, and do according to all that I

have commanded you, and if you keep My statutes
and My judgments,

18 "then I will establish the throne of your kingdom, as I covenanted with David your father, saying,
'You shall not fail *to have* a man as ruler in Israel.'

19 "But if your turn away and forsake My statutes
and My commandments which I have set before you,
and go and serve other gods, and worship them,

20 "then I will uproot them from My land which I
have given them; and this house which I have sanctified for My name I will cast out of My sight, and will
make it a proverb and a byword among all peoples.

21 "And *as for* this house, which is exalted, everyone who passes by it will be astonished and say, 'Why
has the LORD done thus to this land and this house?'

22 "Then they will answer, 'Because they forsook
the LORD God of their fathers, who brought them out
of the land of Egypt, and embraced other gods, and
worshiped them and served them; therefore He has
brought all this calamity on them.'"

2 Chron. 6:12–7:22

This section moves from Solomon's public prayer to God's private
answer, not directly but via a fresh endorsement of the temple on
God's part and an engaging in worship on Israel's part.

1. *Temple prayer.* Solomon mounts a huge platform, to be heard
and seen better, and prays on the people's behalf. The prayer, apart
from its conclusion, follows 1 Kings 8:22–53 closely. It is a prayer
about prayer, and it inaugurates the role of the temple as a house of
prayer. We had occasion to note earlier that biblical prayers tend to
begin with adoration of God. Here God is praised as one who keeps
His promises. The statements of verses 4 and 10 are turned into
praise and made pointers to the unique faithfulness of God. The
prayer encourages a petition that another, related promise may be
kept, the promise of 1 Chronicles 17:12, "He shall build Me a house,
and I will establish his throne forever." This promise of a permanent
Davidic dynasty is dear to the Chronicler, and doubtless as he wrote
he prayed the petition over again in his heart, ever a royalist. There
is an interesting stylistic variation in verse 16. Instead of writing
three times of walking *"before"* God (6:14, 16), the Chronicler varies
the second with *"in My law,"* in contrast to his source in 1 Kings

8:25. To *"walk before"* God is to adopt a way of life which complies with the will of God. In the Chronicler's idiom this spells Torah. The term "Torah" or *"law"* is a metaphor which pictures life as a journey. It means literally *"directions."* The related verb is used in this literal sense in the Hebrew of Genesis 46:28, *"*to point out (the way to Goshen)." So the Torah was God's guiding principles for His people's lives. There is an indication of this in 6:27, where the related Hebrew verb is employed: more literally one might render 'that You may direct them to the good way in which they should walk." I am reminded of a New Testament text which affirms that God has laid out in advance a mode of living for His new people, namely *"good works"* to *"walk in"* (Eph. 2:10).

6:16–17 have launched Solomon's first petition. 6:22–39 present a whole flotilla of petitions, each anchored to a particular situation of need, which prompts an S.O.S. prayer to God. Solomon prays about various people praying and asks that their prayers may be answered. It is all very relevant to the temple because its courts are visualized as the location of prayer, uttered facing the temple. The only exception is, naturally, when those who pray are detained outside the country or its capital; their corresponding pose is to pray facing Jerusalem and the temple. Daniel 6:10 fits into this category. Daniel prayed *"in his upper room, with his windows open toward Jerusalem,"* guaranteeing his consignment to the lions' den, yet obeying God rather than human orders. The temple became the appointed house of prayer in the precise sense that it was God's earthly agency—one might say, the mail box into which all prayers were to be dropped. As the location of God's special presence, it was the point through which to channel prayer.

By way of introduction, 6:18–21 explore this relationship between the temple and prayer. God's dwelling in the temple is essentially to be interpreted as a spiritual metaphor, as the Chronicler affirmed in 2:6. God would indeed have to be small to fit inside the temple: it might be a great temple for a great God (2:5), but it was not that great! J. B. Phillips once wrote a provocative book called *Your God Is Too Small.* God is really too big for so many things. Too big to fit into my own present conception of Him, too big to fit into my church, too big to fit into my denomination—too big to fit into anything human. He is a veritable Gulliver in our Lilliputian world. Yet the Old Testament holds in tension the greatness of God and His grace to a little

231

people. The New Testament attempts the harder task of holding in tension a God who is supercosmic and yet contracted to a span. Since New Testament times even a child can spread tiny arms and say truly, "God is this big." In the temple era one had somehow to relate God to a building ninety feet long and thirty feet wide. The solution envisaged at the beginning and end of the prayer (6:20, 40) is that His *"eyes"* are on it and His *"ears"* listen to the temple prayers. Or, as 7:16 will state, His *"heart will be there"*; indeed, His *"name"* is there, a statement which, as in Deuteronomy 12:11–12, signifies a real but limited presence. At this point scriptural revelation is moving in the direction of incarnation, and it is no coincidence that John 2:19–21 relates Jesus to the temple.

The seven petitions envisaged in 6:22–39 are all framed in the same multiple pattern, which describes (1) a situation of need, (2) temple-centered prayer and requests for (3) a divine hearing, and (4) a reversal of the situation. It is noticeable that in four cases out of the seven the basic situation is explicitly linked with human sinning (6:22, 24, 26, 36), while in a fifth case the accompanying note of forgiveness (6:30) implies it. The motif of forgiveness is pervasive, although it is absent from the first case in 6:22–23, where the concern is for social justice among God's people. In practically every case except that of 6:32–33 there is an emphasis on God's grace to the undeserving. In fact, the instance of the foreigner there is similar, inasmuch as it concerns one who cannot claim help but nevertheless asks for it. The only instance that does not accord with this program is in 6:34–35, the request for victory in a war approved by God. Probably its role is to serve as a foil for the final case of national defeat and even deportation instigated by God (6:36–39), to enhance its shocking and degenerate nature. The note of human sin and so of divine grace is remarkable. It breaks the orderly, normal arrangement calmly envisaged in 6:14, of divine and human partners in the covenant who gentleman-like both keep their side of the bargain. An adequate theology must cater for the abnormal, because sinning is an essential part of the human condition: *"there is no one who does not sin"* (6:36). The British king Charles II once called Presbyterianism *"not a religion for gentlemen."* He was speaking in social terms; in a stricter moral sense a religion for gentlemen would eventually have no honest subscribers left. The Chronicler was no stranger to this realistic viewpoint. In his Davidic prototype of temple prayer God answered a sinner's plea (1 Chron. 21:26).

The theology of the temple frankly faces up to this factor in the lives of individual believers and of God's people as a whole. The Chronicler took the space to copy out this long prayer from Kings because it illustrates so well his image of a God who took sinners back. Sin is not condoned: there is a stress on repentance in 6:24–26 (they *"turn from their sin"*), 6:29, 37–38 (*"return to You with all their heart and with all their soul"*). In 6:37 the rendering of NKJV, *"come to themselves,"* adopted from the Jerusalem Bible, nicely evokes the parable of the prodigal son (Luke 15:17), but it is a little loose, and a closer idiomatic rendering would be "think again" or "have second thoughts." The NEB renders "learn their lesson" and the New Jerusalem Bible "come to their senses." The Hebrew phrase means recalling what one did when carried away by self-will and reconsidering it in the cold light of day. In the central scenario there is emphasis on sincerity and God's ability to read the human mind (6:30), while the final one features a wholehearted response (v. 38). As the jingle goes,

> It's not enough to say
> " I'm sorry and repent,"
> And then to go on afterwards
> Just as you always went.

Repentance is a matter of heart and mind; it is a mental and spiritual realignment with God's will. Divine forgiveness requires it as a human condition or, more exactly, requires person-to-person prayer that gives expression to it. In the Chronicler's presentation of Solomon's temple, and in Chronicles generally, penitent prayer, rather than sacrifice, tends to be the God-appointed way of reconciliation.

One of the scenarios makes those of us who are Gentiles feel at home in this predominantly Israelite setting. Verse 32 portrays a foreigner who is drawn as by a magnet to the temple because of God's exploits on behalf of His people. The urging of God to honor such a prayer in verse 33 significantly regards it as a stimulus to universal faith. Isaiah 56:7 speaks of the temple in similar terms as "a house of prayer for all nations." According to Mark 11:17 Jesus cited that text in condemning the blatant commercialization in the Court of the Gentiles: it presented a poor testimony to Gentiles frequenting that area of the temple to which they were allowed access.

After the final request concerning a theology of temple prayer (6:40), which recapitulates the initial 6:20, the prayer ends in a different way in the Chronicles version. Basically it is a quotation of Psalm 132:8–10. It accords with the preceding prayer in that it associates, without identifying, God with the ark. The quotation fittingly echoes David's description of the temple as "a house of rest" in 1 Chronicles 28:2. The concept of God's rest introduces a note of finality which suited a revelatory era that stretched from David to the Chronicler's day and, as he believed, was to usher in the kingdom of God centered in the temple and a restored Davidic monarchy. It was not to be: God fulfills His word in ways often surprising to the human mind. However, the expectation which this formal assumption of a resting place implies did not fall into the limbo of disappointed dreams. Hebrews 3:7–4:13 renews its relevance, insisting that "there remains . . . a rest for the people of God," a rest which is the corollary of God's rest. The writer to the Hebrews associates this note of finality not with Psalm 132 but mainly with another royal psalm. The promise which Christ inherited, to "sit at My right hand, / Till I make Your enemies Your footstool" (Ps. 110:1), was related to His presence in heaven after taking His seat in the heavenly sanctuary (Heb. 8:1; 10:11, 12). By this session He has become "the finisher of our faith" (Heb. 12:2). The divine promise to Christ makes the future hostage to His will. A similar note of finality underlies the idea of a resting place here, whereby God is invited to take His seat, as it were, in the temple. It will involve the dawn of a temple era in which its personnel would be mediators of God's *salvation.* This term is employed as it is in the psalms of lament and thanksgiving in the Psalter, to refer to God's rescuing from a situation of human crisis. So here it fittingly describes the granting of need-oriented petitions requested in the body of Solomon's prayer. The priests were the transmitters of this salvation, inasmuch as they passed on God's favorable answers and promises of restoration (see Pss. 22:21; 85:8, 9). The reference to God's *saints* (6:41) could allude in this context to the Levites whose role it was to sing joyfully of God's goodness (5:13). However, *saints* means strictly "recipients of the steadfast love" of God and so more appropriately here refers to the people, who were described in similar terms in verse 14. The people's singing of the Levites' chorus in 7:3 supports this interpretation, for it seems to be picking up 6:41. Further support comes from the mention of the people's joy and God's goodness in the same breath at 7:10. In making this emphasis the Chronicler was doubtless not only thinking in purely historical terms but himself rejoicing in a spiritual opportunity that still availed for him and his contemporaries. In turn we Christians may rejoice that we may "find grace to help in time of need" from a God who is "able to save" (Heb. 4:16; 5:7).

The final verse of the prayer blends Psalm 132:10 with a phrase from Isaiah 55:3. It becomes Solomon's appeal to God to hear his royal prayer on the basis of God's "steadfast love" to his father. The covenant God made with David in 1 Chronicles 17 envisaged both Solomon's building of the temple and the establishment of a permanent dynasty as lying within the will of God. Since temple and dynasty were intertwined, the temple prayer ends as it began in 6:16–17, with a petition that God might fulfill the dynastic promise He made to David. The Kings version of the prayer ends with a reference to "Your Servant Moses" (1 Kings 8:53) and to the Exodus. Significantly Moses is here eclipsed by *"Your servant David"* as the founder under God of a new era, an era of steadfast love. As Acts 13:34 declares, it was an era that would culminate in the resurrection of Jesus as God's act of proclamation concerning His messianic role.

2. *Temple worship.* God answers Solomon's prayer in stages. First, there is a symbolic answer to his call to formally take up His resting place (6:41) and to endorse the installation of the ark. There is *"fire . . . from heaven"* (7:1) in acceptance of the sacrifices of worship offered in 5:6 immediately after the ark was installed. The miracle is an echo of 1 Chronicles 21:26 where the temple site was divinely sanctioned in this way. The temple, approved then in principle, is now finally designated by God as His. It is God's seal of approval on the work of David and Solomon as stewards of the temple and its associated era.

This is an endorsement further to that of 5:13, 14. The two are connected; indeed, 7:1b might be rendered "and the glory of the Lord was (still) filling the temple." Verse 3 introduces a new note. Whereas the revelation of 5:13, 14 affected only the priests, as 7:1b–2 serves to remind us, this revelation is observed by *"all the children of Israel"* (7:3). Seeing the fire on the altar of burnt offering and now also the glory *"on* (rather than 'in') *the temple,"* they receive assurance of the divine role of the temple, to which they may bring their praise and prayers. God was making known to His people His commitment to the temple as focus of His glory and grace. The Chronicler wants us to think of Leviticus 9:23–24 where the sacrifices of the tabernacle were authenticated by supernatural fire before all the people. The recapitulation of the attestation of the tabernacle serves to confirm that the temple is a divine institution that has taken its place. The double attestation of the temple, in 5:13, 14 and 7:1–3a, reminds me of the twofold divine endorsement of Jesus, with a voice from heaven at His baptism and a voice from the cloud of glory at His transfiguration (Mark 1:11; 9:7). In both Chronicles and the Gospel story readers are left in no doubt as to the focus of God's will thereafter.

The people respond to the revelation with further worship. If in chapter 5 revelation was a gracious response to worship, here it is its inspiration. God's consecration of the temple warrants a service of dedication (7:5). The people take up the Levitical chorus of 5:13, and indeed *"rejoice in* [God's] *goodness,"* in terms of 6:41. They celebrate the "steadfast love" (RSV) of God, not only as a feature of the national covenant which antedated David (6:14, compare Deut. 7:9), but now enriched by the Davidic covenant which inaugurated a new era of grace (6:42). Nor can one detach the term from Solomon's virtual invocation of God's grace in the forgiveness of sins in 6:27 and following verses. The temple enshrined the grace of God.

According to 7:8–10 the service of dedication, celebrated so enthusiastically that the altar of burnt offering proved too small to accommodate the sacrifices (7:7), lasted a week and was then followed by the Feast of Tabernacles. This festival provided a further week of worship, which reached a climax on the eighth day. The Chronicler is here using 1 Kings 8:65–66; but he carefully aligns it with the Torah's requirements for the festival, in Leviticus 23:34–36, 39–43. The Torah's festivals continued in the new era, receiving a new rendezvous. For the Chronicler the Kings reference to the northern and southern parameters of *"the entrance of Hamath"* and *"the Brook of Egypt"* (7:8) takes on added significance. It draws a parallel with David's assembly for the initial transportation of the ark (1 Chron. 13:5). It also reinforces a theme beloved by the Chronicler and so often expressed, as here, in the phrase *"all Israel."* Here is the challenge of the whole of God's people united in worshiping God. It should have spoken volumes to a divided people in the post-exilic period when the Chronicler wrote. Should it say less to a divided church? It also portrays for the Chronicler a future ideal which he believed God would in His own time establish, the ideal of the people of God occupying the land of Israel to its furthest frontiers and united both in worship and under a king of David's line. Luke to some extent took up this hope in the archangel's message to Mary that one day Jesus would *"reign over the house of Jacob forever"* (Luke 1:33).

All good things come to an end. Reluctantly, one feels, the Chronicler records Solomon's formal dismissal of the people. In combining references to *"David"* and *"Solomon"* (7:10) he wants to remind us that their reigns were two halves of a single episode of divine revelation (compare 11:17; 35:4). He adds verse 11: here was a further step in the completion of the temple. The success invoked by David for its building had been duly enjoyed: *"successfully accomplished"* renders the Hebrew verb translated "prosper" in 1 Chronicles 22:11. "Mission accomplished," reports the Chronicler.

3. *Temple theology.* The resurrection of Jesus is sometimes called the Father's "Amen" to the Son's 'It is finished." Verses 12–22 certainly present God's "Amen" to Solomon's finishing the temple (7:11). More precisely they are a response to his prayer in 6:14–42, in a private revelation. The Chronicler's account is an amplification of 1 Kings 9:2–9. What was expressed in symbol in verse 1 is now expressed in word. The Temple is God's *"chosen" "house of sacrifice"* (7:12). Sacrifice was a prime role of the temple, so much so that its dedication (7:5) could be called *"the dedication of the altar"* (7:9). Solomon had himself summed up the temple's purpose in such terms at 2:6. This meant for the Chronicler that the temple was the accredited place of worship. It reflected the greatness of God not only in its static splendor but through its ongoing sacrifices. Sacrifice was a symbolic expression of worship. This is why there is mention of myriads of sacrificial victims at 7:5. In 5:6 God's ineffable greatness was honored by innumerable gifts of sacrifice. The writer to the Hebrews followed in the Chronicler's train when he mentioned the Christian obligation to offer to God *"the sacrifice of praise,"* except that the concept of sacrifice is changed from a material symbol of praise to a metaphor for praise, *"the fruit of our lips"* (Heb. 13:15). Praise is

surely in mind also at 1 Peter 2:5: the local church is a "spiritual" temple in which "spiritual sacrifices" are offered.

I remember in my late teens being impatient with what was called in my religious circle "the worship meeting," which culminated in the Lord's Supper every Sunday morning. Why not shorten it and give practical teaching to the congregation, very many of whom seemed to attend only that service? Perhaps there was some validity in my objections, but there was more wrong with my own attitude than with the service. With the restless energy of youth I wanted to be up and doing or at least learning how one should live the Christian life: worship went over the same old ground week after week. Yet what better ground to occupy than to sit before the Lord in worship? The activist cannot keep going without recharging his batteries: he needs to learn above all that "the joy of the Lord is your strength" (Neh. 8:10). The Lord's Supper, celebrated with a worshipful heart becomes for the worshiper "bread that strengthens and wine that cheers," as a communion hymn affirms.[1] One mentions such byproducts of worship not to justify worship but as an *argumentum ad hominem*, so that expediency, if nothing else, may prod God's people into worshiping Him (see Hos. 2:6, 7 and Luke 15:17, 18!).

If the temple was the chosen place of worship, it was also the chosen place of prayer (7:13–16). The burden of Solomon's praying in 6:18–40 is given divine approval. The needs expressed in verse 13 are a digest of the scenarios portrayed there. The implication, made amply explicit in the royal prayer, is that God's sinning people are suffering the consequences of willful departure from God's will. There is an agenda of human cause and divine effect, of wild sowing and woeful reaping. This agenda, however, at whose justice none can cavil, lies in the background. It gives way to another agenda, presented in 7:14. This is one of the two keys of Chronicles, the other being 1 Chronicles 17:12, a pair of verses which puts the Chronicler's theology into two nutshells. They are God's words of revelation spoken to David and Solomon as pioneers of a new era and through them to the people of God, generation after generation. The Chronicler will construct the rest of his history around this second verse. Its recurring vocabulary will show that its model for spirituality may either be embraced for one's good or rejected at one's peril. Here in 7:14 is another law of cause and effect, a happier one than the former one implied in 7:13. Where sin abounds, grace may superabound. The low road from sin to disaster could be left by a track which wound back to a high road from obedience to blessing. This track ran alongside the temple, where God's gracious provision of prayer was available. If disobedience had been rampant, all was not lost: there was an opportunity for obeying God's law of restoration. If every rule in the book had been broken, one more ruling is revealed, vibrant with grace and hope, here in 7:14.

Prayer could trigger the grace of God, provided that it was humble prayer that abandoned the brazenness of disobedience and came, cap in hand, into God's presence at the temple. The prayer was to be the expression of seeking God's *"face,"* a spiritual attitude that was ready to turn to God and let His will prevail in one's life (see 1 Chron. 16:11). The prayer had to be accompanied by a resolve to start again with God and leave the bad, old lifestyle behind. Such a prayer was a tough option—but it was the only option left. It was far from a glib recital of a formula of confession. It reached to the heart and soul, as 6:38 indicated. One cannot keep using the past tense, for so lavish is the promise that it spills over into Christian experience. Indeed, verse 14 is well known through Jimmy Owens' oratorio "If My People," popular a decade or so ago. Such a prayer opens up the heart and soul to God, allowing Him to penetrate to the core of our wills and put His will there. The Hebrew idiom which underlies *"called by My name"* (7:14) refers to ownership. God owns His people: He has a claim on their lives because they owe to Him their existence as the people of God. His first claim is for obedience to His covenant will. Yet if they turn aside and go down a path of their own choosing, they find Him standing in their way, reaffirming His claim, now shot through with grace since it offers another chance.

God is here promising to honor such prayer and wipe the slate clean. Moreover, He undertakes to bring healing where there was a failure and loss. In Solomon's prayer Israel's land was featured as the area of deprivation and corresponding blessing (6:25, 27, 28, 31). The land functioned as a spiritual thermometer, registering the people's degree of compliance with the will of God. A frowning providence would be replaced by the smile of God's favor. It would bring new growth where before there had been decay.

Here then is the theology of the temple. It is a pastoral theology, for it comes to where people so often are and compassionately points the way back from failure. It is an evangelical theology, for it meets sin with forgiveness, while it safeguards morality by means of repentance. How shortsighted some Christians are in wanting to see a theology of grace in the New Testament and failing to see its presence in the Old! Even the God of the Mosaic covenant proved that He could cope with failure: as soon as the covenant was made, divine grace had to pick up the broken pieces and start again (Exod. 32–34). Thereafter God was celebrated as "merciful and gracious, longsuffering, and abounding in goodness and truth" (or better "steadfast love and faithfulness," Exod. 34:6). In the temple era, so prized by the Chronicler, the temple became a monument to the grace of God as the channel of prayer and pardon. Moreover, as a place of sacrificial praise, it was a monument to the greatness of God. In both roles it witnessed the people's submission to Him as their Lord, whether in relative spiritual health they brought their sacrifices of praise or, falling into spiritual ill health, brought their prayers of repentance. The temple bore theological witness to God's power and to His restoring love.

In 7:17–18 the divine communication turns to respond to Solomon's request made at the beginning and end of his prayer, concerning the dynastic succession of Davidic kings. The condition of building the temple, laid down in 1 Chronicles 17:12, had been met. The other condition of general obedience, reported by David in 1 Chronicles 28:7, was a continuing one. Special service ever moves within an orbit of general obedience. It was the Chronicler's conviction that Solomon did meet the latter condition. His account of Solomon's reign was to end in a glorious sunset of tributes to him and to his God. In 7:18 there is a significant upgrading of a verb: whereas 1 Kings 9:5 used "promised," the Chronicler uses the stronger "*covenanted.*" God had made a solemn pledge which amounted to a new deal for Israel. The Chronicler was one who, like his noble descendants in Luke 2:38, "looked for redemption in Jerusalem," redemption via restoration of David's royal line. There is a clue to this royal hope in the phrase "*as ruler in Israel*" (7:18), which replaces "on the throne of Israel" (1 Kings 9:5). Certainly the paraphrase means the same, but the Chronicler is writing with an eye on the dynastic promise of the pre-exilic prophet Micah (Mic. 5:2), where this language occurs. For him the promise had not been annulled by the Exile. It remained in the counsels of God, awaiting His timing for restoring the monarchy.

In 7:19 the king and people are addressed together—the Hebrew verbs are plural—while the nation is in view in 7:20–22. If 7:17–18 counseled obedience, these warn of disobedience. This negative passage is much longer than the earlier positive one: the human heart is ever more prone to wrong. It is a contrasting echo of 1 Chronicles 28:8, where God promised possession of the land to the obedient. Here its loss is envisaged as a result of disobedience. Shockingly even the temple could be abandoned by God. The rhetorical device of question and answer in 7:21–22 dramatically teaches the folly of turning one's back on God. Exodus, ungratefully forgotten, would give way to Exile in Israel's experience. Israel refused to listen, and it will be the Chronicler's sad task to recount the sorry tale of the people's disobedience and its sequel of disaster. There are two redeeming features, however. The first is the dynastic promise: once Solomon's reign is over, it stands as a perpetual guarantee for the future. Any hint that Israel's disobedience would lead to forfeiture of the promised line of kings is totally lacking. The second is the conception of God presented in 6:18–7:16. Despite the dire words of 7:20, the earlier passage had shown God to be one who could take Exile in His gracious stride. 6:24–25 had dared to speak of a positive future beyond banishment. Obedience or doom-laden disobedience were not the only options open to God's people. Repentance that led to restoration was a third option made available by a God of grace. It will be the Chronicler's recurring testimony in later chapters not only that his people's history is littered with the wrecks of sin but that God came to their rescue in response to their conscience-stricken cries for help.

There is a tension in these chapters which the New Testament and the Christian pastor also know. On the one hand God issues a solemn call for compliance and integrity; on the other hand there is fervent assurance of forgiveness and a fresh chance. There is inconsistency in this double message. Untidy as it is, it is true to life and so to God's realistic program. It poses a problem, however, in that the faithful preacher of morality can sound legalistic and the preacher of forgiveness can give the impression that sinning does not matter. Yet both messages are necessary. The underlying logic of the double message is supplied in 1 John 2:1: "I am writing this . . . so that you may not sin; but if any one does sin . . ." (RSV). For the Chronicler, as for the editor of Kings, the moral issue was resolved to a certain degree by a stress on repentance; as a second best God is prepared to take the thought for the deed and to accept conscience in place of constancy. Another relevant factor is an emphasis that runs through the Old Testament prophets, that God's way with His people is a sequence of judgment and salvation. In the scenarios of chapter 6 sin leads to suffering, which is brought to a premature end by God's gracious reversal. Perhaps human psychology demands such scenarios. Until we fall on the banana skin of failure, we are apt to walk with a jaunty air of self-confidence, imagining ourselves masters and mistresses of our destiny. If God is to have His way with us, it seems that we have first to fall and humbly realize our need for help from outside ourselves. The wonder is that the grim either-or of verses 17–22 is not God's only word; beyond just deserts lies undeserved grace.

A BLUEPRINT FOR GOD'S KINGDOM

8:1 It came to pass at the end of twenty years, when Solomon had built the house of the LORD and his own house,

2 that the cities which Hiram had given to Solomon, Solomon built them; and he settled the children of Israel there.

3 And Solomon went to Hamath Zobah and seized it.

4 He also built Tadmor in the wilderness, and all the storage cities which he built in Hamath.

5 He built Upper Beth Horon and Lower Beth Horon, fortified cities *with* walls, gates, and bars,

6 also Baalath and all the storage cities that Solomon had, and all the chariot cities and the cities of the cavalry, and all that Solomon desired to build in Jerusalem, in Lebanon, and in all the land of his dominion.

7 All the people *who were* left of the Hittites, Amorites, Perizzites, Hivites, and Jebusites, who *were* not of Israel—

8 that is, their descendants who were left in the land after them, whom the children of Israel did not destroy—from these Solomon raised forced labor, as it is to this day.

9 But Solomon did not make the children of Israel servants for his work. Some *were* men of war, captains of his officers, captains of his chariots, and his cavalry.

10 And others *were* chiefs of the officials of King Solomon: two hundred and fifty, who ruled over the people.

11 Now Solomon brought the daughter of Pharaoh up from the City of David to the house he had built for her, for he said, "My wife shall not dwell in the house of David king of Israel, because *the places* to which the ark of the LORD has come are holy."

12 Then Solomon offered burnt offerings to the LORD on the altar of the LORD which he had built before the vestibule,

13 according to the daily rate, offering according to the commandment of Moses, for the Sabbaths, the New Moons, and the three appointed yearly feasts—the Feast of Unleavened Bread, the Feast of Weeks, and the Feast of Tabernacles.

14 And, according to the order of David his father, he appointed the divisions of the priests for their service, the Levites for their duties (to praise and serve before the priests) as the duty of each day required, and the gatekeepers by their divisions at each gate; for so David the man of God had commanded.

15 They did not depart from the command of the king to the priests and Levites concerning any matter or concerning the treasuries.

16 Now all the work of Solomon was well-ordered from the day of the foundation of the house of the LORD until it was finished. So the house of the LORD was completed.

17 Then Solomon went to Ezion Geber and Elath on the seacoast, in the land of Edom.

18 And Hiram sent him ships by the hand of his servants, and servants who knew the sea. They went with the servants of Solomon to Ophir, and acquired

four hundred and fifty talents of gold from there, and brought it to King Solomon.

9:1 Now when the queen of Sheba heard of the fame of Solomon, she came to Jerusalem to test Solomon with hard questions, *having* a very great retinue, camels that bore spices, gold in abundance, and precious stones; and when she came to Solomon, she spoke with him about all that was in her heart.

2 So Solomon answered all her questions; there was nothing so difficult for Solomon that he could not explain it to her.

3 And when the queen of Sheba had seen the wisdom of Solomon, the house that he had built,

4 the food on his table, the seating of his servants, the service of his waiters and their apparel, his cupbearers and their apparel, and his entryway by which he went up to the house of the LORD, there was no more spirit in her.

5 Then she said to the king: "*It was* a true report which I heard in my own land about your words and your wisdom.

6 "However I did not believe their words until I came and saw with my own eyes; and indeed the half of the greatness of your wisdom was not told me. You exceed the fame of which I heard.

7 "Happy *are* your men and happy *are* these your servants, who stand continually before you and hear your wisdom!

8 "Blessed be the LORD your God, who delighted in you, setting you on His throne *to be* king for the LORD your God! Because your God has loved Israel, to establish them forever, therefore He made you king over them, to do justice and righteousness."

9 And she gave the king one hundred and twenty talents of gold, spices in great abundance, and precious stones; there never were any spices such as those the queen of Sheba gave to King Solomon.

10 Also, the servants of Hiram and the servants of Solomon, who brought gold from Ophir, brought algum wood and precious stones.

11 And the king made walkways *of* the algum wood for the house of the LORD and for the king's house,

also harps and stringed instruments for singers; and there were none such *as these* seen before in the land of Judah.

12 Now King Solomon gave to the queen of Sheba all she desired, whatever she asked, *much more* than she had brought to the king. So she turned and went to her own country, she and her servants.

13 The weight of gold that came to Solomon yearly was six hundred and sixty-six talents of gold,

14 besides *what* the traveling merchants and traders brought. And all the kings of Arabia and governors of the country brought gold and silver to Solomon.

15 And King Solomon made two hundred large shields of hammered gold; six hundred *shekels* of hammered gold went into each shield.

16 *He* also *made* three hundred shields of hammered gold; three hundred *shekels* of gold went into each shield. The king put them in the House of the Forest of Lebanon.

17 Moreover the king made a great throne of ivory, and overlaid it with pure gold.

18 The throne *had* six steps, with a footstool of gold, *which were* fastened to the throne; there were armrests on either side of the place of the seat, and two lions stood beside the armrests.

19 Twelve lions stood there, one on each side of the six steps; nothing like *this* had been made for any *other* kingdom.

20 All King Solomon's drinking vessels *were* gold, and all the vessels of the House of the Forest of Lebanon *were* pure gold. Not *one was* silver, for this was accounted as nothing in the days of Solomon.

21 For the king's ships went to Tarshish with the servants of Hiram. Once every three years the merchant ships came, bringing gold, silver, ivory, apes, and monkeys.

22 So King Solomon surpassed all the kings of the earth in riches and wisdom.

23 And all the kings of the earth sought the presence of Solomon to hear his wisdom, which God had put in his heart.

24 Each man brought his present: articles of silver

and gold, garments, armor, spices, horses, and mules, at a set rate year by year.

25 Solomon had four thousand stalls for horses and chariots, and twelve thousand horsemen whom he stationed in the chariot cities and with the king at Jerusalem.

26 So he reigned over all the kings from the River to the land of the Philistines, as far as the border of Egypt.

27 The king made silver *as common* in Jerusalem as stones, and he made cedar trees as abundant as the sycamores which *are* in the lowland.

28 And they brought horses to Solomon from Egypt and from all lands.

29 Now the rest of the acts of Solomon, first and last, *are* they not written in the book of Nathan the prophet, in the prophecy of Ahijah the Shilonite, and in the visions of Iddo the seer concerning Jeroboam the son of Nebat?

30 Solomon reigned in Jerusalem over all Israel forty years.

31 Then Solomon rested with his fathers, and was buried in the City of David his father. And Rehoboam his son reigned in his place.

2 Chron. 8:1–9:31

In commenting on chapter 1 we observed that the triple pattern of worship, wisdom, and wealth developed in the interests of the temple finds a parallel at the end of the account, now with reference to Solomon's royal role. In the initial patterning there were sideglances at his rule, in 1:10–11 and later in the mention of his building a palace at 2:1–2. This minor motif occurred too in 7:11. Now his secular kingship comes to the fore. Temple concerns remain in view but now as a subsidiary theme. Solomon wore two hats, as temple-builder and as empire-builder. This latter concern of Solomon as the architect of a world power does not lack spiritual value. The key verse of this section is 9:8, the Queen of Sheba's commendation of Solomon's kingly role, which functions as a parallel to Hiram's declaration in 2:12 concerning his temple role. God set Solomon *"on His throne."* Here then was a manifestation of the kingdom of God, a model for its re-establishment, as the Chronicler hoped, in God's good time. To use T. S. Eliot's words, "time future" was "contained in time past."

The Chronicler makes use of 1 Kings 9:10–10:29, adding his own emphases. Solomon's building work is reviewed in 8:1–10, as an achievement brought about with the help of the labor force levied in 2:2, 17–18. The secular close of the negotiations pursued with Hiram in 2:3–16 is noted in verse 2. There is a conscious parallelism in chapters 8–9 with chapters 1–2, to show the complementary nature of Solomon's double work for God. In 8:1–10 Solomon functions as Israel's champion, forwarding God's purposes for His people. Just as David's kingship was consciously exercised as a divine mandate for the sake of Israel (1 Chron. 14:2), so Israel's interests are stressed as a goal of Solomon's rule at the beginning and end, in 8:2, 9.

1. *Worship*. While the motif of building runs over into 8:11–12, and 16, it cannot resist turning back into a temple-oriented one. Solomon's religious and secular roles are intertwined in these final chapters devoted to his reign. Verse 11 presents his concern for the holiness of the temple, even while proudly parading his association with the world power of Egypt. In reminiscence of Israel's territorial frontiers in 7:8, Solomon's sphere of political influence is noted as expanding to include Hamath in the north and Egypt in the south. The religious concern to move his Egyptian wife from proximity to the temple at first sight runs counter to the openheartedness of 6:32, 33 to foreign worship. The Chronicler has at the back of his mind the sinister narrative of 1 Kings 11:1–8: she did not fall into the category of a foreign proselyte but maintained her national faith. To such the temple with its blessings was out of bounds, and the concern was rather to put an appropriate distance between it and the devotee of an alien religion.

In 8:12–16 this religious concern is further exemplified in the establishment of a regular system of worship, which serves as a supplement to the temple account, rounding it off (8:16). Solomon sets going the clock of religious worship which was to operate for centuries into post-exilic times, transcending the hiccup of the Exile. Year in, year out, day in, day out, it would keep ticking away to the glory of God, in a tradition of worship which gave a great God pride of place in human hearts and in a human society. The Chronicler's aim was to show that it rested on the double foundation of two men of God, *"the commandment of Moses"* and also of *"David"* (8:13–14).

The sacrificial and festal system was taken over intact from the old era of God's dealings with Israel. To it were added the arrangements concerning temple administration inaugurated by David, including the Levites' duties of assisting the priests and singing God's praises. Israel's religious faith stood firmly on this double foundation, the old and the new. In like manner the church must never forget that its faith is founded solidly on God's double revelation in the Old Testament and the New.

2. *Wisdom.* From now on the motifs of wisdom and wealth run in tandem, with now one and now the other predominating. The *"four hundred and fifty talents of gold"* in 8:18 connect with the *"one hundred and twenty talents of gold"* in 9:9 (compare *"gold in abundance,"* 9:1) and *"six hundred and sixty-six talents of gold"*—no apocalyptic reference intended!—of 9:13. In 9:1–9 Solomon's wealth is only one of two dominant themes. The Arabian queen comes bearing tribute, as the Chronicler emphasizes in 9:1 and 9:9, but it is his wisdom that takes her breath away (9:3–6). The breakdown of this wisdom in terms of the splendor of his palace lifestyle leads to a testimony to the hand of God in all this (9:8). Again, as in 2:11, God so *"loved Israel"* that He gave them Solomon: God's forwarding of His people's interests continues to be a concern for the Chronicler. The account of Solomon's secular greatness is not intended as glorification of a human leader nor as a nostalgic memory of imperial status to beat a patriotic drum. It is no less than a glimpse of the kingdom of God, a drawing back of the veil of the future when, as the prophets encouraged the Chronicler to believe, God's king would *"be great to the ends of the earth"* (Mic. 5:4). In 1 Chronicles 16:31 David's desire was that it would be said *"among the nations, 'The Lord reigns.'"* Here is that testimony, foreshadowing the end times. Indeed, if God is to come to *"judge the earth"* (1 Chron. 16:33), already that judging was anticipated by Solomon's establishment of *"justice and righteousness"* within Israel's frontiers (9:8) in a prefiguring of that just society to be set up by the coming Davidic king (see Isa. 9:7; 11:1–5). Indeed, tribute from Sheba was a promise of one of the royal psalms (Ps. 72:10), which in the post-exilic Psalter are already imbued with future hope. There is a stress on fabulous newness in Solomon's reign (9:9, amplified in 9:11), which inaugurates future expectation. His reign, although so long for the Chronicler, was a window on God's eventual plans for His people. His purpose was *"to establish*

them forever" (9:8), a notion with which Paul wrestled in Romans 9–11 and eventually affirmed.

3. *Wealth.* The overarching motif which binds together 8:17–9:28 is Solomon's wealth in various forms, such as *"precious stones"* (9:1, 9–10) and *"spices"* (9:1, 9, 24), as well as *"gold"* (8:18; 9:1, 9, 13–24). The whole passage is a kaleidoscope of opulence. Gold, silver, ivory, spices, and precious stones—each is featured in turn, alone or in combination. It is a symbol of royal power, all the more magnificent against a backdrop of post-exilic austerity. If Solomon's reign was marked by uniqueness in relation to the past (9:9, 11), it was also characterized by uniqueness in respect of contemporary kingdoms (9:10, 22). 9:21 strikes an exotic note not only in its list of fabulous imports but also in its mention of *"Tarshish,"* which caught the Hebrew imagination, being the equivalent of Timbuktu for the Victorians or of Cathay for the Venetians.

9:22–28, into which the Chronicler has enlarged his source in 1 Kings 10 by working in references to 1 Kings 4:21 and 26 at 9:26 and 9:25b respectively, explicitly relate Solomon's wealth and wisdom to his royal power. Tribute and esteem are, relatively speaking, universal. The section begins with *"all the kings of the earth,"* has *"all the kings"* at its heart, and closes with *"all lands."* This position of universal power and prestige is traced back to God's endowment in the case of Solomon's wisdom (9:23). Again, the account is intended to transcend history. It foreshadows the coming time when not only would the *"kings of Tarshish"* and *"Sheba"* bring tribute, but *"all kings"* would *"fall down"* and *"all nations serve"* the restored Davidic king (Ps. 72:10–11). The reader of the first Gospel is familiar with prodigious history of this type. The Magi came from the east bearing gifts of gold, frankincense, and myrrh to the infant Jesus in His role as King of the Jews (Matt. 2:1–12). They *"fell down and worshiped"* (or *"served"*) Him. Implicit in Matthew's account is a fulfillment of Psalm 72 (see also Isa. 60:5, 6). It is not of course intended as a complete fulfillment but as an anticipatory one. It pointed beyond its own time to the future role of the Child, just as the Triumphal Entry of Jesus proclaimed His kingship in prophetic principle (Matt. 21:1–11). *"A greater than Solomon"* was *"here"* (Matt. 12:42). He is the one to whom *"all authority has been given . . . in heaven"* as well as *"on earth"* (Matt. 28:18). The world has yet to see the fullness of His glory. If the church has already glimpsed what "eye has not seen, nor ear heard" (1 Cor. 2:9; compare 2 Chron. 9:6), what will be the splendor of the kingdom of God in its fullness?

The epilogue to Solomon's reign in 9:29–31 brings us back to earth. It tells us firmly that the topic of the kingdom is marked by a "not yet." The Chronicler uses 1 Kings 11:41–43. The narratives of 1 Kings 11:1–40 are conspicuous by their absence in Chronicles, although the Chronicler was aware of them, as we have seen and shall see further. Notably he did not include the story of Solomon's backsliding in 1 Kings 11:1–8. Did the charge not convey to him the heinousness there associated with it? Perhaps he was countering it in 8:11. In Chronicles Solomon rides into a glorious sunset, his double mission accomplished—the temple built and the Davidic dynasty secured (see 13:5–8; 21:7). In the epilogue the Chronicler necessarily changes the source reference from the one used by the Kings editor to his own. It refers in prophetic terms to 1 Kings, with its initial involvement of *"Nathan the prophet"* (1 Kings 1) and its final prophecy of *"Ahijah"* (1 Kings 11:29–39; according to Josephus, *"Iddo"* was the name of the anonymous prophet of 1 Kings 13:1–10). The basic narrative of Solomon was a prophetic narrative for the Chronicler, like that of David (1 Chron. 29:29). Our historian stood foursquare on the foundation of the Law and the Prophets, true to the revelation associated with Moses on the one hand and David and Solomon on the other. They spoke to him with divine authority. We live in an age which has experienced a crisis of authority. It is adrift, floating toward the rapids of subjectivity and relativism, rather than steering upstream to truth and the absolute. The Chronicler beckons us in his direction, assuring us from his example that the human mind is not thereby passively locked into the thinking of the past but may find ample stimulation to creative reflection and contextualization.

NOTE

1. I am unable to give the author. The hymn begins "Jesus, Lord, we know Thee present" and appears in *Hymns of Light and Love* (Bath: Echoes of Service, n.d.).

CHAPTER ELEVEN

The Parting of the Ways

2 Chronicles 10:1–12:16

A sigh must have escaped the Chronicler's lips as he reached this point in his history of the Israelite monarchy. The heyday of his story is over. With the death of Solomon the history of God's people takes on a more mundane and certainly a less colorful hue. Gone is the glorious unity of the people of God. In chapters 10–28 the Chronicler narrates the fortunes of the truncated kingdom of Judah after the breakaway of the northern tribes to form a separate state. Unlike Kings, which keeps pace with both states by switching between north and south, Chronicles focuses on the southern state, as the habitat of the temple and of the Davidic throne. The twin institutions of temple and dynasty have been set among the covenant people as focal points of God's purposes. How will the human stewards of these institutions treat the means of grace entrusted to them as generation succeeds generation? In their varied responses lie lessons for the post-exilic community of faith, and perchance for Christians too.

The reign of David was the occasion for God's revelation of a theology linking palace and temple (1 Chron. 17:12), while Solomon's reign saw the revelation of a theology of repentance and restoration (2 Chron. 7:14). The coming chapters presuppose the first theology and find it necessary to invoke the second, especially in the reign of Rehoboam, Solomon's immediate successor. From now on the reigns of David and Solomon become the standard against which to measure subsequent reigns, as the closing statement in 11:17 illustrates: "they walked in the way of David and Solomon for three years." Most of the reigns of the southern kings are found wanting. Rehoboam's reign is used to portray contrasting scenarios: obedience spells divine blessing, while disobedience brings disaster. That is not to be the end of the story, however. God's ultimate will is positive rather than negative: He is just a prayer away, ever ready to answer a call from the contrite heart. The Chronicler is not interested in history for its own sake. His concern has to do with the perennial ways of God with His people. This makes his writings a good read for any Christian.

THE VALUE OF LISTENING

10:1 And Rehoboam went to Shechem, for all Israel had gone to Shechem to make him king.

2 So it happened, when Jeroboam the son of Nebat heard *it* (he was in Egypt, where he had fled from the presence of King Solomon), that Jeroboam returned from Egypt.

3 Then they sent for him and called him. And Jeroboam and all Israel came and spoke to Rehoboam, saying,

4 "Your father made our yoke heavy; now therefore, lighten the burdensome service of your father and his heavy yoke which he put on us, and we will serve you."

5 So he said to them, "Come back to me after three days." And the people departed.

6 Then King Rehoboam consulted the elders who stood before his father Solomon while he still lived, saying, "How do you advise *me* to answer these people?"

7 And they spoke to him, saying, "If you are kind to these people, and please them, and speak good words to them, they will be your servants forever."

8 But he rejected the advice which the elders had given him, and consulted the young men who had grown up with him, who stood before him.

9 And he said to them, "What advice do you give? How should we answer this people who have spoken to me, saying, 'Lighten the yoke which your father put on us'?"

10 Then the young men who had grown up with

him spoke to him, saying, "Thus you should speak to the people who have spoken to you, saying, 'Your father made our yoke heavy, but you make *it* lighter on us'—thus you shall say to them: 'My little *finger* shall be thicker than my father's waist!

11 'And now, whereas my father put a heavy yoke on you, I will add to your yoke; my father chastised you with whips, but I *will chastise you* with scourges!'"

12 So Jeroboam and all the people came to Rehoboam on the third day, as the king had directed, saying, "Come back to me the third day."

13 Then the king answered them roughly. King Rehoboam rejected the advice of the elders,

14 and he spoke to them according to the advice of the young men, saying, "My father made your yoke heavy, but I will add to it; my father chastised you with whips, but I *will chastise you* with scourges!"

15 So the king did not listen to the people; for the turn *of events* was from God, that the LORD might fulfill His word, which He had spoken by the hand of Ahijah the Shilonite to Jeroboam the son of Nebat.

16 Now when all Israel *saw* that the king did not listen to them, the people answered the king, saying:

"What share have we in David?

We have no inheritance in the son of Jesse.

Every man to your tents, O Israel!

Now see to your own house, O David!"

So all Israel departed to their tents.

17 But Rehoboam reigned over the children of Israel who dwelt in the cities of Judah.

18 Then King Rehoboam sent Hadoram, who *was* in charge of revenue; but the children of Israel stoned him with stones, and he died. Therefore King Rehoboam mounted *his* chariot in haste to flee to Jerusalem.

19 So Israel has been in rebellion against the house of David to this day.

11:1 Now when Rehoboam came to Jerusalem, he assembled from the house of Judah and Benjamin one hundred and eighty thousand chosen *men* who were warriors, to fight against Israel, that he might restore the kingdom to Rehoboam.

2 But the word of the LORD came to Shemaiah the man of God, saying,

3 "Speak to Rehoboam the son of Solomon, king of Judah, and to all Israel in Judah and Benjamin, saying,

4 'Thus says the LORD: "You shall not go up or fight against your brethren! Let every man return to his house, for this thing is from Me."'" Therefore they obeyed the words of the LORD, and turned back from attacking Jeroboam.

2 Chron. 10:1–11:4

This passage, largely taken over from 1 Kings 12:1–24, falls into two halves, 10:1–16 and 10:17–11:4. The halves begin respectively with Rehoboam's endeavor to become *"king"* over *"all Israel"* (10:1) and with his severely limited success in this endeavor (10:17). They end with instances of the same Hebrew verb, set in negative and positive statements respectively. First, Rehoboam refuses to *"listen to"* his northern constituents (10:15–16). Finally, he and Judah are constrained to listen to God's words ("obeyed," 11:4). In one of Shakespeare's royal plays Falstaff speaks of the human "disease of not listening." For Rehoboam it was a malady that led to tragic loss. He was forced to swallow a bitter remedy that left his kingdom a shadow of what it had been under David and Solomon. "Won't listen" was made to listen.

The story is a classic one, well worth the Chronicler's repeating it. In the overall context of his history the opening sentence rings a Davidic bell. Did not *"all Israel"* gather *"to make"* David *"king"* at Hebron (1 Chron. 11:3)? What is missing here is the third party in a triad of references, God Himself. This narrative, unlike that of 1 Chronicles 11, runs rigidly along a horizontal plane of human negotiations. References to God are conspicuous by their absence. God is not absent, however, even if uninvited. He broods over the entire scene with His providential presence, as the initial climax of the passage makes clear and the final punchline repeats: the whole affair turns out to be *"from God"* (10:15; *"from Me,"* 11:4). The Chronicler does not explain this appeal to divine providence, apart from retaining in 10:15 the Kings comment that God's earlier prophetic revelation is here realized. The Kings narrative is more lucid (see 1 Kings 11:29–39), but it will not do to read all that material into the narrative here, except for Ahijah's prediction that Jeroboam would become king of ten of the tribes of Israel. In Kings it is portrayed as reprisal for Solomon's wrongdoing, whereas the Chronicler's concern in his presentation of Solomon's reign has been to play down negative factors. In his present narrative God's will is a mysterious element in control of human behavior.

The divine will takes on a special function in his overall history. At 1 Chronicles 10:14 and 12:23 mention was made of God's turning Saul's kingdom over to David, in the second case with a reference to Samuel's two predictions to this effect. A noun related to the verb used there occurs here: *the turn of events was from God* (10:15). There is explicit reference to the prophetic medium by which this truth was communicated. The effect of these parallel statements is to isolate the material about David and Solomon from what preceded in Israelite history and from what was to follow. God's prophets bore witness that David's and Solomon's reigns constituted a special period of divine revelation, unequaled before or since to the Chronicler's knowledge. With David's accession the outgoing tide turned and brought special revelation on its crest. With Solomon's death the tide turned again and went out. It left on Israel's shores three witnesses to the dynamic presence of God during that period: the Davidic dynasty, the temple, and—in memory at least—the union of God's people. These are ideals dear to the Chronicler's heart. In his day the temple still stood as a center of worship, or rather had been rebuilt on the same site. Restoration of Davidic kingship and of a united people were elements that belonged to his vision of a God-ordered future, although hope of reunion was something to strive for even now with ecumenical fervor.

To this latter element the Chronicler implicitly testifies in 10:17 (*the children of Israel who dwelt in the cities of Judah*) and similarly in 11:3. After the division of the kingdom there was in Judah only a partial representation of *Israel.* The Chronicler never forgot that twelve tribes, not two, were God's ideal. He refused to equate Judah and Benjamin with the whole people of God. There was an ache in his heart, as in Paul's heart, over his unconverted Jewish brothers and sisters. Like Paul in Romans 9–11, he had a dream that one day God would be glorified by a larger entity of his people. This conviction is expressed in a stylistic peculiarity that pervades chapters 10–12. The Chronicler is careful to attach the same religious labels to southerners and northerners. If the southern kingdom is *all Israel*, so is the northern one (10:16; 11:13). If the southerners are *the children of Israel* (10:17), so are the northerners (10:18)—and that means elect children of promise (see 1 Chron. 16:13). If the south is "Israel" (12:6), so is the north (10:16, 19; 11:1). These standard designations can be used of both groups equally. From a southern perspective the northerners were separated brethren, but they remained *brethren* (11:4). The Chronicler will not mince his words in criticizing the northern state, but his ecumenical spirit never allows him to disown estranged members of God's family.

I recall some years spent in fellowship with Christians who worshiped at a little free church which was extremely Anabaptist and basically suspicious of what they sectarianly called "the denominations." However, the church leaders and a number of its members were rising above such fears. Some of this group attended an interdenominational breakfast and prayer meeting held once a month on a Saturday morning. The church even hosted the gathering when its turn came around. In my daily work I rubbed shoulders with Christians of many denominations, and I was fully in favor of the venture. Unfortunately, a narrow group in the church frowned on the dangerous fraternization with Anglicans, Baptists, Salvationists, and so on. One of the narrow group would persistently remove from a noticeboard the card advertising the time and place of fellowship. I had no formal authority in the church but took it upon myself to get a supply of cards and to replace the card each time it was missing. Looking back, I like to think that I was wearing the Chronicler's shoes, although I suspect that he would have been more vocal than I usually dared to be. An opportunity came when an aged brother died, who had "come out" of the Church of England without rancor or resentment and publicly used to enthuse over his boyhood experience as a chorister at Durham Cathedral. Apparently he had asked that I, being a kindred spirit, should conduct the funeral service. Before a congregation that included the more sectarian members, I was able to testify, as he would have done, to the wideness of the Church of God, as far beyond sectional parameters, and to announce the hymn in which Frederick W. Faber attested that "the love of God is broader than the measures of man's mind."

Rehoboam suffered from immaturity and did nothing to compensate for this defect. At 13:7 he is to be described as "young and inexperienced." The same adjectives were used of Solomon twice, in 1 Chronicles 22:5 and 29:1, when David expressed his anxieties about handing over the reins of power to his son. Rehoboam, however, was no second Solomon. The new king, bolstered by advice from his contemporaries, had a high and mighty conception of royal power. One can imagine the advice: "Put your foot down from the start, or else they will rule you," "Begin as you mean to go on." Rehoboam is urged to behave like a novice schoolteacher. His subjects are not schoolchildren, however. One cannot put an old head on young shoulders, but one can expect that advice from experienced leaders will be courteously listened to and seriously considered. Rehoboam does not bother. A generation gap and peer pressure—and perhaps an inflated sense of his own importance—combine to do their worst. He fails to appreciate that his people are weary of their part in Solomon's building and other projects, which for them involved both subscription and conscription. Like Britain rejecting Churchill after the Second World War, they want a new kind of leadership and judge the time for it to be ripe. Rehoboam refuses to listen to suggestions that his policy should be one of tact and conciliation. His threats are an overreaction born of his personal sense of insecurity. He hears the people's conditions as threats to his authority and reacts with counter-threats. Where is that insight which David had, that the monarchy was meant to foster the interests of Israel (1 Chron. 14:2)? Power to Rehoboam was force, to be exercised "roughly" (10:13), without regard for feelings or understanding of the situation that confronted him. He tramples on delicate issues uncaringly. He asks for advice, but listens only to the advice that makes him feel big. The incident is a warning to any who embark on new tasks involving authority over others.

I still tremble inside when I recall the six months when I worked under a hospital sister who ruled ruthlessly over the staff of her surgical ward. She loved her patients but with her piercing Welsh eyes and sharpest of tongues she gave the impression that she disliked and distrusted her staff. I can hardly remember her addressing me with a kindly word. She ran a tight ship, but efficiency was achieved at an unnecessarily heavy price.

Rehoboam underestimates the power in the hands of his constituents. Their anti-Davidic slogan (10:16) functions as a reversal of the affirmation of loyalty of 1 Chronicles 12:18. Rehoboam undoes at a stroke the achievements of David and alienates his subjects. The new king is so out of touch with the situation that he sends the person in charge of conscription as his representative (10:18). Hadoram is lynched, and Rehoboam, earlier so rigidly standing on his dignity, is forced to retreat with unseemly haste to the safety of Jerusalem. The Chronicler agrees with Kings that thereafter *Israel has been in rebellion against the house of David* (10:19), but one suspects that for him *"Israel"* is not merely a political term. It pains him that here were members of the chosen nation at loggerheads with God's chosen dynasty. The statement of verse 19 jerks the reader back to the contrast of the union of David and all Israel in 1 Chronicles 11:1, 4, 10 and 12:38. Here was a travesty of what should be. Never was a writer more out of step with his material than here in 11:1, where a show of force is Rehoboam's single-track answer to the situation. It takes a prophet to convince him that the harm done cannot be mended by such violent means. The term *"brethren"* (11:4) is an incriminating word. Rehoboam, who lacked a listening ear and could not hear what his constituents had to say, was forced to listen to God. "It is the privilege of wisdom to listen," Oliver Wendell Holmes once wrote. And fools must bear the consequences when they do not.

THE VIRTUE OF OBEDIENCE

11:5 So Rehoboam dwelt in Jerusalem, and built cities for defense in Judah.

6 And he built Bethlehem, Etam, Tekoa,

7 Beth Zur, Sochoh, Adullam,

8 Gath, Mareshah, Ziph,

9 Adoraim, Lachish, Azekah,

10 Zorah, Aijalon, and Hebron, which are in Judah and Benjamin, fortified cities.

11 And he fortified the strongholds, and put captains in them, and stores of food, oil, and wine.

12 Also in every city *he put* shields and spears, and made them very strong, having Judah and Benjamin on his side.

13 And from all their territories the priests and the Levites who *were* in all Israel took their stand with him.

14 For the Levites left their common-lands and their possessions and came to Judah and Jerusalem, for Jeroboam and his sons had rejected them from serving as priests to the LORD.

15 Then he appointed for himself priests for the high places, for the demons, and the calf idols which he had made.

16 And after *the Levites left,* those from all the tribes of Israel, such as set their heart to seek the LORD God of Israel, came to Jerusalem to sacrifice to the LORD God of their fathers.

17 So they strengthened the kingdom of Judah, and made Rehoboam the son of Solomon strong for three years, because they walked in the way of David and Solomon for three years.

18 Then Rehoboam took for himself as wife Mahalath the daughter of Jerimoth the son of David, *and of* Abihail the daughter of Eliah the son of Jesse.

19 And she bore him children: Jeush, Shamariah, and Zaham.

20 After her he took Maachah the granddaughter of Absalom; and she bore him Abijah, Attai, Ziza, and Shelomith.

21 Now Rehoboam loved Maachah the granddaughter of Absalom more than all his wives and his concubines; for he took eighteen wives and sixty concubines, and begot twenty-eight sons and sixty daughters.

22 And Rehoboam appointed Abijah the son of Maachah as chief, *to be* leader among his brothers; for he *intended* to make him king.

23 He dealt wisely, and dispersed some of his sons throughout all the territories of Judah and Benjamin, to every fortified city; and he gave them provisions in abundance. He also sought many wives *for them.*

2 *Chron.* 11:5-23

If in the previous section a show of human force was seen to be ineffective and opposed to the will of God, in this section the strength that comes from complying with God's will is the keynote. The passage falls into three parts, verses 5-12, 13-17, and 18-23. In the first two parts strength is the explicit theme (vv. 11 ["made strong," RSV], 12, 17), while in the third the king's vigor in producing a family strikes a similar chord. The spiritual secret of Rehoboam's success is given away in verse 17: now he and the people *"walked in the way of David and Solomon."* This is indeed an accolade from the Chronicler. Their joint reigns provided a model for their successors: to do it right was to do it David's and Solomon's way. The New Testament is no stranger to this notion of a modeling role, when it urges Christians, "Let this mind be in you which was also in Christ Jesus" (Phil. 2:5) and commends the self-giving of the One who "though . . . rich, yet for your sakes He became poor" (2 Cor. 8:9). In turn Paul exhorted his converts "Imitate me, just as I also imitate Christ" (1 Cor. 11:1). Psychologists assure us of the need for good role models if life is to be lived aright. Both the Chronicler and the apostle Paul were aware of this need.

1. *Garrisons of defense.* It is usually acknowledged that the Chronicler was following in verses 5–12 a source other than Kings. In the books of Chronicles such building operations as those listed here function as a successful enterprise which represents God's blessing for obedience. The Lord was building and guarding through Rehoboam, on the lines of Psalm 127:1 which envisages Him sharing in human building and guarding. The royal task was to make the borders safe against enemy attack, and so garrisons were built on Judah's eastern, southern, and western frontiers. The security of a good defense system was not regarded as inconsistent with trust in God. The attacks on armaments and military power in the Old Testament are prompted by a sinister shift whereby they are regarded as substitute objects of faith: see, for example, Isaiah 31:1. For the believing heart the things of earth may be the means of furthering the work of God. Nehemiah happily availed himself of an escort of Persian cavalry troops on his perilous journey from Persia to Judah (Neh. 2:9). Interestingly, in a similar situation Ezra was embarrassed about asking for guards, feeling it inconsistent with his earlier testimony to the protective power of God (Ezra 8:22). Obviously it was a matter of spiritual discernment, but in terms of Romans 14:1–15:6 Nehemiah's attitude was the more natural one, to be set aside only for good reasons.

2. *Gains from worshiping aright.* The Chronicler's account of the division of the kingdom laid little, if any, blame on Jeroboam. Now, however, the situation changes drastically, in verses 13–17. If in

chapter 10 Rehoboam was the foolish villain and Jeroboam was the agent of divinely inspired prophecy (see 10:15), now the roles of saint and sinner are reversed. On the basis of 1 Kings 12:26–33 the Chronicler presents the pernicious religious innovations made by Jeroboam. In consequence the priests and Levites defect to the south. They are prepared to lose their land holdings and homes for the sake of religious truth. It is an illustration of the sacrifices sometimes necessary in taking a stand for conscience and for God (see Mark 10:28–30). Northern pilgrims—for such they seem to be rather than immigrants—flock to Jerusalem, preferring the traditional and orthodox worship of the temple to Jeroboam's perversions of the faith. The Chronicler graces their action with his prime word for spirituality: they are wholeheartedly prepared to *"seek"* God (v. 16). We sometimes use the term *"seeker"* to refer to someone who has not yet found God. In Chronicles those who seek God have previously found Him and keep coming back. Seeking is the attitude of the committed believer. It is by no means a vague, optimistic sentiment, but is linked with concrete actions and a positive venture. In the Chronicler's terms to seek God is to resort to the temple as the God-ordained place of worship and prayer. To seek God is associated with making up one's mind (*"set their heart"*). It is to come to decisions and to carry them out. For these northerners their seeking resulted in a clearcut stance that made a difference to their lives. The Chronicler was here not only writing in historical terms but also thinking in terms of his own day. Five centuries later this was what he wanted to see in post-exilic Judah, an influx of northern pilgrims who recognized that the temple was God's appointed place of worship. It was his appeal to contemporary members of the northern tribes—and to his fellow Judeans to receive them warmly. In our own day, of course, there is no such material focus of worship, in the light of John 4:20–24. Yet the fellowship of God's people which transcends denominational frontiers is a continuing ideal. Psalm 133 is a testimony to such united fellowship.

3. *God's gift of children.* This story of polygamy and concubinage, including Rehoboam's intent to name a son of his favorite wife his heir, strikes a discordant note for the modern Christian. One must try to rise above cultural prejudice, even when it seems well grounded, and appreciate the concerns of the text. In the Old Testament period polygamy was an accepted form of marriage, and concubines did not

lack legal rights. Indeed in Judaism today, while monogamy is the prescribed form in Western and other countries which so legislate, polygamy is still permitted for Jews residing in Muslim states. In practice, at least from post-exilic times, economic factors probably made monogamy more expedient. However, the cultural custom of polygamy is so integrated into the Old Testament that in the allegory of Ezekiel 23 God is represented as having two wives, Samaria and Jerusalem. Similarly, in the New Testament the cultural phenomenon of slavery can be used as a model for Christian service (Rom. 6:16–22). God condescended to use these cultural models as part of His self-revelation in particular historical contexts.

The intent of the text is to refer to God's gift of children. In the Old Testament the process of fertility is traced back to His providential blessing, while infertility is regarded as an unnatural and so divinely related phenomenon, as 1 Samuel 1:6, 11 illustrates. Modern men and women in their sophisticated rationalism have put asunder God and nature. Most of the people of the ancient world equated nature and deity, while Israel viewed nature as God's providential means of working out His will. Too close and too remote a correlation between God and the natural world has its dangers, but that there is some relation is a necessary Christian belief. Young parents rejoicing over a new baby respond to a wise spiritual instinct when they praise God for the gift of a child.

In ancient royal circles sons of the harem were trained as civil and military leaders, and this is what happened here (v. 23). Family bonds were judged likely to ensure the loyalty of persons in high positions, and in this respect Rehoboam dealt *wisely.* By this and other means he gradually consolidated his royal power, as 12:1a states by way of summary.

THE VANQUISHING OF SELF-WILL

12:1 Now it came to pass, when Rehoboam had established the kingdom and had strengthened himself, that he forsook the law of the LORD, and all Israel along with him.

2 And it happened in the fifth year of King Rehoboam *that* Shishak king of Egypt came up against

Jerusalem, because they had transgressed against the LORD,

3 with twelve hundred chariots, sixty thousand horsemen, and people without number who came with him out of Egypt—the Lubim and the Sukkiim and the Ethiopians.

4 And he took the fortified cities of Judah and came to Jerusalem.

5 Then Shemaiah the prophet came to Rehoboam and the leaders of Judah, who were gathered together in Jerusalem because of Shishak, and said to them, "Thus says the LORD: 'You have forsaken Me, and therefore I also have left you in the hand of Shishak.'"

6 So the leaders of Israel and the king humbled themselves; and they said, "The LORD is righteous."

7 Now when the LORD saw that they humbled themselves, the word of the LORD came to Shemaiah, saying, "They have humbled themselves; therefore I will not destroy them, but I will grant them some deliverance. My wrath shall not be poured out on Jerusalem by the hand of Shishak.

8 "Nevertheless they will be his servants, that they may distinguish My service from the service of the kingdoms of the nations."

9 So Shishak king of Egypt came up against Jerusalem, and took away the treasures of the house of the LORD and the treasures of the king's house; he took everything. He also carried away the gold shields which Solomon had made.

10 Then King Rehoboam made bronze shields in their place, and committed them to the hands of the captains of the guard, who guarded the doorway of the king's house.

11 And whenever the king entered the house of the LORD, the guard would go and bring them out; then they would take them back into the guardroom.

12 When he humbled himself, the wrath of the LORD turned from him, so as not to destroy him completely; and things also went well in Judah.

13 Thus King Rehoboam strengthened himself in Jerusalem and reigned. Now Rehoboam was forty-one

years old when he became king; and he reigned seventeen years in Jerusalem, the city which the LORD had
chosen out of all the tribes of Israel, to put His name
there. His mother's name *was* Naamah, an Ammonitess.

14 And he did evil, because he did not prepare his
heart to seek the LORD.

15 The acts of Rehoboam, first and last, *are* they
not written in the book of Shemaiah the prophet,
and of Iddo the seer concerning genealogies? And
there were wars between Rehoboam and Jeroboam all
their days.

16 So Rehoboam rested with his fathers, and was
buried in the City of David. Then Abijah his son
reigned in his place.

2 Chron. 12:1–16

It is a mark of the Chronicler's spiritual realism that he paints
neither the northern kingdom in darker hues nor the southern in
lighter hues than the truth warrants. If Jeroboam committed religious infidelity, so does Rehoboam in due course. Ironically the
Judean king fails to match up to the standards of the northerners
who trek south seeking God (11:16; 12:1, 5). The old immaturity of
chapter 10 raises its ugly head again. There are spiritual maladies
which, unlike measles, we never outgrow. Their viruses, once introduced to the human system, are ever apt to attack unless precaution-
ary measures are taken. The references to self-humbling later in the
chapter suggest that Rehoboam falls into a trap of self-sufficiency,
arguing and believing that "my power and the might of my hand
have gained me this wealth" or strength (Deut. 8:17). Indeed, the
proof that the king has forsaken God lies in the fact that he has
forsaken His Torah or *"law"* (vv. 1, 5). Here the Chronicler has in
mind the basic text of 1 Kings 14:23 with its reference to Judeans
worshiping at high places and using the paraphernalia of Canaanite
religion. In referring to the Torah he is thinking specifically of
Deuteronomy 12:2–14. There is a refreshing down-to-earthness
about the Old Testament. To seek God is to worship in His temple; to
forsake God means to forsake His Torah (compare 7:19, 22). There
are certain objective standards of right and wrong, and to defy them
is no different than defying God. The Chronicler is implicitly issuing

a warning to his Judean contemporaries. They have the Torah and the temple, but these are no guarantee that they will stay within the will of God. Religious traditions can become ornaments, like china and crystal in a glass-fronted cabinet, too good to use.

In fact, both temple and Torah are profaned in this case. Forsaking in the Chronicler's vocabulary is related to irregular worship or the blatant worship of foreign gods, as it is here in the light of the Kings text. Rehoboam is castigated with strong language: he and his people are "unfaithful to the Lord" (v. 2, RSV). It is the term the Chronicler has used earlier of Saul and in connection with the exile of the northern and southern kingdoms (1 Chron. 5:25; 9:1; 10:13; 2 Chron. 36:14). It speaks of backsliding to the point of apostasy. Like Saul, Rehoboam—son of David though he is—finds that unfaithfulness exposes him to military defeat. The *"fortified cities"* which featured so prominently in chapter 11 as the medium of the king's trust in God to protect Judah, now crumble (12:4). They are only as strong as their builder's faith. In the absence of true trust they become houses built on sand. Rehoboam can no longer expect God's protective presence: God forsakes those who forsake Him (v. 5; compare 1 Chron. 28:9). There is a striking double use of the verb "forsake" in the Hebrew of verse 5, although the inflexibility of the English language does not permit its repetition: compare the RSV "You abandoned Me, so I have abandoned you to the hand of Shishak." There is spiritual logic at work here. The Chronicler's theology has a strongly moral tone: throughout his history he insists that God keeps short accounts and that to backslide is to forfeit His blessing in a life-shattering way. Did he believe it as a blanket principle? Would he have argued with the modifications of the principle made in Psalm 73 and the Book of Job? He seems to be writing as a pastoral theologian rather than as a purely systematic one, issuing incentives and sanctions as motives to keep his readers on the straight and narrow path of obedience to God.

The Chronicler makes use of 1 Kings 14:25 in verse 2, although he appears to be using another literary account in his historically correct reference to the *"Sukkiim"* in verse 3. The mention of *"sixty thousand horsemen,"* however, seems to be a further instance of what we earlier called rhetorical mathematics. The following *"without number"* is a clue to this factor, like the "beyond measure" of 1 Chronicles 22:14. Whereas the Kings narrative places religious apostasy and foreign invasion side by side without comment, it seems to be implicitly inviting its readers to draw a moral, and the Chronicler is one reader who does. Shemaiah, the bold anti-establishment prophet of 11:2–4 appears once more and addresses the government leaders huddled in a harassed Jerusalem. In God's name he preaches a devastating sermon (v. 5).

Rehoboam has allowed himself to be sucked into the fatal vortex of 1 Chronicles 10:13 and 28:9: death and being cast off forever loom ominously near. In fact the gracious revelation of 2 Chronicles 7:14 comes to his rescue. He does not fall to his merited doom. Near the top of the precipice God has provided a cleft in the rock, a foothold from which he may call for help. "Where sin abounded, grace abounded much more" (Rom. 5:20): this is the good news of the Chronicler and the apostle alike. Self-humbling, prayer, and repentance are for the Chronicler God's appointed way back to Himself and to a new lease on life. Four times he tells his readers about Rehoboam's and his ministers' humbling themselves (vv. 6, 7, 12). It is surely his call to whoever has ears to hear that the gospel of 7:14 is true and that, as it worked for Rehoboam, it can work for anybody else. The liturgical formula *"The Lord is righteous"* (v. 6) is a confession of sin, implying that He is in the right and correspondingly they are in the wrong and receiving their just deserts (compare Exod. 9:27; Dan. 9:14).

As Jacob was left with a limp as a material reminder of his fight with God, so Rehoboam evidently becomes a vassal of Shishak, although the capital and throne are spared. The king is to be taught a lesson by this partial *"deliverance"* (v. 7). Having quit God's loyal service, he will learn that His yoke is easy in comparison with the *"service"* of a foreign power. The experience will enable him to differentiate between the two options and prefer the former (v. 8). Verses 7–8 are carefully phrased to cover a double agenda. They not only speak about Rehoboam and Shishak. They also allude to the experience of post-exilic Judah, restored to their land and to God's favor, but still subject to Persia (see Ezra 9:8, 9; Neh. 9:36). We can learn from this experience, the Chronicler seems to be saying; it should make us appreciate God all the more and induce a prayer of faith to Him for full restoration and liberation.

The reference to *"the kingdoms of the nations"* (v. 8) strikes a discordant note in comparison with the ideal of 1 Chronicles 29:30. The awed respect of the nations was David's fortune, and its potential was to be realized by a later Davidic king, Jehoshaphat (17:10; 20:29). Rehoboam, however, sadly lacks the blessing enjoyed by his grandfather. Another discordant note, this time explicit, is sounded in verse 9, in the account of Rehoboam's payment of tribute, taken over from 1 Kings 14:26–28: *the gold shields which Solomon had made* (9:15, 16) are handed over to the Egyptian overlord. Rehoboam, forsaking the way of David and Solomon (11:17), has forfeited their divine blessings.

In verse 12 the Chronicler sums up the situation. Rehoboam's self-humbling had averted the operation of God's destructive *"wrath."* Like a brand plucked from the burning, he had survived—*"yet so as through fire"* (1 Cor. 3:15), suffering loss. The last clause seems to be a religious reference, as the parallel in 19:3 suggests. The humbling of the Judean leaders presumably resulted in the termination of Judah's religious unfaithfulness described in verse 2. So on this plane *"there were good things in Judah,"* as the Hebrew may be rendered. This was the redeeming feature of a painful experience.

Verses 13–14, based on the introduction to Rehoboam's reign in 1 Kings 14:21–22, appear to be a flashback to verse 1, to judge from the repeated opening words. The Chronicler uses the Kings material to reflect on the tragedy. In the heart of the kingdom, in *"the city"* in which *"the Lord had chosen"* (v. 13) to manifest His authority, Rehoboam opted to reject God and to do *"evil"* (v. 14). Here was perfidy, that one so close to God should stray so far away. Later in his history the Chronicler is to state concerning Jehoshaphat that he set his *"heart to seek God"* (19:3). Rehoboam functions as his negative image, dark where he should have been light. This was the skeleton in his closet, and for the Chronicler it is the punchline of his historical sermon. He is warning Judeans of his own day not to presume on their heritage but to let geographical proximity to the temple be the measure of their proximity to God. A saner aptitude than Rehoboam's is supplied in Isaiah 33:14–16, to listen with respectful awe to the demands the God of Zion makes on the lives of His followers: "The sinners in Zion are afraid; . . . / 'Who among us shall dwell with the devouring fire?' . . . / He who walks righteously . . . / His place of defense will be the fortress of rocks."

CHAPTER TWELVE

Relying on God

2 Chronicles 13:1–16:14

The Chronicler intended these chapters to be read together. They are dominated by the theme of reliance on God. Forms of the key-word "rely" occur here five times and nowhere else in Chronicles. They are found in 13:18; 14:11 (NKJV "rest"); and 16:7, 8. The occurrences of the term split up the material into three sections which respectively revolve around the trust in God exercised by Abijah and Judah (13:18) and Asa's initial trust (14:11; compare 16:8) and subsequent lack of trust (16:7). The reigns of Abijah and Asa are for the Chronicler mirrors of fidelity and infidelity. He uses them to teach lessons about the nature and necessity of faith. If reliance is the unique thread that binds these chapters together, it is interwoven with two other threads which are common terms in the spiritual vocabulary of Chronicles, "forsaken" (13:10, 11) and "seek" (14:4, 7; 15:2, 4, 12, 15; 16:12). In this kaleidoscope of spirituality three scenarios are presented, of which the first has a built-in contrast and the other two function as external contrasts: (a) a profession of trust in God, which is vindicated because it is supported by lives committed to God, while those who forsake Him lose out; (b) trust in God which He honors because it is exercised by those who seek Him; and (c) a spurious trust which eventually leads to ruin because its practitioners do not seek God. History is used to preach a series of three sermons which are variations on a single theme.

FIDELITY VERSUS INFIDELITY

13:1 In the eighteenth year of King Jeroboam, Abijah became king over Judah.

2 He reigned three years in Jerusalem. His mother's name *was* Michaiah the daughter of Uriel of Gibeah. And there was war between Abijah and Jeroboam.

3 Abijah set the battle in order with an army of valiant warriors, four hundred thousand choice men. Jeroboam also drew up in battle formation against him with eight hundred thousand choice men, mighty men of valor.

4 Then Abijah stood on Mount Zemaraim, which *is* in the mountains of Ephraim, and said, "Hear me, Jeroboam and all Israel:

5 "Should you not know that the LORD God of Israel gave the dominion over Israel to David forever, to him and his sons, by a covenant of salt?

6 "Yet Jeroboam the son of Nebat, the servant of Solomon the son of David, rose up and rebelled against his lord.

7 "Then worthless rogues gathered to him, and strengthened themselves against Rehoboam the son of Solomon, when Rehoboam was young and inexperienced and could not withstand them.

8 "And now you think to withstand the kingdom of the LORD, which is in the hand of the sons of David; and you *are* a great multitude, and with you are the gold calves which Jeroboam made for you as gods.

9 "Have you not cast out the priests of the LORD, the sons of Aaron, and the Levites, and made for yourselves priests, like the peoples of *other* lands, so that whoever comes to consecrate himself with a young bull and seven rams may be a priest of *things that are* not gods?

10 "But as for us, the LORD *is* our God, and we have not forsaken Him; and the priests who minister to the LORD *are* the sons of Aaron, and the Levites *attend* to *their* duties.

11 "And they burn to the LORD every morning and every evening burnt sacrifices and sweet incense; *they* also *set* the showbread *in order on* the pure *gold* table, and the lampstand of gold with its lamps to burn every evening; for we keep the command of the LORD our God, but you have forsaken Him.

12 "Now look, God Himself is with us as *our* head,
and His priests with sounding trumpets to sound the
alarm against you. O children of Israel, do not fight
against the LORD God of your fathers, for you shall
not prosper!"

13 But Jeroboam caused an ambush to go around
behind them; so they were in front of Judah, and the
ambush *was* behind them.

14 And when Judah looked around, to their surprise the battle line *was* at both front and rear; and
they cried out to the LORD, and the priests sounded
the trumpets.

15 Then the men of Judah gave a shout; and as the
men of Judah shouted, it happened that God struck
Jeroboam and all Israel before Abijah and Judah.

16 And the children of Israel fled before Judah,
and God delivered them into their hand.

17 Then Abijah and his people struck them with a
great slaughter; so five hundred thousand choice
men of Israel fell slain.

18 Thus the children of Israel were subdued at that
time; and the children of Judah prevailed, because
they relied on the LORD God of their fathers.

19 And Abijah pursued Jeroboam and took cities
from him: Bethel with its villages, Jeshanah with its
villages, and Ephrain with its villages.

20 So Jeroboam did not recover strength again in
the days of Abijah; and the LORD struck him, and he
died.

21 But Abijah grew mighty, married fourteen wives,
and begot twenty-two sons and sixteen daughters.

22 Now the rest of the acts of Abijah, his ways,
and his sayings *are* written in the annals of the
prophet Iddo.

2 Chron. 13:1–22

In 1 Kings 15:1–8 Abijah, there called Abijam, is a nonentity who
does so little to enhance the Davidic line that its survival is credited
solely to God's gracious covenant with David. One of the few significant points of contact between the Kings account and Chronicles is
mention of war between him and Jeroboam. Some noteworthy scholars have postulated that the Chronicler had access to a historical

source which specified a campaign in which Abijah won a victory over the north in the terms of verse 19; on this basis he was able to present a more positive picture of the king as faithful to God, on the premise that virtue underlay victory. In 13:1-2 the Chronicler reproduces 1 Kings 15:1, 2, 6. He never elsewhere transmits from Kings the chronological relation between a southern king and his northern counterpart. He does so here in verse 1 because the whole chapter hangs on the respective relations of the southerners and northerners to God. The people of God had been split into two. The initial split was ratified by the prophetic word, while on the human plane the folly of Rehoboam was warrant enough for the bulk of his subjects to reject him. The Chronicler knew, however, that the perpetuation of the northern line of kings was dependent on Jeroboam's fidelity to God (see 1 Kings 11:37, 38). In fact he had signally failed in this respect, as his religious innovations proved (2 Chron. 11:14, 15). Accordingly the death of foolish Rehoboam and the accession of a new Judean king afforded an opportunity to the northerners to reject Jeroboam and revert to allegiance to the true, Davidic king.

In verses 4–12 Abijah lays the issues squarely before them, and then in verses 13–19 a Judean victory makes it abundantly clear that right is on Judah's side. Finally, in verses 20–22 two contrasting vignettes of the rival kings are drawn. The debate was no academic one for the Chronicler: it concerned the warrant of post-exilic Judah to regard itself as the preserver of true faith and worship. Abijah's speech expresses the Chronicler's theological convictions about Judah's status before God.

1. *The issues presented.* There are some surprising parallels between the New Testament and the Old. Did you know that there is an Ethiopian eunuch in both the Old and New Testaments (Jer. 38:7–13; Acts 8:27–38)? And were you aware that the Old Testament has its Sermon on the Mount? Here it is, in the light of verse 4. The punchline at the end of verse 12 gives the main point of the "sermon," that the northerners should recognize that God is on Judah's side. What precedes is a two-pronged argument to this end, in verses 5–8a and 8b–12. The first prong is the legitimacy of the Davidic dynasty. Expressed here is a conviction of the divine right of the Davidic line of kings, such as we have heard before. David and his heirs enjoyed a God-given right to rule. We do not know how the expression *"covenant of salt"* (v. 5) originated, but we may safely surmise that it

271

refers to a perpetual covenant, in the light of Numbers 18:19. The word *"forever"* spoke volumes to the Chronicler, as it does to the Christian. It was for the Chronicler the basis of a sure hope that a descendant of David would once again rule over God's people. For the Christian it is amplified by New Testament claims that Jesus is the significant Son of David who has inherited the Davidic covenant. The reference to *"worthless rogues"* in verse 7 is probably to Rehoboam's young men who *"gathered to him"* (= Rehoboam) and prevailed over (NKJV *"against"*) him, persuading him to adopt a high-handed attitude. The Jewish historian Josephus so interpreted the verse, probably rightly since the phrase *"worthless rogues"* suggests a small group, rather than "Jeroboam and all Israel" (10:3). Abijah is admitting that an awful mistake has been made and is apologizing for it. Rehoboam was led astray in his immaturity. Now that he had died, there was no excuse for persisting in secession. The rule of David's sons was no less than God's rule (see 1 Chron. 17:14; 29:23). Although Abijah was prepared to lose face by a moral apology over his father's behavior, he could not give way on the ideological level.

As the speech proceeds, Abijah increasingly bypasses Jeroboam. He is jointly addressed at the start (v. 4), then mentioned obliquely in the third person (vv. 6, 8), and at the end only the people are addressed (v. 12). The message is that Jeroboam no longer counts, just as Rehoboam has ceased to be a material factor in the contemporary situation. The reason is to be given in verses 8b–12a. Before we consider it, let us reflect on the concept of self-determination presented here, a theme dear to the Chronicler's heart and mind. He would have strongly approved of Romeo and Juliet marrying despite the feud of their houses Montague and Capulet! The Chronicler considers that each generation has a fresh start and can decide anew how to live. His emphasis on the value of sacred history and tradition does not mean that for him the whole of life was locked into the past. Let bygones be bygones is his summons. Sadly there have been small communities and even churches which have never heard of this liberating truth. Family feuds have had a divisive influence long after the original cause was perpetrated. Increased social mobility, for all its attendant problems, has had one good effect in displacing such stale air. The Chronicler's call is to bury the hatchet and smoke a pipe of peace. He may perhaps be judged over-optimistic and idealistic. Even so, it is refreshingly positive. The world would be a better place if it were heeded more. It is a message too for the church with its denominational demarcations and also for the local church. There is a type of conservatism which is best forgotten, when principles can no longer be differentiated from prejudices.

The religious group among which I grew up tragically split into two over issues with which personality had more to do than principle, and love and humility were conspicuously absent. The split occurred around the year 1845, and thereafter to this day those who aspire to membership of the narrower group are solemnly asked "Have you judged the question?" The sad thing is not simply that a question first posed over a hundred and thirty years ago is still mooted, but that the right answer is assumed to be an unwavering one. Samuel Johnson's words to a Quaker are worth pondering: "Oh, let us not be found when our Master calls us, ripping the lace off our waistcoats, but the spirit of contention from our souls and tongues." A prime need for the Christian is to judge which moments in the past history of the church are sacred history and which are all too human and best forgotten.

In fact the Chronicler walks a tightrope of conciliation and conservatism. Recently in modern Israel a tied election resulted in a coalition government in which each political party provided a prime minister alternately. The Chronicler could never have made such a concession in the royal or religious issues affecting Judah and Israel. The sacred history of David and Solomon had established standards from which he could not deviate. There are two unchangeable factors in his ideology, both of which he held to be divinely sanctioned: commitment to the Davidic dynasty and perpetuation of the worship of the Jerusalem temple.

Jeroboam's fall from grace is explained in verses 8b–12. It concerns the religious innovations of which the reader was historically informed in chapter 11. Now their theological significance is considered. The new era established by David and Solomon determined criteria of worship for God's people. The reader of Chronicles is no stranger to these criteria, proper personnel and four typical features of worship (vv. 10b, 11a). These were the tangible evidences to which the Chronicler clung as embodiments of true religion. Their presence or absence determined whether God had been *forsaken* or not (vv. 10a, 11b). Faith was no vague belief, but was essentially clothed in religious forms. A striking thing about the ancient culture of which the Chronicler spoke and to which he still belonged is that for both sides religious forms stood at the forefront of controversy. Many people today who would call themselves Christians are like the man Samuel Johnson wryly described: "I am afraid he has not been in the inside of a church for many years; but he has never passed a church without pulling off his hat. This shows that he has principles." If "faith without works is dead" (James 2:26), so is faith without religious habits. Those who rely on God (v. 18) are also those who prize institutional forms of the faith which accord with God's self-revelation.

Abijah's challenge comes at the end of verse 12. It is an appeal for reunification. The address *"children of Israel"* is no mere political label. Mention of *"the Lord God of your fathers"* confirms that it is as resonant with spirituality as it was in 1 Chronicles 2:1, where it is rendered *"sons of Israel."* The northerners have *"forsaken"* God, but so did Rehoboam (12:1, 5) and a door of repentance was open for him (12:6). So it was for the northerners: they were part of God's family. In New Testament terms they were the prodigal sons of Luke 15, rather than the dead branches broken from the olive tree of Romans 11. The distinction may be a difficult one for us Christians to grasp because we are so used to applying the parable of the prodigal son in a general evangelistic sense. Strictly Jesus told it to those who belonged within the covenant circle and still had opportunity to return to the God from whom they had strayed. Paul in his metaphor of the olive tree judged that a decisive break had occurred and that the Jewish people stood now outside the covenant, though not permanently so in God's long-term plans. In the Chronicler's mind such a break had not taken place: the northerners were prodigal sons, but sons still. God's arms were open to welcome them back, and so were the Chronicler's in his own day. In a historical environment of religious resentment, not untinged with political and economic factors, he refused to budge from this ideal.

History did not stand beside him, but took a downward path to the point where Jews had *"no dealings with Samaritans"* (John 4:9). In principle Jesus was affirming the Chronicler's stand when He built bridges between Himself and the Samaritan community of Sychar (John 4:39–41). He insisted on the historical priority of Jerusalem, like the Chronicler, but was able to announce a new era of worship, centered in Himself and based on criteria of *"spirit and truth"* (John

4:22–26). It is by these criteria that our own worship forms are to be judged, even as the Chronicler made those of the era of David and Solomon his standards.

The warning against being found fighting against God has a striking parallel in Gamaliel's caution to the Sanhedrin who were minded to kill the apostles: "If it is of God, you cannot overthrow it—lest you even be found to fight against God" (Acts 5:39). Just as the apostles were bravely determined to "obey God rather than men" (Acts 5:29), so Abijah, leading an outnumbered army (v. 3), stands staunchly by his principles.

2. *The issues put to the test.* In verses 13–19 truth is on trial. The description of the battle has an old world ring about it: it is written in the style of Holy War, like the military narratives of Joshua and Judges. The only soldiers the Chronicler and his first readers ever saw wore Persian uniforms. In historical terms the tale he tells reads like a bout of medieval jousting described in a modern book or seen on the television screen. What he wants to get across to his readers is a spiritual perspective. It is a spirit of faith and hope which Paul shares in his testimony "When I am weak, then I am strong" (2 Cor. 12:10) and "we are more than conquerors through Him who loved us" (Rom. 8:37). It is a David and Goliath story which encourages a faithful minority to hold on to the truth. The key to the narrative occurs in verse 18: *"They relied on the Lord God of their fathers."* It refers back to the shout of faith in verse 15 and identifies it in terms of the keyword of these chapters. To rely is literally to lean; a related noun occurs in Psalm 18:18, where David attested that "the Lord was my support." Both contexts indicate that the term belongs to a situation of desperate crisis.

"Faith is a desperate action," my colleague H. Newton Malony has written. "It is not a lighthearted, casual act. It is an important activity in which a person invests heavily. It is serious, critical, decisive, risky, strategic behavior. It occurs when the data are unclear and the situation is ambiguous. It goes beyond the evidence and makes a judgment without clear proof."[1] The same note of desperate decisiveness is struck here. Life throws crises in our path, which are meant to elicit from us a cry of faith. This is not fox-hole religion. Rather, it draws credit from a spiritual bank account already set up and regularly used. It leans back in weakness on the One who in times of lesser need has already been a conscious support. In this case the

275

southerners *"prevailed"* (v. 18), finding in God deliverance that matched their need and a power that proved the sufficiency of His grace (see 2 Cor. 12:9).

3. *Issues of life and death.* In verses 20–22 the moral is drawn in plain terms. Jeroboam has trodden the way that leads to death. The verb *"struck"* (v. 20) is significantly repeated from verse 15. The battle scenario is replayed on a personal level, in the northern king's experience. On the other hand, Abijah's fortunes are represented by a vignette of life and blessedness: he is another Rehoboam—in his early period—in terms of power and a large family (see 11:17–21). It is the Chronicler's way of affirming that the path of obedience is a path of blessing, while the path of disobedience illustrated by Rehoboam leads to destruction, in the absence of repentance which saved Rehoboam at the brink (12:12). The Chronicler presents, as he did in his contrast of the reigns of Saul and David, two possibilities which lay before the people of God in his own day. In New Testament terms the choice remains, "the goodness and severity of God," either to "continue in His goodness" or to "be cut off" (Rom. 11:22).

TRUE FAITH

14:1 So Abijah rested with his fathers, and they buried him in the City of David. Then Asa his son reigned in his place. In his days the land was quiet for ten years.

2 Asa did *what was* good and right in the eyes of the LORD his God,

3 for he removed the altars of the foreign *gods* and the high places, and broke down the *sacred* pillars and cut down the wooden images.

4 He commanded Judah to seek the LORD God of their fathers, and to observe the law and the commandment.

5 He also removed the high places and the incense altars from all the cities of Judah, and the kingdom was quiet under him.

6 And he built fortified cities in Judah, for the land had rest; he had no war in those years, because the LORD had given him rest.

7 Therefore he said to Judah, "Let us build these cities and make walls around *them,* and towers, gates,

and bars, *while* the land *is* yet before us, because we have sought the LORD our God; we have sought *Him*, and He has given us rest on every side." So they built and prospered.

8 And Asa had an army of three hundred thousand from Judah who carried shields and spears, and from Benjamin two hundred and eighty thousand men who carried shields and drew bows; all these *were* mighty men of valor.

9 Then Zerah the Ethiopian came out against them with an army of a million men and three hundred chariots, and he came to Mareshah.

10 So Asa went out against him, and they set the troops in battle array in the Valley of Zephathah at Mareshah.

11 And Asa cried out to the LORD his God, and said, "LORD, *it is* nothing for You to help, whether with many or with those who have no power; help us, O LORD our God, for we rest on You, and in Your name we go against this multitude. O LORD, You *are* our God; do not let man prevail against You!"

12 So the LORD struck the Ethiopians before Asa and Judah, and the Ethiopians fled.

13 And Asa and the people who *were* with him pursued them to Gerar. So the Ethiopians were overthrown, and they could not recover, for they were broken before the LORD and His army. And they carried away very much spoil.

14 Then they defeated all the cities around Gerar, for the fear of the LORD came upon them; and they plundered all the cities, for there was exceedingly much spoil in them.

15 They also attacked the livestock enclosures, and carried off sheep and camels in abundance, and returned to Jerusalem.

15:1 Now the Spirit of God came upon Azariah the son of Oded.

2 And he went out to meet Asa, and said to him: "Hear me, Asa, and all Judah and Benjamin. The LORD *is* with you while you are with Him. If you seek Him, He will be found by you; but if you forsake Him, He will forsake you.

3 "For a long time Israel *has been* without the true God, without a teaching priest, and without law;

4 "but when in their trouble they turned to the LORD God of Israel, and sought Him, He was found by them.

5 "And in those times *there was* no peace to the one who went out, nor to the one who came in, but great turmoil *was* on all the inhabitants of the lands.

6 "So nation was destroyed by nation, and city by city, for God troubled them with every adversity.

7 "But you, be strong and do not let your hands be weak, for your work shall be rewarded!"

8 And when Asa heard these words and the prophecy of Oded the prophet, he took courage, and removed the abominable idols from all the land of Judah and Benjamin and from the cities which he had taken in the mountains of Ephraim; and he restored the altar of the LORD that *was* before the vestibule of the LORD.

9 Then he gathered all Judah and Benjamin, and those who dwelt with them from Ephraim, Manasseh, and Simeon, for they came over to him in great numbers from Israel when they saw that the LORD his God was with him.

10 So they gathered together at Jerusalem in the third month, in the fifteenth year of the reign of Asa.

11 And they offered to the LORD at that time seven hundred bulls and seven thousand sheep from the spoil they had brought.

12 Then they entered into a covenant to seek the LORD God of their fathers with all their heart and with all their soul;

13 and whoever would not seek the LORD God of Israel was to be put to death, whether small or great, whether man or woman.

14 Then they took an oath before the LORD with a loud voice, with shouting and trumpets and rams' horns.

15 And all Judah rejoiced at the oath, for they had sworn with all their heart and sought Him with all their soul; and He was found by them, and the LORD gave them rest all around.

16 Also he removed Maachah, the mother of Asa the king, from *being* queen mother, because she had made an obscene image of Asherah; and Asa cut down her obscene image, then crushed and burned *it* by the Brook Kidron.

17 But the high places were not removed from Israel. Nevertheless the heart of Asa was loyal all his days.

18 He also brought into the house of God the things that his father had dedicated and that he himself had dedicated: silver and gold and utensils.

19 And there was no war until the thirty-fifth year of the reign of Asa.

2 Chron. 14:1–15:19

In 1 Kings 15 Asa is judged to be a good king. The Chronicles picture of him is different: two contrasting cameos of good and bad periods are presented in schematic fashion. Seemingly the Chronicler fastened on two features mentioned in 1 Kings 15, alliance with Syria and a disease of his feet in his old age. Interpreting these negative factors in terms of moral providence, he reasoned back to a radical change in Asa's spiritual stand, a shift from reliance on God to non-reliance (see especially 16:7, 8). There are chronological difficulties in the different presentations of Asa's reign in 1 Kings and Chronicles (contrast 2 Chron. 16:1 with 1 Kings 16:6, 8) which are perhaps best explained by judging that the Chronicler has reshuffled the events and timing of Kings so as to present a clearcut division into a long period of divine blessing for fidelity and a short period of infidelity. The account of Asa's reign reads as a powerful two-part sermon of spiritual greatness and a tragic fall.

1. *Faith at work.* In 14:1–8 the terms *"quiet"* and *"rest"* in 14:1 and 5b–7 provide a framework. It is a blessing *"given"* by God (14:6). The term *"rest"* is resonant with overtones of Deuteronomy. Rest from enemies was an ancient promise associated with God's gift of the promised land (see Deut. 12:10). It is noteworthy that *"the land"* is mentioned three times in this passage. For the Chronicler rest had been realized in the reign of Solomon, marking the onset of a new era of grace (1 Chron. 22:9). It was a heritage which each succeeding king had the potential to enjoy, but its enjoyment was conditional on meeting two God-given obligations, again successfully discharged

by Solomon, which centered in the temple and the Torah (1 Chron. 28:7–10). God's gifts of rest and responsibilities went together as a package deal. Asa is portrayed in 14:1–8 as a second Solomon, living up to the obligations laid on him and so living in peace. In this phase of his life he matches up to the Solomonic model associated with the beginning of the new era.

If the framework of the passage is divinely given peace, its core is Asa's faithful discharge of the associated obligations. The accolade of 14:2 is unpacked in 14:3–5a. His concern for the temple is illustrated in 14:3, 5a. Only Solomon could build the temple: his successor's task was to maintain it as the focal point of worship. The priority given to the temple in the Chronicler's representation of the reigns of David and Solomon had revealed God's will for the new age. Its religious monopoly was violated by Judah's recourse to alternative sanctuaries and paraphernalia. Such fidelity to the temple as verses 3 and 5a exhibit was a measure of fidelity to God. The Christian reader may be tempted to dismiss this theme as a typical Old Testament stress on the material, which in the New is replaced by emphasis on the spiritual. In such passages as this one the material and spiritual co-exist. John 4:21–26 announces a new, messianic era in which the temple is superseded; yet still the spirit of worship can be revealed only in material ways, and the inner attitude of the heart only in external forms. Belonging to a spiritual temple carries with it the obligation of communal worship and of commitment to a local congregation of believers (Heb. 13:15; 1 Pet. 2:5). In this religious context the New Testament recognizes that there are parameters within which the Christian must remain: there are idols and false prophets in Christendom of which he or she must beware (1 John 4:1; 5:21).

If the temple was important, it was part of a wider claim, summed up in the Torah, "the law and the commandment" (14:4). The Chronicler's spiritual catchword, to "seek" God, reappears here. There is a beautiful correlation between traditional faith and personal commitment in the phrase "seek the Lord God of their fathers." A new generation lays claim to a spiritual heritage and accepts the claims of the old faith in an ever-living God. Spirituality, in this case spiritual renewal, is measured by adherence to God's guidelines for life. When John in his first letter called Christians to keep God's commandments in token of their love for Him (1 John 5:2, 3), we may regard it as a fresh application of the Chronicler's message. "Love

God and do what you will," preached St. Augustine. He spoke tongue in cheek, implying the subordination of the human will to the divine. In the church to which John wrote there were people flying spiritual blimps as they claimed to love God. In his letter he called their bluff by demanding that spiritual claims be grounded in keeping His commandments, a good Old Testament phrase. There is a whole gamut of obligations, moral, social, and religious, entailed in the biblical call to love God and one's neighbor.

The references to building *"fortified cities"* in 14:6–7 and to the *"army"* in verse 8 represent in the Chronicler's idiom God's blessings in response to royal faithfulness. We noted earlier that the reference to rest implicitly uses Solomon as a measuring rod to evaluate Asa. The same comparison probably underlies the theological explanation of 14:7b: *"Because we have sought the Lord our God, He has sought us"* (NEB). The last clause has been so rendered in accord with the ancient Greek version's interpretation of the Hebrew consonantal text. It aligns with David's message to Solomon: "If you seek Him, He will be found by you; but if you forsake Him, He will cast you off forever" (1 Chron. 28:9). The grim corollary is to be repeated in 15:2: "if you forsake Him, He will forsake you." This way of thinking, which has been called "mirror-image theology," reappears in the teaching of Jesus, as an incentive to fulfill God-given obligations. It always has an unexpected ring about it, pulling up its hearers short, shaking them out of their complacency, and making them think again. There are Christians who refuse to pray the Lord's Prayer because it asks God to "forgive us our debts, as we forgive our debtors." They speak of this as legal ground and contrast it with the grace of the Christian God who forgives freely. Certainly God takes the initiative in forgiveness, but His forgiveness sets up an obligation to forgive in turn, an obligation which, unheeded, can damage the relationship and impede further forgiveness. So taught Jesus in his great parable of forgiveness (Matt. 18:21–35), which serves to explain the petition for forgiveness in His great prayer (Matt. 6:12). Mirror-image theology is the norm in God's dealings with His people. He also has an emergency system, as the Chronicler is well aware from his key text, 2 Chronicles 7:14. Grace is available like a lifeboat ever ready to launch a rescue operation. But what sailor worth his salt would say "Let's sail dangerously; there's always the lifeboat"? The New Testament equivalent of 14:7b and 15:2 is the

solemn either-or message to Christians in Galatians 6:7–9 concerning exact recompense. Paul can marry it with his doctrine of justifi-
cation by faith proclaimed earlier in Galatians, ill-matched though
the marriage looks in terms of human logic.

2. *The victory of faith.* In 14:9 the peace and quiet of verses 1–8 are
rudely shattered. Foreign invasion brings Judah's idyllic rest to an
abrupt end. Here is another of the battle scenes the Chronicler loves
to depict, alien though they were to the political realities he and his
first readers knew in a Judah which was part of a stable Persian
empire. Their message is a spiritual call to faith and a portrayal of
God as able to meet any need, however great the human odds. In
this case the odds are grandiloqently represented as a thousand
thousand foes (*"a million men,"* 14:9). Fundamentally the Chronicler
has a realistic view of life. Foes do not appear on the horizon merely
as divine agents of retribution. Fond though he is of preaching providential causality, he is too good a student of life to promise a bed of
roses to the faithful believer. Crisis is a fact of life. Yet God is able to
deal with crisis when it comes: for the believer it is an opportunity
to prove God's power in a new way.

At first sight one would be inclined to argue from 14:7–8 that God
had already provided the answer to Asa's problem. Perhaps that is
often true in human experience, but in this case fortifications and
troops prove inadequate. There has to be a fresh turning of the heart
to God rather than trusting in what He has provided previously. The
lesson of renewed and direct contact with God is a valuable one.
Like yesterday's manna, old resources will not do, impressive though
they may be. There has to be a new recourse to God, to obtain grace
to help in time of need. "Let us therefore come boldly to the throne
of grace" (Heb. 4:16) is the Chronicler's implicit message.

God's *"help"* (14:11) is triggered by prayer, prayer which admits to
human helplessness and lays claim to God's patronage (*"our God"*
twice) and to His unique prayer. The power of 14:11 is beautifully
structured, beginning and ending with appeals to God and setting
human faith in the middle, surrounded by the protective power of
the covenant God. Asa's prayer is well-known to Christian congregations in the form of the lovely hymn of Edith G. Cherry, "We rest
on Thee, our Shield and our Defender," happily enhanced by its musical setting, Sibelius's *Finlandia.* The verb in the clause *"we rest on
You"* is better rendered "rely" (RSV) since it echoes the terminology,

and the context, of 13:18. The hymn may have influenced the NKJV to retain *"rest,"* confusing though it is in view of the triple occurrence of the English word in quite a different sense in 14:6–7. As in 13:18, this kind of faith is not an everyday matter, but that which is exercised at the end of one's tether, when ordinary spiritual resources have been exhausted. It is the faith which is so eloquently affirmed in the laments of the Book of Psalms, blending praise and petition in ardent prayer. In response God proves to be One who can be depended on when crisis comes.

3. *God's word of commendation and challenge.* In 15:1–7 the lessons of the previous narrative are drawn out through the medium of Azariah's prophetic message. In 15:8 the prophet seems disconcertingly to turn into his father, but the text is in a little disorder. The smooth rendering *"the prophecy of Oded the prophet"* conceals the fact that the equivalent of *"of"* is missing in the Hebrew (see RSV margin). *"Oded the prophet"* seems to have been a misplaced marginal reference to verse 1, intending to add *"the prophet"* to the phrase ending in *"Oded"* there.

The message takes the form of a Levitical sermon, like 1 Chronicles 28:2–10. After identifying its audience, it supplies a text, a historical illustration, and an application. The text (15:2b) is taken from Jeremiah 29:13–14, a favorite of the Chronicler. The experience of king and country was that, after seeking God (14:4, 7), they did find Him (14:12–14)—a very present help in trouble. Overwhelming proof of the text has been provided, in terms of its positive portion. Its negative element might seem irrelevant: in the overall context of Asa's reign it points forward to Asa's spiritual declension and warns against it. The twosidedness of the text is illustrated from the period of the Judges. In verse 3 there is no Hebrew verb. The historical perspective suggests *"was"* (RSV) rather than *"has been."* The double possibility of seeking God (15:3–4) or deserting Him and meeting only *"turmoil"* and *"adversity"* (15:5–6) was not foreign to Israel's experience. The Book of Judges presents the history of Israel as a wheel of fortune turning round and round, a wheel segmented into declension, invasion, repentance, divine deliverance, and peace (Judg. 2:11–16; 3:7–11; 10:6–16). In the sermon these segments are used to illustrate the double message. In declension Israel forsook God and His Torah in favor of pagan religion (see Judg. 2:12; 17:5–6). Yet they were able to bypass the divine law of cause and effect by seeking

God and finding Him there to help. Then the wheel turned on, and crises loomed again, with danger lurking on every journey, so strong was the enemy (Judg. 5:6; compare 6:2). In the absence of a turning back to God things went from bad to worse. The sermon closes with an application, encouraging the hearers to keep up the good *"work"* and urging them not to rest on their laurels.

The illustration is an instance of the use of previous spiritual history as a spur to a life of faith. It is a microcosm of what the whole of Chronicles was written to convey. The method is found elsewhere in the Bible as a means of teaching moral and spiritual lessons. Psalm 95 is an example: it harks back to the wilderness period of Israel's history. The psalm is re-used in Hebrews 3:7–4:13. Paul also used that period for *"examples"* or warnings to believers (1 Cor. 10:1–11). Christian biographies have the same function of presenting fortune, failure, and faith in human lives. The hero of this historical study is God, as the answer to human inadequacy. The fault it deprecates is not moral or economic failure, but failure in such circumstances to turn to God for help. To fall is human; to lift up divine.

The Chronicler has craftily woven into the sermon material from Zechariah 8:10 in 15:5–6. It is his way of challenging his post-exilic readers. How about us, he whispers to them. Have not we been suffering national distress after our return from exile? Have we been forsaking God and incurring His chastisement? Ought not we in turn seek the Lord and find in Him the answer to our needs? Just as Azariah is exhorting pre-exilic Judah by referring to the past, so implicitly the Chronicler is challenging post-exilic Judah and preaching his own sermon via Azariah's. The proclaimed word spans the centuries, living and powerful (Heb. 4:12).

4. *Obeying God's word.* 15:8–15 is marked by practical amens to the prophetic word. In 15:8 *"took courage"* echoes in the Hebrew *"be strong"* in 15:7, which accordingly is better rendered "take courage" (RSV). The seeking and finding of 15:12 and 15:15 pick up the terms of the sermon text and illustration (15:2, 4). King and country are a model congregation any preacher would be proud to have, first listening to the message and then living it out. It triggers a veritable revival, a deepening of the spiritual life of the nation. In its light some things had to be thrown out of their lives (15:8a). The altar of worship needed repairing (v. 8b). The Feast of Weeks provided an opportunity for a special service of recommitment to God. Verses

9–15 are marked by expressions of totality and enthusiasm. Verse 9 speaks of the wholeness of God's people, a sentiment dear to the Chronicler's heart. The worship of sacrifice (15:11) is a thank offering indicating their indebtedness to God in the previous battle. God's grace had given them victory, and so to God must be the glory. It is an opportunity for the community to dedicate themselves afresh to Him. The royal command of 14:4 is now enthusiastically honored. The repeated phrases *"with all their heart and with all their soul"* (15:12, 15; slightly varied in the Hebrew: see RSV) reflect the restoration of old-time religion (see Deut. 6:5). So does the somber note of verse 13, which relates to those who clung to pagan faiths and refused to acknowledge the God of Israel (see Deut. 13:1–10; 17:2–7). The communal pledge of allegiance is taken to the accompaniment of hallelujahs and musical blasts, which externalize the fervor of human hearts. For the Chronicler this was a model of temple worship, a scene of spiritual commitment in which religious forms reflected the worship of the heart. Here was God's Word dwelling in them richly, prompting true praise and thankfulness to God, on the lines of Colossians 3:16. It was one time at least when the people's hearts were in the right place. The passage ends on the note that in seeking God they were not disappointed. They enjoyed His blessing in the renewal of peace (15:15).

15:16–19 echo 15:8–15 in their motifs of reform, thankfulness to God, and peace. The Chronicler is falling back on 1 Kings 15:13–15. He quotes partly to capture the note of Asa's loyalty and the lengths to which it went (15:16, 17b). In the Judean monarchy the rank of queen mother was an official appointment, as the habitual naming in Kings attests: see 1 Kings 22:41; 2 Kings 14:1. Maachah by her Canaanite form of religion proved unworthy of the appointment and had to be dismissed. It must have caused a public scandal, and a lesser king would have done a cover-up. Painful as the incident was, consistency demanded it. If the heart is committed to God, it will not shrink from making necessary changes, however radical and disturbing.

COUNTERFEIT FAITH

16:1 In the thirty-sixth year of the reign of Asa, Baasha
king of Israel came up against Judah and built Ramah,

that he might let none go out or come in to Asa king of Judah.

2 Then Asa brought silver and gold from the treasuries of the house of the LORD and of the king's house, and sent to Ben-Hadad king of Syria, who dwelt in Damascus, saying,

3 *Let there be* a treaty between you and me, as there was between my father and your father. See, I have sent you silver and gold; come, break your treaty with Baasha king of Israel, so that he will withdraw from me.*

4 So Ben-Hadad heeded King Asa, and sent the captains of his armies against the cities of Israel. They attacked Ijon, Dan, Abel Maim, and all the storage cities of Naphtali.

5 Now it happened, when Baasha heard *it,* that he stopped building Ramah and ceased his work.

6 Then King Asa took all Judah, and they carried away the stones and timber of Ramah, which Baasha had used for building; and with them he built Geba and Mizpah.

7 And at that time Hanani the seer came to Asa king of Judah, and said to him: *Because you have relied on the king of Syria, and have not relied on the LORD your God, therefore the army of the king of Syria has escaped from your hand.

8 *Were the Ethiopians and the Lubim not a huge army with very many chariots and horsemen? Yet, because you relied on the LORD, He delivered them into your hand.

9 *For the eyes of the LORD run to and fro throughout the whole earth, to show Himself strong on behalf of *those* whose heart *is* loyal to Him. In this you have done foolishly; therefore from now on you shall have wars.*

10 Then Asa was angry with the seer, and put him in prison, for *he was* enraged at him because of this. And Asa oppressed *some* of the people at that time.

11 Note that the acts of Asa, first and last, are indeed written in the book of the kings of Judah and Israel.

12 And in the thirty-ninth year of his reign, Asa

became diseased in his feet, and his malady was severe; yet in his disease he did not seek the LORD, but the physicians.

13 So Asa rested with his fathers; he died in the forty-first year of his reign.

14 They buried him in his own tomb, which he had made for himself in the City of David; and they laid him in the bed which was filled with spices and various ingredients prepared in a mixture of ointments. They made a very great burning for him.

2 Chron. 16:1-14

Chapter 16 is a negative re-run of the previous two chapters. It is a hellish perversion of their themes. Victory is now won by unworthy means, God's word is rejected, and the compounding of infidelity is the dreary climax. In penning this chapter, the first and last of whose three parts are derived from 1 Kings 15, the Chronicler probably has one eye on Ezekiel 18. There three spiritual case histories are examined. The Chronicler appears to look at a number of Judean kings in the light of Ezekiel's models. Here the case of a righteous person who "turns away from his righteousness" (Ezek. 18:24-26) is relevant. Asa fits into this category in the Chronicler's eyes, and he tells the story as a warning against backsliding. His implicit message is that of the apostle Paul after he had surveyed the downhill journey of Israel from Exodus redemption to death in the wilderness: "Therefore let him who thinks he stands take heed lest he fall" (1 Cor. 10:12).

1. *Victory falsely won.* In verses 1-6 the Chronicler lets 1 Kings 15:17-22 speak for itself. He will reserve comment until the speech of Hanani in verses 7-10. However, his underlying sense of outrage is easily appreciated. Where now is the spirit of faith of 14:11? How can treasures consecrated to God, including Asa's own gifts to Him (see 15:18), be grabbed and used as payment for unnecessary help? Asa's expedient works, but at what a cost, material and spiritual!

2. *God's word of rebuke rejected.* Hanani is a second Azariah, but unfortunately he has a far different message to bring, a message of accusation and judgment. If Asa is congratulating himself on the success of his stratagem, he needs to be told how shortsighted he has been: Syria would have fallen into his lap! The seer's rebuke is enhanced by a contrast with Asa's earlier victory: *"You relied on the king*

of Syria, and have not relied on" God, whereas before *"you relied on the Lord"* (vv. 7–8). The keyword of the section bombards Asa's ears and the reader's eyes, recalling 14:11. Again crisis had been an opportunity to prove God but this time faith had been put in human aid. The wrong emergency button was pressed. The Chronicler seems to have in mind Isaiah 10:20, which speaks of relying (NKJV "depend") on God instead of Assyria. Isaiah regarded reliance on foreign aid a besetting sin of the Judean monarchy (Isa. 30:1–2; 31:1) and Hosea had earlier berated the northern kingdom for this perversity (Hos. 7:8–12; 14:3). In God's nation, where religion and politics were one, human expediency was a denial of true faith and a switch from God to humanity as the object of trust. Verse 9 cites Zechariah 4:10, assuring the universality of God's protection, whether danger loomed from the south, as in chapter 14, or from the north, as in the case of Baasha. From wherever crisis comes, God is aware of it and ready to respond to faith with proof of His power. In this instance, however, faith had been replaced by folly. In divine reprisal Asa's lot would not be peace, as before, but warfare.

Asa, the model sermon hearer in chapter 15, perversely rejects the divine message. He takes out on Hanani his resentment against God, and puts him in the prison *"stocks"* (v. 10, RSV), a fate which Jeremiah suffered (Jer. 20:2). Others, presumably supporters of Hanani, are tortured ("treated . . . with brutality," NEB). The incident is a reminder of the courage needed to witness for God in a hostile or potentially hostile environment. The writer to the Hebrews, addressing a Christian group which had previously suffered persecution and was likely to do so again, challenged them to recall the persecution and torture the Old Testament saints endured for the sake of the faith (Heb. 10:32–35; 11:35–37). Supremely he pointed to the example of Jesus (Heb. 12:3).

3. *Infidelity compounded.* If Asa failed to rely on God in his military crisis, he failed to *"seek"* Him in a personal crisis (v. 12). The royal malady might have been gangrene, but the description is not clear enough for a sure diagnosis. The Chronicler's concern is to draw attention to Asa's reaction. There may be a wordplay underlying the surface of the text. Asa's name means "He (God) heals," yet here was Asa resorting to physicians! For the Chronicler it is another recourse to human aid. Backslider as he was, his disease should have been a warning of God's displeasure. This malady went too deep for

doctors to cure, irrespective of the fact that ancient medical lore was limited. Asa's recourse to physicians represented an evasive tactic and a failure to *"seek"* God. It was like treating a decayed tooth with a pain-reliever from the drugstore instead of going to the dentist. The New Testament too envisages cases of sickness linked with unfaithfulness to God (1 Cor. 11:30). It would have been remiss for those sick Christians at Corinth to seek medical help rather than putting the spiritual malady right. There is no warrant to see here an absolute denial of the value of doctors. In the intertestamental book of Ecclesiasticus there is an interesting passage about how God heals through the agency of doctors (Ecclus. 38:1–15). Paul's warm reference to Luke as *"the beloved physician"* (Col. 4:14) points in this direction.

Asa dies, whether of his foot trouble we do not know. Significantly there is a more elaborate note of his burial than in 1 Kings 15:24. He is given an honorable burial with the traditional *"burning"* of spices being performed on a *"very great"* scale (v. 14; compare 21:19). In fairness the Chronicler wants his readers to remember that, if he fell from grace in his latter years, earlier he had been a good king. The fact remains that Asa suffered shipwreck concerning the faith (1 Tim. 1:19). The warning is worth repeating: *"Let him who thinks he stands, take heed lest he fall."* What counts is not a decision made for God in one's youth or last year but a decision made today. Ordinary days bring with them a call to live out one's commitment to God. Times of crisis summon us to exercise the emergency faith of reliance. Temptations to forsake God and to rely on other expedients may well confront us. *"See then that you walk circumspectly, not as fools but as wise"* (Eph. 5:15).

NOTE

1. H. Newton Malony, *Living the Answers* (Nashville: Abingdon, 1979), pp. 38f.

CHAPTER THIRTEEN

Keeping the Right Company

2 Chronicles 17:1–20:37

The next four chapters are devoted to the reign of Jehoshaphat, who is thus shown to be an important king in the Chronicler's eyes and one worthy of his close study. In his presentation of the divided monarchy in 2 Chronicles 10–28, Jehoshaphat's reign stands at the literary midpoint. It provides the Chronicler with the opportunity to present both the potential and the limitations of this period of the history of God's people. In his treatment of Jehoshaphat's reign he gives the most positive portrayal of any king in this period; he was a great and good king (compare 21:12; 22:9). However, as a child of his age, Jehoshaphat lived under the shadow of the divided monarchy. Almost inevitably he fell victim at times to the temptation of collaborating with his northern counterparts, who were religious apostates. These chapters have two contrasting themes, the alternatives of staying within the circles of fellowship with God or straying outside in wrongful alliance with wicked kings of the north, Ahab and Ahaziah. The presence of the Lord in blessing and help is mentioned four times, at 17:3; 19:6, 11, and 20:17. The motif of impious alliance is mentioned at 18:1 and 20:35–37. Prominence is given to each of these controlling motifs in their respective contexts. The Chronicler has used Jehoshaphat's reign to preach a powerful sermon, exploring the outworking of faith and implicitly challenging his readers to walk with God.

GOD'S PRESENCE IN BLESSING

17:1 Then Jehoshaphat his son reigned in his place,
and strengthened himself against Israel.

2 And he placed troops in all the fortified cities of Judah, and set garrisons in the land of Judah and in the cities of Ephraim which Asa his father had taken.

3 Now the LORD was with Jehoshaphat, because he walked in the former ways of his father David; he did not seek the Baals,

4 but sought the God of his father, and walked in His commandments and not according to the acts of Israel.

5 Therefore the LORD established the kingdom in his hand; and all Judah gave presents to Jehoshaphat, and he had riches and honor in abundance.

6 And his heart took delight in the ways of the LORD; moreover he removed the high places and wooden images from Judah.

7 Also in the third year of his reign he sent his leaders, Ben-Hail, Obadiah, Zechariah, Nethanel, and Michaiah, to teach in the cities of Judah.

8 And with them *he sent* Levites: Shemaiah, Nethaniah, Zebadiah, Asahel, Shemiramoth, Jehonathan, Adonijah, Tobijah, and Tobadonijah—the Levites; and with them Elishama and Jehoram, the priests.

9 So they taught in Judah, and *had* the Book of the Law of the LORD with them; they went throughout all the cities of Judah and taught the people.

10 And the fear of the LORD fell on all the kingdoms of the lands that *were* around Judah, so that they did not make war against Jehoshaphat.

11 Also *some* of the Philistines brought Jehoshaphat presents and silver as tribute; and the Arabians brought him flocks, seven thousand seven hundred rams and seven thousand seven hundred male goats.

12 So Jehoshaphat became increasingly powerful, and he built fortresses and storage cities in Judah.

13 He had much property in the cities of Judah; and the men of war, mighty men of valor, *were* in Jerusalem.

14 These *are* their numbers, according to their fathers' houses. Of Judah, the captains of thousands: Adnah the captain, and with him three hundred thousand mighty men of valor;

15 and next to him *was* Jehohanan the captain, and with him two hundred and eighty thousand;

16 and next to him *was* Amasiah the son of Zichri, who willingly offered himself to the LORD, and with him two hundred thousand mighty men of valor.

17 Of Benjamin: Eliada a mighty man of valor, and with him two hundred thousand men armed with bow and shield;

18 and next to him *was* Jehozabad, and with him one hundred and eighty thousand prepared for war.

19 These served the king, besides those the king put in the fortified cities throughout all Judah.

2 Chron. 17:1–19

In Kings the account of Jehoshaphat's reign has a northern orientation (1 Kings 22; 2 Kings 3). In Chronicles, however, Jehoshaphat is considered in his own right. This chapter functions as an introductory and basic one in the description of his reign. The chapters that follow it either endorse its high assessment of the king or else provide exceptions to the general tenor of his rule. The gist of chapter 17 is provided in summary form in verses 1–5. It is carefully structured with verses 3b–4 at its heart. Jehoshaphat's life was characterized by loyalty to God. The accolade of spirituality is bestowed on him: he *"sought"* God. A similar testimony to his faith is given in 22:9 as one who "sought the Lord with all his heart."

Here the observation is clarified by a comparison and a contrast. He is compared with Asa in his *"former"* period of faith (chaps. 14, 15) as distinct from his later period of declension (chap. 16). In the standard Hebrew text *"David"* appears, but it is rightly not present in the Greek version and in certain Hebrew manuscripts (see RSV). The Chronicler seems to have had in mind 1 Kings 22:43, which refers to Asa, and the adjective *"former"* confirms this reference, whereas David's reign was not split into two periods. Probably at some stage in the history of the present Hebrew text, "David his father"—such is the Hebrew order—was written in the margin of a Hebrew manuscript as a synoptic comment expanding "David" in 16:14 in line with the parallel "David his father" in 1 Kings 15:24. Then because of the repeated *"he did not seek"* in 16:12 and 17:3 the comment slipped and was taken as an amplification of *"his father"* in 17:3. The Hebrew text over the ages has not been immune to such ravages here and there, and the commentator has to be alert to the totality of witnesses to the ancient Hebrew. Textual criticism is an evangelical task, committed as it is to the basic work of establishing as far as possible the original text of the Word of God.

If Jehoshaphat is related positively to his father, negatively he is related to Ahab, in oblique terms. The Chronicler assumes that his readers know the final chapters of 1 Kings and the northern king's shocking adherence to Canaanite religion. By contrast Jehoshaphat stood out as a witness to the true faith. His lifestyle was governed by the *"commandments"* of God in the Torah. It was *"because"* of this commitment that *"the Lord was with Jehoshaphat."* Evidence of this supporting presence has been provided in verse 2. As in 11:5–12, the king's defense system, to be amplified at the end of the chapter, is for the Chronicler a mark of God's blessing. It makes Judah a strong nation which under God can hold its own in the world. If verses 2–3a pave the way for verses 3b–4, verse 5 further explains them with its *"therefore."* This further evidence of God's blessing is His consolidation of the king's rule and the gifts of *"riches and honor."* So the message of verses 1–5 is seeking and finding. The king's prosperity is traced back to his commitment to God. Seeking God, he found evidence of God's goodness flooding into his life. For the Chronicler a living faith and well-being went hand in hand.

In the rest of the chapter particular evidence of Jehoshaphat's spiritual concern (vv. 6–9) is followed by evidence of blessing (vv. 10–19). The Hebrew verb underlying *"took delight"* is an unusual one, as if the Chronicler was straining to portray the exceptional nature of the king's spirituality. The verb means to be high, and elsewhere with "heart" it has the bad sense of a high and mighty attitude. Here it refers to his high ideals or spiritual ambition to follow God's *"ways,"* especially as it corresponds to seeking God (v. 3). A similar expression in the New Testament occurs in the exhortation which may literally be rendered "Think high things" ("Set your mind on things above," Col. 3:2). In the original Greek this is the motto of the London Bible College, where I was privileged to serve for over twenty years. A better motto for young people training for the Lord's work would be difficult to find. Ambition is a virtue when practiced within the guidelines of *"the ways of the Lord"* (v. 6). Jehoshaphat knew nothing of an "Oh to be nothing, nothing" religious mentality: that would have been to bury in the ground the talent entrusted to him.

His high aims were achieved in the two areas which in Chronicles are the twin expressions of God's will, temple and Torah. As for the temple, he safeguarded it from challenges from elsewhere (v. 6b). As for the Torah, he instigated an itinerant team of teachers. Here the Chronicler seems to have had available a source other than Kings from which he draws. In the light of 15:3 teaching and Torah go together—naturally so since Torah relates to directions for life's journey. A team of religious personnel and laypersons is dispatched throughout Judah, to carry out a teaching ministry among the people, Bible in hand (v. 9). Presumably the Pentateuch is in view, and one is reminded of Ezra's similar commission from the Persian king (Ezra 7:6, 11–26). Here is another instance of Jehoshaphat's high ideals, that the people should be instructed in God's revelation so that it might take root and bear fruit in their lives.

The text moves from Jehoshaphat's concern for the things of God to an elaboration of God's blessings in terms of peace, foreign *"tribute"* (v. 11; compare v. 5), building projects, and military power (compare v. 2). The chapter comes around full circle to the themes of its opening verses as a portrayal of obedience and blessing. The blessings are those appropriate to a member of the Davidic dynasty, reflecting the power and affluence of a true theocracy (vv. 5, 10). In line with this conception is the description of Amasiah as one who *"willingly offered himself to the Lord"* (v. 16). He was a soldier who evidently volunteered and rose to a responsible rank, but his work is described in religious terms. The wording is reminiscent of the royal Psalm 110:3, which speaks of the people being *"volunteers"* to serve the Davidic king in his divinely backed campaigns. With different associations but similar effect the New Testament urges slaves to serve their masters *"with good will doing service, as to the Lord"* (Eph. 6:7). "Happy is the man whose job is his hobby," Bernard Shaw once said. Perhaps happier still is the person whose daily work is dedicated to God and done to please Him.

WRONGFUL ALLIANCE

18:1 Jehoshaphat had riches and honor in abundance;
and by marriage he allied himself with Ahab.
    2 After some years he went down to *visit* Ahab in

Samaria; and Ahab killed sheep and oxen in abundance for him and the people who were with him, and persuaded him to go up *with him* to Ramoth Gilead.

3 So Ahab king of Israel said to Jehoshaphat king of Judah, "Will you go with me *against* Ramoth Gilead?" And he answered him, "I *am* as you *are*, and my people as your people; *we will be* with you in the war."

4 Also Jehoshaphat said to the king of Israel, "Please inquire for the word of the LORD today."

5 Then the king of Israel gathered the prophets together, four hundred men, and said to them, "Shall we go to war against Ramoth Gilead, or shall I refrain?" So they said, "Go up, for God will deliver it into the king's hand."

6 But Jehoshaphat said, "*Is there* not still a prophet of the LORD here, that we may inquire of Him?"

7 So the king of Israel said to Jehoshaphat, "*There is* still one man by whom we may inquire of the LORD; but I hate him, because he never prophesies good concerning me, but always evil. He *is* Micaiah the son of Imla." And Jehoshaphat said, "Let not the king say such things!"

8 Then the king of Israel called one *of his* officers and said, "Bring Micaiah the son of Imla quickly!"

9 The king of Israel and Jehoshaphat king of Judah, clothed in *their* robes, sat each on his throne; and they sat at a threshing floor at the entrance of the gate of Samaria; and all the prophets prophesied before them.

10 Now Zedekiah the son of Chenaanah had made horns of iron for himself; and he said, "Thus says the LORD: 'With these you shall gore the Syrians until they are destroyed.'"

11 And all the prophets prophesied so, saying, "Go up to Ramoth Gilead and prosper, for the LORD will deliver *it* into the king's hand."

12 Then the messenger who had gone to call Micaiah spoke to him, saying, "Now listen, the words of the prophets with one accord encourage the king. Therefore please let your word be like *the word of* one of them, and speak encouragement."

13 And Micaiah said, "*As* the LORD lives, whatever my God says, that I will speak."

14 Then he came to the king; and the king said to him, "Micaiah, shall we go to war against Ramoth Gilead, or shall I refrain?" And he said, "Go and prosper, and they shall be delivered into your hand!"

15 So the king said to him, "How many times shall I make you swear that you tell me nothing but the truth in the name of the LORD?"

16 Then he said, "I saw all Israel scattered on the mountains, as sheep that have no shepherd. And the LORD said, 'These have no master. Let each return to his house in peace.'"

17 And the king of Israel said to Jehoshaphat, "Did I not tell you he would not prophesy good concerning me, but evil?"

18 Then *Micaiah* said, "Therefore hear the word of the LORD: I saw the LORD sitting on His throne, and all the host of heaven standing on His right hand and His left.

19 "And the LORD said, 'Who will persuade Ahab king of Israel to go up, that he may fall at Ramoth Gilead?' So one spoke in this manner, and another spoke in that manner.

20 "Then a spirit came forward and stood before the LORD, and said, 'I will persuade him.' The LORD said to him, 'In what way?'

21 "So he said, 'I will go out and be a lying spirit in the mouth of all his prophets.' And *the LORD* said, 'You shall persuade *him* and also prevail; go out and do so.'

22 "Therefore look! The LORD has put a lying spirit in the mouth of these prophets of yours, and the LORD has declared disaster against you."

23 Then Zedekiah the son of Chenaanah went near and struck Micaiah on the cheek, and said, "Which way did the spirit from the LORD go from me to speak to you?"

24 And Micaiah said, "Indeed you shall see on that day when you go into an inner chamber to hide!"

25 Then the king of Israel said, "Take Micaiah, and

return him to Amon the governor of the city and to
Joash the king's son;

26 "and say, 'Thus says the king: "Put this *fellow* in
prison, and feed him with bread of affliction and
water of affliction, until I return in peace."'"

27 But Micaiah said, "If you ever return in peace,
the LORD has not spoken by me." And he said, "Take
heed, all you people!"

28 So the king of Israel and Jehoshaphat the king
of Judah went up to Ramoth Gilead.

29 And the king of Israel said to Jehoshaphat, "I
will disguise myself and go into battle; but you put
on your robes." So the king of Israel disguised himself, and they went into battle.

30 Now the king of Syria had commanded the captains of the chariots who *were* with him, saying,
"Fight with no one small or great, but only with the
king of Israel."

31 So it was, when the captains of the chariots saw
Jehoshaphat, that they said, "It *is* the king of Israel!"
Therefore they surrounded him to attack; but Je-
hoshaphat cried out, and the LORD helped him, and
God diverted them from him.

32 For so it was, when the captains of the chariots
saw that it was not the king of Israel, that they
turned back from pursuing him.

33 Now a certain man drew a bow at random, and
struck the king of Israel between the joints of his
armor. So he said to the driver of his chariot, "Turn
around and take me out of the battle, for I am
wounded."

34 The battle increased that day, and the king of
Israel propped *himself* up in *his* chariot facing the
Syrians until evening; and about the time of sunset
he died.

19:1 Then Jehoshaphat the king of Judah returned
safely to his house in Jerusalem.

2 And Jehu the son of Hanani the seer went out
to meet him, and said to King Jehoshaphat, "Should
you help the wicked and love those who hate the
LORD? Therefore the wrath of the LORD *is* upon you.

3 "Nevertheless good things are found in you, in

> that you have removed the wooden images from the
> land, and have prepared your heart to seek God."
>
> *2 Chron. 18:1–19:3*

Most of this material concerning Jehoshaphat's involvement in a joint military campaign with Ahab is taken from 1 Kings 22. The Chronicler uses it to demonstrate an unfortunate lapse on the part of the Judean king, and adds his own introduction and conclusion to the narrative (18:1; 19:1–3), which reveal his understanding of it. The introduction is resonant with fury just beneath the surface. What a fool Jehoshaphat was—on three scores.

1. *A needless alliance.* Despite the gains God had lavished on him (cf. 18:5), he ventured into a "marriage alliance" (18:1, RSV), which as in medieval times was contracted among royalty for political ends.

2. *Alliance with an apostate king.* His partner in this scheming was none other than Ahab. The name spoke volumes to anyone who had read the account of his reign in Kings: the Chronicler's comments in 21:6 and 22:2, 3 are indications of his low estimate of Ahab. Jehoshaphat who had resolutely trodden a path of religious purity (17:3) now entangled himself with an apostate. The result was to affect not only himself but the royal house and his people. In the marriage of the crown prince Jehoram to Athaliah, the daughter of Ahab and Jezebel, a viper was introduced into the Judean nest, as the Chronicler's history will disclose in chapters 21–23. It has already been hinted in 17:3 that Ahab sanctioned Canaanite religion. The Chronicler has made clear in chapter 13 his distinction between the people of the northern kingdom, Judah's brothers and sisters and God's children, and their kings who led them astray. Ahab was a particularly obnoxious example as one who not merely introduced innovations into Israel's faith but sanctioned an alien religion.

3. *A naïve association.* Dazzled by the extravagance of his state visit to Samaria, Jehoshaphat is swept off his feet and falls an ingenuous victim to Ahab's wishes. The Hebrew word rendered *"persuaded"* is a strong one: it is used in Deuteronomy 13:6 of enticement to apostasy and so it connotes leading someone spiritually astray. The motif of enticing or persuading becomes in the Chronicles version of the story a key one. The same term, lacking in 1 Kings 22, recurs in 18:31 (*"diverted,"* RSV "drew . . . away"), while a verb of similar meaning runs through 18:19–21 (*"persuade,"* RSV "entice").

The whole story is made to revolve around the concept of manipulation, human and divine.

The narrative of 18:3–34 follows 1 Kings 22:4–35, apart from 18:31b. Jehoshaphat joins in a campaign to capture Ramoth Gilead, a border town between Syria and Israelite territory in the north Transjordan, currently in Syrian hands. The compliant words of Jehoshaphat in 18:3 sound willfully foolish in view of the Chronicler's accent on the northern king's apostasy. In 18:4, 6 Jehoshaphat comes over in a comparatively good light in his insistence on a prophetic inquiry: literally the verb means *"seek"* (19:3). It is noteworthy, however, that when his request is honored and defeat is foretold, he persists in the military venture. A fool and his principles are soon parted! The scene involving the prophets in 18:5–27 is a fiasco from beginning to end, or more strictly a game which Ahab wrongly thinks he wins, ignoring the checkmate move of his prophetic opponent.

Jehoshaphat sees through the glib reply to Ahab's prophetic yes-men. With a cynical comment Ahab has Micaiah fetched. Micaiah refuses to toe the party line (18:12, 13). Nevertheless he gives the stock answer—but evidently in such sarcastic tones as to make it clear that he is only mimicking his colleagues. Ahab gets the truth he claims he wants in the form of an account of a prophetic vision of the heavenly council chamber. The statement that God had been manipulating the compliant prophets to lure Ahab to his doom is heavily ironic. In fact, of course, there is no deception. Ahab knows the truth (18:15), but chooses to go his own way, his ego bolstered by his court prophets (see 18:12). The point is that they play a part in God's providential plan. Ahab, master of manipulation (18:2), has met his match. His ploy has been followed by God's counterploy. Ahab still has some cards to play—throwing Micaiah into prison and donning a disguise. His true opponent is not Syria, but God, who plays a trump card. Ahab is killed by a *"random"* (18:33) arrow, which just happens to hit him! Such are the ways of an overriding providence.

Jehoshaphat, on the other hand, maliciously thrust into danger, has nothing more than a close shave with death. The Chronicler interprets the Judean king's cry in 1 Kings 22:32 as a prayer and adds his own amplification. The S.O.S. prayer of this believer, although he is in trouble of his own making, is charitably answered with divine help. The Chronicler is urging the power of prayer, or rather the efficacy of prayer in triggering the powerful grace of God in time of need. Something else he wants to draw attention to is the divine manipulation of events. The Hebrew verb of verse 2 occurs again in 18:31, with God as subject (NKJV, *"diverted"*). Ahab had wanted Jehoshaphat to die in his place (18:29–30), but God foils his scheme and makes the Syrian troops recognize that this royal figure is not their intended quarry. One great lesson for the Chronicler is the mystery of divine providence, whereby God protects His own and repays wrongdoing. From a tangle of human mistakes and machinations the Lord is able to weave eventually a tapestry which glorifies His moral will. This is the truth of Romans 8:28: "all things work together"—or perhaps better with the NEB "in everything . . . he [the Spirit] co-operates for good with those who love God." Charles Spurgeon testified, as he looked back over his own life: "I can see a thousand chances, as men would call them, all working together like wheels in a great piece of machinery, to fix me where I am."[1]

The Chronicler has yet to supply the main lesson of the passage via the prophetic post-mortem of 19:1–3. Jehoshaphat had indeed had a providential escape (19:1) in fulfillment of the divine word of 18:16, fruitlessly defied by Ahab (18:27). The Judean king is properly taken to task for the folly of his political and military association with Ahab. It has to be made clear that divine mercy does not condone wrongdoing. *"Love"* is used in the idiomatic Hebrew sense of political alliance, but it is here tellingly coupled with *"hate"* as a term of religious antagonism. Spiritually the two kings were as different as chalk and cheese, and no good could have come of the venture. The reference to God's *"wrath"* is not easy to explain, since it has no verb with it in the Hebrew. The RSV may be correct in interpreting "wrath has gone out," in which case the reference is to Jehoshaphat's humiliating defeat (see 18:16 and compare 20:37). Many commentators find a forward-looking reference here, judging that the king is under a sword of Damocles, which is kept aloft by his deeds of repentance in 19:4–20:30, but eventually falls on him in 20:1 or 20:35–37. In the latter passage, however, God's judgment has its own adequate reasons, and in Jehoshaphat's prayer of 20:6–12 there is no expected confession of sin.

Did the Chronicler have in mind a situation in the post-exilic age, comparable to Jehoshaphat's ill-advised venture? He may have been thinking of mixed marriages between the faithful and those who avowed a polytheistic form of faith. He would not have taken the narrow, racial stand of Ezra and Nehemiah, necessary though it evidently was in their special circumstances, but he too would have counseled separation when the "God of their fathers" was not honored as exclusive Lord. Paul inherited this tradition: "Do not be unequally yoked together with unbelievers. . . . What accord has Christ with Belial?" (2 Cor. 6:14, 15).

GOD'S PRESENCE IN SOCIAL REFORM

19:4 So Jehoshaphat dwelt at Jerusalem; and he went out again among the people from Beersheba to the mountains of Ephraim, and brought them back to the LORD God of their fathers.

5 Then he set judges in the land throughout all the fortified cities of Judah, city by city,

6 and said to the judges, "Take heed to what you are doing, for you do not judge for man but for the LORD, who *is* with you in the judgment.

7 "Now therefore, let the fear of the LORD be upon you; take care and do *it,* for *there is* no iniquity with the LORD our God, no partiality, nor taking of bribes."

8 Moreover in Jerusalem, for the judgment of the LORD and for controversies, Jehoshaphat appointed some of the Levites and priests, and some of the chief fathers of Israel, when they returned to Jerusalem.

9 And he commanded them, saying, "Thus you shall act in the fear of the LORD, faithfully and with a loyal heart:

10 "Whatever case comes to you from your brethren who dwell in their cities, whether of bloodshed or offenses against law or commandment, against statutes or ordinances, you shall warn them, lest they trespass against the LORD and wrath come upon you and your brethren. Do this, and you will not be guilty.

11 "And take notice: Amariah the chief priest *is* over you in all matters of the LORD; and Zebadiah

> the son of Ishmael, the ruler of the house of Judah,
> for all the king's matters; also the Levites *will be* offi-
> cials before you. Behave courageously, and the LORD
> will be with the good.'
>
> *2 Chron. 19:4–11*

Jehoshaphat's assurance and prayerful wish concerning the Lord's presence, at the beginning of his first speech and the end of his second (vv. 6, 11), supply the keynote of this passage. It brings us out of the shadows of chapter 18 and back into the sunshine of chapter 17 (17:3). The Chronicler seems to be following a source other than Kings in his description of a judicial reform instigated by Jehoshaphat. Underlying the reform is a shift from the old tribal system of justice to centralized royal administration. The mention of *"the fortified cities"* (v. 5), which were under royal control, is thus historically feasible. The whole enterprise is described as stimulating a return to covenant standards (v. 4). The Chronicler probably had in mind especially Deuteronomy 16:18–20 and 17:8–13, on which Jehoshaphat's speeches draw heavily. A revival takes place, in the matter-of-fact form of social ethics. The spirituality of *"a loyal heart"* (v. 9) has to be worked out in details of social behavior. Again there is evidence of the king's concern for the people, as in 17:9. It is a grass-roots implementation of faith: to administer justice was a king's divinely sanctioned duty (1 Chron. 18:14; Ps. 72:1–4, 12–14). Judges are appointed for the Judean towns, while in Jerusalem both a lower court (v. 8, rendering *"and for controversies of the inhabitants of Jerusalem"* with the Greek version; cf. NEB) and a court of appeal (v. 10) are established, with separate presidents for civil and religious cases.

In his two speeches Jehoshaphat characterizes the judges as God's representatives before society (v. 6; cf. Deut. 1:17) and representatives of society before God (v. 10). They are to judge by divine standards of morality, uncorrupted by human failings. Should they fail, they would not only be misinterpreting God but themselves incur His punishment. Jehoshaphat is sensitive to the providential will of God—he has learned his lesson, for now at least.

The passage pushes forward into the New Testament at three points.

1. *Ephesians 6:9.* The warning that Christians in positions of authority have their own impartial Master in heaven is an extension of the principles laid down here.

2. *Romans 13:1-7.* God is the Lord of social order in the wider secular world. In principle, governing authorities are God's ministers in their enforcement of law and order. A Christian who cheats when filling in his tax forms is obstructing God's purpose for society.

3. *Romans 2:11.* Paul may have had 2 Chronicles 19:7 in mind, for only here in the Hebrew Bible does the noun *"partiality"* occur. The Chronicler argues from theology to the practical dimension of a legal system. The apostle stays on a theological level but develops the basic truth by arguing for an inclusive principle which affects Jews and Gentiles alike.

GOD'S PRESENCE IN DELIVERANCE

20:1 It happened after this *that* the people of Moab with the people of Ammon, and *others* with them besides the Ammonites, came to battle against Jehoshaphat.

2 Then some came and told Jehoshaphat, saying, "A great multitude is coming against you from beyond the sea, from Syria; and they are in Hazazon Tamar" (which *is* En Gedi).

3 And Jehoshaphat feared, and set himself to seek the LORD, and proclaimed a fast throughout all Judah.

4 So Judah gathered together to ask *help* from the LORD; and from all the cities of Judah they came to seek the LORD.

5 Then Jehoshaphat stood in the assembly of Judah and Jerusalem, in the house of the LORD, before the new court,

6 and said: "O LORD God of our fathers, *are* You not God in heaven, and do You *not* rule over all the kingdoms of the nations, and in Your hand *is there not* power and might, so that no one is able to withstand You?

7 *"Are* You not our God, *who* drove out the inhabitants of this land before Your people Israel, and gave it to the descendants of Abraham Your friend forever?

8 "And they dwell in it, and have built You a sanctuary in it for Your name, saying,

303

9 'If disaster comes upon us—sword, judgment, pestilence, or famine—we will stand before this temple and in Your presence (for Your name *is* in this temple), and cry out to You in our affliction, and You will hear and save.'

10 "And now, here are the people of Ammon, Moab, and Mount Seir—whom You would not let Israel invade when they came out of the land of Egypt, but they turned from them and did not destroy them—

11 "here they are, rewarding us by coming to throw us out of Your possession which You have given us to inherit.

12 "O our God, will You not judge them? For we have no power against this great multitude that is coming against us; nor do we know what to do, but our eyes *are* upon You."

13 Now all Judah, with their little ones, their wives, and their children, stood before the LORD.

14 Then the Spirit of the LORD came upon Jahaziel the son of Zechariah, the son of Benaiah, the son of Jeiel, the son of Mattaniah, a Levite of the sons of Asaph, in the midst of the assembly.

15 And he said, "Listen, all you of Judah and you inhabitants of Jerusalem, and you, King Jehoshaphat! Thus says the LORD to you: 'Do not be afraid nor dismayed because of this great multitude, for the battle *is* not yours, but God's.

16 'Tomorrow go down against them. They will surely come up by the Ascent of Ziz, and you will find them at the end of the brook before the Wilderness of Jeruel.

17 'You will not *need* to fight in this *battle.* Position yourselves, stand still and see the salvation of the LORD, who is with you, O Judah and Jerusalem!' Do not fear or be dismayed; tomorrow go out against them, for the LORD *is* with you."

18 And Jehoshaphat bowed his head with *his* face to the ground, and all Judah and the inhabitants of Jerusalem bowed before the LORD, worshiping the LORD.

19 Then the Levites of the children of the

Kohathites and of the children of the Korahites stood up to praise the LORD God of Israel with voices loud and high.

20 So they rose early in the morning and went out into the Wilderness of Tekoa; and as they went out, Jehoshaphat stood and said, "Hear me, O Judah and you inhabitants of Jerusalem: Believe in the LORD your God, and you shall be established; believe His prophets, and you shall prosper."

21 And when he had consulted with the people, he appointed those who should sing to the LORD, and who should praise the beauty of holiness, as they went out before the army and were saying:

"Praise the LORD,
For His mercy *endures* forever."

22 Now when they began to sing and to praise, the LORD set ambushes against the people of Ammon, Moab, and Mount Seir, who had come against Judah; and they were defeated.

23 For the people of Ammon and Moab stood up against the inhabitants of Mount Seir to utterly kill and destroy *them.* And when they had made an end of the inhabitants of Seir, they helped to destroy one another.

24 So when Judah came to a place overlooking the wilderness, they looked toward the multitude; and there *were* their dead bodies, fallen on the earth. No one had escaped.

25 When Jehoshaphat and his people came to take away their spoil, they found among them an abundance of valuables on the dead bodies, and precious jewelry, which they stripped off for themselves, more than they could carry away; and they were three days gathering the spoil because there was so much.

26 And on the fourth day they assembled in the Valley of Berachah, for there they blessed the LORD; therefore the name of that place was called The Valley of Berachah until this day.

27 Then they returned, every man of Judah and Jerusalem, with Jehoshaphat in front of them, to go back to Jerusalem with joy, for the LORD had made them rejoice over their enemies.

28 So they came to Jerusalem, with stringed instruments and harps and trumpets, to the house of the LORD.

29 And the fear of God was on all the kingdoms of *those* countries when they heard that the LORD had fought against the enemies of Israel.

30 Then the realm of Jehoshaphat was quiet, for his God gave him rest all around.

2 Chron. 20:1–30

This is a classic story of faith. Twenty years and more ago it used to fall to my regular lot to conduct a short morning service of hymn, reading, and prayer for Christian students. This passage was my choice more than once, so eloquent is its summons to spiritual commitment. Again the keynote is the formula *"The Lord is with you"* (v. 17), which comes at the climax of a prophet's speech of assurance.

It is the situation of Asa and Zerah (14:9–15) all over again, but the narrative is more complex. The Chronicler seemingly followed a tradition of a successful military engagement located to the northwest of the Dead Sea (vv. 2, 16, 20). The enemies are represented as a coalition of *"Moab," "Ammon,"* and *"Meunites"* (v. 1, RSV, following the Greek version: cf. 26:7), invading Judah by advancing up the west side of the Dead Sea. *"Jehoshaphat feared"* (v. 3)—a very natural reaction. Eventually he will hear from God's servant the message *"Do not fear"* (v. 17). It has been said—I have not checked—that this counsel occurs 365 times in the Bible, enough for each day's quota of fearful situations.[2] Believers are not exempt from fear, but they have a God to take their fears to. It is a situation that calls for seeking God (vv. 3, 4), here in the sense of taking specific religious measures to deal with the situation. The measures comprise total representation in reflection of the immensity of the crisis, fasting as an accompaniment to prayer to show the earnestness of those who pray, and communal prayer in front of the temple. These measures are traditional ones, which find illustration in Joel 2:12–17. At times of crisis religious forms are vehicles of spiritual comfort.

The prayer is a beautiful expression of human despair and dependence on God. It follows the general structure of the communal laments found in the Psalter, such as Psalms 44 and 83. It recounts God's favors in the past (vv. 6, 7), affirms confidence in God (vv. 8,

9), narrates the human predicament (vv. 10, 11), and turns to God in a final plea and an affirmation of trust (v. 12). An unusual feature is the barrage of rhetorical questions, which serve to reinforce the certainty of what is said. Two issues are at stake, the promised land as God's gift (vv. 7, 11) and the temple as the place where God answers prayer (v. 9)—and for the Chronicler and his first readers both issues were very relevant still. Israel's occupation of the land constituted a moment of sacred history which revealed God's ongoing purposes for His people. The reference to the temple harks back to Solomon's prayer in chapter 6, which received an affirmative answer from God in 7:12–16. The building of the temple marked a new era for Israel as a provision of grace for a needy people. Through temple-centered prayer grace to help in time of need was available for God's people. The great promise of 7:14 was valid as long as the temple stood. The old era, instituted by Moses and Joshua and grounded in the divine promises to the patriarchs, had its own sign of grace in the gift of the promised land. Jehoshaphat is portrayed as having one foot in each era, laying every possible claim to the grace of God. The Christian has inherited the temple theology of 7:14 and 20:8, 9 in the provision of a heavenly sanctuary where Jesus is the royal high priest (Heb. 4:14–16). The land has no obvious analogy in New Testament theology. Continued enjoyment of the land corresponds in general to the power of God to help His own who have been saved by the work of Christ, which has a timeless relevance (see Rom. 5:1–11; 8:31–39).

The crisis was a dire one and could not be wished away. Since it constituted a reversal of God's declared will, His intervention is not unreasonably claimed. If *"we"* are powerless, *"our God"* is all-powerful. The final appeal, *"our eyes are upon You"* (v. 12), is a lovely expression of hope and faith, reminiscent of Psalm 123:2.

In the temple system a prayer of need was regularly answered by a prophetic message in God's name: compare Joel 2:18–27. So it is here in verses 14–17. These verses also introduce the literary tradition of Holy War, which pervades verses 14–25. With the inspired oracle of the Levitical prophet the Chronicler means us to contrast the travesty and confusion of 18:4–27. Jahaziel's pedigree is traced back a number of generations, probably to David's time as a reminder of the new era of grace established by the provision of the temple. The message of salvation delivered by Jahaziel is made up of three standard elements, the identifying of the addressees (v. 15a), the formula *"Do not be afraid"* (v. 15b), and its backing with a specific promise (vv. 16–17a). For good measure these elements are repeated (v. 17b): anxious hearts appreciate the repetition of a reassuring message. Reserved for the climax is the keynote of the overall section, the promise of God's protective presence: *"the Lord is with you."* These elements may be usefully compared with a passage possessing the same literary form, Isaiah 41:8–13. The prophetic oracle is resonant with echoes of Scriptures, which bring their own comfort to those who know them. Verse 15 recalls 1 Samuel 17:47—here indeed is another David and Goliath situation. Verse 17a cites Exodus 14:13, a great promise of a divine miracle. The God who smote Pharaoh and the Philistine was still Israel's God.

The prophetic message of assurance is followed by worship and praise. Here again is a traditional practice. In temple procedure a prayer of lament was followed by a song of thanksgiving, at a later time when the crisis that prompted the prayer had been resolved. Before that happy time, immediately after an affirmative answer had been received from God via a temple prophet or priest, the thanksgiving song was anticipated by interim praise which by faith took the divine word seriously, though the external situation remained unchanged as yet. A good example is Psalm 22, where the lamenting prayer of verses 1–21a is followed by the grateful cry "You have answered me" (Ps. 22:21b) and then by praise which anticipates eventual thanksgiving (Ps. 22:22–31). So here in verses 18–19 we find the praise of faith which dares to take God at His word.

Jehoshaphat's battle speech on the morrow places a premium on faith. It echoes the message of Isaiah in a similar context of military threat, a message rendered more effectively by its Hebrew wordplay: "Have firm faith, or you will not stand firm" (Isa. 7:9, NEB). In expression of such faith orders are given for anticipatory praise to be sung afresh, as on the day before in the temple precincts. The praise looks forward to a manifestation of God's "steadfast love" (RSV), promised *"forever"* (v. 21) and so for today. The praise here replaces the shout associated with Holy War (see Judg. 7:20; 2 Chron. 13:15). It accentuates the fact that the people's part was not to fight but to be spectators of the divine defeat of the foe, in accord with the prophet's promise (vv. 15, 17).

God's role is here greater than in the Holy War accounts of

13:13-17 and 14:12-13; the enormous amount of booty reflects the greatness of the God-given victory. The people gather for a service of thanksgiving. Centuries later its venue, *"the Valley of Berachah,"* could still be visited in commemoration of this victory. *"Berachah"* or *"blessing"* is used in the sense of praise, as in Nehemiah 9:5. In the phrase *"until this day"* (v. 26) there is the thrill of a link between now and then, such as visitors to the Holy Land always feel as they stand in places hallowed by sacred memories. Finally, after a festive procession to the temple, thanksgiving is fittingly rendered in the very place where prayer had been offered. Like the single leper of Luke 17:15-16, the people come back to give thanks.

In the accounts of the victories of David and the extensive power and prestige of Solomon we noticed that the Chronicler was at the same time pursuing another agenda. He was providing a model for Israel's future hope. The same phenomenon appears to be the case here. Just as *"all the kingdoms of the lands"* in 1 Chronicles 29:30 and *"all the kings of the earth"* in 2 Chronicles 9:22, 23 related David's and Solomon's realms to the coming kingdom of God, so here in 20:29 does *"all the kingdoms of the countries"* (RSV), especially as it echoes mention of God's *"rule over all the kingdoms of the nations"* in Jehoshaphat's prayer (v. 6; cf. Dan. 7:14, 27). The victory is intended as a type of earnest of the end-time when God would intervene in human history and set up His kingdom over the world.

The post-exilic community prized the message of salvation which they found present in the canonical books of the prophets. The Chronicler's word to his generation is transparent in the exhortation of verse 20: *"Believe His prophets."* Israel's future was bound up with the divine hope revealed in the prophetic books. The call to God's people was to wait in faith for God's intervention. Herein lies the relevance of this version of the Holy War, which leaves everything to God. Many centuries later in Jewish history orthodox Jews opposed the rise of Zionism as *"flying in the face of Heaven"* by usurping the role of the Messiah in taking Israel back to their land. For the Chronicler the model of the Holy War that left everything to God and dispensed with human cooperation was a prefiguring of the end-time. Correspondingly the call was to wait for God to intervene, rather than try to help Him by abortive rebellion against the secular power. Significantly in verse 22 *"ambushes"* is literally *"ambushers,"* and evidently refers to supernatural agents.

In similar vein the New Testament distinguishes between the work that God has done and will do in Christ and what He shares with His people. It looks forward to the Second Advent as a dynamic breaking into human history. In Revelation 19:11–21 it is "the King of Kings" and His celestial army who fight against the forces of evil, human and superhuman. There is a liberal brand of the Christian faith which reinterprets this event as gradual growth of the kingdom which the church achieves under God. This view is a rationalistic reduction under the influence of a now old-fashioned theory of human society as able to improve itself. The church must ever beware of hitching its wagon to a humanistic star.

The New Testament recognizes other applications of the holy war theme. Just as the Chronicler distinguished between manifestations in which God helped His fighting people (13:14–17) and this manifestation in which He fought without their participation, so the New Testament knows a similar differentiation. It speaks on the one hand of the once-for-all campaign Christ fought against principalities and powers (Col. 2:15) and on the other hand of the ongoing fight of the Christian in the Lord's strength against those principalities and powers (Eph. 6:10–17). The church puts its trust in a work that only its Lord has done and which He will consummate. Within these parameters God's people strenuously "fight the good fight of faith" (1 Tim. 6:12).

WRONGFUL ALLIANCE AGAIN

> 20:31 So Jehoshaphat was king over Judah. *He was* thirty-five years old when he became king, and he reigned twenty-five years in Jerusalem. His mother's name *was* Azubah the daughter of Shilhi.
>
> 32 And he walked in the way of his father Asa, and did not turn aside from it, doing *what was* right in the sight of the LORD.
>
> 33 Nevertheless the high places were not taken away, for as yet the people had not directed their hearts to the God of their fathers.
>
> 34 Now the rest of the acts of Jehoshaphat, first and last, indeed they *are* written in the book of Jehu the son of Hanani, which *is* mentioned in the book of the kings of Israel.

35 After this Jehoshaphat king of Judah allied himself with Ahaziah king of Israel, who acted very wickedly.

36 And he allied himself with him to make ships to go to Tarshish, and they made the ships in Ezion Geber.

37 But Eliezer the son of Dodavah of Mareshah prophesied against Jehoshaphat, saying, "Because you have allied yourself with Ahaziah, the LORD has destroyed your works." Then the ships were wrecked, so that they were not able to go to Tarshish.

2 Chron. 20:31-37

There is an ambiguity about human life such as Victorian biographers of the great and good were loath to admit. Jehoshaphat was basically righteous (v. 32). Yet, for all his virtues, he was not immune from a besetting sin, to which he was to surrender again (vv. 35-37). The Chronicler, who in verses 31-34 follows in the main 1 Kings 22:41-45, allows verse 32 to stand as a generalization. The tenor of the king's life was good, despite temporary lapses. "God is not unjust to forget" his "work and labor of love" (Heb. 6:10). The reassurance brings comfort to us all. A similar lapse is recorded in the case of the people (v. 33). In the light of 17:6 evidently worship at the unorthodox high places was revived. Jehoshaphat had given the example of a spiritual stand in preparing "his heart to seek God" (19:3). In the Hebrew the phrase *"directed their hearts"* (v. 33) is the same as in 19:3 and echoes it. One can lead a horse to water . . . ! A good example and good teaching are not enough when those who see and hear do not commit themselves in turn. Implicitly the Chronicler is contrasting the ideal triad of unity in his Davidic narratives, when king, people, and God were one. This shadow across Jehoshaphat's reign reads as a warning to the flock to follow the lead of their spiritual shepherds and not go their own willful way.

There is a shadow of the king's making too. In verses 35-37 the Chronicler appears to reinterpret 1 Kings 22:48-49 in terms of seeking a human ally instead of God. Possibly he had another literary source available for this incident. The king blots his copybook again, in this maritime venture. The formula of the Lord's presence is absent from his passage, as in 18:1-19:3; it is replaced by the triple mention of human alliance. The pull of the northern kingdom draws this good king into its strong magnetic field. In the absence of the unity of south and north which God desired, the best of kings was caused to stumble. The implicit lesson is the paramount need of the unity of the people of God. Again, as in 19:1–3, a prophet intervenes, here forecasting failure. The Hebrew verb rendered *"has destroyed"* (v. 37) has a connotation of divine wrath as it did in 1 Chronicles 13:11–15. It is *pāraṣ*, which played an important role in 1 Chronicles 13–15. Jehoshaphat had not learned his lesson from the experience of chapter 18. He made the same old mistake; he slipped on the same banana skin. The Chronicler is warning his readers that there are paths to avoid, paths down which the Lord will not accompany them.

NOTES

1. Charles Spurgeon, *The Early Years* (London: Banner of Truth, 1962), p. 176.
2. Paul Tournier, *The Strong and the Weak* (Philadelphia: Westminster, 1963), p. 93.

CHAPTER FOURTEEN

God's Royal Lamp

2 Chronicles 21:1-23:21

If Jehoshaphat's reign marked a zenith in the fortunes of the Judean monarchy during the period of the divided kingdom, the period of the next two reigns of Jehoram and Ahazariah registers an all-time low. Indeed the Chronicler polarizes the two periods in 21:12 and 22:9. The influence of northern kingship, which like the proverbial camel poked its nose into the Judean royal tent in Jehoshaphat's reign, now makes its presence so blatantly felt that the Davidic dynasty is almost obliterated. Almost, for God checks the downward plunge away from His will and turns it into a U-curve by rescuing the endangered line of promise. Not unnaturally the pervading theme of these three chapters is the Davidic covenant. References to it occur in 21:7 and 23:3 as a divine promise and in 21:12 as a spiritual challenge. Closely related to this theme is the era of worship associated with the Davidic monarchy, which is re-established in 23:18. Over against this royal path of God's choosing looms the threat of a pernicious alternative, "the house of Ahab" (21:6, 13; 22:3, 4), whose influence increases and whose interests are represented in the person of the witch-like Athaliah (21:6; 22:2, 3, 10–12; 23:12–15, 21). The twin leitmotifs of the house of David and the house of Ahab run through these chapters, with the latter rising to a crescendo until it is silenced by a resurgence of the sweeter melody. In precise musical terms this saga of a growing threat and its eventual dissipation is reminiscent of Rimsky-Korsakov's arrangement of Mussorgsky's "A Night on the Bald Mountain." The strident and increasingly deafening music of the powers of evil represented in the dance of the witches is stilled by the dawning of a new day and the tolling of a church bell. Corresponding to that finale is the closing paragraph,

23:16–21, which speaks of the triumph of good and the enjoyment of rest. God is the eventual winner in this terrible struggle, and the Davidic line and the temple are beneficiaries in His victory.

THE FLICKERING LAMP

21:1 And Jehoshaphat rested with his fathers, and was buried with his fathers in the City of David. Then Jehoram his son reigned in his place.

2 He had brothers, the sons of Jehoshaphat: Azariah, Jehiel, Zechariah, Azaryahu, Michael, and Shephatiah; all these *were* the sons of Jehoshaphat king of Israel.

3 Their father gave them great gifts of silver and gold and precious things, with fortified cities in Judah; but he gave the kingdom to Jehoram, because he *was* the firstborn.

4 Now when Jehoram was established over the kingdom of his father, he strengthened himself and killed all his brothers with the sword, and also *others* of the princes of Israel.

5 Jehoram *was* thirty-two years old when he became king, and he reigned eight years in Jerusalem.

6 And he walked in the way of the kings of Israel, just as the house of Ahab had done, for he had the daughter of Ahab as a wife; and he did evil in the sight of the LORD.

7 Yet the LORD would not destroy the house of David, because of the covenant that He had made with David, and since He had promised to give a lamp to him and to his sons forever.

8 In his days Edom revolted against Judah's authority, and made a king over themselves.

9 So Jehoram went out with his officers, and all his chariots with him. And he rose by night and attacked the Edomites who had surrounded him and the captains of the chariots.

10 Thus Edom has been in revolt against Judah's authority to this day. At that time Libnah revolted against his rule, because he had forsaken the LORD God of his fathers.

11 Moreover he made high places in the mountains of Judah, and caused the inhabitants of Jerusalem to commit harlotry, and led Judah astray.

12 And a letter came to him from Elijah the prophet, saying,

Thus says the LORD God of your father David: Because you have not walked in the ways of Jehoshaphat your father, or in the ways of Asa king of Judah,

13 but have walked in the way of the kings of Israel, and have made Judah and the inhabitants of Jerusalem to play the harlot like the harlotry of the house of Ahab, and also have killed your brothers, those of your father's household, *who were* better than yourself,

14 behold, the LORD will strike your people with a serious affliction—your children, your wives, and all your possessions;

15 and you *will become* very sick with a disease of your intestines, until your intestines come out by reason of the sickness, day by day.

16 Moreover the LORD stirred up against Jehoram the spirit of the Philistines and the Arabians who *were* near the Ethiopians.

17 And they came up into Judah and invaded it, and carried away all the possessions that were found in the king's house, and also his sons and his wives, so that there was not a son left to him except Jehoahaz, the youngest of his sons.

18 After all this the LORD struck him in his intestines with an incurable disease.

19 Then it happened in the course of time, after the end of two years, that his intestines came out because of his sickness; so he died in severe pain. And his people made no burning for him, like the burning for his fathers.

20 He was thirty-two years old when he became king. He reigned in Jerusalem eight years and, to no one's sorrow, departed. However they buried him in the City of David, but not in the tombs of the kings.

22:1 Then the inhabitants of Jerusalem made Ahaziah his youngest son king in his place, for the raiders who

came with the Arabians into the camp had killed all
the older *sons.* So Ahaziah the son of Jehoram, king of
Judah, reigned.

2 Ahaziah *was* forty-two years old when he became king, and he reigned one year in Jerusalem. His
mother's name *was* Athaliah the granddaughter of
Omri.

3 He also walked in the ways of the house of
Ahab, for his mother advised him to do wickedly.

4 Therefore he did evil in the sight of the LORD,
like the house of Ahab; for they were his counselors
after the death of his father, to his destruction.

5 He also followed their advice, and went with
Jehoram the son of Ahab king of Israel to war against
Hazael king of Syria at Ramoth Gilead; and the Syri-
ans wounded Joram.

6 Then he returned to Jezreel to recover from the
wounds which he had received at Ramah, when he
fought against Hazael king of Syria. And Azariah the
son of Jehoram, king of Judah, went down to see Jehoram the son of Ahab in Jezreel, because he was
sick.

7 His going to Joram was God's occasion for
Ahaziah's downfall; for when he arrived, he went
out with Jehoram against Jehu the son of Nimshi,
whom the LORD had anointed to cut off the house of
Ahab.

8 And it happened, when Jehu was executing
judgment on the house of Ahab, and found the
princes of Judah and the sons of Ahaziah's brothers
who served Ahaziah, that he killed them.

9 Then he searched for Ahaziah; and they caught
him (he was hiding in Samaria), and brought him to
Jehu. When they had killed him, they buried him,
"because," they said, "he is the son of Jehoshaphat,
who sought the LORD with all his heart." So the
house of Ahaziah had no one to assume power over
the kingdom.

10 Now when Athaliah the mother of Ahaziah saw
that her son was dead, she arose and destroyed all
the royal heirs of the house of Judah.

11 But Jehoshabeath, the daughter of the king,

took Joash the son of Ahaziah, and stole him away from among the king's sons who were being murdered, and put him and his nurse in a bedroom. So Jehoshabeath, the daughter of King Jehoram, the wife of Jehoiada the priest (for she was the sister of Ahaziah), hid him from Athaliah so that she did not kill him.

12 And he was hidden with them in the house of God for six years, while Athaliah reigned over the land.

Chron. 21:1–22:12

These two reigns of Jehoram and Ahaziah are presented as a pair: the addition of *"also"* (22:3; cf. 21:6) indicates a correlation of the evil reigns. The importance of this evil pair for the Chronicler is demonstrated by his more than doubling the material allotted to them, in comparison with Kings. They are the first reigns to be judged in totally negative terms; as such they form a dark backdrop to God's redeeming purpose (21:7). "Where sin abounded, grace abounded much more" (Rom. 5:20).

1. *An evil reign.* The echo of 1 Kings 22:50 in 21:1 is amplified in 21:2–4 by a grim commentary of fratricide, which the Chronicler evidently knew from another source. As the *"firstborn,"* Jehoram had been marked for kingship, but the father's love had been shared among all his sons (21:3). Not content with the throne, the new king jealously wants to protect his own interests. He has his brothers murdered, evidently suspicious of potential rivals and perhaps resenting his father's favors to them. In this narrative the Chronicler is introducing a theme that will run through these chapters, that of a threat to the royal family, which puts at risk the very purposes of God. Here it is a threat from within, a multiplication of a Cain and Abel crime. It was a wrong that would not go unpunished. Just as politically Richard III eventually lost his throne because he scandalously murdered the princes in the Tower of London, so here providentially Jehoram was to suffer harm because of his brutal act.

First, however, Jehoram proceeds to chalk up further crimes on his black slate. The Chronicler cites 21:5–10a from 2 Kings 8:17–22. 21:6 mentions the influence of *"the house of Ahab"* on his reign in the person of his wife Athaliah, *"the daughter of Ahab."* Here was the grim legacy of a mistake made by his father (18:1). Jehoshaphat, for all his virtues (21:12), blotted his copybook in the matter of fraternization with the kings of the north. It was a lapse that mushroomed into disproportionate consequences. The northern monarchy gained a foothold in the Judean palace. The rival dynasty in the north, the first lasting dynasty to be established there, having extended its tentacles to the court, gradually claimed the crown. The destiny of the Davidic line was at stake, not simply for political reasons but on providential grounds, because the present occupant of the throne *"did"* such rampant *"evil."* Significantly the Chronicler changes "Judah" in 2 Kings 8:19 to *"the house of David,"* blatantly juxtaposing it with *"the house of Ahab."* In logical terms the former had chameleon-like so donned the character of the latter that it deserved the fate of Ahab's house (see 1 Kings 21:22, 29; 2 Kings 9:7–9). However, grace in the form of the *"covenant"* promises made by God to David (see 1 Chron. 17:12) intervened, altering the wages of sin into eternal life for the Davidic dynasty. If chapter 20 commemorated one of the key texts of Chronicles, 2 Chronicles 7:14, chapter 21 exalts the other, 1 Chronicles 17:12.

The metaphor of a lamp for the lasting existence of the dynasty is taken over from Kings (see 1 Kings 11:36; 15:4, as well as 2 Kings 8:19), but for the Chronicler it seems to have had a heightened significance. In speaking of the lamps in Solomon's temple he had singled them out by specifying that their form was *"as prescribed"* by David (4:7, 20, RSV). In 13:11 he mentioned *"the lampstand of gold"* being in the temple as an ingredient of legitimate worship in a passage which replaces reference to the dynastic lamp metaphor in 1 Kings 15:4. The Chronicler seems to have consciously related the metaphor and the religious ritual of the everburning lamp: instead of referring to lampstands in the plural as elsewhere, he mentioned only one. It is probable that he viewed the perpetually burning light of the lampstand(s) as a symbol of the perpetuity of the Davidic line. And it was burning still in his own lifetime! Now, in post-exilic times, it burned on the single many-branched lampstand of the second temple (see 1 Macc. 1:21; 4:50). The building of the temple constituted a guarantee of the continuance of the Davidic line (1 Chron. 17:12). Evidently in the very ritual of the temple the Chronicler saw a confirmation of this truth. The everburning lamp spoke to him of God's irrevocable promise and undergirded his theological hope of the restoration of the Davidic monarchy. There was a witness to the truth of the divine promise within the temple, sustaining the people of God through dark king-less days until their Messiah came.

Continuing with the Kings narrative, the Chronicler records the revolt of Edom, which led to a campaign in which the king escaped by the skin of his teeth, and also the revolt of Libnah on the Philistine border. He adds in 21:10b his theological interpretation of these territorial losses, using his distinctive vocabulary: Jehoram *"had forsaken"* Judah's traditional faith. If Jehoshaphat's virtue was to seek God (17:4; 19:3; 22:9), his son's vice was to forsake Him. The Chronicler's view of moral providence was a high one: he delights to demonstrate how God keeps short accounts in the payment of moral debts. So if the reward of his father's seeking God was the consolidation of his kingdom (17:5), Jehoram's own recompense for forsaking Him was its depletion. Evil does not go unpunished.

The Chronicler drives another nail into Jehoram's coffin by accusing him of disparaging the temple by constructing *"high places"* (21:11) as alternative places of worship. He goes on to use a significant term, the first of two that refer to another religious sin, polytheism: he *"caused the inhabitants of Jerusalem to commit harlotry"* (21:11). It is significant because it echoes the use of the same Hebrew verb in 1 Chronicles 5:25: the northern tribes *"played the harlot"* in a religious sense by being unfaithful to the true God. That the Chronicler has the northern kingdom at the back of his mind is indicated by his language in verse 16: the Lord *"stirred up . . . the spirit"* of foreign powers. The same phrase was used in 1 Chronicles 5:26 with reference to Assyria's deportation of the northerners. The correlation of north and south in moral state and sinister fate indicates that Judah under Jehoram had sunk as low as its northern neighbor. If the north was apostate, so was the south. If the northerners were prodigal sons, needing to return to God in repentance, as chapter 13 taught, so now were the Judeans. Ironically north and south were united—in unfaithfulness to God! There is a tragic leveling down at this point, the opposite of a leveling up to spirituality, for which the Chronicler yearned. Was the Chronicler preaching against the Judah of his day, a proud elder brother who despised the northern prodigals? Was he reminding them that in their past and in their wicked potential they too were prodigal sons, needing the same grace from a forgiving Father? Paul had a similar word of rebuke for the Jew-despising Gentile Christian in Romans 11:17–22.

In 21:12–15 the Chronicler cites a letter from Elijah. In historical terms it raises problems: Kings seems to suggest that the northern prophet was dead by this time (2 Kings 3:11). The theological point the Chronicler is making is an intensification of his equation of south and north. Verses 11 and 16 are the significant frame of the prophetic message. Elijah was the great protagonist of Ahab for his moral and religious enormities (1 Kings 18–21). Those criticisms were applicable to Ahab's son-in-law Jehoram in view of his copycat attitude. The letter follows the standard threefold form of a prophetic message of judgment: the divine authority of the prophetic word (v. 12), accusation of wrongdoing (vv. 12, 13), and announcement of punishment (21:14, 15). The wording of the initial messenger formula advances the motif so prominent in these chapters by describing the Lord as *God of your father David* (21:12). The *"covenant"* between God and David (21:7) called for a two-way commitment, making moral and religious claims even as it extended gracious care. The accusation echoes the terms of verses 6 and 11 and cites the fratricide of 21:4 as a case of the worst man winning. The announcement of divine reprisal predicts that the people and the royal family will suffer as the result of invasion and that the king will be punished by a severe and prolonged intestinal illness.

21:16–19 records the fulfillment, for whose details the Chronicler may well have had a historical source. If the king had killed his brothers to gain their possessions, now these were lost. If it was to secure his own life against threat, now his selfishness was repaid by a premature and painful death. *"Whoever desires to save (or keep safe) his life will lose it"* (Mark 8:35). The severity and also the mercy (21:7) of God are demonstrated in the survival of a single son, here called Jehoahaz but elsewhere Ahaziah with a reversal of the two elements that make up the Hebrew name. Both forms of the name mean *"Yahweh has taken hold."* The verb can refer to God's taking hold of someone in judgment (Job 16:12), and the Chronicler may have found this significance in it.

21:20a repeats 21:5 from 2 Kings 8:17. It repeats the following *"and he walked"* (v. 6 = 2 Kings 8:18) but uses the Hebrew verb in a new, fatal sense *"and . . . departed."* It is as if the Chronicler were saying "There is a way which seems right to a man, but its end is the way of death" (Prov. 14:2). The phrase *"to no one's sorrow"* refers on the surface to Jehoram's deserved unpopularity, which the end of verse 19 illustrates: there were no regrets at his passing. It has been observed that usually the royal epilogues of Chronicles contain at this point a reference to sources of further information (cf. 20:34). By omitting such a reference the Chronicler is recording his own conviction that Jehoram was not worthy of further investigation. He was best forgotten. It is a tragic obituary of a wasted life and a failure to live up to one's heritage.

2. *Another evil reign.* The lamp of the Davidic lineage flickered again in the next reign (22:1–9). Ahaziah is another Jehoram in his pursuit of *"the ways of the house of Ahab"* (22:3). The queen mother had a recognized position of privilege and influence in the Davidic monarchy, with a seat of honor at the king's right hand (see 1 Kings 2:19). Unfortunately in this case she was none other than *"Athaliah"* (22:2). She exploits her position to the full as his counselor. Presumably at her suggestion other members of *"the house of Ahab"* are invited to Jerusalem to add weight to her counsel. It is they who advise him to ally himself with his northern counterpart in a military campaign at Ramoth Gilead. It is a story we have read before in chapter 18! It is not difficult to catch the overtones of horror which accompany the words. 22:1b–6 follow 2 Kings 8:26–29 quite closely, but the Chronicler has introduced and stressed the theme of evil counsel. Three times in as many verses there is mention of counseling. Every king—like every president and every prime minister—had to depend on advisors. In this case it led to wickedness and destruction (22:3, 4). Ahaziah might have pleaded that he was not to blame. He might have excused himself as the pawn of stronger personalities. To no avail: the responsibility was his for acting on the proffered advice. Harry Truman, it is said, had on his desk a notice "The buck stops here." The dice of heredity and environment were loaded against Ahaziah, but weakly he it was who plunged the dynasty into danger. A moral doctrine of personal responsibility is here sounded clearly. Any note of repentance, which could have made all the difference, is quite lacking.

The writing was on the wall for the northern dynasty, and Ahaziah gets caught up in its destruction. In 22:7–9 the Chronicler assumes a knowledge of 2 Kings 9:1–28; 10:12–14. He abbreviates and adapts his source, supplying an interpretive framework at beginning and end, in 22:7a, 9b. He brings to the fore the providential work of God, which effects the destruction that inevitably lay at the end of Ahaziah's self-chosen path. The mention of Jehoshaphat's spirituality, which allows the royal corpse a decent burial, enhances the radical difference between grandfather and grandson. The reforming zeal of Jehu, commissioned by Elisha to crusade in God's name against the house of Ahab, extended not only to the ally Ahaziah but also to his nephews. It meant a further depletion of the house of David. Evidently there was no obvious successor, no one of sufficient maturity and influence to take over. The Davidic dynasty has been brought to the brink of extinction. Is all lost?

3. *The illicit queen and the secret king.* At first it seems so. The wicked queen mother fills the vacancy by usurping the throne. Now the throne is occupied by a daughter of Ahab. The house of Ahab, extirpated from the north, has turned up at the Judean court! In four hundred years of rule this was the only break in the Davidic line. Fortunately it was a brief one. Fortunately? Providently, rather: the hand of God rests on the episode of verses 10–12, unseen but silently at work. The wicked queen kills off all the male heirs to consolidate her position. The theme of the whittling down of the royal family here reaches a horrifying climax.

One heir is missed. This is a rescue narrative which is a link in a biblical chain, beginning with the secreting of baby Moses in the bulrushes and culminating in the spiriting of Jesus from the infanticidal wrath of King Herod. Whether it is a Pharaoh, an Athaliah, or a Herod, they meet their match in the providential working of God. They do their worst and think they have triumphed, unaware of the loophole that spells their failure. In this episode is won in principle a victory which, like the moral victory of Dunkirk in World War II, allows another victorious encounter to be mounted at a later stage (chap. 23). It is a crystallization of the remnant theme which runs through the Bible and through the history of the church. It speaks to the people of God whenever they feel themselves a beleaguered minority.

The episode is a tale of two women. On the one hand Athaliah is in control, indulging to the full her opposition to the true God (cf. 24:7) and thinking she had dealt to the house of David Jehu's death blow to the house of Ahab. On the other side is Jehoshabeath, the princess born to Ahaziah by another wife according to the Jewish historian Josephus. She takes on herself the hazardous mission of preserving the Davidic line in the person of a helpless baby. In the next chapter the main action will pass to her husband Jehoiada, but it must not be forgotten that she spent six long years tending her secret in the temple precincts. While Athaliah represents a regime of wanton usurpation and cruel oppression, Jehoshabeath is the heroine of a resistance movement, risking her life that good may eventually triumph. This tale of two women presents contrasted cameos of self-seeking exploitation and unselfish heroism.

There is another contrast here. Over against the female usurper is the figure of a baby king. Significantly, before the boy Joash is crowned, the Chronicler already gives him his royal title (23:3), regarding him as the legitimate Davidic king even during Athaliah's usurpation. The house of David lives on! A baby, the epitome of weakness—is this the king? Yes, the Chronicler would reply, just as assuredly as Matthew in whose Gospel the baby Jesus was represented as the recipient of royal gifts. As in Matthew 2:1-18 King Herod is pitted against the true King of the Jews, so here the non-Davidic queen mother and the rescued child are rival figures. Power and weakness oppose one another. For the Chronicler and his first readers this event must have preached its own message of courageous hope during "a day of small things" (Zech. 4:10). Truly "God has chosen the weak things of the world to put to shame the things which are mighty" (1 Cor. 1:27). The Christian too knows of hiddenness and awaits the revelation of his King as the key to truth and right (Col. 3:1-4).

THE LAMP RELIT

23:1 In the seventh year Jehoiada strengthened himself, *and made a* covenant with the captains of hundreds: Azariah the son of Jeroham, Ishmael the son of Jehohanan, Azariah the son of Obed, Maaseiah the son of Adaiah, and Elishaphat the son of Zichri.

2 And they went throughout Judah and gathered the Levites from all the cities of Judah, and the chief fathers of Israel, and they came to Jerusalem.

3 Then all the assembly made a covenant with the king in the house of God. And he said to them, "Behold, the king's son shall reign, as the LORD has said of the sons of David.

4 "This *is* what you shall do: One-third of you entering on the Sabbath, of the priests and the Levites, *shall be* keeping watch over the doors;

5 "one-third *shall be* at the king's house; and one-third at the Gate of the Foundation. All the people *shall be* in the courts of the house of the LORD.

6 "But let no one come into the house of the LORD except the priests and those of the Levites who serve. They may go in, for they *are* holy; but all the people shall keep the watch of the LORD.

7 "And the Levites shall surround the king on all sides, every man with his weapons in his hand; and whoever comes into the house, let him be put to death. You are to be with the king when he comes in and when he goes out."

8 So the Levites and all Judah did according to all that Jehoiada the priest commanded. And each man took his men who were to be on duty on the Sabbath, with those who were going *off duty* on the Sabbath; for Jehoiada the priest had not dismissed the divisions.

9 And Jehoiada the priest gave to the captains of hundreds the spears and the large and small shields which *had belonged* to King David, that *were* in the temple of God.

10 Then he set all the people, every man with his weapon in his hand, from the right side of the temple to the left side of the temple, along by the altar and by the temple, all around the king.

11 And they brought out the king's son, put the crown on him, *gave him* the Testimony, and made him king. Then Jehoiada and his sons anointed him, and said, "*Long* live the king!"

12 Now when Athaliah heard the noise of the people running and praising the king, she came to the people *in* the temple of the LORD.

13 When she looked, there was the king standing by his pillar at the entrance; and the leaders and the trumpeters *were* by the king. All the people of the land were rejoicing and blowing trumpets, also the singers with musical instruments, and those

who led in praise. So Athaliah tore her clothes and said, "Treason! Treason!"

14 And Jehoiada the priest brought out the captains of hundreds who were set over the army, and said to them, "Take her outside under guard, and slay with the sword whoever follows her." For the priest had said, "Do not kill her in the house of the LORD."

15 So they seized her; and she went by way of the entrance of the Horse Gate *into* the king's house, and they killed her there.

16 Then Jehoiada made a covenant between himself, the people, and the king, that they should be the LORD'S people.

17 And all the people went to the temple of Baal, and tore it down. They broke in pieces its altars and images, and killed Mattan the priest of Baal before the altars.

18 Also Jehoiada appointed the oversight of the house of the LORD to the hand of the priests, the Levites, whom David had assigned in the house of the LORD, to offer the burnt offerings of the LORD, as *it is* written in the Law of Moses, with rejoicing and with singing, *as it was established* by David.

19 And he set the gatekeepers at the gates of the house of the LORD, so that no one *who was* in any way unclean should enter.

20 Then he took the captains of hundreds, the nobles, the governors of the people, and all the people of the land, and brought the king down from the house of the LORD; and they went through the Upper Gate to the king's house, and set the king on the throne of the kingdom.

21 So all the people of the land rejoiced; and the city was quiet, for they had slain Athaliah with the sword.

2 Chron. 23:1-21

This is the story of how the Davidic line in the person of Joash was restored to its rightful place on the throne. If it is compared with its source in 2 Kings 11:4–20, it is evident that the Chronicler has followed it closely apart from working into it two particular interests of his. The first is a replacement of the role of the foreign royal bodyguard by Levites. By the Chronicler's time there was a firm regulation that foreigners were not allowed inside the temple (contrast Ezek. 44:6–8). Its sanctity is preserved on the lines of verse 6: only temple personnel were allowed inside and all others had to "keep the charge of the Lord" (RSV) not to enter. The Chronicler's concern for the temple, here in terms of its sanctity, shines out at this point. It is a reflex of his sense of the holiness of God, which casts its distinctive aura on earthly things dedicated to its glory. The other interest worked into the narrative is the pervasive stress on *all the people*" (v. 6). The Chronicler takes the references in 2 Kings 11:13–14 as his cue to project them into the whole story. The unity of king and people under God, so gloriously set forth as an ideal at David's coronation (1 Chron. 11–12) finds a fitting echo throughout this chapter and especially in verses 3 and 16. Just as David depended on the help of his supporters who pledged themselves to him and to God, so the boy king is backed by a loyal populace. True, it is not the whole people of north and south, but it is a representative group of those who are loyal to God and so loyal to His royal purposes. The coup is the triumph of God's word concerning *the sons of David*" (v. 3). The statement picks up in triumphant vindication God's promise of a perpetual dynasty "to David and his sons" (21:7). There is a new beginning, grounded in God's old promise.

The coronation takes place in two phases, the defiant crowning and anointing in the temple (v. 11) and the triumphant procession from temple to palace, escorting the new king to his rightful throne (v. 20). In between occurs the intervention of Athaliah and her execution. Life for the king (v. 11) means death for the usurper (v. 15). Her cry *Treason! Treason!*" (v. 13) expresses unconscious irony. She is the traitor. Pointing a finger of criticism at Joash, she points three at herself.

The *covenant*" to carry out the plot to enthrone Joash (v. 3) is fittingly followed by a *covenant*" of renewed commitment to God as their exclusive Lord (v. 16). In a period of religious declension, that commitment had to take the form of religious reform. Negatively those things that were not of God were swept away (v. 17), for God brooks no rivals. After this basic principle is re-established, there remains the positive task of restoring the proper means for the worship of God. The rites of the temple, which rested on the double foundation of Moses as to sacrifice and David as to the worship of song, are given their proper place again. Torah and temple are honored afresh. Davidic worship at the temple and Davidic representation on the throne meant the fulfillment of ideals dear to the Chronicler's heart.

A mass of such favorite themes crowds into this chapter. It is a glorious moment of revelation honored and potential attained. It corresponds to the Chronicler's picture of what ought always to be and also his picture of what was yet to be. It is no wonder that the chapter ends on the notes of joy and peace (v. 21): they are inspired by the recognition of the true king of David's line. In like spirit the angelic song of peace and joy resounded at the birth of the Davidic Messiah, in fulfillment of God's ancient Word (Luke 1:69, 70; 2:4–14).

CHAPTER FIFTEEN

How to Be a Loser

2 Chronicles 24:1–26:23

In John Bunyan's *Pilgrim's Progress* Christian and his friend Hopeful at one point saw a frightening sight, a man whom seven devils had bound with strong cords being carried off to a door in the side of a hill, which opened into a byway to hell. Christian could not see who it was because the man hung his head in shame, but he "thought it might be one Turnaway, that dwelt in the town of Apostasy." At the sight both pilgrims "began to tremble." The incident evokes the mood in which we are to read these next three chapters. They belong together as a distinct section: all three concern Judean kings whose reigns started well but ended in apostasy. The Chronicler uses them as grim warnings against abandoning the true faith. Each of these kings "ran well" for a time, to use the metaphor of Galatians 5:7, but they failed to finish the race. Did the Chronicler have at the back of his mind the case of "a righteous man" who "turns away from his righteousness and commits iniquity"—and so dies (Ezek. 18:24–26)? He is writing from a pastor's heart, using history as illustrations for a sermon which sounds a triple warning against giving up the faith.

LISTENING TO THE WRONG VOICES

24:1 Joash *was* seven years old when he became king, and he reigned forty years in Jerusalem. His mother's name *was* Zibiah of Beersheba.

2 Joash did *what was* right in the sight of the LORD all the days of Jehoiada the priest.

3 And Jehoiada took two wives for him, and he had sons and daughters.

4 Now it happened after this *that* Joash set his heart on repairing the house of the LORD.

5 Then he gathered the priests and the Levites, and said to them, "Go out to the cities of Judah, and gather from all Israel money to repair the house of your God from year to year, and see that you do it quickly." However the Levites did not do it quickly.

6 So the king called Jehoiada the chief *priest*, and said to him, "Why have you not required the Levites to bring in from Judah and from Jerusalem the collection, *according to the commandment* of Moses the servant of the LORD and of the assembly of Israel, for the tabernacle of witness?"

7 For the sons of Athaliah, that wicked woman, had broken into the house of God, and had also presented all the dedicated things of the house of the LORD to the Baals.

8 Then at the king's command they made a chest, and set it outside at the gate of the house of the LORD.

9 And they made a proclamation throughout Judah and Jerusalem to bring to the LORD the collection *that* Moses the servant of God *had imposed* on Israel in the wilderness.

10 Then all the leaders and all the people rejoiced, brought their contributions, and put *them* into the chest until all had given.

11 So it was, at that time, when the chest was brought to the king's official by the hand of the Levites, and when they saw that *there was* much money, that the king's scribe and the high priest's officer came and emptied the chest, and took it and returned it to its place. Thus they did day by day, and gathered money in abundance.

12 The king and Jehoiada gave it to those who did the work of the service of the house of the LORD; and they hired masons and carpenters to repair the house of the LORD, and also those who worked in iron and bronze to restore the house of the LORD.

13 So the workmen labored, and the work was completed by them; they restored the house of God to its original condition and reinforced it.

14 When they had finished, they brought the rest of the money before the king and Jehoiada; they made from it articles for the house of the LORD, articles for serving and offering, spoons and vessels of gold and silver. And they offered burnt offerings in the house of the LORD continually all the days of Jehoiada.

15 But Jehoiada grew old and was full of days, and he died; *he was* one hundred and thirty years old when he died.

16 And they buried him in the City of David among the kings, because he had done good in Israel, both toward God and His house.

17 Now after the death of Jehoiada the leaders of Judah came and bowed down to the king. And the king listened to them.

18 Therefore they left the house of the LORD God of their fathers, and served wooden images and idols; and wrath came upon Judah and Jerusalem because of their trespass.

19 Yet He sent prophets to them, to bring them back to the LORD; and they testified against them, but they would not listen.

20 Then the Spirit of God came upon Zechariah the son of Jehoiada the priest, who stood above the people, and said to them, "Thus says God: 'Why do you transgress the commandments of the LORD, so that you cannot prosper? Because you have forsaken the LORD, He also has forsaken you.'"

21 So they conspired against him, and at the command of the king they stoned him with stones in the court of the house of the LORD.

22 Thus Joash the king did not remember the kindness which Jehoiada his father had done to him, but killed his son; and as he died, he said, "The LORD look on *it*, and repay!"

23 So it happened in the spring of the year *that* the army of Syria came up against him; and they came to Judah and Jerusalem, and destroyed all the leaders of the people from among the people, and sent all their spoil to the king of Damascus.

24 For the army of the Syrians came with a small

company of men; but the LORD delivered a very great army into their hand, because they had forsaken the LORD God of their fathers. So they executed judgment against Joash.

25 And when they had withdrawn from him (for they left him severely wounded), his own servants conspired against him because of the blood of the sons of Jehoiada the priest, and killed him on his bed. So he died. And they buried him in the City of David, but they did not bury him in the tombs of the kings.

26 These are the ones who conspired against him: Zabad the son of Shimeath the Ammonitess, and Jehozabad the son of Shimrith the Moabitess.

27 Now *concerning* his sons, and the many oracles about him, and the repairing of the house of God, indeed they *are* written in the annals of the book of the kings. Then Amaziah his son reigned in his place.

2 Chron. 24:1–27

By and large the Chronicler seems to have read the same amount of Joash's reign as is available to us in 2 Kings 12, but he interpreted it a little differently. He understood 2 Kings 12:2 in a restrictive sense, like NKJV "Jehoiada did what was right . . . all the days in which Jehoiada the priest instructed him" (contrast RSV). He was encouraged to do this by the disasters which marked the end of the king's reign, namely foreign invasion and an internal conspiracy which led to his assassination. He divided Joash's reign into two phases, before and after Jehoiada's demise, the first marked by obedience and blessing and the second by disobedience and unmitigated disaster.

1. *Joash the reformer.* The sympathetic reader of chapters 21–23 has laid them down with a sigh of relief and contentment, echoing in his heart the joy and quiet of 23:21. Now surely the ship of state has resumed its proper course and will calmly follow its compass bearings until the haven looms into view. And so it seems at first. Joash had everything going for him, the loyalty of a committed people (23:16) and lessons in leadership from a man of God. Verses 2–3 present a vignette of obedience and blessing. After the ravages suffered by the royal family in earlier chapters the increase of verse 3 is bounty indeed. It makes up, one may say, for the years the locusts had eaten.

Joash's obedience is illustrated in verses 4–14 by his concern for the temple and the Torah. An emphasis on the temple comes to the fore: the *"house"* of God is mentioned no less than ten times. The Chronicler had an essentially practical understanding of spirituality. The *"heart"* (v. 4) is where one's hands and feet are. He will never allow us simply to make generalized professions of faith or even to propound our theology in learned tones. His spirituality is down to earth, concerned with repairs and renovation of fabric and stones. The passage begins and virtually ends in the Hebrew with the same vocabulary of renovating and needs strengthening (vv. 3, 4, 12), while fresh terms are supplied for the same activities at the close: *"they restored"* the temple *"to its original condition and reinforced it"* (v. 13). In a human environment the instruments of faith have a built-in obsolescence, like the modern automobile. The new becomes old and requires renovation. What is initially stable becomes wobbly and weak, and needs strengthening. The maintenance of a practical spirituality is like going up a down escalator; one has to move to stay at the same place, to offset the downward pull of the earthly and temporary. The silver chalice requires polishing; tarnished door handles need cleaning. Anyone who has a house and garden knows how much time has to be spent in maintenance work. A church too, whether we understand it in terms of place or people, needs positive measures of effort and industry to counteract the wear and tear that occur naturally.

I recall being taught this lesson at the most practical of levels. At the church I was then attending there was difficulty in replacing a custodian who had attained the age of honorable retirement. A deacon stood up at the Sunday morning service and announced that the membership list had forthwith been turned into a cleaning rota and only a doctor's certificate of ill health could grant exemption! The congregation's laughter was a cover-up for less jubilant thoughts that were dominating every one's mind, and certainly mine. Several Saturday mornings' labor over the next year made me look with new eyes at elements of the church I had previously taken for granted— and it introduced me to a new dimension of fellowship as a member of a work force. If we are the "living stones" of a spiritual temple (1 Pet. 2:5), then we too need to refurbish and renovate ourselves and each other regularly.

In the case of the temple there was a special factor which made repairs necessary, the defilement and damage done in the reign of the *"wicked"* Queen Athaliah (v. 7). The repair work inaugurated by Joash represents a spiritual new broom, beginning the implementation of a fresh commitment to God (see 23:16). The negative work of 23:17 needed a positive counterpart. The undoing of religious wrong had to be succeeded by the doing of *"what was right in the sight of the Lord"* (24:2). Reformation involves not only removing vice but replacing it with virtue. Any definition of a Christian which is confined to negative terms, as one who does not do this or that, is sadly deficient. In the case of Joash refurbishing was followed by regular worship of a godly nature (v. 14b).

If Joash was aware of the needs of the temple, he was also alert to the relevant stipulations of the Torah. In the wilderness days of Israel the tabernacle had been maintained by an annual tax of a half shekel, according to Exodus 30:11-16. The Chronicler takes over Joash's reintroduction of this tax from 2 Kings 12:4, but characteristically he accentuates a reference to the Torah by twice naming God's *"servant"* *"Moses"* (vv. 6, 9) as its venerable originator. In the account of the initial dilatoriness of the temple personnel and the eventual glad giving of leaders and people, one senses that strong hints are being dropped to the Chronicler's own generation. Interestingly there is indirect evidence of a reluctance to contribute the temple tax in the post-exilic period, which is not surprising in view of its persistent economic problems. A pledge to pay it was written into the covenant of national rededication to God in Nehemiah 10 (vv. 32, 33). Accordingly the Chronicler doubtless intended verse 10—like 1 Chronicles 29—to be a model for his readers, with its expression of joyful giving to God's work.

Paul appears to have translated the temple tax into a corresponding obligation laid upon his missionary churches to support the headquarters church in Jerusalem, which was going through a period of economic stringency (see Rom. 15:25-28, 31; 2 Cor. 8-9). Both Paul and the Chronicler were applying a typological principle. The Chronicler emphasized that the obligation laid down in the Torah to maintain the tabernacle in the old dispensation was still relevant in the new era of the temple. Paul in turn moved from a temple-oriented liability to a corresponding one in the Christian epoch. This typologizing insists that dipping regularly into pocket and purse remains a measure of the believer's spirituality. "God" still "loves a cheerful giver" (2 Cor. 9:7).

2. *Joash the renegade.* The Chronicler insists that the king's spiritual zeal lasted only as long as Jehoiada's lifetime (vv. 2, 14). He pauses to note the priest's honorable burial after longevity that reflected the blessing of God for his *"good"* deeds (vv. 15, 16). Then he has a shockingly different tale to tell. The king's lifestyle, deprived of his mentor's good influence, degenerates into a vicious circle of wrongdoing. Joash lends his ear to less worthy counsels proposed by national leaders who seemingly hankered after precedents set by Athaliah. The offense incurs divine *"wrath"* (v. 18). Yet God in His grace gives a second chance by sending *"prophets"* (v. 19) to His prodigal sons and daughters, urging them to repent. The verb *"bring. . . back"* (v. 19) is a cue for the people to claim the grace of God on the lines of 7:14: in the Hebrew it is a transitive form of the verb there rendered "turn."

When these warnings go unheeded, God gives a third chance, not willing that any should perish (see Ezek. 33:11; 2 Pet. 3:9). The opportunity, which comes together with accusation of a broken Torah, leads only to further incrimination, for in reprisal the son of the venerated Jehoiada is lynched, with the active connivance of the king. Standing on a platform in the temple court, the prophet is an easy target for the stones hurled by the crowd, who are undeterred by the sanctity of the location. The Chronicler, who may well be following a tradition other than Kings in his reference to *"Zechariah"* (v. 20) and in his later account of the Syrian attack on Jerusalem, lays responsibility for the murder squarely on the king's shoulders, finding in it a terrible return for Jehoiada's loyal service (v. 22).

The dying prophet's last words are a grim prayer of requital, addressed to God as Judge. At this point the knowledgeable Christian reader cannot help thinking of two or three New Testament texts for comparison. The first passage that comes to mind is Luke 11:47–51, where one of the "woes" uttered by Jesus specifies "the blood of all the prophets . . . from the blood of Abel to the blood of Zechariah who perished between the altar and the temple." There is a reference to the canon of the Hebrew Bible, which starts with Genesis and finishes with Chronicles. God's Word from beginning to end is chock-full of evidence of His people's rejection of His messengers. "This generation," warns Jesus, would have to pay the price for the backlog of those martyrdoms. The repetition of the phrase "this generation" at Luke 21:32 in the context of a prediction of the fall of Jerusalem clarifies this reference and directs the reader's mind to the events of A.D. 70 (cf. Matt. 23:35; 24:2). The incident of Chronicles is regarded as the culmination of the Old Testament record of human rejection of God.

Another New Testament passage that may come to the reader's mind is a contrasting one. It relates the gracious prayer of Jesus on the Cross: "Father, forgive them, for they do not know what they do" (Luke 23:34). Comparable is the last cry of Stephen, the first Christian martyr: "Lord, do not charge them with this sin" (Acts 7:60). These calls for forgiveness are strikingly different from Zechariah's plea for vengeance. However, it will not do simply to contrast New Testament grace with Old Testament wrath, in view of Luke 11:47–51—and also Revelation 6:10; 19:2. Zechariah was praying not a personal prayer of vengeance but a formal one as God's representative. The overtures He made had been spurned time after time, and the fate of the wayward king and people was sealed by this last, wanton rejection. They had lost their last chance, and it could hardly be said that they did not know what they were doing. The Chronicler took pains to show how God gave every opportunity for a change of heart, in line with its key text of 7:14, but there came a point when defeat had to be admitted.

The punishment does not take long in coming. The Chronicler makes plain the precise correspondence between offense and reprisal. The "wrath" of God is realized via foreign invasion and a domestic coup. The "leaders" of Israel, Joash's evil counselors, suffer to a man via the Syrian attack (vv. 17, 23). Conspiracy against Zechariah, in which the king played a leading role, is requited by a court conspiracy against Joash (vv. 21, 25, 26). The king who "killed" Zechariah was himself "killed" (vv. 22, 25). The forsaking of God is repaid (vv. 20, 24). It is made very plain that what one sows must eventually be reaped. Ironically the tables are turned on Judah by the victory of a small Syrian force in fighting "a very great army" (v. 24). Once again God shows Himself on the side of the outnumbered, as in 13:3–18 and 14:8–15, but this time He is backing Judah's foes! The grim passage is rounded off with mention of the king's burial, a markedly less prestigious affair than that of Jehoiada at the end of the preceding passage (v. 16).

In fact the figure of Jehoiada, who dominated the first half of the chapter (vv. 2, 14–16), also haunts the second half, in verses 17, 20, 22, 25. Likewise *the house* of God, so prominent in verses 2–16, finds further mention in verses 18 and 21. At the close of the chapter the Chronicler manages to find a good word to say about Joash, in specifying the *repairing of the house of God* (v. 27), but it functions as a distant memory and serves to enhance the heinousness of verses 18 and 21. Both the priest and temple stand as symbols of a gracious and holy God which, rejected, bring judgment in their train. The grim message the Chronicler is preaching in this narrative is akin to that which the writer to the Hebrews proclaimed more explicitly in predicting dire punishment for one "who has trampled the Son of God underfoot, counted the blood of the covenant by which he was sanctified a common thing, and insulted the Spirit of grace" (Heb. 10:29).

Another term that haunts verses 17–26 is the verb "forsake." The passage falls into four sections, verses 17–19, 20–22, 23–24, and 25–26. Each of these sections has in it a mention of this key term, which is rendered in NKJV either as *left* or *has/have/had forsaken.* First, in verse 18 the forsaking of the temple marks the abandoning of the true, traditional faith. In verse 20 that act is interpreted as the forsaking of God Himself, which incurs the awful curse of being forsaken by Him. We have encountered earlier, in 1 Chronicles 28:9 and 2 Chronicles 12:5, 15:2 this mirror-image theology of reaping what one sows and getting as good—or as bad—as one gives. The third instance is in verse 24, which reiterates the sin of verses 18 and 20, now as the reason for Judah's punishment. The last case, in verse 25, refers to the king as *left* badly wounded by the attacking troops. Since they feature as agents of divine retribution, the act showed that Joash was truly God-forsaken. If the chapters concerning Jehoshaphat highlighted fellowship with God, Joash's latter period brings to the fore its polar opposite, God-forsakenness.

FINDING A NEWFANGLED FAITH

25:1 Amaziah *was* twenty-five years old *when* he became king, and he reigned twenty-nine years in Jerusalem. His mother's name *was* Jehoaddan of Jerusalem.

2 And he did *what was* right in the sight of the LORD, but not with a loyal heart.

3 Now it happened, as soon as the kingdom was established for him, that he executed his servants who had murdered his father the king.

4 However he did not execute their children, but *did* as *it is* written in the Law in the Book of Moses, where the LORD commanded, saying, "The fathers shall not be put to death for their children, nor shall the children be put to death for their fathers; but a person shall die for his own sin."

5 Moreover Amaziah gathered Judah together and set over them captains of thousands and captains of hundreds, according to *their* fathers' houses, throughout all Judah and Benjamin; and he numbered them from twenty years old and above, and found them to be three hundred thousand choice *men, able* to go to war, who could handle spear and shield.

6 He also hired one hundred thousand mighty men of valor from Israel for one hundred talents of silver.

7 But a man of God came to him, saying, "O king, do not let the army of Israel go with you, for the LORD *is* not with Israel—*not with* any of the children of Ephraim.

8 "But if you go, be gone! Be strong in battle! *Even so*, God shall make you fall before the enemy; for God has power to help and to overthrow."

9 Then Amaziah said to the man of God, "But what *shall we* do about the hundred talents which I have given to the troops of Israel?" And the man of God answered, "The LORD is able to give you much more than this."

10 So Amaziah discharged the troops that had come to him from Ephraim, to go back home. Therefore their anger was greatly aroused against Judah, and they returned home in great anger.

11 Then Amaziah strengthened himself, and leading his people, he went to the Valley of Salt and killed ten thousand of the people of Seir.

12 Also the children of Judah took captive ten

thousand alive, brought them to the top of the rock, and cast them down from the top of the rock, so that they all were dashed in pieces.

13 But as for the soldiers of the army which Amaziah had discharged, so that they would not go with him to battle, they raided the cities of Judah from Samaria to Beth Horon, killed three thousand in them, and took much spoil.

14 Now it was so, after Amaziah came from the slaughter of the Edomites, that he brought the gods of the people of Seir, set them up *to be* his gods, and bowed down before them and burned incense to them.

15 Therefore the anger of the LORD was aroused against Amaziah, and He sent him a prophet who said to him, "Why have you sought the gods of the people, which could not rescue their own people from your hand?"

16 So it was, as he talked with him, that *the king* said to him, "Have we made you the king's counselor? Cease! Why should you be killed?" Then the prophet ceased, and said, "I know that God has determined to destroy you, because you have done this and have not heeded my advice."

17 Now Amaziah king of Judah asked advice and sent to Joash the son of Jehoahaz, the son of Jehu, king of Israel, saying, "Come, let us face one another *in battle.*"

18 And Joash king of Israel sent to Amaziah king of Judah, saying, "The thistle that *was* in Lebanon sent to the cedar that was in Lebanon, saying, 'Give your daughter to my son as wife'; and a wild beast that *was* in Lebanon passed by and trampled the thistle.

19 "Indeed you say that you have defeated the Edomites, and your heart is lifted up to boast. Stay at home now; why should you meddle with trouble, that you should fall—you and Judah with you?"

20 But Amaziah would not heed, for it *came* from God, that He might give them into the hand *of their enemies*, because they sought the gods of Edom.

21 So Joash king of Israel went out; and he and Amaziah king of Judah faced one another at Beth Shemesh, which *belongs* to Judah.

22 And Judah was defeated by Israel, and every man fled to his tent.

23 Then Joash the king of Israel captured Amaziah king of Judah, the son of Joash, the son of Jehoahaz, at Beth Shemesh; and he brought him to Jerusalem, and broke down the wall of Jerusalem from the Gate of Ephraim to the Corner Gate—four hundred cubits.

24 And *he took* all the gold and silver, all the articles that were found in the house of God with Obed-Edom, the treasures of the king's house, and hostages, and returned to Samaria.

25 Amaziah the son of Joash, king of Judah, lived fifteen years after the death of Joash the son of Jehoahaz, king of Israel.

26 Now the rest of the acts of Amaziah, from first to last, indeed *are* they not written in the book of the kings of Judah and Israel?

27 After the time that Amaziah turned away from following the LORD, they made a conspiracy against him in Jerusalem, and he fled to Lachish; but they sent after him to Lachish and killed him there.

28 Then they brought him on horses and buried him with his fathers in the City of Judah.

2 Chron. 25:1-28

Here is another person who bears the name of Turnaway; indeed, the very phrase occurs in verse 27. Once again the reign is split down the middle by an initial period of favor and then a fall from grace.

1. *The pious winner.* The characterization of qualified approval in verse 2 seems to apply not to the whole reign but to the initial period. The hesitation *"not with a loyal* (literally 'whole') *heart"* which the Chronicler has added is looking ahead to the wobbliness of verses 6 and 9. The historical definition of this flawed spirituality is given in two incidents which are narrated in verses 3–4 and 5–13. The first episode is taken over, along with verses 1–2a, from 2 Kings 14:1–3, 5, 6. The reference to compliance with the Torah obviously coincided with one of the Chronicler's interests. Although the murderers of Amaziah's father had been agents of divine providence, their recourse to illegality could not be condoned. The Torah citation about limiting reprisals is taken from Deuteronomy 24:16. The note

of moderation is one that correspondingly speaks to all in a position of authority. Many a mother or father knows the temptation to crack the nut of a child's offense with a sledgehammer of fury. Police eyeing a surging crowd of demonstrators have to make the difficult decision whether and when to resort to a vehement crackdown. On the spur of the moment human nature urges excess, while wiser counsels advocate a moderate course. Who does not sympathize with the angry desire of James and John to call down fire from heaven to destroy the Samaritan villagers who rejected Jesus? And who does not on reflection agree with Jesus' refusal of this extreme step as an overreaction (Luke 9:52–56; cf. an Old Testament counterpart, 2 Sam. 16:5–13)?

The second incident in verses 5–13 concerns a successful campaign against Edom. It is an expansion of a single verse, 2 Kings 14:7, which is echoed at verse 11. The reference to the attempted use of mercenaries from the northern state and the damage they inflicted on Judah are presumably derived from another source at the Chronicler's disposal. The supplementing of Amaziah's own national army with northern mercenaries becomes the object of a prophetic rebuke. It is the story of Jehoshaphat's alliance in chapter 18 all over again. Defeat is forecast as the price to pay for such fraternizing. As long as the northerners persisted in their present attitude of rejecting God, they were out of fellowship with Him, as the Chronicler had explained in 13:4–12 (cf. 15:2).

The first half of verse 8 is notoriously difficult and the text seems to have suffered a little damage. A feasible reconstruction is "But if with them you are about to act strongly in war, God . . . " (cf. NEB). It is a warning that numerical superiority must give way to the more powerful will of God, who can grant victory or defeat, irrespective of numbers. Paradoxically this ill-conceived augmenting of Amaziah's troops was a sure way to guarantee defeat. It is to Amaziah's credit that he complied with the prophetic criticism, though not without a grumble. The king's complaint is all too human. Obviously the cost had to be written off as the price of experience. It was a costly mistake indeed, but one from which a crucial lesson could be learned. How many of us look back at experiences in our past and regret the expending of resources to no good purpose? At least such experiences have left us somewhat wiser, if sadder. The prophet's reply is that God can compensate for losses incurred as the cost of making good. The one who is the loser becomes an eventual winner under God. The loss is here the price of putting right a mistake. That God promises renumeration in such a case is a mark of His grace. We have not heard the last of the mercenaries, however. With their expectation of loot from the coming campaign denied them, they turn elsewhere for their prerequisites. The following campaign and eventual victory is marred by the accompanying reports of the mercenaries' reprisals in verses 10b and 13. Even when amends have been made, mistakes sometimes cast long shadows down the corridors of human life and diminish their perpetrators' potential.

The account of that victory in verses 11–12, taken in part from 2 Kings 14:7, has a bloodthirsty ring. One must take into account the longstanding hostility between Judah and Edom, which in post-exilic times was exacerbated by the failure of the Edomites to stand by Judah in the crushing defeat of 586 B.C. and by their infiltration into the southern territory of Judah during the Exile. The prophecy of Obadiah reflects this animosity and so does the passionate Psalm 137. Consequently in the conception of the coming kingdom of God the subjugation of Edom played a key role, as Amos 9:12 and Obadiah 21 indicate. Edom becomes a cipher for human opposition to the people of God and so to God Himself. This prophetic understanding seems to be the animating force behind the virulence of the text.

2. *The apostate loser.* If so, the sequel to the campaign in verse 14 is an ironic disappointment. One expects God-given victory to be succeeded by the worship of grateful hearts, as in 20:26–28. Instead, Amaziah becomes a convert to Edomite religion! The narrative reminds me of the self-styled Messiah of the seventeenth century A.D., Shabbatai Zevi. He gained an enormous Jewish following by his reputed signs and wonders. Eventually he had an audience with the Turkish Sultan, who gave him an ultimatum, to become a Muslim or die. To his followers' chagrin he chose the former option.

Nowhere more than in the glory and shame of Amaziah is the dual potential of humanity polarized. He illustrates Alexander Pope's definition of human ambiguity:

He hangs between; . . .
In doubt to deem himself a god, or beast; . . .

341

> Created half to rise, and half to fall;
> Great lord of all things, yet a prey to all;
> Sole judge of truth, in endless error hurl'd;
> The glory, jest, and riddle of the world![1]

Now the degenerate period of Amaziah's reign is in view. The defeat of Judah in verses 17–24 and his violent death in verses 25–28 are taken over from 2 Kings 14:8–20. The Chronicler has prefaced the account with a new beginning, middle, and end: the theological introduction in verses 14–17 and further theological comments in verses 20–27. The royal defeat and murder are providential reprisals for his apostasy. In verse 15 the divine *"anger,"* expressed in the prophetic challenge, has the function of a warning, seeking to turn Amaziah from his folly. Gods whose weakness had been proven in battle must come a poor second to the true God who gives powerful help (v. 8b). The prophet is silenced, in spite of his testimony to the truth and his implicit call to the king to see the error of his ways. In the Chronicler's mind this was the greater crime. It meant that a second chance had been spurned. The king's fate is sealed not so much by his espousal of a spurious faith as by his refusal to heed the prophet's counsel.

In the Hebrew, verses 16 and 17a contain a fourfold play with the concept of counsel. The king rejects the prophet's right to take part in the royal deliberations and threatens death. In reply the prophet blames the king for refusing to listen to his sound deliberations. He announces that in reprisal God Himself has deliberated (*"determined"*) Amaziah's destruction. The king's threat of death for the prophet turns into a boomerang of an eventual violent death for himself, as verse 27 will narrate. Lastly the king proceeds to deliberate a foolish military confrontation with the northern state of *"Israel"*: for the readers it is an ironic echo of the divine decision and points to a significant stage in its providential outworking. Divine wisdom and human wisdom are contrasted, and the latter is shown to be arrogant folly. "Has not God made foolish the wisdom of this world?" (1 Cor. 1:19–20).

The northern king's reply to Amaziah's puny challenge was as sensible as the prophet's reasoning earlier, but Amaziah was not prepared to listen to reason. He paid as little *"heed"* (v. 20) as to the prophet. As the saying goes, there's none so deaf as he who does not want to hear. One cannot help thinking of Dryden's couplet: "For those whom God to ruin has design'd, / He fits for fate, and first destroys their mind."[2] To Amaziah Joash's diagnosis of his over-weening temerity is like the proverbial red rag to a bull; perversely it provokes him to initiate the campaign. And, adds the Chronicler, it was the outworking of a providential purpose, in punishment of Amaziah's apostasy. People, king, and capital all suffer in a terrible foreshadowing of the later conquests of 597 and 586 B.C. Twice the Chronicler has mentioned Jerusalem's exposure to enemy attack, in 24:23 and here, both deliberately repeated from Kings. For the Chronicler the phenomenon of exile was a recurring one, rather than a culminating climax. It functioned as a theological image of divine punishment to which he deemed any generation of God's people liable, should they rebel against His will. For Amaziah apostasy proves to be a slippery slope toward destruction (v. 27). He lives on, but eventually his fate is the same as his predecessor's. His flight from fatality only delays it, for the wages of sin is death.

The story preaches its own message. Implicitly the Chronicler is pleading with his readers in every generation not to "cast away" their "confidence," but to confess with him that "we are not of those who draw back to perdition, but of those who believe to the saving of the soul" (Heb. 10:35, 39).

OVERSTEPPING GOD'S LIMITS

26:1 Now all the people of Judah took Uzziah, who *was* sixteen years old, and made him king instead of his father Amaziah.

2 He built Elath and restored it to Judah, after the king rested with his fathers.

3 Uzziah *was* sixteen years old when he became king, and he reigned fifty-two years in Jerusalem. His mother's name was Jecholiah of Jerusalem.

4 And he did *what was* right in the sight of the LORD, according to all that his father Amaziah had done.

5 He sought God in the days of Zechariah, who had understanding in the visions of God; and as long as he sought the LORD, God made him prosper.

6 Now he went out and made war against the Philistines, and broke down the wall of Gath, the wall of Jabneh, and the wall of Ashdod; and he built cities *around* Ashdod and among the Philistines.

7 God helped him against the Philistines, against the Arabians who lived in Gur Baal, and against the Meunites.

8 Also the Ammonites brought tribute to Uzziah. His fame spread as far as the entrance of Egypt, for he became exceedingly strong.

9 And Uzziah built towers in Jerusalem at the Corner Gate, at the Valley Gate, and at the corner buttress of the wall; then he fortified them.

10 Also he built towers in the desert. He dug many wells, for he had much livestock, both in the lowlands and in the plains; *he also had* farmers and vine-dressers in the mountains and in Carmel, for he loved the soil.

11 Moreover Uzziah had an army of fighting men who went out to war by companies, according to the number on their roll as prepared by Jeiel the scribe and Maaseiah the officer, under the hand of Hananiah, *one* of the king's captains.

12 The total number of chief officers of the mighty men of valor *was* two thousand six hundred.

13 And under their *was* an army of three hundred and seven thousand five hundred, that made war with mighty power, to help the king against the enemy.

14 Then Uzziah prepared for them, for the entire army, shields, spears, helmets, body armor, bows, and slings to *cast* stones.

15 And he made devices in Jerusalem, invented by skillful men, to be on the towers and the corners, to shoot arrows and large stones. So his fame spread far and wide, for he was marvelously helped till he became strong.

16 But when he was strong his heart was lifted up, to *his* destruction, for he transgressed against the LORD his God by entering the temple of the LORD to burn incense on the altar of incense.

17 So Azariah the priest went in after him, and

with him were eighty priests of the LORD—valiant men.

18 And they withstood King Uzziah, and said to him, *"It is* not for you, Uzziah, to burn incense to the LORD, but for the priests, the sons of Aaron, who are consecrated to burn incense. Get out of the sanctuary, for you have trespassed! You *shall have* no honor from the LORD God."

19 Then Uzziah became furious; and he *had* a censer in his hand to burn incense. And while he was angry with the priests, leprosy broke out on his forehead, before the priests in the house of the LORD, beside the incense altar.

20 And Azariah the chief priest and all the priests looked at him, and there, on his forehead, he *was* leprous; so they thrust him out of that place. Indeed he also hurried to get out, because the LORD had struck him.

21 King Uzziah was a leper until the day of his death. He dwelt in an isolated house, because he was a leper; for he was cut off from the house of the LORD. Then Jotham his son *was* over the king's house, judging the people of the land.

22 Now the rest of the acts of Uzziah, from first to last, the prophet Isaiah the son of Amoz wrote.

23 So Uzziah rested with his fathers, and they buried him with his fathers in the field of burial which *belonged* to the kings, for they said, "He is a leper." Then Jotham his son reigned in his place.

2 Chron. 26:1-23

In Chronicles Amaziah's father, Amaziah himself, and Amaziah's son are all three tarred with the same brush as first faithful to God and then faithless. The royal trilogy is meant as a powerful sermon to believers to "hold the beginning of" their "confidence steadfast to the end" (Heb. 3:14).

The name *"Uzziah"* appears to be an alternative form of "Azariah," which this king bears in the Davidic genealogy of 1 Chronicles 3:12 and—mostly—in 2 Kings 14-15. About seven verses in this chapter have been copied from the corresponding Kings narrative. At the beginning of the chapter verses 1-2 are taken from 2 Kings 14:21-22, and verses 3–4 from 2 Kings 15:2–3. At the end of the chapter the last clause of verse 20 and verses 21–22 are derived from 2 Kings 15:5–6a, while verse 23, apart from *"for they said, 'He is a leper'"* harks back to 2 Kings 15:7. Uzziah's long reign is regarded by historians as a prosperous one, although Kings devoted only nine verses to it. He was the Judean counterpart of the equally long-reigning and even more prosperous Jeroboam II of Israel in the eighth century B.C. The wresting of *"Elath"* (v. 2) from Edomite control gave access to the sea trade of Arabia, Africa, and India. The accounts of his conquests in verses 6–8 and of his agricultural enterprises and military developments in verses 9–15 are all feasible in principle and appear to have been taken from a source other than Kings. The Chronicler also seems to know from elsewhere a mentor called *"Zechariah"* (v. 5) and the king's officiating in the temple (v. 16).

Despite his successes the Kings narrative refers to Uzziah's succumbing to leprosy. The comparison of his reign with that of Amaziah (v. 4 = 2 Kings 15:3) would have confirmed the Chronicler's impression that Uzziah's reign had a Jekyll and Hyde sequence of blessing and backsliding.

1. *Uzziah's blessing.* The Chronicler took the religious assessment of verse 4 as a reference to the first, happy period of his rule and developed it in two ways, in terms of foreign affairs (vv. 6–8) and internal matters (vv. 9–15). First, however, he provided an introduction to this positive period, in verse 5. It was the situation of the pious Jehoiada's mentorship of Joash (24:2–16) all over again. Uzziah was like Joash too in that prosperity depended on a positive attitude toward God (24:20). The Chronicler tends to work with a theology of prosperity, although he does allow for crisis breaking into the obedient believer's life, as precursor to a new experience of trust in God as one who saves as well as one who blesses (see 20:1–30). He writes as a pastoral theologian in advocating spirituality as the hallmark of the lives of his fellow-believers and using the prospect of well-being as an incentive to that end. We fickle humans seem to need such an incentive as much as the donkey needs its dangled carrot.

The Chronicler's repetition of his King's source in verse 2 has already specified Uzziah's capture of the key port of Elath. It conjures up Solomonic associations, for he too controlled Elath (8:17). From another source the Chronicler was able to supply details of successful campaigns, mainly in the south and southwest of Judah. He supplies the spiritual secret of Uzziah's success in verse 7a. The end product of immense power (*"he became exceedingly strong,"* v. 8), which resulted in widespread prestige (*"his fame spread"*), was due not to Uzziah's sole efforts but to the divine help he received. The accolade of prestige has a Davidic ring, for it directs the careful reader back to 1 Chronicles 14:17. So here is a worthy king who is walking in the footsteps of both the Chronicler's heroes. Moreover, strength was a repeated motif in the description of the early, prosperous period of Rehoboam's reign (11:11, 12, 17; 12:1). Uzziah had positive qualities associated with the early Davidic monarchy. From a literary standpoint the references to strength and help appear to be wordplays on the king's two names, *"Uzziah"* ("Yahweh is my strength") and *"Azariah"* ("Yahweh helps"). In the second case the same Hebrew verb is used, while in the first instance a more common synonym in the Chronicler's vocabulary is used. These are the blessings that accrue to Uzziah. His power and prestige depend on the backing of his divine Patron.

The same message is delivered at the end of the next paragraph, in verse 15b. Now the king's internal exploits are in view: his building work (vv. 9, 10), ever an indication of blessing in Chronicles, and his military manpower and material (vv. 11–15a). The agricultural exploits of verse 10 presumably relate to the royal estates of 1 Chronicles 27:25–31. Readers who are keen gardeners will warm to the description of Uzziah as one who *"loved the soil."* In this context of divine blessing they will not be able to resist thinking of Dorothy F. Gurney's couplet from "God's Garden":

> One is nearer God's heart in a garden
> Than anywhere else on earth.

The mention of growing sophistication of ancient warfare (v. 15a) strikes a more somber note, although the Chronicler regarded it positively as further evidence of divine blessing. Old Testament theology is a triangle with three corners, the land, God's people, and God Himself. Inclusion of the land necessarily brought territorial security into the sphere of the things of God. The advancement featured here concerns siege warfare. The Israeli general and scholar Yigael Yadin has plausibly identified the *"devices"* (v. 15) with special structures added to towers and battlements. Such structures were in evidence at Lachish at the end of the eighth century according to the scenes of the siege of the Judean city of Lachish depicted on the reliefs of the Assyrian king Sennacherib. They were wooden frames into which round shields were inserted to form a protective barrier behind which archers and stone-throwers could safely stand instead of crouching awkwardly.[3]

2. *Uzziah's backsliding.* The success story, accentuated by the repeated reference to power and prestige, dependent still on the supernatural (*"marvelously,"* v. 15) factor of help, changes abruptly into a tragedy. Uzziah's strength becomes a catchword linking success with self-centeredness. The Chronicler views the king as another Rehoboam, who perverted strength into a willful facility for transgression (12:1, 2), as here in verse 16. There is a sense of anticlimax as success gives way to failure. In the Chronicler's eyes to commit blatant sin against God meant forfeiting His generous gifts. One could not have the gifts without allegiance to the Giver, an allegiance which involved staying within the moral and religious parameters of the Torah. His thinking is reminiscent of that of John who for pastoral ends declared in equally categorical terms that "whoever hates his brother is a murderer, and you know that no murderer has eternal life abiding in him" (1 John 3:15). Similarly Paul listed a catalog of sins that excluded their perpetrators from inheriting "the kingdom of God" (1 Cor. 6:9, 10). However, Paul went on to envisage a divine work of renewal which could remove the disqualification. So did the Chronicler in Rehoboam's case: mention of self-humbling in 12:6, 7, 12 alludes to the gracious provision laid down in 7:14. In the case of Uzziah, however, it is to be stressed that an opportunity for repentance was given—and lost.

Uzziah's lifting up of his *"heart"* (v. 16) is a repetition of his father's pride (25:19). It implicitly contrasts with the self-humbling essential for the procuring of divine forgiveness. Moreover, it is stressed in verse 19 that judgment strikes not when Uzziah commits a religious sin by usurping the role of the Aaronic priesthood, but when he reacts to the high priest's reprimand with wrath instead of repentance. In each of the cases of the three apostate kings there is a concern on the Chronicler's part to stress God's patience in giving an opportunity for rethinking and repenting. There is ever a divine reluctance to punish, and punishment materializes only as a last resort. First, there is an endeavor to touch the sinner's conscience by challenging him (24:19, 20; 25:15; 26:18). Only when that expedient fails does the ax fall.

Uzziah's sin is that of pride in wanting to extend his power from the secular to the religious sphere. His power goes to his head. No longer content with legitimate authority, he oversteps the mark by extending it in an illegitimate direction, to enhance his own glory ("honor"). In the Chronicler's mind it constituted a double offense, against the temple and the Torah: the priestly prerogatives laid down in the Torah (cf. Exod. 30:7-9; Num. 18:1-7) applied to the temple. In the Hebrew the offense is twice described in extreme terms as unfaithfulness (vv. 16, 18 NKJV "transgressed," "trespassed"), in echo of the sin of Saul (1 Chron. 10:13) and of the sin which was to send both Israel and Judah to Exile (1 Chron. 5:25; 9:1; 2 Chron. 36:14). Again, the cautionary message of the Chronicler is that the peril of Exile and so of excommunication from the Lord's presence lies within the potential of every generation of His people. Here that fate finds illustration in the "leprosy" of Uzziah, which is hauntingly mentioned no less than five times in verses 19-23. In the Bible leprosy is not the malady which now popularly bears the name and technically is called Hansen's Disease. It can be identified only as a severe skin complaint whose direness lay in its rendering the victim ritually unclean (cf. Lev. 13:44-46).

He who trespasses into the temple is henceforth excluded from it (v. 21) and evidently from society. His overweening ambition robs him of his previous legitimate power. For the rest of his reign his royal authority is delegated to his son as regent. Even in his burial his royal rank stands in some question, for he is laid to rest not in the royal cemetery but in crown property adjoining it. He who wanted too much ends up with less than he previously had. Yet the Chronicler desires his readers to appreciate that, great as his sin was, his fate was not irrevocable until it was sealed by willful refusal to climb down from his high and mighty attitude. In retrospect the incident casts a chilling shadow over the narrative of 1 Chronicles 13. David's recourse to anger to express his frustration over the transporting of the ark was a dangerous one, but in his case it gave way to a proper reverence for God (1 Chron. 13:12, 13). Ultimately to be a man or woman after God's own heart entails compliance not with the law of His moral will but with His gospel of a second chance.

These three chapters have a painful message, and it is only out of a pastoral concern that the Chronicler presents it, using three variations on a common theme in sermonic fashion. His positive desire is that of the writer to the Hebrews in his passages of dire warning. The overall intent of both pastoral authors is the same: "Beware, brethren, lest there be in any of you an evil heart of unbelief in departing from the living God; but exhort one another daily . . . , lest any of you be hardened through the deceitfulness of sin" (Heb. 3:12, 13).

NOTES

1. Alexander Pope, *An Essay on Man,* ep. 2, 1.7–12.
2. John Dryden, *The Hind and the Panther,* pt. 3, 1.1093.
3. Yigael Yadin, *The Art of Warfare in Biblical Lands* (New York: McGraw-Hill, 1963), 2:324–26, 431, 434.

CHAPTER SIXTEEN

Images of Right and Wrong

2 Chronicles 27:1–28:27

The previous three chapters of Chronicles have warned that human fortunes can tumble when spirituality ceases to be a priority. A contrast between good and evil was worked out in each of the reigns of three successive kings. Now the Chronicler uses a different format to preach the same message: two reigns are set back to back as examples of right and wrong respectively. A pair of kings are polarized, Jotham the Good and Ahaz the Bad. The Chronicler may have had at the back of his mind the case histories of Ezekiel 18:5–9, 10–13, where a good father is succeeded by an immoral wretch of a son. A glance at the respective lengths of chapters 27 and 28 reveals that the latter contains a much fuller treatment of its theme. Is it because human nature leans toward evil and so in practice "Don't do that" has to be stated more loudly and often than "Do this"? Perhaps so, but a second agenda is being pursued in chapter 28, which explains its size to some extent. Chapters 10–28 of 2 Chronicles form a distinct section, concerning the history of the divided kingdom. The Chronicler takes the opportunity to round it off by pointing out a surprising contrast between the opening factors and the final ones. While we read on, the Chronicler, as ever, wants to whisper in our ears, "How about you? Where do you stand?"

A SUCCESS STORY

27:1 Jotham *was* twenty-five years old when he became king, and he reigned sixteen years in Jerusalem. His mother's name *was* Jerushah the daughter of Zadok.

2 And he did *what was* right in the sight of the
LORD, according to all that his father Uzziah had
done (although he did not enter the temple of the
LORD). But still the people acted corruptly.

3 He built the Upper Gate of the house of the
LORD, and he built extensively on the wall of Ophel.

4 Moreover he built cities in the mountains of Judah, and in the forests he built fortresses and towers.

5 He also fought with the king of the Ammonites
and defeated them. And the people of Ammon gave
him in that year one hundred talents of silver, ten
thousand kors of wheat, and ten thousand of barley.
The people of Ammon paid this to him in the second
and third years also.

6 So Jotham became mighty, because he prepared
his ways before the LORD his God.

7 Now the rest of the acts of Jotham, and all his
wars and his ways, indeed they *are* written in the
book of the kings of Israel and Judah.

8 He was twenty-five years old when he became
king, and he reigned sixteen years in Jerusalem.

9 So Jotham rested with his fathers, and they
buried him in the City of David. Then Ahaz his son
reigned in his place.

2 Chron. 27:1–9

The first story with a moral is short and sweet. The reign of Jotham
is presented as a neat vignette of obedience and blessing. The message that God honors commitment to moral and spiritual excellence
is preached clearly and concisely. The chapter is structured in a sym-
metrical fashion. At its heart lie two evidences of God's favor in
verses 3–4 and 5. This twinned element is surrounded by the secret
of Jotham's success in verses 2 and 6. Encircling that are the initial
and closing formulas of his reign in verses 1 and 7–9, each including
a statement of his sixteen years' reign, a repetition which finds a
parallel in the case of Jehoram at 21:5, 20. We shall find that chapter
28, similar in form but diverse in content, functions as the negative
counterpart of chapter 27.

The Chronicler has made use of the short account of Jotham's
reign in 2 Kings 15:32–38 in verses 1–2a, 3a, 7–9. He has been able

to amplify that account with details of further building operations in verses 3b–4 and with a reference to a successful Ammonite campaign in verse 5, both of which he seems to have gleaned from another source. He has suppressed the reference to initial invasion from the north in 2 Kings 15:37, in the interests of a sharper contrast between the blessed reign of Jotham the Good and the blighted regime of Ahaz the Bad.

At the center of the chapter lies double evidence of the blessing of security and protection bestowed by God. As in previous reigns, the topics of building operations and military victory belong to the Chronicler's standard code for divine blessing. Jotham takes after his father Uzziah not only in his piety (v. 2) but also in his receipt of Ammonite tribute (see 26:8) and his building of cities and towers (26:6, 10). For a weak Judah in post-exilic times, harassed by neighbors and eking out a bare economic existence, such operations had a mouth-watering appeal. The message is that God can meet His people at the point of their need, developing potential in the spheres where now there is failure.

If God is the unnamed benefactor in verses 3–5, such blessing is explicitly grounded in the king's honoring of God, at verses 2 and 6. Obedience is the way forward, preaches the Chronicler, and God certainly cannot be expected to bless when it is absent. In verse 2 Jotham's goodness shines out all the brighter by being set against a drab background of contrasting ills, perpetrated by his predecessor and by the people. It is a goodness that takes its cue from the will of God. In the books of Judges and Proverbs an opposite principle is featured, doing what is right in one's own eyes (Judg. 17:6; 21:25; Prov. 12:15; cf. 30:12). The hallmark of biblical faith is to look at life through God's eyes. The fact that "He has shown you, O man, what is good" (Mic. 6:8) is taken seriously. Neither expediency nor any other form of self-interest is to lie at the root of the believer's motivation for living. Faith has a practical flowering when God is accepted as the arbiter of right and wrong. The result may often coincide with the ideals of the noble pagan—which may well be post-Christian relics—but not necessarily so. The norms of society have constantly to be brought to the bar of biblical ethics before the believer can endorse them in his or her attitudes. In New Testament terms his principle is enshrined in the challenge "Do not be conformed to this world, but be transformed by the renewing of your mind, that you may prove what is that good and acceptable and perfect will of God" (Rom. 12:2).

In verse 6 the Chronicler redefines the Kings formula of verse 2 in his own words. The key to Jotham's power was that *"he prepared his ways before the Lord his God."* Now a personal faith and a conscious dependence on God come to the fore. Not that God is Big Brother whose sinister gaze and secret microphones curb and curtail with his ruthless will the development of his subjects. Submission to God meant for the Chronicler the realization of God-given potential: it was a positive force, as the means whereby Jotham *"became mighty."* That meant in practice a life based on the Torah as the revelation of God's will for His people. The Chronicler would have added his own Amen to the prayerful wish of the psalmist who, using the same Hebrew verbal phrase as here, longed "Oh, that my ways were directed to keep Your statutes" (Ps. 119:5)! For the psalmist there was often a tantalizing gap between goals and performance. The Chronicler would not have denied that a subtle combination of utter trust and earnest effort was necessary to reach those goals (cf. Phil. 2:12, 13), but he would have affirmed its worthwhileness.

As C. Stacey Woods, formerly General Secretary of the International Fellowship of Evangelical Students, has written:

> Psychologists tell us that usually the difference between success and failure is not so much caused by intelligence, personality, or appearance, but rather by motivation. Many are millionaires in terms of natural ability, talent, opportunity, and possibility, but they never amount to anything. They are failures, even in this life. Whereas many others of mediocre ability and limited opportunity become tremendous successes. Why is this? The reason is motivation. God is the great motivator. . . . Like Christ feeding the five thousand when He took a boy's lunch, five barley rolls, and a couple of pickled or dried fish, and fed a multitude, Christ can take you and me, very limited and circumscribed though we may be, and can—I dare say *will*—use us to a degree far beyond any natural expectation. . . . God loves me and desires more ardently than I do my self-realization and self-expression under His holy will and purpose. He calls me to "the courage to be" according to His Word and His Spirit. Only as I accept myself according to His will,

can I be a real person. In all of this He promises me His strength and guidance.[1]

A TALE OF WOE

28:1 Ahaz *was* twenty years old when he became king, and he reigned sixteen years in Jerusalem; and he did not do *what was* right in the sight of the LORD, as his father David *had done*.

2 For he walked in the ways of the kings of Israel, and made molded images for the Baals.

3 He burned incense in the Valley of the Son of Hinnom, and burned his children in the fire, according to the abominations of the nations whom the LORD had cast out before the children of Israel.

4 And he sacrificed and burned incense on the high places, on the hills, and under every green tree.

5 Therefore the LORD his God delivered him into the hand of the king of Syria. They defeated him, and carried away a great multitude of them as captives, and brought *them* to Damascus. Then he was also delivered into the hand of the king of Israel, who defeated him with a great slaughter.

6 For Pekah the son of Remaliah killed one hundred and twenty thousand in Judah in one day, all valiant men, because they had forsaken the LORD God of their fathers.

7 Zichri, a mighty man of Ephraim, killed Maaseiah the king's son, Azrikam the officer over the house, and Elkanah *who was* second to the king.

8 And the children of Israel carried away captive of their brethren two hundred thousand women, sons, and daughters; and they also took away much spoil from them, and brought the spoil to Samaria.

16 At the same time King Ahaz sent to the kings of Assyria to help him.

17 For again the Edomites had come, attacked Judah, and carried away captives.

18 The Philistines also had invaded the cities of the lowland and of the South of Judah, and had taken Beth Shemesh, Aijalon, Gederoth, Sochoh with its

villages, Timnah with its villages, and Gimzo with its villages; and they dwelt there.

19 For the LORD brought Judah low because of Ahaz king of Israel, for he had encouraged moral decline in Judah and had been continually unfaithful to the LORD.

20 Also Tiglath-Pileser king of Assyria came to him and distressed him, and did not assist him.

21 For Ahaz took part *of the treasures* from the house of the LORD, from the house of the king, and from the leaders, and he gave *it* to the king of Assyria; but he did not help him.

22 Now in the time of his distress King Ahaz became increasingly unfaithful to the LORD. This *is that* King Ahaz.

23 For he sacrificed to the gods of Damascus which had defeated him, saying, "Because the gods of the kings of Syria help them, I will sacrifice to them that they may help me." But they were the ruin of him and of all Israel.

24 So Ahaz gathered the articles of the house of God, cut in pieces the articles of the house of God, shut up the doors of the house of the LORD, and made for himself altars in every corner of Jerusalem.

25 And in every single city of Judah he made high places to burn incense to other gods, and provoked to anger the LORD God of his fathers.

26 Now the rest of his acts and all his ways, from first to last, indeed they *are* written in the book of the kings of Judah and Israel.

27 So Ahaz rested with his fathers, and they buried him in the city, in Jerusalem; but they did not bring him into the tombs of the kings of Israel. Then Hezekiah his son reigned in his place.

2 Chron. 28:1–8, 16–27

Chapter 27 used a target-like structure with concentric rings, the outermost ring of a sixteen years' reign narrowing into another of obedience to God and then into the central circle of His blessing. The closing stress on the length of reign neatly dovetails into the next, equally long reign (28:1), but that similarity only emphasizes the gap between the two kings. Sixteen good years were followed by sixteen wasted years. Another similarity is that the Hebrew verb meaning "be strong" or "strengthen" occurs three times in these two chapters, twice in 27:5-6 in a positive sense ("defeated," RSV "prevailed"; "became mighty") and in 28:20 in a negative context ("*assist*," RSV "strengthening"). After a king who "did what was right in the sight of the Lord" (27:2) came one who "*did not do what was right*" (28:1). The Chronicler would have his readers view the reigns side by side as a challenge for them—and so for us—to decide which king is to be the role model to follow.

In this chapter there is a similar structure of concentric rings. The opening and closing formulas in verses 1 and 26-27 feature the absence of "*what was right*" and its final corollary, the lack of burial in the royal cemetery. The next ring features changes of religious loyalty in verses 2-4 and 22-25, each with mention of sacrifice and burning incense. Further into the chapter appear two pairs of military defeats, at the hands of Syria and Israel in verses 5-8 and of Edom and Philistia in verses 17-19. The latter pair of national catastrophes is set in its own framework of turning to Assyria for help, which brings harm rather than help in its train (vv. 16, 20-21). At the heart of the chapter is a successful prophetic appeal to the people of the northern kingdom to repatriate their Judean prisoners of war (vv. 9-15). The success of the appeal shows up in an even worse light the unmitigated rejection of the true God on the part of the Judean king. Style and subject matter are matched in a telling fashion.

The Chronicler has based his version of Ahaz's reign on the unsavory account of this wicked king in 2 Kings 16:1-20. This framework is reflected at the beginning and end, being largely followed in verses 1-4, 5a, 6a and 24a, 26-27 and also in verses 16a and 21a. The second pair of invasions in verses 17-19 are generally judged feasible and based on a tradition other than Kings, while the specifications of the personal names in verse 12 and the place name "Jericho" in verse 15 also appear to have been taken from a separate source. The Chronicler has woven various pieces of historical information into a powerful piece of writing which makes liberal use of his own interpretative terms.

The historical background is what is generally called the Syro-Ephraimite War. It sprang from an attempt to form a sort of N.A.T.O. alliance against threat of attack from the eastern world power,

Assyria. Judah, nestling quietly in its out-of-the-way hills, refused to cooperate, judging discretion to be the better part of valor and hoping not to antagonize Assyria, if an attack did materialize. This policy provoked Syria and Israel to put increasing pressure on Judah, culminating in an attack on Jerusalem with the intent of deposing the Davidic monarch and replacing him with a Syrian puppet king. There are various, divergent accounts of this complex conflict in the Old Testament, in 2 Kings 15:37, 16:5, Isaiah 7, Hosea 5:8–6:6, and here. Each account is written from its own angle and the Chronicles material complements the others in a feasible fashion. Ahaz's appeal to the Assyrian empire builder Tiglath-Pileser to intervene in the local struggle was nothing less than an invitation to be sucked into the vortex of vassal kingship.

The Chronicler links religious apostasy and military defeat as cause and effect. Ahaz breaks the first two of the Ten Commandments by using images in his perverse worship of alien gods. He incurs the covenant curse of defeat in battle. The Chronicler portrays separately the attacks of the allies Syria and Israel in verses 5a and 5b-8. The Judean defeat at the hands of Israel is interpreted in passionate terms as reprisal for the fact that Judah *"had forsaken the Lord God of their fathers"* (v. 6), while in the next paragraph the defeat is credited to His anger toward Judah (v. 9). In verses 16–21, which correspond to verses 5–8, Ahaz's apostasy in being *"continually unfaithful to the Lord"* and his social evil of encouraging in Judah *"moral decline"*—in the Hebrew more strictly moral laxity—lead to God's use of neighboring states to inflict His punishment (v. 19). These errors are compounded by his grave sin of seeking help, in a situation of military crisis, not from God but from a human source. His religious unfaithfulness, as if verses 2–4 were insufficient, is increased in verse 22, which verses 23–25 proceed to amplify, culminating in the fresh notice that God had been *"provoked to anger."*

Taking his cue from Kings, the Chronicler views Ahaz as an Old Testament version of Judas. No other Davidic king is portrayed in such disparaging terms: he is another Saul or Athaliah. Ahaz's reign is a picture of the potential of human nature to debase itself and crash headlong into a barrier of providential reprisal. Davidic kingship reaches its lowest point in the person of Ahaz. It is not surprising therefore that a motif of exile runs all through this chapter. In 1 Chronicles 10 the end of Saul's reign was described in terms of exile and loss of land. The same phenomenon occurs here. Judean prisoners of war are deported by Syria, Israel, and Edom (vv. 5, 8, 17), while the Philistines take over Judean territory (v. 18)—as they had done in Saul's day (1 Chron. 10:7). Post-exilic Judah tended to look back on the Babylonian conquest of Jerusalem and exile of the people in 586 B.C. as the ultimate in woes, in tune with the representation in Kings and the pre-exilic prophets' threats of divine judgment. The Chronicler also viewed exile as the worst of calamities, but he refused to envisage it as an isolating chasm separating the pre-exilic and post-exilic communities. Rather, it was experienced at a number of points in Judean history. Dire as it was, each time God managed to take it in His forbearing stride and created a new beginning as its positive aftermath. One gets the impression that for the Chronicler each generation contained within it the seeds of exile, which it might cultivate into noxious weeds or with God's help firmly suppress. The former, negative potential finds sinister illustration in the reign of Ahaz. Indeed, God's help was so disdained that the Assyrian king—and later *"the gods of Damascus"* (v. 23)—was put in His place, and to that end *"the house of the Lord"* (v. 24) was plundered. However, Judah found that it had leapt out of the frying pan only to land in an Assyrian fire. The Chronicler is preaching a strong warning of the awful fate that can overwhelm the apostate. It is "written for" his readers' "admonition. . . . Therefore let him who thinks he stands take heed lest he fall" (1 Cor. 10:11–12). Or, in another's words, "Let us therefore be diligent . . . lest anyone fall according to the same example of disobedience" (Heb. 4:11).

A REVERSAL OF ROLES

28:9 But a prophet of the LORD was there, whose name *was* Oded; and he went out before the army that came to Samaria, and said to them: "Look, because the LORD God of your fathers was angry with Judah, He has delivered them into your hand; but you have killed them in a rage *that* reaches up to heaven.

10 "And now you propose to force the children of Judah and Jerusalem to be your male and female slaves; *but are* you not also guilty before the LORD your God?

11 "Now hear me, therefore, and return the captives, whom you have taken captive from your brethren, for the fierce wrath of the LORD *is* upon you."

12 Then some of the heads of the children of Ephraim, Azariah the son of Johanan, Berechiah the son of Meshillemoth, Jehizkiah the son of Shallum, and Amasa the son of Hadlai, stood up against those who came from the war,

13 and said to them, "You shall not bring the captives here, for we *already* have offended the LORD. You intend to add to our sins and to our guilt; for our guilt is great, and *there is* fierce wrath against Israel."

14 So the armed men left the captives and the spoil before the leaders and all the assembly.

15 Then the men who were designated by name rose up and took the captives, and from the spoil they clothed all who were naked among them, dressed them and gave them sandals, gave them food and drink, and anointed them; and they let all the feeble ones ride on donkeys. So they brought them to their brethren at Jericho, the city of palm trees. Then they returned to Samaria.

2 Chron. 28:9–15

The Chronicler has written his work of theological history in a series of four blocks. Thus far we have read together three of them, the genealogies of 1 Chronicles 1–9, the establishment of the Davidic dynasty and the Solomonic temple in 1 Chronicles 10 to 2 Chronicles 9, and Judean history in the period of the divided kingdom in 2 Chronicles 10–28. This last portion is now brought to a fitting close. The Chronicler seems to assume that in the course of the period covered by chapter 28 the series of northern kings came to an end with the collapse of the northern state and the deportation of many of its inhabitants to the other side of the Assyrian empire (cf. 30:6). From now on until the fall of Judah there was only one royal personage for the covenant people. The Chronicler appears to be making a threefold declaration of this new phenomenon toward the end of the chapter by calling Ahaz "king of Israel" (v. 19) and speaking of his subjects as "all Israel" (v. 23)—but in a bitterly negative context—and even calling the span of Judean monarchs "*kings of Israel*" (v. 27).

So chapter 28 brings to a close an important phase of the history of the covenant nation. The Chronicler signals it by contrasting the end of this phase with its beginnings. Verses 9–15 especially convey this contrast, though it does spill over into their context. In two negative aspects a comparison could also be drawn. Rehoboam at one stage in his reign "forsook" God by being "unfaithful to the Lord" (RSV), and in consequence he had to rob the temple coffers to pay an indemnity to the invading king of Egypt, Shishak (12:2, 5, 9). Ahaz too brought Judah to defeat because they "had forsaken the Lord" (28:6) and he was "increasingly unfaithful" (28:19, 22). He too had to ransack the temple, in this case to pay for Assyria's dubious help. These comparisons only throw into relief the fact that, whereas in Rehoboam's case divine "wrath" was averted by the king's and princes' humbling themselves (12:6, 7, 12), in the case of Ahaz there was no such self-humbling, and divine "anger" wrought disaster and ominously remained unsatisfied at the end of his reign (28:9, 25).

In 11:4 and in 28:11 (cf. v. 8) a prophet chides his hearers for unworthy treatment of their "*brethren.*" However, in the former case it is a southern army that is taken to task for preparing to fight the northerners, while in the latter instance it is a northern army that is criticized for capturing southerners. It is clear that power has passed from Judah to Israel, and in the privilege of receiving a prophetic caution against misusing this power in unbrotherly conduct, Israel is functioning as the favored nation.

The stereotype of the southerners as good guys and the northerners as bad guys, which the Chronicler has partially taken over from his contemporaries, is surprisingly discarded and even reversed at some points. In 28:5 Ahaz experienced "a great slaughter," which was the fate of the northerners at the hands of Abijah and his people in 13:17. Moreover, formerly Judah received the ministry of the prophet Shemaiah and repented in self-humbling in accord with the model of 7:14 (12:5, 6)—and Israel rejected Abijah's implicit counsel to the northern army to cease their backsliding. Now Israel was privileged to hear the prophet Oded and took a step in the right direction by confessing their backlog of sin and complying with his counsel to "*return*" the prisoners (28:9–15). It is not difficult to see here subtle echoes of the injunction of 7:14 to "turn from their wicked ways." Back in 13:16 God "delivered" Israel into Judah's "hand," but now He "*delivered*" Judah into Israel's "*hand*" (28:9). In

28:19 the Lord "brought Judah low," whereas in 13:18 "the children of Israel were subdued." Behind the different renderings lies a repetition of the same Hebrew verb. Judah had lost its position of privilege: while earlier the temple was a center of orthodox worship (13:10, 11), now its "doors" were "shut up" (28:24; cf. 29:7).

It is clear that the pro-Judah and anti-Israel impressions of chapters 11–13 have been reversed for the reader. I cannot help thinking of the parable of the prodigal son in Luke 15:11–32. The "Pharisees and scribes" are represented as the elder brother caviling at the welcome extended to the prodigal, who stands for the repentant "tax collectors and sinners" (15:1, 2). The former, who conceived of themselves as faithful to God, are portrayed in a bad light for criticizing the gracious overtures of Jesus, who is claiming that His work of love is a God-given mission. The Chronicler was playing the same tune as Jesus in His parable. One senses that the Judeans of the post-exilic period disowned members of the northern tribes who had escaped deportation. Mention of brotherhood in 28:8 and 11 serves as a reminder of the family relationship that bound the two communities and of their intrinsic unity as the people of God. Judah, as self-righteous as the elder brother, is bidden remember the skeletons in its own closet. The Father's prophetic overtures to the northerners met with confession and fraternal repatriation. Correspondingly the Judeans should be prepared to unbend and make warm advances to their northern brothers and sisters, instead of isolating themselves in a castle of proud rectitude with the drawbridge tightly closed.

Paul had occasion to criticize the same spirit of arrogant withdrawal among certain believers in his own day. In his case it was an outbreak of virtual anti-Semitism (Rom. 11:13–22). Gentile Christians were glorying in their own response to the gospel and their role as members of God's people. In contrast they looked down at the Jews as spiritual has-beens; they themselves had taken the place of the Jews as God's current favorites. For Paul it was a dangerous half-truth. He was finding among Gentile Christians little sympathy with his own passion for Jewish converts. Instead, they shrugged their shoulders at him for flogging a dead horse. Yet privilege never warrants pride, let alone prejudice or presumption. Arrogance and faith make poor bedfellows, for divine love and human humility are simultaneously affirmed by faith and denied by arrogance. "Do not boast," warned Paul, or else these smart alecks would find the present fate of the Jews their own.

This lesson is one which I have had to learn and learn again, as one who was brought up among a rather sectarian group of Christians who in their heart of hearts regarded themselves as the true church and expressed doubts about those who were in "the denominations." I can now find divine irony in the fact that I went on to find a haven and happy fellowship at a church which contained comparatively few evangelicals, within the Methodist denomination which among my former coreligionists had met with suspicions only surpassed by those reserved for Roman Catholics. In my new fellowship I had to change my religious vocabulary and work much harder at sermons, to prove the relevance of the Bible. I had to learn to let the drawbridge down. My hardness of heart had to be melted by the love of God: it is a lesson I am still learning. Christian exclusivism imparts a comfort and a sense of security perilously close to complacency and self-sufficiency. I recall a classmate at grammar school, a staunch Anglo-Catholic, loftily admitting to me, "It's better to be a Plymouth Brother or to attend the Methodist chapel in one's Sunday best than not to go to church at all." I was amazed at his cocksureness. "Of course, he's wrong" thought I, "and hopelessly prejudiced. But still, I suppose it's better to be an Anglo-Catholic than not to go to church at all!" I thank God that I have moved a little further along the pilgrim path since then. I have learned to appreciate the truth of Luke 9:49, 50. Jesus had to correct John, when he and the other disciples forbade a man they saw casting out demons in His name "because he does not follow with us."

The Christian reads verse 15 with a sense of déjà vu. He recalls the parable of the Good Samaritan in Luke 10:25–37. Really the boot is on the other foot: this passage seems to have provided Jesus with literary inspiration for His parable. He spoke it in a century when religious relations between Judah and Samaria had degenerated much further. Yet in the parable it was the Good Samaritan, as we call him, who reflected the love of God in neighborly love, rather than the Judean priest or Levite who both "passed by on the other side." There is the same reversal of roles as in the Chronicler's overall story, and both it and our Lord's parable expound each other well. The northerners' actions were "works befitting repentance" (Acts 26:20) or "fruits worthy of repentance" (Matt. 3:8). Actions speak louder than words—and, one may add, louder than pretentious poses, which in the case of both Judah and the priest and Levite proved to be hollow.

Another part of Jesus' oral ministry which may well have been influenced by this passage is His teaching about the basis of the Last Judgment in Matthew 25:31–46. Those who had clothed, or given food or drink to, a follower of His find themselves honored, for they are accounted as doing it to Him. It is a measure of the premium that Jesus ever set on loving actions. "Show me your faith without your works," said James in a provocative challenge to this very end, "and I will show you my faith by my works" (James 2:14–18). His challenge hit the nail on the head.

NOTE

1. C. Stacey Woods, *Some Ways of God* (Downers Grove: Inter-Varsity Press, 1975), pp. 128–30.

CHAPTER SEVENTEEN

Potential Attained

2 Chronicles 29:1–32:33

With Hezekiah a fresh and final stage begins in the Chronicler's history of the pre-exilic monarchy. From the reign of Rehoboam to that of Ahaz the Davidic throne had presided over a truncated realm. There had been northern kings ruling over ten of Israel's tribes and separate shrines for worship. Now the handicap of rival monarchies had been removed, with the Assyrian defeat of the northern state, dissolution of its monarchy, and deportation of its upper class. In the Chronicler's eyes it spells a new lease on life for the Davidic monarchy. Here was an opportunity for it to recapture the ancient—and future—ideal of a people united in worship at God's chosen shrine. The focus in this account is on the relations between king, people, and God. In comparison with the account of Hezekiah's reign in 2 Kings there is a shift of emphasis. Salvation from crisis was the primary theme of the Kings narrative, in a context of political threat and military invasion. This is indeed a theme dear to the Chronicler, and he does find room for it. Crisis, however, is only one of life's many experiences, and his account goes beyond such emergency conditions. It is set within a wider framework of spiritual restoration, united worship, religious reformation, and in conclusion, divine blessing in response to royal obedience. It is made plain that a respect for God's will dominated the king's rule and dictated his direction of national life.

The Chronicler's concern is to provide a role model for the people of God in his own day. David and Solomon, the human founders of God's new era, were the ultimate models. Hezekiah, in modeling himself on their ideals, constituted a challenge for God's later people to take to heart. "Imitate me, just as I also imitate Christ," Paul urged

the young Christians of Corinth (1 Cor. 11:1). His task as a missionary was to teach by example as well as by exhortation. With his
deeper experience he was able to reflect the standards originally set
by the Lord and apply them to specific situations which faced him
and his converts. Such is the Christian's reverence for the Lord that
His glory has a blinding effect. Was He not an overwhelmingly special person? May any of us mere mortals, we humbly ask, hope to
attain His standards? Such piety can put a distorted distance between the Lord and His followers. Paradoxically human reverence
can nullify one of the explicit roles of Jesus in His earthly ministry:
"I have given you an example, that you should do as I have done to
you" (John 13:15). Paul, as a wise teacher, realized that one of his
prime tasks had to be to teach his converts to apply to their own
situations the lead given by his Lord, in this case His desire to at-
tract people to God rather than put unnecessary stumbling blocks in
their way (1 Cor. 10:32, 33).

The Chronicler faced a similar situation. There was a danger that
David and Solomon were so highly venerated as heroes of the faith
and inspired founders of a new epoch that their exemplary roles
could not be appreciated by ordinary folk. The Chronicler presents
King Hezekiah as the link person between the golden age of religious giants and an inglorious present. That is why in Chronicles
more space is devoted to him than to any other king apart from
David and Solomon. Our author will draw parallels not only with
their glorious reigns but also with post-exilic conditions.

Usually the Chronicler helps his readers by employing a clear-cut
structure, and this account is no exception despite its lengthiness.
The first two verses of chapter 29 are taken over from 2 Kings
18:2-3. The second verse, "And he did what was right . . . ," has a
structural function in the account of Hezekiah's reign. It serves to
summarize not only the rest of the chapter but also chapters 30 and
31. Indeed, it is resumed in an expanded form in 31:20. In turn the
last clause of 31:21, "So he prospered," is a virtual summary of the
content of chapter 32, by way of introduction; it too is resumed at its
close, "Hezekiah prospered in all his works" (32:30). The Chronicler
provides his readers with headlines before elaborating them in detail. "He did what was right . . ." and "So he prospered" are the gist
of his presentation of the reign.

SPIRITUAL RESTORATION

29:1 Hezekiah became king *when he was* twenty-five years old, and he reigned twenty-nine years in Jerusalem. His mother's name *was* Abijah the daughter of Zechariah.

2 And he did *what was* right in the sight of the LORD, according to all that his father David had done.

3 In the first year of his reign, in the first month, he opened the doors of the house of the LORD and repaired them.

4 Then he brought in the priests and the Levites, and gathered them in the East Square,

5 and said to them: "Hear me, Levites! Now sanctify yourselves, sanctify the house of the LORD God of your fathers, and carry out the rubbish from the holy *place.*

6 "For our fathers have trespassed and done evil in the eyes of the LORD our God; they have forsaken Him, have turned their faces away from the dwelling place of the LORD, and turned *their* backs *on Him.*

7 "They have also shut up the doors of the vestibule, put out the lamps, and have not burned incense or offered burnt offerings in the holy *place* to the God of Israel.

8 "Therefore the wrath of the LORD fell upon Judah and Jerusalem, and He has given them up to trouble, to desolation, and to jeering, as you see with your eyes.

9 "For indeed, because of this our fathers have fallen by the sword; and our sons, our daughters, and our wives *are* in captivity.

10 "Now *it is* in my heart to make a covenant with the LORD God of Israel, that His fierce wrath may turn away from us.

11 "My sons, do not be negligent now, for the LORD has chosen you to stand before Him, to serve Him, and that you should minister to Him and burn incense."

12 Then these Levites arose: Mahath the son of

Amasai and Joel the son of Azariah, of the sons of the Kohathites; of the sons of Merari, Kish the son of Abdi and Azariah the son of Jehallelel; of the Gershonites, Joah the son of Zimmah and Eden the son of Joah;

13 of the sons of Elizaphan, Shimri and Jeiel; of the sons of Asaph, Zechariah and Mattaniah;

14 of the sons of Heman, Jehiel and Shimei; and of the sons of Jeduthun, Shemaiah and Uzziel.

15 And they gathered their brethren, sanctified themselves, and went according to the commandment of the king, at the words of the LORD, to cleanse the house of the LORD.

16 Then the priests went into the inner part of the house of the LORD to cleanse *it*, and brought out all the debris that they found in the temple of the LORD to the court of the house of the LORD. And the Levites took *it* out and carried *it* to the Brook Kidron.

17 Now they began to sanctify on the first *day* of the first month, and on the eighth day of the month they came to the vestibule of the LORD. So they sanctified the house of the LORD in eight days, and on the sixteenth day of the first month they finished.

18 So they went in to King Hezekiah and said, "We have cleansed all the house of the LORD, the altar of burnt offerings with all its articles, and the table of the showbread with all its articles.

19 "Moreover all the articles which King Ahaz in his reign had cast aside in his transgression we have prepared and sanctified; and there they *are*, before the altar of the LORD."

20 Then King Hezekiah rose early, gathered the rulers of the city, and went up to the house of the LORD.

21 And they brought seven bulls, seven rams, seven lambs, and seven male goats for a sin offering for the kingdom, for the sanctuary, and for Judah. Then he commanded the priests, the sons of Aaron, to offer *them* on the altar of the LORD.

22 So they killed the bulls, and the priests received the blood and sprinkled *it* on the altar. Likewise they killed the rams and sprinkled the blood

on the altar. They also killed the lambs and sprinkled the blood on the altar.

23 Then they brought out the male goats *for* the sin offering before the king and the assembly, and they laid their hands on them.

24 And the priests killed them; and they presented their blood on the altar as a sin offering to make an atonement for all Israel, for the king commanded *that* the burnt offering and the sin offering *be made* for all Israel.

25 And he stationed the Levites in the house of the LORD with cymbals, with stringed instruments, and with harps, according to the commandment of David, of Gad the king's seer, and of Nathan the prophet; for thus *was* the commandment of the LORD by his prophets.

26 The Levites stood with the instruments of David, and the priests with the trumpets.

27 Then Hezekiah commanded *them* to offer the burnt offering on the altar. And when the burnt offering began, the song of the LORD *also* began, with the trumpets and with the instruments of David king of Israel.

28 So all the assembly worshiped, the singers sang, and the trumpeters sounded; all *this continued* until the burnt offering was finished.

29 And when they had finished offering, the king and all who were present with him bowed and worshiped.

30 Moreover King Hezekiah and the leaders commanded the Levites to sing praise to the LORD with the words of David and of Asaph the seer. So they sang praises with gladness, and they bowed their heads and worshiped.

31 Then Hezekiah answered and said, "Now *that* you have consecrated yourselves to the LORD, come near, and bring sacrifices and thank offerings into the house of the LORD." So the assembly brought in sacrifices and thank offerings, and as many as were of a willing heart *brought* burnt offerings.

32 And the number of the burnt offerings which the

assembly brought was seventy bulls, one hundred rams, *and* two hundred lambs; all these *were* for a burnt offering to the LORD.

33 The consecrated things *were* six hundred bulls and three thousand sheep.

34 But the priests were too few, so that they could not skin all the burnt offerings; therefore their brethren the Levites helped them until the work was ended and until the *other* priests had sanctified themselves, for the Levites were more diligent in sanctifying themselves than the priests.

35 Also the burnt offerings *were* in abundance, with the fat of the peace offerings and *with* the drink offerings for *every* burnt offering. So the service of the house of the LORD was set in order.

36 Then Hezekiah and all the people rejoiced that God had prepared the people, since the events took place so suddenly.

2 Chron. 29:1–36

The Chronicler wanted to illustrate in three ways the headline of verse 2. His first example occurs in verses 3–36 and is summarized in verse 35: *"So the service of the house of the Lord was set in order."* The sentence is composed as an echo of 8:16, where Solomon's building and dedication of the temple are similarly described in conclusion, using the same Hebrew verb: "Now all the work of Solomon was well-ordered." In his concern for the temple Hezekiah was walking in Solomon's footsteps. His own role could not be that of the architect and builder, but it was the contemporary counterpart of Solomon's inauguratory work, as necessary now as his was then. The temple had a sacramental value in the life of God's people. It was the touchstone of their reverence for Him, as the place where God's honor was most evidently demonstrated. A right regard for Him was no abstraction for God's people, but was grounded in pure and regular worship at the temple. Hezekiah at the beginning of his reign found the temple in a shocking state of neglect and misuse. It was a mirror of the people's condition before God. So two related tasks were necessary, to put the temple aright and to use it for a service which the people—or at least a representative number—could get right with God again.

370

1. *A restored temple* (vv. 3–19). A closing note with reference to
Ahaz's reign, in 28:24, had drawn attention to the atrocious attitude
of Hezekiah's predecessor toward the temple. Now the need was to
rectify Ahaz's abuses and neglect. Hezekiah gave it top priority, *"in
the first month"* of his *"first year"* (v. 3). For the people of God a
locked temple was a contradiction in terms: the temple spelled access to God. In the letter to the Ephesians the Christian's access to
the Father and position within the spiritual temple of the church are
mentioned side by side (Eph. 2:18–22), while Hebrews celebrates the
privilege of entering the heavenly tabernacle won by Jesus for His
followers (Heb. 10:19–22). Strictly only the priests could enter the
temple hall, as verse 16 emphasizes, while the people were re-
stricted to its courts, to the sacred area surrounding the temple. The
priests entered, however, on the people's behalf. Moreover, here
the reference to the temple doors probably includes the outer doors
to the temple area (cf. 4:9). An open temple meant that worship and
prayer could proceed in its courts and that God's grace and blessing
could be invoked. Inside the temple the showbread was offered and
the lamps gave their light and the incense its fragrance, while in the
inner court the burnt offerings were sacrificed (vv. 7, 18)—all to
the glory of God. The supreme task of God's people was to worship
their God, both indirectly through the regular rites of the temple and
directly by their participation.

This priority of worship comes over into the Christian era. The
role of local believers can be described as "to offer up spiritual sacrifices acceptable to God" and to "proclaim the praises" of a gracious
God (1 Pet. 2:5, 9), and "the prayers of the saints" are represented in
a vision as incense (Rev. 5:8). In turn the lives of believers are to
comprise "a living sacrifice, holy and acceptable to God, which is
your spiritual worship" (Rom. 12:1, RSV). For Christians worship
spills over into the marketplace and the home. It is an obligation to
be met both as a member of a church congregation and as a citizen,
employee, and family member. Perhaps, though, there is danger in
translating the Chronicler's concern too diffusely. Incurable individ-
ualists as we are by culture, many of us have a tendency to shy away
from the congregational and the institutional. Yet, just as for the Old
Testament believer the togetherness of temple worship was the
prime source of blessing and vitality in his or her everyday world
(see Ps. 133:1, 3), so the writer to the Hebrews could not conceive of

enjoying the privilege of access to God apart from faithful attendance at Christian meetings for mutual encouragement (Heb. 10:19,
25). The implicit call of the Chronicler to his own generation was to
rally around the temple as a key priority; the simplest and so best
translation of his call is in terms of supporting the Christian place of
congregational prayer and praise.

In practice the work of restoring the temple had to fall on its official personnel, and to this end Hezekiah summons them to a meeting, in a square outside the uncleansed temple area. The speech that
follows in verses 5–11 takes the form of the so-called Levitical sermon with its initial call to hear, and specification of the audience
(v. 5), biblical text (v. 8), and closing exhortation (v. 11). The Chronicler uses it to address his own generation, for it is carefully phrased
to cover both historical situations. Most obviously the speech is a
summons to the Levites, and implicitly to the priests too, to clean
up the temple and reconsecrate its defiled equipment. Woven into
the speech, however, is a theological explanation. At its heart is
the sermon text of verse 8b, which can be recognized as Jeremiah
29:18. The three Hebrew terms rendered *"trouble," "desolation,"* and
"jeering" (better translated *"hissing,"* as in Jer. 29:18) all occur there
too. In fact Jeremiah 29 is a chapter dear to the Chronicler: he has
used 29:12–14 on a number of occasions, for instance in 15:2.
Jeremiah was prophesying the climactic fall of Jerusalem, which occurred in 586 B.C., and the subsequent exile of the Judeans. The
Chronicler reapplies Jeremiah's words to the exile-like conditions of
Hezekiah's reign in the eighth century, after many subjects had been
killed or deported by their enemies (28:5, 8, 17; 29:9). Along with
this experience of physical exile went a spiritual exile, even when
the bulk of the Judeans were still occupying the land. The catalog of
negative terms in verse 6, including being *"unfaithful"* (RSV; NKJV
"trespassed"), doing *"evil,"* and forsaking God are stock terms in the
Chronicler's vocabulary for a spiritual exile. Most notably the first
term recalls Saul's unfaithfulness (1 Chron. 10:13), which was associated with physical exile for his subjects (1 Chron. 10:7). Like David
whose reign betokened spiritual restoration, it was Hezekiah's task
to recall his people from their spiritual exile, which was evidenced
especially in their abandoning of temple worship. His eventual aim
to lead a service solemnly renouncing this sinful state (v. 10), which
will be realized in verses 20–36, required a preliminary task, the

cleansing of the defiled and debris-ridden temple. So the Levites and the priests had a crucial task to do in preparing for the community's rededication of their lives to God.

In this sermon the Chronicler is using the historical situation of Hezekiah as a means of preaching to his contemporaries. They were heirs of the prophetic message of Jeremiah 29:18 whose context pinpointed the nation's backsliding as the reason for the Babylonian exile. Although they had returned from exile, they had relatives who had not returned and knew family stories of a previous generation who had perished in the fall of Jerusalem. The rigors of post-exilic life had nourished a conviction that they were still under the wrath of God and for that reason the golden age forecast by the prophets had not materialized (cf. Neh. 9:32–37; Ps. 126). In response the Chronicler offers the success story of Hezekiah's reign as a timely assurance that such negativism may be reversed. The Chronicler turns their eyes to the temple as the focus of true and necessary spirituality. The priests and especially the Levites he regards as exercising a key, God-given role (v. 11) in supervising the worship of the temple so that it assumes pride of place in the community's life and is carried on decently and in order, in spirit and in truth. *"Do not be negligent"* is the Chronicler's exhortation to them, or in other words *"get on with the good work."*

The Chronicler's message may be updated with little difficulty as a call to ministers of the church, to be aware of the God-given responsibility that rests on their shoulders, taking care of God's people and encouraging them to worship at His shrine. There are many Christians who badly need the example of godly lives and reverent service, so that their hearts may be turned toward God in acknowledgment of His claim on their lives. The minister has a key role in God's purposes for His people: to him or her comes the call mediated with affection (*"my sons,"* v. 11) to get on with the good work or, in the words of one Christian minister to another, *"that you may know how you ought to conduct yourself in the house of God, which is the church of the living God"* (1 Tim. 3:15). The spirituality of God's people depends to a large degree on the spirituality of its religious leaders, in fulfillment of their ministry.

Heartened by Hezekiah's explanation of the prime part they had in God's positive purposes for His people, the temple staff worked with a will, obeying not only the king but the God whose prophetic word had been brought to their notice (v. 15). It is stressed that all the main groups of the Levites, including the choral families, were represented (vv. 12–14; cf. 1 Chron. 15:5–8; 25:1). They spent a week working in the courts and another week in the sanctuary, and *"on the sixteenth day"* the task was done (v. 17). In the closing verbal reports emphasis is laid on the various temple *"vessels"* (NEB; NKJV *"articles"*). In the post-exilic temple the *"vessels"* were especially prized, for in the rebuilt sanctuary they alone provided continuity with the pre-exilic temple (cf. Ezra 1:7–11; 6:5). Doubtless the aura of their pristine sanctity pervaded the second temple, ensuring that it too was regarded as the true house of God. The vessels were a heritage that went back to the inspired temple builder Solomon (chap. 4). Likewise in a spiritual sense we Christians receive the communion cup ultimately from the hand of Jesus who first passed it to His disciples, and we take the morsel of bread broken first by the fingers of the incarnate Lord, while by faith we hear His voice whispering to us across the centuries *"This do in remembrance of Me."*

2. *A restored people* (vv. 20–36). Hezekiah was now ready for the next phase in bringing the relationship between the people and their God back to normal, if normal is defined as the high ideal attained in the foundational ministry of David and Solomon. There was still a wide gap, not yet bridged by the goodwill and efforts of the king and the temple staff. The next step was a ceremony of rededication to God. It took the form of two sets of sacrifices, one set described in verses 20–24 and the other in verses 31–36.

a. *Sacrifices for sin* (vv. 20–24). The first set has an atoning and purifying purpose. They are offered on behalf of the royal house (*"the kingdom"*), the temple personnel (*"the sanctuary"*), and the people at large (v. 21). These sacrifices are brought by the national leaders, including the king, as representatives of the whole community. According to the details of verses 22–24 the *"bulls,"* *"rams,"* and *"lambs"* are brought as burnt offerings and the *"male goats"* as sin offerings. The burnt offerings here have an atoning value—unlike the burnt offerings of verses 32 and 35. The appropriate ritual is laid down in Leviticus 1:3–17; the present account, although shorter, seems to concur with that procedure. Here there is a focus on the treatment of the blood. After the offerers had killed the animals, the blood was drained out of the bodies and collected in a basin. Then the blood was splashed against the sides of the altar of burnt offering that stood in the main court of the temple. Although the incineration of the victims followed, the Chronicler's partial description is true to the Old Testament's ritual principle that the blood had a crucial role in the sacrificial ceremony of atonement.

Next came the sin offerings. The Hebrew term for sin offering is more literally a de-sinning or purification offering: a verb related to this noun is rendered "purge" in Psalm 51:7. Its ritual is described in Leviticus 4:1–5:13, although there it is prescribed for inadvertent sins and sins of omission caused by forgetfulness, whereas here it has a much more comprehensive coverage, as it does in the Day of Atonement ritual described in Leviticus 16. The theory behind the sin offering was that human sin had a polluting effect on the sanctuary. Its perpetrators "defile My tabernacle that is among them," declared God (Lev. 15:31). The opposite effect of the sin offering on the sanctuary was to "cleanse it, and consecrate it from the uncleanness of the children of Israel" (Lev. 16:19). Again, the treatment of the blood was the important element in the sin offering, but there was a different procedure than that of the burnt offering. After the blood had been drained, most of it was poured out at the foot of the altar, but a little was put in a basin and either smeared or sprinkled on parts of the sanctuary. Here the altar of burnt offering is specified, as in Leviticus 4:25.

An earlier detail is also highlighted by the Chronicler, the laying on of hands. This is specified in Leviticus 4:24, and indeed was an element of the burnt offering ritual according to Leviticus 1:4. In each of these instances "laid (their hands)" is a little weak: "pressed" would convey the meaning better, for the Hebrew verb has the sense of leaning one's weight. In this way there was a self-identification of the offerer with the animal which was to be killed, and the sin of the offerer was transferred to it so that it died as a substitute. Interestingly in the Day of Atonement ceremony it is linked with a prayer of confession (Lev. 16:21). Animal sacrifice was never intended as an impersonal, mechanical way of dealing with sinning. Both the laying on of hands and the accompanying prayer were personal affirmations of one's sinful status before God and sincere desire to have the broken spiritual relationship mended. In this account the king and the leaders pressed their hands on the goats not only for their own sakes but as representatives of the rest of the people. This is made clear in verse 24, *"to make an atonement for all Israel."*

Much scholarly ink has been spilled over the significance of the Hebrew verb *kippēr* which in the Old Testament underlies the verb "atone" or the phrase "make atonement." The explanation currently preferred is the sense "pay a ransom." The sacrificial victim was a ransom price as the sinful offerer's alternative to losing his or her own life. In the overall context of this passage one can hardly exclude a propitiatory value for these atoning sacrifices. They are meant as an answer to divine wrath, to which Hezekiah's speech had drawn attention as resting destructively on the nation (vv. 8–10).

The Chronicler underlines the comprehensive scope of these offerings: twice in verse 24 he mentions that they were made on behalf of *"all Israel."* It is clear, especially in the light of the next chapter, that wider coverage is intended here than in verse 21. Already the Chronicler wants to bring out Hezekiah's ecumenical concern for the whole people of God, including the unexiled citizens of the old northern state. He would not rest content until his separated brothers and sisters were visibly reunited in common worship of their one God.

At first sight verses 21–24 are an account of antiquated rites and ceremonies which are irrelevant for the Christian. On the contrary, it forms a necessary background to the thought, though not the practice, of the New Testament. A vital role of the Old Testament is to function as a theological dictionary for the New. In expressing the significance of such a key Christian event as the crucifixion, the New Testament draws heavily on the concept of sacrifice. The issue of sinning had not gone away by the first century A.D. nor has it by the twentieth. The early church lived and thought in a period when religious sacrifice still was common, not least in a Jewish context, as a means of dealing with sinfulness. Although such ritual is absent from modern culture, the theology of the church cannot dispense with this dynamic concept, whose roots delve deep into the Old Testament. The regular description of the death of Jesus in terms of "blood" labels it as sacrificial. The atoning value of the burnt offering is echoed in a number of important New Testament passages, even though the actual term is not used. In Mark 10:45 it underlies the explanation that Jesus came "to give His life a ransom for many." The definition of the devoted love of Christ in Ephesians 5:2 makes use of it: He "has . . . given Himself for us, an offering and a sacrifice to God for a sweet-smelling aroma." In 1 Peter 1:18–19 Christians are similarly described as "ransomed (RSV) . . . with the precious blood of Christ, like that of a lamb without blemish or spot."

The sense of propitiation which is implied in 2 Chronicles 29 is unconsciously echoed in the letter to the Romans. Just as atoning sacrifices were the God-given answer to the dark shadow of divine wrath which covered His people, so "God set forth" Jesus "as a propitiation by His blood," as God's own solution to the wrath which barred humanity from His presence (Rom. 1:18; 2:5; 3:25).

As to the de-sinning offering, the writer to the Hebrews was aware of its importance in the Old Testament economy: "according to the law almost all things [in the sanctuary] are purified with blood, and without shedding of blood there is no remission" (Heb. 9:22). He uses especially its role in the Day of Atonement ritual to describe in chapters 9–10 the work of Christ in dying and ascending alive to heaven. Just as the sanctuary was sprinkled with the blood of the purification offering, so there are spiritual counterparts which have been purified through His sacrificial death, namely the bad consciences and sinful hearts of those who have availed themselves of God's provision (Heb. 9:14, 23; 10:22; cf. 1 John 1:7, 9).

Here in 2 Chronicles 29:23 this appropriation is symbolized by the pressure of the offerer's hands, a practice elsewhere explicitly accompanied by confession. This act of self-identification lies at the heart of the Christian gospel as the personal means of turning the bad news of human sinfulness into the good news of divine forgiveness. In 1 John 1:9 the oral aspect of this appropriation is made explicit: "If we confess our sins, He is faithful and just to forgive us our sins and to cleanse us from all unrighteousness." Significantly the promise is related not simply to the beginning of the Christian life but to its continuation, as a means of maintaining fellowship with God.

In conclusion, it may be said that the theology of sacrifice used in the Chronicler's narrative is vital for the Christian faith. Paradoxically, to delve into the intricacies of a bygone religion is to enrich one's understanding of the New Testament theology upon which the church must ever stand.

b. *Musical accompaniment and worship* (vv. 25–30). The Chronicler draws special attention to the music and singing of the Levites. Evidently, as verses 27–29 imply, their performance was simultaneous with the offering of the atoning sacrifices described in verses 21–24.

This accompaniment is mentioned separately in order to give prominence to the Levites' role. Underlying the passage is the depiction of Hezekiah as a second Solomon, living up to ancient precedent: according to 7:6 Solomon used the musical institution set up by David at the dedication of the temple. A more obvious, and not unrelated, underlying concern for the Chronicler is to present the whole ceremony as truly biblical. The Torah was the implicit basis for the priestly sacrifices (cf. 1 Chron. 16:40). David's institution of the Levitical music was by prophetic authorization, as verse 25 emphasizes, while the content of the singing was the biblical Psalms (v. 30). Law, Prophets, and Psalms—this is the scriptural basis for worship which the Chronicler means to commend to his readers. His message is that God has specified in His word practices and texts which were to be perpetuated in His people's worship. For post-exilic Jews, so remote from the origins of their faith, this was to be the anchor securing them to divine revelation and so keeping them true to God. The Chronicler's particular concern is to underscore the ministry of the Levites as part of Israel's Bible-based worship.

Obviously the Christian reader—and the modern Jewish reader—cannot follow the Chronicler all the way in this respect, as we discussed when commenting on 1 Chronicles 15. There is no such precise blueprint available to the local church. As to practices, the Lord's Supper and engaging in prayer (cf. Acts 2:42) will come to mind; but it is the New Testament principles of worshiping in spirit and truth and decently and in order that have applicability to every Christian meeting. The chanting or singing of psalms or at least hymnic paraphrases has been a healthy tradition in the church down the ages, presumably on the authority of Ephesians 5:19, which might be described as a New Testament counterpart to 2 Chronicles 29:25–30. A biblical content for church services in such elements as public reading, sermon, and song seems to be a logical application of the Chronicler's concept of worship as Psalms-based.

While the national leaders, the priests, and assisting Levites were involved with sacrificing and the Levitical musicians and singers and the priestly trumpeters were adding their accompaniment, the congregation did not stand idly by. They *"worshiped"* and in due course they were joined in this activity by the royal party (vv. 28–30). There hardly seems reason to deny that this refers to a meaningful posture of worship, especially after *"bowed their heads"* (cf. 1 Cor. 14:25; Rev.

5:14). Islam has perpetuated the particular posture described by the verb, which is more literally "did obeisance" or "prostrated themselves." Even more specifically it refers to an act of kneeling with one's head touching the ground. Members of the older Christian denominations know of the value of kneeling, to which the so-called "evangelical crouch" comes a poor second. A culture which has abandoned the masculine bow and the feminine curtsy not unnaturally finds it difficult to express religious deference by means of physical posture. Yet one wonders whether the modern emphasis on harmony between body and mind, evidenced for instance in the study of body language, will extend eventually to Christian worship and lead to a rediscovery of this biblical posture, along with the posture of leading prayer by standing with uplifted hands (Ps. 134:2; 1 Tim. 2:8). The charismatic renewal movement has served to remind us how apt we are to restrict worship to cerebral activity—and perhaps how difficult it is for many of us to learn to do otherwise. It is true that it would be easy to go through the motions as in an aerobics class, without the concentration of the heart and mind, as the challenge to "rend your heart, and not [merely] your garments" (Joel 2:13) serves to teach. Static immobility, however, does not guarantee spirituality. Every preacher has noticed a glazed look on the faces of his congregation and realized that he must re-engage their attention if he is not to continue talking to the air. And everyone who has slumped in prayer with closed eyes has learned at times how conveniently indistinguishable that position is from indulging in a doze!

Let us never forget that the Chronicler worship was characterized by *"gladness"* (v. 30). Correspondingly there must ever be in Christian worship a leap of the heart, as in the hymn by H. F. Lyte:

> Ransomed, healed, restored, forgiven,
> Who like thee his praise should sing?

c. *Sacrifices of worship* (vv. 31–36). The final phase of this model service is now narrated. The account thus far has been on bridging the sin-created gap between the community and their God. The gladness and praise of verse 30 convey a joyful recognition that the gap had been closed. The way was open for individuals to bring their testimonies of praise via sacrifices of a different kind, now that they had *"consecrated"* themselves afresh to God (v. 31). The Hebrew verbal phrase normally refers to the consecration of a new priest by offering his first sacrifice; in 1 Chronicles 29:5 it was used metaphorically of commitment to God's work by the gift of money. Here it relates to recommitment to God's service now that the burden of guilt had been removed and they could walk tall again. The echoing of David's phrase suggests that Hezekiah is portrayed as a second David, as verse 2 implied.

The sacrifices now to be brought are *"the peace offerings"* of verse 35. The precise translation of this phrase in the Old Testament is uncertain, but their general function is clear. This was a large category of voluntary offerings brought for the sheer joy of it, like giving an unbirthday present to a favorite uncle. There are many Christians who categorize the religion of the Old Testament as bondage to formality—one hopes that some of them will read Chronicles carefully and eat their words! This category included *"thank offerings,"* so that the compound phrase in verse 31 seems to mean *"sacrifices and [spe-cifically] thank offerings."* These were all partial offerings in that only the *"fat"* (v. 35), kidneys, and liver were actually sacrificed and the rest of the animal was returned to the offerer to eat with his family at a festival meal. Some people, however, perhaps about a tenth of the household heads present in the light of the comparative figures of verses 32–33, went so far as to bring *"burnt offerings."* This was a larger gift, as the whole animal went up in smoke and there were no returns. It was not the burnt offering brought to secure atonement but reflected another usage as a superior form of worship offering. The earlier burnt offering moved within the orbit of confession and divine forgiveness, while this one expresses individual gratitude and praise to God. It is this type of burnt offering which underlies the summons in Romans 12:1, *"Present your bodies a liv-ing sacrifice."* The believers' *"sacrifices"* of *"giving thanks"* and doing good and sharing in Hebrews 13:15–16 correspond in general to the so-called peace offerings, with the first echoing the thank offering.

The Chronicler, ever ready to call attention to the Levites, finds occasion to note that *"too few"* priests responded to the call of verse 5, whereas the Levites had been more prompt. Doubtless he was conveying a contemporary challenge. Being a professional in the Lord's work by no means guarantees alacrity.

The chapter closes on the glad note that now normal service had been resumed. A restored temple and a restored people offering worship to their Lord—here indeed was spiritual normality. The ritual clock had been wound up and had once more started to tick regularly to the glory of God. This switch from apostasy to spirituality had been marked by unnatural speed, taking place in less than three weeks. The king and the congregation gave the credit to God. He, they concluded, must have been at work in their midst. For them it was a miracle of grace: they had been dead, and now *"suddenly"* they have come to life. They do not forget to thank God for it, with the joy of grateful praise. When one life is committed to Him (v. 3), God can work wonders in a wider circle.

UNITED CELEBRATION

30:1 And Hezekiah sent to all Israel and Judah, and also wrote letters to Ephraim and Manasseh, that they should come to the house of the LORD at Jerusalem, to keep the Passover to the LORD God of Israel.

2 For the king and his leaders and all the assembly in Jerusalem had agreed to keep the Passover in the second month.

3 For they could not keep it at the regular time, because a sufficient number of priests had not consecrated themselves, nor had the people gathered together at Jerusalem.

4 And the matter pleased the king and all the assembly.

5 So they resolved to make a proclamation throughout all Israel, from Beersheba to Dan, that they should come to keep the Passover to the LORD God of Israel at Jerusalem, since they had not done *it* for a long *time* in the *prescribed* manner.

6 Then the runners went throughout all Israel and Judah with the letters from the king and his leaders, and spoke according to the command of the king: "Children of Israel, return to the LORD God of Abraham, Isaac, and Israel; then He will return to the remnant of you who have escaped from the hand of the kings of Assyria.

7 "And do not be like your fathers and your

brethren, who trespassed against the LORD God of their fathers, so that He gave them up to desolation, as you see.

8 'Now do not be stiff-necked, as your fathers *were, but* yield yourselves to the LORD; and enter His sanctuary, which He has sanctified forever, and serve the LORD your God, that the fierceness of His wrath may turn away from you.

9 'For if you return to the LORD, your brethren and your children *will be treated* with compassion by those who lead them captive, so that they may come back to this land; for the LORD your God *is* gracious and merciful, and will not turn *His* face from you if you return to Him.'

10 So the runners passed from city to city through the country of Ephraim and Manasseh, as far as Zebulun; but they laughed at them and mocked them.

11 Nevertheless some from Asher, Manasseh, and Zebulun humbled themselves and came to Jerusalem.

12 Also the hand of God was on Judah to give them singleness of heart to obey the command of the king and the leaders, at the word of the LORD.

13 Now many people, a very great assembly, gathered at Jerusalem to keep the Feast of Unleavened Bread in the second month.

14 They arose and took away the altars that *were* in Jerusalem, and they took away all the incense altars and cast *them* into the Brook Kidron.

15 Then they slaughtered the Passover *lambs* on the fourteenth *day* of the second month. The priests and the Levites were ashamed, and sanctified themselves, and brought the burnt offerings to the house of the LORD.

16 They stood in their place according to their custom, according to the Law of Moses the man of God; the priests sprinkled the blood *received* from the hand of the Levites.

17 For *there were* many in the assembly who had not sanctified themselves; therefore the Levites had charge of the slaughter of the Passover *lambs* for everyone *who was* not clean, to sanctify *them* to the LORD.

18 For a multitude of the people, many from Ephraim, Manasseh, Issachar, and Zebulun, had not cleansed themselves, yet they ate the Passover contrary to what was written. But Hezekiah prayed for them, saying, "May the good LORD provide atonement for everyone

19 *who* prepares his heart to seek God, the LORD God of his fathers, though *he is* not *cleansed* according to the purification of the sanctuary."

20 And the LORD listened to Hezekiah and healed the people.

21 So the children of Israel who were present at Jerusalem kept the Feast of Unleavened Bread seven days with great gladness; and the Levites and the priests praised the LORD day by day, *singing* to the LORD, accompanied by loud instruments.

22 And Hezekiah gave encouragement to all the Levites who taught the good knowledge of the LORD; and they ate throughout the feast seven days, offering peace offerings and making confession to the LORD God of their fathers.

23 Then the whole assembly agreed to keep *the feast* another seven days, and they kept it *another* seven days with gladness.

24 For Hezekiah king of Judah gave to the assembly a thousand bulls and seven thousand sheep, and the leaders gave to the assembly a thousand bulls and ten thousand sheep; and a great number of priests sanctified themselves.

25 The whole assembly of Judah rejoiced, also the priests and Levites, all the assembly that came from Israel, the sojourners who came from the land of Israel, and those who dwelt in Judah.

26 So there was great joy in Jerusalem, for since the time of Solomon the son of David, king of Israel, *there had* been nothing like this in Jerusalem.

27 Then the priests, the Levites, arose and blessed the people, and their voice was heard; and their prayer came *up* to His holy dwelling place, to heaven.

31:1 Now when all this was finished, all Israel who were present went out to the cities of Judah and broke the sacred pillars in pieces, cut down the

wooden images, and threw down the high places and
the altars—from all Judah, Benjamin, Ephraim, and
Manasseh—until they had utterly destroyed them
all. Then all the children of Israel returned to their
own cities, every man to his possession.

2 Chron. 30:1–31:1

Already in 29:24 we noticed the Chronicler's interest in observing
Hezekiah's concern for *"all Israel."* It was a concern that the king
was to follow up as soon as the initial tasks of cleansing the temple
and rededicating a nucleus of the people had been completed. The
joint festivals of Passover and Unleavened Bread were an opportunity to invite all members of the covenant people to Jerusalem, to
worship at the temple. The phrase *"all Israel"* finds repetition at significant points in the narrative, in 30:5 and 31:1. Unity for the
Chronicler was primarily a religious unity, worshiping their common
God, the *"God of Israel"* (30:1, 5). This section lays stress not only on
a common faith in the same God but on a vertical continuity from
generation to generation, which the present generation was to take
seriously by playing their part as links in the chain of faith. The
Lord is the God of their common ancestors, *"Abraham, Isaac, and
Israel"* (v. 6), the *"God of their fathers"* (vv. 7, 22; cf. *"God of his fathers,"* v. 19) and now *"your God"* (v. 9). The challenge rings out to
live up to the claims of God and to honor the roots of their common
faith by worshiping together. Hezekiah is the Chronicler's hero in
refusing to write off the northerners as apostates but recognizing
them as brothers and sisters in the faith who were to be welcomed
in the name of God. The owning of the same God made unity
a desirable potential and an essential principle. Hezekiah's ecumenical zeal did not go unopposed—it met with only partial success
(v. 10)—but for the Chronicler it is a principle worth all the effort.
Throughout the narrative he is appealing to his Jewish contemporaries to share his love and his yearning to work for a religiously
undivided Israel. Is the Spirit of God making a comparable appeal to
the Christian reader?

The Chronicler has left far behind the basic text, the second Book
of Kings. He last cited it in 29:1–2 and will echo it briefly in 31:1
and even more briefly in 31:21. We do not know what sources he
had available for these three chapters or to what extent they are

simply his own feasible reconstruction. Certainly the key account of an appeal to the north is historically fitting. The northern kingdom, earlier diminished territorially by the Assyrians, was brought to an end in 721 B.C.; its land was incorporated into their provincial system. Hezekiah's naming his son Manasseh, after a leading northern tribe, impressively indicates his interest in the citizens of the old northern state, halfway through his reign. Moreover, it is now being recognized by biblical scholars that the editors of Kings had an agenda of their own and that religious information about Hezekiah's reign may well have been suppressed in the interests of raising the stock of Josiah, their own hero of the faith.

1. *The summons to reunion* (vv. 1–12). Traditionally the Passover was celebrated during the evening of the fourteenth day of the first month of the year, and the Unleavened Bread on the fifteenth day till the twenty-first. In the perspective of the overall narrative the meeting of verse 2 which resolved to hold the festival(s) took place comparatively late in the first month (cf. 29:17), too late for the regular timing. Accordingly it was resolved to hold it on the same dates in the next month. (There is actually a precedent for this relating to individuals in Numbers 9:6–12). To this end couriers were sent throughout the erstwhile realm of David, *"from Beersheba to Dan"* (v. 5; cf. 1 Chron. 21:2), to proclaim orally and with a reinforcing letter, an invitation to a temple celebration of the Passover. This was to be a religious reliving of the Davidic ideal of a united people. Verse 1 supplies a summary of the procedure, with an unpacking of its details in verses 2–9. *"Ephraim and Manasseh"* are cited in verse 1 (and v. 10) as leading tribes of the earlier northern state. The Chronicler lays typical emphasis on the Torah (v. 5). The *"prescribed manner"* refers to Deuteronomy 16:1–8, where a central festival of sacrifice at the sanctuary is envisaged, rather than to Exodus 12, where the Passover is described as a family celebration at home.

The message cited in verses 6–9 is similar to the so-called Levitical sermon, a form which the Chronicler is fond of using. Its basic scriptural text appears to be Zechariah 1:2–4, echoed in *"return to the Lord . . . ; then He will return"* (v. 6), *"do not be like your fathers"* (v. 7) and perhaps the mention of God's anger in verse 8. Although addressed to both Judah and the northerners, it is angled toward the latter, as the references to Assyrian destruction and exile make clear. Nevertheless Judah too is clearly in mind, in the light of Hezekiah's speech in chapter 29, where Judah was described in remarkably similar terms (29:6, 8–10). There is a deliberate leveling down of Judah to the northerners' position. Judah and Israel stood before their God as sinners both and as common victims of God's fair judgment. Both stood in an exilic situation, especially in a spiritual sense, for in their recent past they had been unfaithful to God, like Saul of old (*"trespassed,"* 29:6; 30:7). There is a call to abandon their stubborn ways and swallow their pride. The verbal phrase *"yield yourselves"* (v. 8) is literally *"give your hand."* It is a gesture indicating affirmation, the proffering of the hand, as for a handshake, to express a promise of commitment. A second Solomon, Hezekiah echoes by way of incentive Solomon's petition for compassionate treatment for exiled relatives (1 Kings 8:50).

The propositional definition of God as *"gracious and merciful,"* derived from Exodus 34:6, was a favorite text of the post-exilic Judean community. It commemorated forgiveness originally extended to those who had broken a brand-new covenant by worship of the golden calf; it also summed up Judah's gratitude for restoration from exile. In this context a loving Father waited for His prodigal daughters and sons in north and south to *"return."* The call to return significantly begins and ends the message (vv. 6, 9) as the precondition of a fresh start promised by a gracious God. This call for renewed commitment has a perennial value in the area of divine-human relations. Dietrich Bonhoeffer wrote eloquently about a formal brand of Christianity which lacks commitment. Cheap grace, a contradiction in terms, is

> the preaching of forgiveness without requiring repentance, baptism without church discipline, communion without confession. . . . Cheap grace is grace without discipleship, grace without the cross, grace without Jesus Christ living and incarnate.[1]

One of the Chronicler's concerns in this chapter is to trace the fulfillment of a Solomonic feature, the revelation of divine grace after a prayer of repentance (7:14). Already this message with its keyword *"return"* has referred to the identical Hebrew verb rendered "turn" in the classic formulation of 7:14. In the narrative of response another prime term *"humbled themselves"* (v. 11) is also an echo. The tribal list of verse 11 is representative rather than complete, in the light of verse 18. There was a mixed response, as to the Christian gospel. Many *"mocked"* (v. 10). The pressures of tradition and convention must not be minimized. Hezekiah was reiterating the claim of Abijah that the Jerusalem temple was the true focus of the ancestral faith (13:10, 11). The decisive sign of returning to God was to *"enter His"* perennial *"sanctuary"* (v. 8). For the northerners it meant going against a current which had been flowing for two centuries in a contrary direction; it meant abandoning an entrenched position within the overall framework of a common faith. Ecumenicity always involves the surrender of that which is emotionally dear and the challenge to re-examine cherished convictions and consider whether we ourselves are not in some respects *"a bundle of prejudices,"* to use Charles Lamb's telling phrase. To put God first means to check for authenticity the images of God enshrined in our minds and hearts.

The Chronicler has to overcome embarrassment in describing Judah's positive reaction to Hezekiah's summons to unity. It is not described as a feather in Judah's cap but attributed to the gracious leading of God. In the context of the northerners' self-humbling, any temptation to pride must be firmly resisted. Verse 13 is like a cartoon advertisement where the hero, basking in the spotlight of success, has a balloon over his head containing the tribute "Thanks to . . ." Here the Chronicler, a Judean himself, will not allow his fellows the credit but thinks "Thanks to God." The reference to *"the word of the Lord"* (v. 12), in the light of the meaning in 29:25, seems to be a reference to the prophetic word of Zechariah 1:2–4, echoed in the oral and written message carried by the couriers.

2. *The united festival of worship* (vv. 13–22). The spiritual commitment of the pilgrims led to reform in the holy city itself, destroying altars built at Ahaz's behest "in every corner of Jerusalem" (28:24). Just as the Levites and priests had cleansed the temple, so the people cleansed the city, each group acting in its respective area. Why had not *"the assembly in Jerusalem"* (v. 2) carried through this reform already? Perhaps because a further step of faith grants insights unappreciated before, and ongoing discipleship finds a further shedding of divine light on human circumstances. "The path of the just is like the shining sun,/That shines ever brighter unto the perfect day" (Prov. 4:18).

The people *"slaughtered"* their *"Passover lambs."* Verse 15b is logically in parenthesis as a prelude to verse 16 with the sense "Now the priests had been put to shame," seeing the enthusiastic participation of so many lay people, and so they prepared to play their traditional part. Opposition to the united festival and to Hezekiah's new broom of reform lay not only among the northerners but at home in the minds of some of the temple staff, as verse 3 had hinted. There were priests and even Levites who stood aloof, until their hardness of heart was melted by the sheer devotion of the massed pilgrims. There are often scruples in the minds of God's servants, scruples which only a demonstration of true spirituality in the lives of other believers can succeed in overcoming. Here the religious authorities had to run to keep up with the zeal of the laity. Perhaps in turn Christian ecumenism can hardly flourish as long as and insofar as it is the sole concern of church leaders. It must light its fire in the hearts of ordinary believers and in local churches. The *"burnt offerings"* (v. 15) brought by the temple personnel on their own behalf have an atoning value, as in 29:20–24: they were only now catching up with the momentum of Hezekiah's reforms.

In verse 16 the Chronicler revels in the vision of obedience to the Torah or *"Law,"* with reference to its priestly passages. Just as penitent pilgrimage gave honor to the Prophets (v. 12), so the ritual paid tribute to the Law: God's written revelation was being lived out, a glorious ideal for the Chronicler. A potential hitch in the proceedings is resolved happily in verses 17–26. There were northern pilgrims who had not undergone the statutory ritual cleansing by the set time of the Passover, perhaps having arrived too late, perhaps through ignorance and/or inadequate briefing. Technically they were unable to participate (cf. Num. 9:6), but love found a way. The Levites killed their Passover lambs for them (v. 17), while the pilgrims received a special dispensation to participate. The Law was not God's last word, although it was the regular norm, as verse 16 serves to stress. The Chronicler knew that in God's economy there was a higher principle of grace—the principle of 7:14—and it was at such a juncture as this that it would come into operation. Hezekiah's prayer in verses 18–19 reflects that Solomonic ideal, the effectiveness of God's revelation of His grace in response to Solomon's prayer in the temple, the house where prayer was heard. Moreover, God had shown that He honors good intentions in the context of David's attempt to transport the ark to Jerusalem (1 Chron. 13–14). Now Hezekiah's plea in their emergency situation is that the principle of 7:14 be honored. Here were those who had humbled themselves, turned back to God, and were seeking His face, and so fitted into the category of the golden text of 7:14. Would God proceed to do His part by forgiving their ritual sin? Indeed, He would and did. He *"listened to"*—literally *"heard,"* as in 7:14—Hezekiah *"and healed the"* unqualified *"people"* (v. 20). The Chronicler uses the final verb as a reflection of his primary text, which he sees here gloriously fulfilled. He has to stretch the bounds of language to squeeze it into the passage, just as he did in his final case of *"left"* (or *"forsook"*) in 28:25. He uses it evidently to refer to some objective evidence of God's affirmative answer. Improper participation should have resulted in a covenant curse on the lines of the lists in Leviticus 26 or Deuteronomy 28 (cf. 1 Cor. 11:29–30); instead, God leaves them unharmed. For the Chronicler the incident is a beautiful illustration of the temple dispensation at work, in that God graciously gives a second chance when the first is missed with regret. Even to the unclean there would come miraculous cleansing. The apostle John was to revel in a kindred truth of the Christian era in 1 John 1:5–2:2.

Verses 21–22 give a brief description of the week of Unleavened Bread festivities, in which Levites with their music and song and the priests with their trumpet blasts played their full part. It was a time of worship and praise, in which the laity participated with their *"peace offerings"* betokening willing worship and with their testimonies of praise. While *"making confession"* is not an illegitimate rendering of the Hebrew verb, in this context the translation *"giving thanks"* (RSV) is fitting, since peace offerings were not sacrifices for sin. The king complimented the Levites, who *"showed good skill"* (RSV). Their standard of musical and choral excellence was not something to be taken for granted, but deserved vocal appreciation of the performers.

In his book *Father and Son* Edmund Gosse described a disappointing experience of ingratitude which dealt his young life a bitter blow. He had managed to save the princely sum of seven shillings and sixpence with the intent of presenting it to a needy couple who had recently professed conversion as a result of witnessing his baptism. One Sunday he set out for their cottage with the money in a bag. "When I reached the cottage," he continues, "husband and wife were at home, doing nothing at all in the approved Sunday style. I was received by them with some surprise, but I quickly explained my mission and produced my linen bag. To my disgust, all John Brooks said was, 'I know'd the Lord would provide,' and after emptying my little bag into the palm of an enormous hand, he swept the contents into his trousers pocket and slapped his leg. He said not a single word of thanks or appreciation and I was absolutely cut to the heart."[2] It seems that in religious circles especially lurks ingratitude, Shakespeare's "marble-hearted fiend." One senses that here the Chronicler was speaking to his own generation. It is not difficult to surmise that the Levites, the second-class servants of the temple, were treated as invisible—until they did something wrong. He who has ears to hear, let him hear!

3. *The joy and challenge of reunion* (vv. 23–31:1). The festivities spilled into a second week of celebration. The Chronicler wants us again to think of his model Solomon, in this case of the two-week festival at the dedication of the temple (7:9). Here too was a welcome overflow of spirituality. So generous were the contributions of Hezekiah and the administration, and so ample now was the supply of priests who identified themselves with Hezekiah's spiritual venture, that the sacrifices superabounded and sacred meals of veal and lamb succeeded them at a happy pace. In his mind's eye the Chronicler surveys the joyful scene of southerners and northerners, priests and Levites, and Gentile proselytes who had traveled from the north or resided in Judah. Pilgrims all and prodigals many, their differences transcended in the worship of their one Lord; they were a mirror of reconciliation. The Chronicler craved such ecumenical healing of religious divisions in his own day.

As a Gentile, I am glad that he thought to include the Gentiles in his survey, although from 1 Chronicles 2–4 and 2 Chronicles 6:32–33 we learned that he was no stranger to their place amid God's people. In this setting they had a well-established Old Testament role: *"sojourners"* (v. 25), or resident aliens who had adopted Israel's faith, were ever welcome at the Passover (see Exod. 12:48–49).

For the Chronicler the occasion was also the reliving of a Solomonic ideal in a special sense. Such a volume of joy had not been heard during the dark ages of the divided kingdom. Verse 27 tells us that the conclusion of the festival was the sacred benediction, an invocation of blessing which built a bridge between the holy season and ordinary life which followed. The invocation was honored by a transcendent God, and the pilgrims departed with the prospect of His bounty crowning their subsequent lives.

Yet the joy of worship has to issue in challenge along the pilgrim way. The concentric circles of reform were now widened to the outer limits of Judah and Israel. Life which had been so signally blessed could not stay unchanged but must banish from its midst that which was not of God.

RELIGIOUS REFORMATION

31:2 And Hezekiah appointed the divisions of the priests and the Levites according to their divisions, each man according to his service, the priests and Levites for burnt offerings and peace offerings, to serve, to give thanks, and to praise in the gates of the camp of the LORD.

3 The king also *appointed* a portion of his possessions for the burnt offerings: for the morning and evening burnt offerings, the burnt offerings for the Sabbaths and the New Moons and the set feasts, as *it is* written in the Law of the LORD.

4 Moreover he commanded the people who dwelt in Jerusalem to contribute support for the priests and the Levites, that they might devote themselves to the Law of the LORD.

5 As soon as the commandment was circulated, the children of Israel brought in abundance the first-fruits of grain and wine, oil and honey, and of all the produce of the field; and they brought in abundantly the tithe of everything.

6 And the children of Israel and Judah, who dwelt in the cities of Judah, brought the tithe of oxen and sheep; also the tithe of holy things which were consecrated to the LORD their God they laid in heaps.

7 In the third month they began laying them in heaps, and they finished in the seventh month.

8 And when Hezekiah and the leaders came and saw the heaps, they blessed the LORD and His people Israel.

9 Then Hezekiah questioned the priests and the Levites concerning the heaps.

10 And Azariah the chief priest, from the house of Zadok, answered him and said, "Since *the people* began to bring the offerings into the house of the LORD, we have had enough to eat and have plenty left, for the LORD has blessed His people; and what is left *is* this great abundance."

11 Now Hezekiah commanded *them* to prepare rooms in the house of the LORD, and they prepared them.

12 Then they faithfully brought in the offerings, the tithes, and the dedicated things; Cononiah the Levite had charge of them, and Shimei his brother *was* the next.

13 Jehiel, Azaziah, Nahath, Asahel, Jerimoth, Jozabad, Eliel, Ismachiah, Mahath, and Benaiah *were* overseers under the hand of Cononiah and Shimei his brother, at the commandment of Hezekiah the king and Azariah the ruler of the house of God.

14 Kore the son of Imnah the Levite, the keeper of the East Gate, *was* over the freewill offerings to God, to distribute the offerings of the LORD and the most holy things.

15 And under him *were* Eden, Miniamin, Jeshua, Shemaiah, Amariah, and Shecaniah, *his* faithful assistants in the cities of the priests, to distribute allotments to their brethren by divisions, to the great as well as the small.

16 Besides those males from three years old and up who were written in the genealogy, they distributed to everyone who entered the house of the LORD his daily portion for the work of his service, by his division,

17 and to the priests who were written in the genealogy according to their father's house, and to the Levites from twenty years old and up according to their work, by their divisions,

18 and to all who were written in the genealogy— their little ones and their wives, their sons and daughters, the whole company of them—for in their faithfulness they sanctified themselves in holiness.

19 Also for the sons of Aaron the priests, *who were* in the fields of the common-lands of their cities, in every single city, *there were* men who were designated by name to distribute portions to all the males among the priests and to all who were listed by genealogies among the Levites.

20 Thus Hezekiah did throughout all Judah, and he did what *was* good and right and true before the LORD his God.

21 And in every work that he began in the service of the house of God, in the law and in the commandment, to seek his God, he did *it* with all his heart. So he prospered.

2 Chron. 31:2–21

A new broom sweeps clean. Yet, as the proverb implies, initial zeal is liable to peter out. The test of a new venture is continuance. I recall with sadness a teenage friend of mine who was a great spiritual challenge in organizing a weekly Bible study with me, checking up on my attitudes and behavior as to whether they were consistent with my Christian profession and urging me to be baptized along with him and become a church member. However, shortly after we had been baptized and received into church fellowship, he departed, never darkened the church's doors again, and dropped me as a friend. It turned out that it was his habit to throw himself vigorously into a new craze until a certain goal was achieved, and then to lose interest in it. This is the nightmare of the evangelist and church planter. It surfaces in Paul's letters at times, for instance in the reservations of Colossians 1:23, "if indeed you continue in the faith, grounded and steadfast, and are not moved away from the hope of the gospel which you heard." In the Chronicler's narrative Hezekiah is marked by stickability, which is evidenced in this chapter. There is a natural thrill about a new venture which is bound to evaporate. In the great prophetic promise to the Jewish exiles about their homeward journey there is a threefold sequence, "mount up with wings," "run," and "walk" (Isa. 40:31). Each clause is accompanied by assurance of corresponding strength supplied by God. "Walk" might be better rendered "keep on going." God would be there in the initial excitement; He would equally be there in the slower pace of steady, persevering progress. The focus of this chapter will be on human dedication to the things of God, as Hezekiah labors at the inglorious but so necessary tasks of religious administration.

1. *Organizing the work* (v. 2). The temple was a complex organization, and efficiency was necessary if it was to be run properly. There is a type of spirituality which seems to place a premium on muddling along and rejects businesslike methods as carnal. The Chronicler would have scorned such thinking. As he was to record in conclusion, Hezekiah's organizational acumen was one fine way in which he endeavored *"to seek his God"* (v. 21). The Chronicler's use of his characteristic language of spirituality shows how he was able to invest the most mundane of religious tasks with an aura of devotion.

Ahaz had shut up the temple, and presumably the system of staffing it had collapsed. Hezekiah implemented the system of coordinating personnel and duties set up by David, like Solomon after the temple was built (8:14; cf. 1 Chron. 23–26). In this as in other themes of this chapter the Chronicler intended to instruct his own generation, urging them to make proper arrangements so that the temple would run like clockwork. The simple structuring of the local church in New Testament times, as a comparatively small group meeting in the home of a member, provides an inadequate model for many modern American churches, with their large plant and range of activities. The principle *"Let all things be done decently and in order"* (1 Cor. 14:40) takes on a new dimension of meaning, but it is one which was already familiar to the Chronicler and based on an ancient religious tradition.

One senses his thrill as he thought back to the glory of the achievements of David and Solomon and back further to the Mosaic tabernacle evoked by the archaic term *"camp"* (v. 2). Here was a precious heritage to be received with devoted appreciation. Here was a sacred privilege indeed. This hive of religious industry called the temple was for him the focus of work done for God and in line with His will. Such is the lofty perspective that animated the Chronicler's thinking, and he commended it to every priest and Levite involved in their everyday, repetitive tasks.

2. *Providing the materials* (v. 3). If for the Chronicler the temple duty rosters were a mark of God's new era for His people that went back to its foundation under David and Solomon, the provision of *"burnt offerings"* was a responsibility carried over from the old

dispensation of the Torah. The sacrificing of burnt offerings was a staple ingredient in the complex temple calendar. Morning by morning, evening by evening, week by week, month by month, festival by festival, as laid down in Numbers 28–29, it symbolized the perennial offering of worship to God. It was a costly responsibility, and Hezekiah offered to pay for the necessary top-quality animals from *"his"* own *"possessions."* Again this was no innovation: a Solomonic precedent was being followed (see 8:12–13). Likewise in the program for re-establishing temple worship in Ezekiel 45:17 it is a responsibility assigned to the royal *"prince."* Presumably in the non-monarchical Judah which the Chronicler knew, he was arguing that this burden should be borne by state funds rather than by temple resources (cf. Ezra 6:9, 10). We may compare such concessions as apply in the American situation, the exemption of church buildings from property taxes and the parsonage allowance for ministers. For another perspective, one may think of the obligation of the British Royal Family to devote time, effort, and money to charitable organizations, such as Princess Anne's sponsorship of children's welfare work. Noblesse oblige, and *"everyone to whom much is given, from him much will be required"* (Luke 12:48).

3. *Funding the staff* (vv. 4–19). Significantly most of this chapter is concerned with providing regular support for the temple staff. Since such support was given largely in kind, the necessary administration must have been akin to that of thrift shops run by a modern charity as part of its fund-raising activities.

The amount of space the Chronicler devoted to this concern is doubtless linked with the fact that in the post-exilic period the temple work seems to have been hampered by the difficulty of maintaining full-time staff in the absence of adequate support, in an age of economic stringency (see Neh. 13:10–13; Mal. 3:8–10). Every large church and every parachurch organization know all too well the amount of time and energy which must be devoted to raising funds. There have been Christians who have operated on the noble principle *"The Lord will provide,"* notably George Muller who successfully ran a children's orphanage on these lines in Bristol, England, in order to show the effectiveness of such a principle. His story is a refreshing change from the problems of financial spiral from which television evangelists seem characteristically to suffer and which they then have to inflict on their viewers. The Chronicler's axiom, in Paul's words, was that "those who minister the holy things eat of the things of the temple, and those who serve at the altar partake of the offerings of the altar" (1 Cor. 9:13). From this axiom the apostle deduced the comparable tenet for the Christian era that "those who preach the gospel should live from the gospel," grounding it in a command of Jesus Himself (1 Cor. 9:14; cf. Luke 10:7; 1 Tim. 5:18). Accordingly in principle there need be no embarrassment in soliciting funds for Christian work from the Christian public nor should there be resentment over such solicitation as if it were unspiritual and exhibiting lack of faith. Obviously in practice there must be a delicate appropriateness of method, language, and tone which avoid such unfortunate impressions as begging or brashness. Obviously too such funds must be scrupulously allocated and accounted for, a concern to which this passage is no stranger, in verses 11–19. The Christian gospel has not been advanced by tales of lavish personal spending of countless widows' mites.

a. *Contributing* (vv. 4–10). This part of the narrative is an implicit sermon preached by the Chronicler to his contemporaries, with three points: support of the temple personnel was a divine mandate, a human obligation to be discharged with a good grace and a source of divine blessing. The Chronicler's Judean readers would have realized that the specifications of firstfruits and tithes earmarked for such support were derived from the Torah (Lev. 2:11, 12; 27:30–33; Num. 18:8–24; Deut. 12:5, 6; 14:22, 23; 18:1–4). The contributions were given *"to the Lord their God"* (v. 6) with the understanding that they be passed on to His servants to buy, as it were, their time for their Torah-inspired duties by releasing them from the need to support themselves and their families with other work (v. 4; cf. Neh. 13:10). The two months, *"the third"* and *"the seventh,"* (v. 7) were key agricultural periods, marking the grain harvest and the grape and other fruit harvest respectively.

"Abundantly" and *"great abundance"* (vv. 5, 10), strategically placed at the beginning and end of the section describing the people's response, carry an implicit message of "hint, hint!" The copious contributions call forth from Hezekiah and the leaders two exclamations which used different formulas of blessing (v. 8), first "Blessed be God who . . ." (cf. Ruth 4:14) and secondly "May you be blessed by the Lord for . . ." (cf. Ruth 2:20). In fact, before Hezekiah called on

God in this latter prayerful wish, He had already answered, providing such a bumper harvest that the people lost nothing by their gifts (v. 10). Paul advanced a similar argument as an incentive for giving, that God is generous to the generous: "God is able to make all grace abound toward you, that you, always having all sufficiency in all things, may have an abundance for every good work" (2 Cor. 9:8; cf. Phil. 4:19). Obviously the argument is intended not to provide a selfish motivation for giving, but as an assurance that God is no man's debtor but blesses the disinterested giver.

b. *Distributing* (vv. 11–19). Arrangements had to be made first for the storage of the gifts and then for their allocation. Storage space was made available in some of the rooms of the three-story structure built around three sides of the temple. Two Levites with ten assistants were given charge of the stored items (vv. 12–13). Distribution of the gifts and also of sacrificial offerings reserved for the priests' consumption were put in the care of another Levite. He had six helpers who were posted in the tribal areas where the priests and Levites resided when not on duty. While they were on duty at the temple, they received their allowances there, along with their families; evidently they lived in married quarters in Jerusalem during their spell of duty (v. 16). Verses 17–19 further elaborate the rules that were drawn up with thoroughness. Obviously there was a conscientious sense of stewardship in two directions, to faithfully honor the intent of the donors by using the gifts responsibly and to allocate contributions faithfully, according to the number of dependents.

Chapters 29–31 are brought to a conclusion with a summary in verses 20–21. Verse 20a summarizes verses 4–19, and verses 20b–21 pick up 29:2 as a sweeping summary of the intervening material. Hezekiah's devotion to God in all matters of temple and Torah was exemplary. His whole ambition was to apply himself to the revealed will of God and to the right worship of God. The Chronicler could bestow no greater accolade. Hezekiah's prosperity is another story, which he will relate in chapter 32. Here his brief mention carries the message that loyal and devoted service does not go unrewarded by God. In his readers' case too, he implies, "God is not unjust to forget your work and labor of love which you have shown toward His name" (Heb. 6:10).

DIVINE APPROBATION

32:1 After these deeds of faithfulness, Sennacherib king of Assyria came and entered Judah; he encamped against the fortified cities, thinking to win them over to himself.

2 And when Hezekiah saw that Sennacherib had come, and that his purpose was to make war against Jerusalem,

3 he consulted with his leaders and commanders to stop the water from the springs which *were* outside the city; and they helped him.

4 Thus many people gathered together who stopped all the springs and the brook that ran through the land, saying, "Why should the kings of Assyria come and find much water?"

5 And he strengthened himself, built up all the wall that was broken, raised *it* up to the towers, and *built* another wall outside; also he repaired the Millo *in* the City of David, and made weapons and shields in abundance.

6 Then he set military captains over the people, gathered them together to him in the open square of the city gate, and gave them encouragement, saying,

7 "Be strong and courageous; do not be afraid nor dismayed before the king of Assyria, nor before all the multitude that *is* with him; for *there are* more with us than with him.

8 "With him *is* an arm of flesh; but with us *is* the LORD our God, to help us and to fight our battles." And the people were strengthened by the words of Hezekiah king of Judah.

9 After this Sennacherib king of Assyria sent his servants to Jerusalem (but he and all the forces with him *laid siege* against Lachish), to Hezekiah king of Judah, and to all Judah who *were* in Jerusalem, saying,

10 "Thus says Sennacherib king of Assyria: 'In what do you trust, that you remain under siege in Jerusalem?

11 'Does not Hezekiah persuade you to give

yourselves over to die by famine and by thirst, saying, "The LORD our God will deliver us from the hand of the king of Assyria"?

12 'Has not the same Hezekiah taken away His high places and His altars, and commanded Judah and Jerusalem, saying, "You shall worship before one altar and burn incense on it"?

13 'Do you not know what I and my fathers have done to all the peoples of *other* lands? Were the gods of the nations of those lands in any way able to deliver their lands out of my hand?

14 'Who *was there* among all the gods of those nations that my fathers utterly destroyed that could deliver his people from my hand, that your God should be able to deliver you from my hand?

15 'Now therefore, do not let Hezekiah deceive you or persuade you like this, and do not believe him; for no god of any nation or kingdom was able to deliver his people from my hand or the hand of my fathers. How much less will your God deliver you from my hand?' "

16 Furthermore, his servants spoke against the LORD God and against His servant Hezekiah.

17 He also wrote letters to revile the LORD God of Israel, and to speak against Him, saying, "As the gods of the nations of *other* lands have not delivered their people from my hand, so the God of Hezekiah will not deliver His people from my hand."

18 Then they called out with a loud voice in Hebrew to the people of Jerusalem who *were* on the wall, to frighten them and trouble them, that they might take the city.

19 And they spoke against the God of Jerusalem, as against the gods of the people of the earth—the work of men's hands.

20 Now because of this King Hezekiah and the prophet Isaiah, the son of Amoz, prayed and cried out to heaven.

21 Then the LORD sent an angel who cut down every mighty man of valor, leader, and captain in the camp of the king of Assyria. So he returned shamefaced to his own land. And when he had gone into

the temple of his god, some of his own offspring struck him down with the sword there.

22 Thus the LORD saved Hezekiah and the inhabitants of Jerusalem from the hand of Sennacherib the king of Assyria, and from the hand of all *others*, and guided them on every side.

23 And many brought gifts to the LORD at Jerusalem, and presents to Hezekiah king of Judah, so that he was exalted in the sight of all nations thereafter.

24 In those days Hezekiah was sick and near death, and he prayed to the LORD; and He spoke to him and gave him a sign.

25 But Hezekiah did not repay according to the favor *shown* him, for his heart was lifted up; therefore wrath was looming over him and over Judah and Jerusalem.

26 Then Hezekiah humbled himself for the pride of his heart, he and the inhabitants of Jerusalem, so that the wrath of the LORD did not come upon them in the days of Hezekiah.

27 Hezekiah had very great riches and honor. And he made himself treasuries for silver, for gold, for precious stones, for spices, for shields, and for all kinds of desirable items;

28 storehouses for the harvest of grain, wine, and oil; and stalls for all kinds of livestock, and folds for flocks.

29 Moreover he provided cities for himself, and possessions of flocks and herds in abundance; for God had given him very much property.

30 This same Hezekiah also stopped the water outlet of Upper Gihon, and brought the water by tunnel to the west side of the City of David. Hezekiah prospered in all his works.

31 However, *regarding* the ambassadors of the princes of Babylon, whom they sent to him to inquire about the wonder that was *done* in the land, God withdrew from him, in order to test him, that He might know all *that was* in his heart.

32 Now the rest of the acts of Hezekiah, and his goodness, indeed they *are* written in the vision of

Isaiah the prophet, the son of Amoz, *and* in the book
of the kings of Judah and Israel.

33 So Hezekiah rested with his fathers, and they
buried him in the upper tombs of the sons of David;
and all Judah and the inhabitants of Jerusalem honored him at his death. Then Manasseh his son reigned
in his place.

2 Chron. 32:1-33

We have seen that in relation to Kings the Chronicler gave much
more space to temple matters. Correspondingly he heavily reduced
the amount of material Kings devoted to the Assyrian crisis. Especially in verses 1, 9-21, 24, 30-31 he drew on 2 Kings 18-20 extensively but he refashioned it into a narrative of his own which reflects
his distinctive concerns. Besides Kings he seems to have also had at
his disposal another source concerning measures taken to defend
Jerusalem. The whole narrative is set within the framework of
Hezekiah's prosperity (31:21; 32:30). The king is used as a model
of faith and spirituality; yet he is not elevated depressingly beyond
hope of human imitation. An essential part of his faith is a spirit of
repentance that serves to magnify the grace of God. Hezekiah is
portrayed as a winner, but his victories are attained via a traumatic
route of threats and scars.

1. *The triumph of faith* (vv. 1-23). The reign of Hezekiah was best
known to posterity for the glorious occasion of Jerusalem's deliverance from Assyrian invasion. It was celebrated as a tribute to the
power of God in that against all expectations Jerusalem did not fall.
The Chronicler echoed this tradition and even added to the aura of
splendor that surrounded it, but he celebrated it from the perspective of Hezekiah as a person of faith and commitment to God. To the
post-exilic community who tended to think of themselves as losers,
the divine deliverance of 701 B.C. might have been an event that
mocked their impotence. Perhaps for this reason the Chronicler desired to mingle the human and divine factors associated with this
glorious event. What were the human qualities that contributed to
God's intervention? By what means was the king able to let God
be God?

a. *Works of faith* (vv. 1-6a). Faith is not quiescent. Martin Luther
once exclaimed "Oh, it is a living, creative, active, mighty thing—

401

this faith!" Certainly faith waits for God to act and does not usurp His role, but it is ready to pave the way for His intervention. Hezekiah took defensive measures against an Assyrian siege of Jerusalem. Interestingly the prophet Isaiah condemned such measures as indicative of a lack of faith (Isa. 22:8–11). The Chronicler was able to espy an overall consistency, as in the case of Asa (14:6–15), and regarded them rather as the activity of a believer blessed by God. "God helps those who help themselves" is a saying that can have a cynical ring, but it contains a positive truth, to which the repetition *"helped"* (v. 3) and *"help"* (v. 8) seems to point. This stress on help is an echo of the Davidic theme of 1 Chronicles 11–12.

The first of the practical measures taken by Hezekiah was the control of the water supply, here a separate procedure from the building of the Siloam tunnel mentioned in verse 30, an extensive undertaking which must have occurred earlier. The supply from the Gihon spring had been channeled into outlets to irrigate the terraces cultivated on the western slope of the Kidron valley, which then produced a run-off stream at the bottom of the valley. These outlets were blocked off to prevent Assyrian access to the water. A second measure was the improvement of Jerusalem's fortifications and a third was of a military nature, the organization and arming of a conscript force. In principle Hezekiah's twin policy was to "put your faith in God and keep your powder dry."

b. *Words of faith* (vv. 6b–8). The Chronicler uses Hezekiah's morale-building speech to point to the primacy of faith. Fundamentally it expresses a truth that has ever emboldened the believer who has intimidating odds ranged against him, a truth which the Protestant reformer John Knox formulated as "A man with God is always in the majority." Such faith can put natural fears to flight and impart strength to face opposition unflinchingly. In verse 8 the Hebrew term rendered *"were strengthened by"* means literally to lean one's weight on and to find the source of solid support. Such encouragement of God's people is ever the task of their God-appointed leaders.

c. *Threats from the infidel* (vv. 9–19). The Chronicler selectively condensed the two accounts in 2 Kings 18–19 into a single narrative to express a barrage of threats via an oral message (vv. 9–16), a letter (v. 17), and intimidating shouts (v. 18). The transition between verses 8 and 9 brings to the fore a contrast that runs all through verses 1-23, between the God-honoring believer and the blasphemous infidel, between *"Hezekiah king of Judah"* and *"Sennacherib king of Assyria."* To be for or against God is the basic issue for the Chronicler. The shocking nature of Sennacherib's blasphemies underlined in verse 19 is an implicit call to faith designed to put every Jewish reader on his or her mettle and to transform nominal faith into vigorous zeal.

Humanly speaking the Assyrian had an impressive case. Byron captured the emotional impact of Sennacherib's invincibility in his lines: "The Assyrian came down like a wolf on the fold,/And his cohorts were gleaming in purple and gold."[3] A record of victories as long as one's arm is frighteningly impressive—until one remembers the belittling phrase *"an arm of flesh"* (v. 8). The Chronicler points out in his own summary (v. 19) that the Assyrian made the mistake of underestimating God by equating Him with pagan gods, in ignorance of the truth of Judah's monotheism. Theologically Judah thought as contemptuously of such gods—*"the work of men's hands"* (v. 19)—as the Assyrians thought militarily. Where Sennacherib went wrong was in thinking that Judah's God was in the same losing league as they were. The theme tune of his speech mistakenly highlights divine impotence—inability *"to deliver"*—over against human power—*"out of my hand"* (v. 13).

If Sennacherib is the polar counterpart of Hezekiah, he is also the arrogant rival of God Himself, as verse 16 expresses by setting *"his servants"* over against *"His servant Hezekiah."* The Chronicler evidently had at the back of his mind the royal Psalm 2, especially verse 2, "The kings of the earth set themselves . . . against the Lord and against His anointed." He too envisages God as the unseen power behind the Judean throne, guaranteeing the eventual triumph of His people and the downfall of their intimidating foes. Paradoxically, for all its bluster the speech is intended by the Chronicler to have an opposite effect on its Judean readers, to get human opposition into proper perspective, in the light of their distinctive traditional faith. "If God is for us, who can be against us?" (Rom. 8:31).

d. *Prayers of faith* (vv. 20-23). Here is the human factor which tipped the scales from defeat to victory. King Jehoshaphat earlier had spoken of the powerful cry of appeal to God in time of crisis: "You will hear and save" (20:9). Of course, its power has God as its cause. The salvation (*"saved,"* v. 22) which is triggered by Hezekiah's and Isaiah's prayers (= 2 Kings 19:4, 15) takes two appropriate forms: a supernatural defeat of Sennacherib's military power and a proof of the ironic failure of a pagan god to protect his devotee from providential punishment. The menacing *"hand"* so blatantly vaunted in Sennacherib's speech was rendered ineffectual (v. 22).

Hezekiah entered into another aspect of his Solomonic heritage. God had given Solomon *"rest from all his enemies all around"* (1 Chron. 22:9). Here the verb *"guided"* should be changed slightly (in the Hebrew) to "gave them rest" (RSV) with the notable support of the ancient Greek and Latin versions. Like Solomon too (9:23–24), international prestige became Hezekiah's happy lot. One cannot help thinking that, just as Solomon's golden age represented for the Chronicler one end of a rainbow, while its other end rested out of sight in a coming golden age for God's people, so too in Hezekiah's case a sign pointing forward to eschatological splendor is intended. Sacred history is a sure pointer to spiritual hope.

2. *The triumph of grace* (vv. 24–26). If so, Hezekiah is now brought down to earth as a fallible mortal. The Chronicler assumes that his readers know the basic text in 2 Kings 20:1–19, detailing Hezekiah's sickness and the subsequent visit of envoys from Babylon. At death's door the king once more uttered a prayer of faith, which God honored with a miraculous *"sign"* as a pledge of his eventual recovery. In spite of this boon Hezekiah ostentatiously displayed all his wealth to the envoys. Already in Kings this act was condemned as faithless. Here it is characterized as serious indeed, an exhibition of human pride directed against God because it left Him out of account: *"his heart was lifted up"* (v. 25). Hezekiah succumbed to the temptation of going it alone and regarding himself as master of his possessions rather than steward (cf. v. 29).

If Hezekiah's misdeed and its aftermath are hardly Solomonic in terms of the Chronicler's portrayal of Solomon, they are in accord with a Solomonic principle. Once again the gracious provision of 7:14 comes into operation, triggered by that self-humbling which spells repentance and turning from one's wicked ways. Hezekiah and his subjects were spared the onset of divine *"wrath"* (v. 25) which would otherwise have overwhelmed both him and them.

Just as prayer secured for the sick Hezekiah a new lease on life, so now did a compliant attitude which put humility in place of pride. Instead of the finality of death, God's grace opened a new chapter of life for Hezekiah and his people. Was the Chronicler meaning to draw a parallel between them and his contemporary readers who had survived the Exile? If so, it is worth remembering that his Christian readers too are those who are "alive from the dead" (Rom. 6:13).

3. *The triumph of blessing* (vv. 27-31). In the context there seems to be an intended contrast between wrath and the *"riches and honor"* which were the gift of God. Of course, the mention of prosperity picks up the principle of 31:21 that God blesses the obedient. Yet there seems to be a hint that in practice His grace cannot be shut out of the divine-human experience.

The paragraph has been inspired by the mention of Hezekiah's *"riches," "silver," "gold,"* and *"spices"* in 2 Kings 20:13. A further achievement, which the Chronicler reiterated from Kings (20:20) but probably also reinforced from another source, was the engineering exploit of the Siloam *"tunnel"* to bring a supply of water into the city, an exploit which survives to this day with its inscription triumphantly describing the excavations. In verse 31 the NKJV has fudged the link with the last clause of verse 30 by the anomalous rendering *"However"* (= "Howbeit," KJV) instead of a normal *"and so."* The overall meaning appears to be as represented in NEB: "In fact, Hezekiah was successful in everything he attempted, even in the affair of the envoys. . . ." There is a reference back to the incident of 2 Kings 20:12-19 which the Chronicler used earlier in verses 25-26. There he used it both negatively in terms of human sin and divine judgment and positively in terms of eating humble pie. Now he picks up the last, positive element and comments on it in an interesting way: "God left him to himself (RSV) *in order to test him."* In the end the incident showed that Hezekiah's *"heart"* was in the right place by his reverting to God's way of thinking. The Chronicler is repeating an old lesson that is ever worth learning and relearning. The test of a true believer is not that one never falls but that, when it happens, he or she repents sincerely and, drawing on God's grace, continues along the Christian path, chastened but not devastated by the experience. To "walk in the light" includes bringing into God's light the mistakes we make and finding forgiveness and new confidence to carry on (1 John 1:7–2:2). It is such fallibly loyal servants whom God recognizes as men and women after His own heart.

NOTES

1. Dietrich Bonhoeffer, *The Cost of Discipleship* (London: SCM, 1959), p. 36.

2. Edmund Gosse, *Father and Son* (London: Heinemann, 1907), pp. 198–99.

3. Lord Byron, "Destruction of Sennacherib."

CHAPTER EIGHTEEN

Ascents to Glory

2 Chronicles 33:1–35:27

The reign of Hezekiah marked for the Chronicler an ideal to emulate. It represented an attaining of the potential associated with the temple era of divine revelation. His account of Manasseh's reign begins with a violent contrast: instead of a hero of the faith we are confronted with an infernal renegade. Yet, remarkably, there is to be a happy ending. Here is the presentation of another potential, an evangelistic and pastoral potential, that the worst of people may discover salvation and attain excellence. For the Chronicler it was a prime truth of his temple theology. Hugh Redwood, the Christian journalist, used to say that God is able to save from the guttermost to the uttermost. Here is a portrayal of that redemptive power, not in social terms but from a moral and religious perspective.

After presenting Manasseh's fall and rise in 33:1–20, the Chronicler will give a rerun of his thesis, now spread over two generations. Amon, a carbon copy of Manasseh in his pre-conversion days, is succeeded by a son who rises to Hezekiah-like heights of commitment. Perhaps, as we have suggested for earlier chapters, the Chronicler had in mind the range of vignettes in Ezekiel 18. If Hezekiah is in principle the good person of Ezekiel 18:5–9, Manasseh is a trophy to the grace of a God who forgives repentant sinners, forgets their former way of life, and fires a new integrity, on the lines of Ezekiel 18:21–23. In turn Josiah's reversal of Amon's evil reign corresponds to the person who rises above a ruinous background, enabled by grace to break the chains (Ezek. 18:14–18). These two chapters are an exposition of God's liberating grace and of lives radically changed and dedicated to His glory. Wherever sin abounds, superabounding grace and goodness may take its place.

AN APOSTATE REDEEMED

33:1 Manasseh *was* twelve years old when he became king, and he reigned fifty-five years in Jerusalem.

2 But he did evil in the sight of the LORD, according to the abominations of the nations whom the LORD had cast out before the children of Israel.

3 For he rebuilt the high places which Hezekiah his father had broken down; he raised up altars for the Baals, and made wooden images; and he worshiped all the host of heaven and served them.

4 He also built altars in the house of the LORD, of which the LORD had said, "In Jerusalem shall My name be forever."

5 And he built altars for all the host of heaven in the two courts of the house of the LORD.

6 Also he caused his sons to pass through the fire in the Valley of the Son of Hinnom; he practiced soothsaying, used witchcraft and sorcery, and consulted mediums and spiritists. He did much evil in the sight of the LORD, to provoke Him to anger.

7 He even set a carved image, the idol which he had made, in the house of God, of which God had said to David and to Solomon his son, "In this house and in Jerusalem, which I have chosen out of all the tribes of Israel, I will put My name forever;

8 "and I will not again remove the foot of Israel from the land which I have appointed for your fathers—only if they are careful to do all that I have commanded them, according to the whole law and the statutes and the ordinances by the hand of Moses."

9 So Manasseh seduced Judah and the inhabitants of Jerusalem to do more evil than the nations whom the LORD had destroyed before the children of Israel.

10 And the LORD spoke to Manasseh and his people, but they would not listen.

11 Therefore the LORD brought upon them the captains of the army of the king of Assyria, who took

Manasseh with hooks, bound him with bronze *fetters,* and carried him off to Babylon.

12 Now when he was in affliction, he implored the LORD his God, and humbled himself greatly before the God of his fathers,

13 and prayed to Him; and He received his entreaty, heard his supplication, and brought him back to Jerusalem into his kingdom. Then Manasseh knew that the LORD *was* God.

14 After this he built a wall outside the City of David on the west side of Gihon, in the valley, as far as the entrance of the Fish Gate; and *it* enclosed Ophel, and he raised it to a very great height. Then he put military captains in all the fortified cities of Judah.

15 He took away the foreign gods and the idol from the house of the LORD, and all the altars that he had built in the mount of the house of the LORD and in Jerusalem; and he cast *them* out of the city.

16 He also repaired the altar of the LORD, sacrificed peace offerings and thank offerings on it, and commanded Judah to serve the LORD God of Israel.

17 Nevertheless the people still sacrificed on the high places, *but* only to the LORD their God.

18 Now the rest of the acts of Manasseh, his prayer to his God, and the words of the seers who spoke to him in the name of the LORD God of Israel, indeed they *are written* in the book of the kings of Israel.

19 Also his prayer and *how* God received his entreaty, and all his sin and trespass, and the sites where he built high places and set up wooden images and carved images, before he was humbled, indeed they *are* written among the sayings of Hozai.

20 So Manasseh rested with his fathers, and they buried him in his own house. Then his son Amon reigned in his place.

2 Chron. 33:1-20

In 2 Kings 21 Manasseh is an unmitigated villain, the king at whose door liability for the Exile is laid, and so a veritable Judas. The

Chronicler put Ahaz or perhaps Zedekiah, if anybody, in that dastardly role. He found reason to view Manasseh rather as a counterpart to Simon Peter, whose blasphemous denial of Christ remarkably did not debar him from distinguished leadership in the early church. It is difficult to imagine that the Chronicler created out of nothing the crucial episode in verses 11 and 13, although we may only surmise how the otherwise unknown incident fits into the history of the Assyrian empire, in which Manasseh had a role as a vassal. There was political unrest in much of its western sector at a certain period, and the otherwise loyal Manasseh might have been caught up in it. If so, the emperor Ashurbanipal's attested lenient treatment of other deviant vassal kings makes Manasseh's restoration to his realm not incredible. For the Chronicler the spiritual significance of Manasseh's fortunes was what mattered. He saw in the incident a pattern of exile and return, and in Manasseh's reign generally an outworking of the temple theology of chapter 7.

1. *The way out of favor* (vv. 1–9). These verses are taken over practically verbatim from the parallel passage, 2 Kings 21:1–9. They are an impassioned piece of writing, well worth repeating. Their double declaration of the flouting of God's express will (vv. 4, 7–8) is impressively enveloped in a refrain, the triple mention of Manasseh's evildoing which sinisterly progresses from *"evil"* to *"much evil,"* to *"more evil"* (vv. 2, 6, 9). Whatever these verses meant in their Kings context, here they form part of the Chronicler's own theological agenda. He has in mind God's revelation to Solomon in chapter 7, which for him represented the theological basis of the era in which he and his contemporaries lived. The clue to this insight comes in verse 4, where the Chronicler changes the wording slightly. In place of *"In Jerusalem I will put My name"* appears *"In Jerusalem shall My name be forever."* The alteration was meant to align with the divine statement of 7:16, that God's intent in His sponsorship of the temple was *"that My name might be there forever."*

However, this was only one clause in the Magna Charta of the temple dispensation. Sadly the promise of God's special presence at the temple—where He would listen to His people's prayers, receive their worship, and bestow His blessing on them—could be retracted under certain conditions. Those conditions, set out in 7:19, were the people's forsaking of God's Torah and their abandoning of exclusive allegiance to Him by serving other gods and worshiping them.

Manasseh became guilty of these very misdemeanors. As for the Torah, the first sentence in verse 6 was in its Kings setting a deliberate echo of Deuteronomy 18:10–11. Neither the Chronicler nor his contemporary readers could have been so poorly versed in the Torah as to miss the allusion. These various prohibited forms of religion were all Canaanite practices designed to manipulate for human ends the divine will and supernatural forces in general. If an explicit directive in the Torah was flouted, the other condition did not go unfulfilled, as the mention of different gods and of the verbs *"worshiped"* and *"served"* in verse 3 was intended to show. Manasseh, then, stood in a precarious position.

The king's religious innovations struck a shocking blow at the purpose of the temple. If Peter denied knowing his Lord, Manasseh by his actions denied the basic truth of the temple, that it was dedicated to God alone and was the focus of His special presence. This terrible denial is demonstrated in verses 4–5, where astral gods are assigned altars in the temple courts, and in verse 7. In the latter verse the English translations miss part of a deliberate and forceful repetition of Hebrew terms. God had declared: *"In this house . . . I will put My name forever."* Manasseh's actions deliberately countermanded this declaration of the divine will: he put *"a carved image . . . in the house of God"* (v. 7). Here was blatant apostasy indeed, as if to assert "Not Thy will but mine be done!"

It has been made plain that Manasseh fell into the traps of 7:20 and, moreover, was totally out of sympathy with God's temple-centered revelation laid down in chapter 7. The divinely appointed fate there prescribed for such spiritual treason was exile: "I will uproot them from My land which I have given them" (7:20). It is this fate that is expressed in the paraphrase in verse 8: *"I will not again remove the foot of Israel from the land . . . —only if they are careful"* to comply with the Torah. The paragraph at its outset has let us hear the rumbling of this volcano: instead of living *"according to"* the Torah (v. 8), Manasseh acted *"according to the abominations of the nations whom the Lord had cast out before the children of Israel"* (v. 2). This was a dangerous move for the king to make: he was already traveling down a road signposted to exile.

Thus far Manasseh alone has been in historical view. In verse 9 his influence on his subjects is broached. Under his pernicious guidance they cooperated in his wrongdoing. The sinister statement is made that they outdid the pre-Israelite *"nations whom the Lord had destroyed"* (v. 9). The verb *"destroyed"* is an intensification of *"cast out"* in the corresponding verse 2. It is a hint that not merely loss of land but loss of life would be a fitting reprisal for the way the king and people spurned their religious heritage.

2. *The way back to God* (vv. 10–13). Verse 10a is the Chronicler's paraphrase of God's prophetic revelation in 2 Kings 21:10(–15), while verse 10b is derived from 2 Kings 21:9a, "But they paid no attention." The Chronicler deliberately specifies the human recipients of God's message as *"Manasseh and his people,"* in line with verse 10, and later on we shall find significance in this specification. After this point in the story of Manasseh the Chronicler leaves the Kings account behind, till verses 18 and 20. However, he remains very much within the orbit of 2 Chronicles 7. When we read the prophetic message in 2 Kings, we receive the impression that it represents a sealing of the nation's fate as a prediction of terrible calamity. The Chronicler has a different perspective. In an earlier chapter he disclosed his theology of prophecy. It was to "bring" the people "back to the Lord" (24:19; cf. 36:15). In other words, prophecy was God's warning appeal to them not to continue on their dangerous path but to "seek" His "face and turn from their wicked ways," as 7:14 declares. (In the Hebrew "turn" and "bring back" are forms of the same verb.)

There is a beautiful inconsistency in the temple theology of chapter 7. It sets up rigorous standards of obedience—and it also provides a loophole, in 7:14, for those who fail to meet them, just like 1 John 2:1 in a Christian setting. This logical weakness is a concession to human infirmity and so is a mark of divine grace. It is such grace that Psalm 103 celebrates:

> He has not dealt with us according to our sins
> Nor punished us according to our iniquities . . .
> For He knows our frame;
> He remembers that we are dust (Ps. 103:10, 14).

Already in verse 10 the Chronicler finds an ingredient of this gospel-like truth, which is a firm part of his complex theology. The sword of Damocles suspended over these sinners' heads had not fallen yet. The motivation for God's prophetic appeal was a truth declared in Ezekiel 18:32: "I have no pleasure in the death of one who dies . . . Therefore turn and live!" Or, as the New Testament rephrases this happy truth: "The Lord is . . . not willing that any should perish but that all should come to repentance" (2 Pet. 3:9).

Reluctantly God had to activate the next phase of providential judgment (v. 11), since His second chance was rejected, as it was in 24:19. The Assyrian invaders whom He *"brought upon them"* were marching in step with the stern part of chapter 7: the language recalls the predictive statement "He has brought all this calamity on them" (7:22). At this point there is another lapse in logic which can hardly escape the reader's notice. In the middle of verse 11 there is a switch from *"Manasseh and his people"* (v. 10) as the focus of concern back to the king. Only Manasseh is exiled to Babylon, not the people. Historically, of course, the Chronicler was evidently bound by his source, which may have spoken in terms of a Gestapo-like delegation of high-ranking security officers with powers to arrest the king and escort him to Babylon, to answer charges of treason. Why to Babylon, when Nineveh was the Assyrian capital? Perhaps the summons to the emperor took place in 648 B.C., when he had suppressed in Babylonia the rebellion of his brother, who had also fomented unrest in the west. Theologically, however, the sole mention of Manasseh must be a pointer to God's mercy in sparing the people, who had shared not only in Manasseh's spiritual infidelity but in his rejection of God's prophetic overtures.

Anyway, for Manasseh there was no hope, we might think. He was suffering his just deserts and had turned down the chance of a reprieve. It is not for nothing that Psalm 103:8 speaks of God as "abounding in mercy." At last Manasseh came to his senses, *"when he was in affliction"* (v. 12). How true to life it is that human stress or frustration is the factor that brings conviction of a need for God! There is an implicit contrast here with Ahaz. In 28:22 a clause which is practically the same in the Hebrew, rendered "when he was in distress," prefaces Ahaz's further decline into apostasy. Manasseh, however, becomes a textbook example of the fulfillment of the golden promise of 7:14. He *"humbled himself"* and *"prayed"* (vv. 12–13) to God for help. God graciously honored His Solomonic promise and *"heard"* Manasseh's prayer. The last two clauses of verse 13 echo one of the scenarios depicted in Solomon's prayer, which of course underlies the promise of 7:14, namely the confession of God's name by victims of sin-caused exile and His bringing them back to their land (6:24, 25). The confession of faith contained in the climactic *"Then Manasseh knew that the Lord was God"* (v. 13) constitutes an about-face. Earlier he had patronized polytheistic substitutes for the true God. Now he confessed the sole claim of God on his life and took his place in the chain of believers down the ages: *"the God of his fathers"* becomes *"his God"* (v. 12). Here the confession is mentioned not as part of the king's prayerful turning to God before he was delivered, as in 6:24, but as an item of thanksgiving after his return. It is an avowal of faith which looks back to God's redeeming power in his life, rather like the post-exilic shout of praise *"The Lord has done great things for us,/And we are glad"* (Ps. 126:3). However, it moves beyond gratitude for deliverance to an underlying theological truth. An experience patently discernible to the eye of faith as the delivering power of God had proved His exclusive claims on the life of His backsliding follower.

In these verses the Chronicler is speaking to his post-exilic contemporaries. He reminds them of God's great demonstration of His power in the re-establishment of the Judean community after the Exile. Manasseh's experience of deportation to Babylon and return was a pilot for Judah's fortunes in the next century. It was also a reminder that God takes the phenomenon of exile in His giant stride. The Exile did not constitute a great gulf for the Chronicler, whereby monarchical Judah gave way to a second-rate post-exilic community. There was an essential continuity in God's dealings with His people. Manasseh's exile and return belonged firmly within the temple era and was a glorious vindication of one of its prime truths. So too the post-exilic people of God belonged to the same temple era, saved by that divine grace which on numerous occasions throughout the history of the monarchy had been at work on Judah's behalf.

God's people sometimes suffer from a second- or third-generation syndrome. It is detectable in Hebrews 13:7–8, where the advice to *"remember"* dead *"leaders, . . . consider the outcome of their life, and imitate their faith"* (RSV) is followed by the triumphant claim, *"Jesus Christ is the same yesterday, today and forever"* (cf. 2 Pet. 3). The momentum of faith is stimulated by a reaffirmation of the Lord's redemptive, protective power as constant and unfailing. The Chronicler seems to be affirming this pastoral truth over against a spiritual depression which dragged down the redeemed into defeatism. The shadow of past failure haunted their minds and cast doubt on their worth in God's service and on His willingness to use their tainted lives for His glory. I chose the title of this subsection, "The way back to God," with care: it reminds me of a children's chorus by E. H. Swinstead I was taught to sing many years ago. Its tune was a soft, haunting melody which fitted its theme beautifully:

> There's a way back to God from the dark paths of
>   sin,
> There's a door that is open and you may go in:
> At Calvary's cross is where you begin
> When you come as a sinner to Jesus.

The words belong as well in a pastoral context of counseling Christians as in an evangelistic setting. Jewish theology significantly uses the concept of being born again as a sequel to any occurrence of repentance. The Chronicler had a concern for the people of God, that their faith in Him might overcome their depressive doubts about themselves. "He is faithful . . . to forgive us our sins and to cleanse us from all unrighteousness" (1 John 1:9). The biblical expositor E. M. Blaiklock realized the truth behind the Chronicler's narrative about Manasseh's rehabilitation when he wrote: "I am glad Elijah, Manasseh, and Peter show me that no failure is final."[1]

3. *The way forward* (vv. 14–20). What follows is a success story. Manasseh steps into the shoes of Rehoboam who after a step of obedience found blessing in the form of building operations (v. 14; cf. 11:5–12). His repentance reaps religious fruit in that God is given back His exclusive role in the temple and in Jerusalem. The king's service of alien gods (v. 3), commended to his people (v. 9), is now countermanded by a directive to *"serve the Lord God of Israel"* (v. 16) alone. There is a touch of irony in v. 17. The high places rebuilt by Manasseh in verse 3 stubbornly retained their popular appeal, although now dedicated exclusively to the Lord. Exasperatingly an unhelpful example tends to be more persuasive than a good one. Overall, though, the Chronicler's message in verses 14–17 is clear, that adequate resources for life and the due honoring of God go hand in hand.

In verses 18–19 the Chronicler goes to the trouble of giving a rather lengthy review of Manasseh's experiences. He develops the source citation formula of 2 Kings 21:17 which specifically mentioned only the sin of Manasseh. In addition the Chronicler has a positive list of mementos of the reign to commend to his readers. True, *"his sin"* not only finds mention but is amplified with the Chronicler's key term for unspirituality, *"unfaithfulness"* (NEB; NKJV *"trespass"*) and also with a recapitulation of verses 3 and 7. Yet the Chronicler wants to make it clear that divine grace triumphed over godlessness. God would not let Manasseh alone, but endeavored to coax him back by His *"seers"* (v. 18; cf. v. 10). Eventually the king succumbed to His persistent love and found in 2 Chronicles 7:14 a prescription for the way back to Him: self-humbling, a *"prayer"* of penitent faith *"to his God"*—mentioned twice, so important a spiritual key was it—and a favorable response from God. The Chronicler's final elaboration of Manasseh's *"sin"* serves as a pastoral reminder that no one is too bad to be welcomed back by a loving God. Did he have partly in mind the hated northerners of his own day whose return to the fold was hampered as much by southern hardness of heart as by their religious unorthodoxy? In turn, the church dares not forget that it is a community of sinners saved by grace, who must echo that grace by restoring the backslider *"in a spirit of gentleness"* (Gal. 6:1).

A SPIRITUAL REVOLUTION

33:21 Amon *was* twenty-two years old when he became king, and he reigned two years in Jerusalem.

22 But he did evil in the sight of the LORD, as his father Manasseh had done; for Amon sacrificed to all the carved images which his father Manasseh had made, and served them.

23 And he did not humble himself before the LORD, as his father Manasseh had humbled himself; but Amon trespassed more and more.

24 Then his servants conspired against him, and killed him in his own house.

25 But the people of the land executed all those who had conspired against King Amon. Then the people of the land made his son Josiah king in his place.

34:1 Josiah *was* eight years old when he became king, and he reigned thirty-one years in Jerusalem.

2 And he did *what was* right in the sight of the LORD, and walked in the ways of his father David; *he* did *not* turn aside to the right hand or to the left.

3 For in the eighth year of his reign, while he was still young, he began to seek the God of his father David; and in the twelfth year he began to purge Judah and Jerusalem of the high places, the wooden images, the carved images, and the molded images.

4 They broke down the altars of the Baals in his presence, and the incense altars which *were* above them he cut down; and the wooden images, the carved images, and the molded images he broke in pieces, and made dust of them and scattered *it* on the graves of those who had sacrificed to them.

5 He also burned the bones of the priests on their altars, and cleansed Judah and Jerusalem.

6 And so *he did* in the cities of Manasseh, Ephraim, and Simeon, as far as Naphtali and all around, with axes.

7 When he had broken down the altars and the wooden images, had beaten the carved images into powder, and cut down all the incense altars throughout all the land of Israel, he returned to Jerusalem.

8 In the eighteenth year of his reign, when he had purged the land and the temple, he sent Shaphan the son of Azaliah, Maaseiah the governor of the city, and Joah the son of Joahaz the recorder, to repair the house of the LORD his God.

9 When they came to Hilkiah the high priest, they delivered the money that was brought into the house of God, which the Levites who kept the doors had gathered from the hand of Manasseh and Ephraim, from all the remnant of Israel, from all Judah and Benjamin, and *which* they had brought back to Jerusalem.

10 Then they put *it* in the hand of the foremen who had the oversight of the house of the LORD; and they gave it to the workmen who worked in the house of the LORD, to repair and restore the house.

11 They gave *it* to the craftsmen and builders to buy hewn stone and timber for beams, and to floor the houses which the kings of Judah had destroyed.

12 And the men did the work faithfully. Their overseers *were* Jahath and Obadiah the Levites, of the sons of Merari, and Zechariah and Meshullam, of the sons of the Kohathites, to supervise. *Others of* the Levites, all of whom were skillful with instruments of music,

13 *were* over the burden bearers and *were* overseers of all who did work in any kind of service. And *some* of the Levites *were* scribes, officers, and gatekeepers.

14 Now when they brought out the money that was brought into the house of the LORD, Hilkiah the priest found the Book of the Law of the LORD *given* by Moses.

15 Then Hilkiah answered and said to Shaphan the scribe, "I have found the Book of the Law in the house of the LORD." And Hilkiah gave the book to Shaphan.

16 So Shaphan carried the book to the king, bringing the king word, saying, "All that was committed to your servants they are doing.

17 "And they have gathered the money that was found in the house of the LORD, and have delivered it into the hand of the overseers and the workmen."

18 Then Shaphan the scribe told the king, saying, "Hilkiah the priest has given me a book." And Shaphan read it before the king.

19 Thus it happened, when the king heard the words of the Law, that he tore his clothes.

20 Then the king commanded Hilkiah, Ahikam the son of Shaphan, Abdon the son of Micah, Shaphan the scribe, and Asaiah a servant of the king, saying,

21 "Go, inquire of the LORD for me, and for those who are left in Israel and Judah, concerning the words of the book that is found; for great *is* the wrath of the LORD that is poured out on us, because our fathers have not kept the word of the LORD, to do according to all that is written in this book."

22 So Hilkiah and those the king *had appointed* went to Huldah the prophetess, the wife of Shallum the son of Tokhath, the son of Hasrah, keeper of the

wardrobe. (She dwelt in Jerusalem in the Second Quarter.) And they spoke to her to that *effect*.

23 Then she answered them, "Thus says the LORD God of Israel, 'Tell the man who sent you to Me,

24 "Thus says the LORD: 'Behold, I will bring calamity on this place and on its inhabitants, all the curses that are written in the book which they have read before the king of Judah,

25 'because they have forsaken Me and burned incense to other gods, that they might provoke Me to anger with all the works of their hands. Therefore My wrath will be poured out on this place, and not be quenched.'"'

26 "But as for the king of Judah, who sent you to inquire of the LORD, in this manner you shall speak to him, 'Thus says the LORD God of Israel: "Concerning the words which you have heard—

27 "because your heart was tender, and you humbled yourself before God when you heard His words against this place and against its inhabitants, and you humbled yourself before Me, and you tore your clothes and wept before Me, I also have heard *you*," says the LORD.

28 "Surely I will gather you to your fathers, and you shall be gathered to your grave in peace; and your eyes shall not see all the calamity which I will bring on this place and its inhabitants."'" So they brought back word to the king.

29 Then the king sent and gathered all the elders of Judah and Jerusalem.

30 The king went up to the house of the LORD, with all the men of Judah and the inhabitants of Jerusalem—the priests and the Levites, and all the people, great and small. And he read in their hearing all the words of the Book of the Covenant which had been found in the house of the LORD.

31 Then the king stood in his place and made a covenant before the LORD, to follow the LORD, and to keep His commandments and His testimonies and His statutes with all his heart and all his soul, to perform the words of the covenant that were written in this book.

32 And he made all who were present in Jerusalem and Benjamin take a stand. So the inhabitants of Jerusalem did according to the covenant of God, the God of their fathers.

33 Thus Josiah removed all the abominations from all the country that *belonged* to the children of Israel, and made all who were present in Israel diligently serve the LORD their God. All his days they did not depart from following the LORD God of their fathers.

35:1 Now Josiah kept a Passover to the LORD in Jerusalem, and they slaughtered the Passover *lambs* on the fourteenth *day* of the first month.

2 And he set the priests in their duties and encouraged them for the service of the house of the LORD.

3 Then he said to the Levites who taught all Israel, who were holy to the LORD: "Put the holy ark in the house which Solomon the son of David, king of Israel, built. *It shall* no longer *be* a burden on *your* shoulders. Now serve the LORD your God and His people Israel.

4 "Prepare *yourselves* according to your fathers' houses, according to your divisions, following the written instruction of David king of Israel and the written instruction of Solomon his son.

5 "And stand in the holy *place* according to the divisions of the fathers' houses of your brethren the *lay* people, and *according to* the division of the father's house of the Levites.

6 "So slaughter the Passover *offerings*, consecrate yourselves, and prepare *them* for your brethren, that *they* may do according to the word of the LORD by the hand of Moses."

7 Then Josiah gave the *lay* people lambs and young goats from the flock, all for Passover *offerings* for all who were present, to the number of thirty thousand, as well as three thousand cattle; these *were* from the king's possessions.

8 And his leaders gave willingly to the people, to the priests, and to the Levites. Hilkiah, Zechariah, and Jehiel, rulers of the house of God, gave to the

priests for the Passover *offerings* two thousand six hundred *from the flock,* and three hundred cattle.

9 Also Conaniah, his brothers Shemaiah and Nethanel, and Hashabiah and Jeiel and Jozabad, chief of the Levites, gave to the Levites for Passover *offerings* five thousand *from the flock* and five hundred cattle.

10 So the service was prepared, and the priests stood in their places, and the Levites in their divisions, according to the king's command.

11 And they slaughtered the Passover *offerings;* and the priests sprinkled *the blood* with their hands, while the Levites skinned *the animals.*

12 Then they removed the burnt offerings that *they* might give them to the divisions of the fathers' houses of the *lay* people, to offer to the LORD, as *it is* written in the Book of Moses. And so *they did* with the cattle.

13 Also they roasted the Passover *offerings* with fire according to the ordinance; but the *other* holy *offerings* they boiled in pots, in caldrons, and in pans, and divided *them* quickly among all the *lay* people.

14 Then afterward they prepared portions for themselves and for the priests, because the priests, the sons of Aaron, *were busy* in offering burnt offerings and fat until night; therefore the Levites prepared portions for themselves and for the priests, the sons of Aaron.

15 And the singers, the sons of Asaph, *were* in their places, according to the command of David, Asaph, Heman, and Jeduthun the king's seer. Also the gatekeepers were at each gate; they did not have to leave their position, because their brethren the Levites prepared portions for them.

16 So all the service of the LORD was prepared the same day, to keep the Passover and to offer burnt offerings on the altar of the LORD, according to the command of King Josiah.

17 And the children of Israel who were present kept the Passover at that time, and the Feast of Unleavened Bread for seven days.

18 There had been no Passover kept in Israel like

that since the days of Samuel the prophet; and none of the kings of Israel had kept such a Passover as Josiah kept, with the priests and the Levites, all Judah and Israel who were present, and the inhabitants of Jerusalem.

19 In the eighteenth year of the reign of Josiah this Passover was kept.

20 After all this, when Josiah had prepared the temple, Necho king of Egypt came up to fight against Carchemish by the Euphrates; and Josiah went out against him.

21 But he sent messengers to him, saying, "What have I to do with you, king of Judah? I *have* not *come* against you this day, but against the house with which I have war; for God commanded me to make haste. Refrain *from meddling with* God, who *is* with me, lest He destroy you."

22 Nevertheless Josiah would not turn his face from him, but disguised himself so that he might fight with him, and did not heed the words of Necho from the mouth of God. So he came to fight in the Valley of Megiddo.

23 And the archers shot King Josiah; and the king said to his servants, "Take me away, for I am severely wounded."

24 His servants therefore took him out of that chariot and put him in the second chariot that he had, and they brought him to Jerusalem. So he died, and was buried in *one of* the tombs of his fathers. And all Judah and Jerusalem mourned for Josiah.

25 Jeremiah also lamented for Josiah. And to this day all the singing men and the singing women speak of Josiah in their lamentations. They made it a custom in Israel; and indeed they *are* written in the Laments.

26 Now the rest of the acts of Josiah and his goodness, according to *what was* written in the Law of the LORD,

27 and his deeds from first to last, indeed they *are* written in the book of the kings of Israel and Judah.

2 Chron. 33:21–35:27

This section is a reiteration of the truth that a dire situation of spiritual betrayal can be gloriously redeemed. The Chronicler is telling his fellows that they need not languish in a low level of living, under the shadow of divine wrath for unfaithfulness inherited from former generations. The transition from Amon to Josiah repeats the good news of God's renewal of lives recommitted to Him.

1. *Apostasy renewed* (vv. 21–25). The Chronicler bases his material on the account of 2 Kings 21:19–24. His careful concern is to present it as a parallel rerun of Manasseh's first, evil period. In fact, *"evil,"* as a perpetual mark of Amon's reign, echoed that of *"his father"* earlier (vv. 2, 22). An innovation the Chronicler makes is to replace Kings' characteristic vocabulary for apostasy (2 Kings 21:21, 22) with his own terms borrowed from verse 19. With hindsight verse 19 can be seen to fulfill a second agenda, to recapitulate negative elements which were to resurface in the reign of Amon, in order to parallel the two periods. *"Carved images"* are *"served"* (v. 22; cf. v. 19 and also v. 3) in token of the fact that once more exclusive allegiance to the Lord is shockingly disdained. Self-humbling before God, the low door to achievement of a high potential, is conspicuous by its absence (vv. 19, 23).

The convoluted political maneuverings of verses 24–25 are for the Chronicler an implicit description of the providential retribution and re-ordering instigated by God, like the regicidal conspiracies of 24:25 and 25:27. Noteworthy is the role of *"the people"* in verse 25. (Although the Chronicler copied from Kings the longer appellation *"people of the land,"* he probably attached to it no special meaning such as scholars suspect it had but are unable to define with certainty.) Under Manasseh they were the willing dupes of his evil genius (v. 9); later they lagged somewhat behind the momentum of his new spirituality, just making a passing grade (v. 17). Now they have got the message and instigate a turn for the better, as if provoked by Amon's regressiveness to prefer Manasseh's better way at last.

2. *Spirituality restored* (34:1–35:27). The people retained and consistently developed this new spirit of commitment, as the comment in 34:33b attests. In this exemplary pilgrimage they had the encouragement and role modeling of Josiah (34:33a), whose reign is now described. For the Chronicler it is a grander version of Manasseh's

new lease on life. Self-humbling features in both periods (33:12, 19, 23; 34:27); so too does the approved offering of sacrifices *on the altar of the Lord* (33:16; 35:16), while Josiah's insistence that the people serve only Him is an echo of Manasseh's command (33:16; 34:33). Moreover, if the first period of Manasseh was marked by failure to keep the Torah (33:8), Josiah's reign is characterized not only by an admission of such failure but by a resolve to give the Torah its due priority and so to submit to God's will in the life of the community (34:14, 21, 31). A devout spirit of self-humbling before God and a desire to honor the temple as the means of proper worship and the Torah as an appropriate way of life—these were ideals dear to the Chronicler which he desired to see given pride of place among his contemporaries. This is the spirituality he commends to his readers.

a. *Clean-up operations* (34:1–13). If Amon was a negative model of spiritual exile, Josiah was a shining example of restoration and renewal. The Chronicler takes over the introduction to his reign in verses 1–2 from 2 Kings 22:1–2 and uses verse 2 as a headline for verses 3–13 (*"For . . ."*). The Davidic idealism of verse 2 is reinforced in verse 3, with the help of the Chronicler's key term for spirituality, *"seek."* In Chronicles David is the founder of a new divine dispensation, whose faith laid down guidelines for believers thereafter. In similar vein for Christians the new era inaugurated by Jesus means that God cannot be recognized as other than the God and Father of our Lord Jesus Christ and that Jesus is the Teacher from whom they learn of God.

In Kings the record of Josiah's reforms clusters around the eighteenth year of his reign, 622 B.C., and his discovery of the Torah book, so that reform takes its motivation and direction from the find. In 2 Chronicles 34, on the other hand, the reform is staggered over two stages and the book has a much lesser role in it. The language of verses 4–7, applied to Josiah's twelfth year (628 B.C.), is patently borrowed from the phrase of reform following the finding of the book described in 2 Kings 23:4–20—in the eighteenth year—as the repetition of *"he returned to Jerusalem"* (v. 7 = 2 Kings 23:20) shows. There is no indication in the Chronicler's material that he was using a different source at this point. However, in redating this material or rather spreading it over two periods (cf. v. 33a), the Chronicler might have been aware of an independent tradition which placed some elements of reform earlier.

Historically Assyria was growing weaker as an imperial power from the 630s onward and was increasingly beset with problems inside and outside its empire. Consequently it lost control of the western parts, where Egypt gradually took its place. By the late 630s and early 620s Egypt was in control of the coastal highway of Palestine and Syria. There may well have been a political vacuum sufficient for Josiah to exercise some control over the mountainous hinterland, specifically part of the northern territory of Israel, as the reform account implies (v. 6). Moreover, the editors of Kings had a vested interest in the discovery of the lawbook, evidently a form of the Book of Deuteronomy. Deuteronomy was the theological key they used to unlock the meaning of history. So their emphasis on the lawbook as the springboard for Josiah's reform is not necessarily to be taken at its face value. Their own ideology may well have motivated the chronological order in Kings, whereas the Chronicler, with no such ax to grind, may have been pursuing an independent tradition.

The homiletic use to which the Chronicler puts the tradition of the earlier dating, if such it was, is reminiscent of the "first year" and the "first month" emphasis in his account of Hezekiah's reforms (29:3). Spiritual priorities must dominate the believer's life. The significance of *the twelfth year* (v. 3), when Josiah was twenty years old, seems to have been that it marked his reaching the age of majority. The reference in 31:17 to this age as the time when Levites began their life's work so suggests. Now Josiah was able to dispense with a regent and to rule in his own right. At the first opportunity Josiah put a new broom to work. It meant the fruiting of spiritual aspirations which had already blossomed in his *eighth year,* when he was sixteen. Many Christians look back to their teen-age years or even earlier as the period when faith first found a place in their hearts and decisions were made which determined the course of their later lives. What tremendous potential lies in Christian work among young people! I myself look back with gratitude to God for dedicated youth leaders, especially Mr. Leonard Wood and Dr. Maurice Packer, who in Bible class and elsewhere devoted much time and effort to helping me and other young fellows and girls to *seek* God in a life commitment and in Christian service.

The reforms of verses 3–7 are summed up in verse 8 as the purging of *"the land and the temple."* The account itself is written in generalized terms which do not mention the temple: it describes two parallel prongs of a reforming operation, first in *"Judah and Jerusalem"* (vv. 3b–5) and then at northern shrines (vv. 6, 7) and so *"throughout all the land of Israel"* (v. 7). The Chronicler is asserting that in Israel's land the Lord must be honored as God and worshiped aright. John's vision of the New Jerusalem develops this theme of religious purity: *"nothing unclean shall enter it, nor any one who practices abomination"* (Rev. 21:27, RSV). Paul made use of this motif when he wrote of the need for a moral purge of the Christian community, illustrating his point from the Passover practice of searching for leaven: *"purge out the old leaven . . . of wickedness"* (1 Cor. 5:7, 8). He too laid claim for his Lord to areas belonging to His domain, urging the detection and expulsion of that which was alien to His moral purposes.

In verses 8–13 repair work in the temple is undertaken with funds garnered from God's people. The Chronicler emphasizes that they all, from north and south, contributed to the upkeep of the sanctuary (v. 8). Both groups had a stake in the temple (contrast Ezra 4:1–3; cf. 2 Chron. 34:21). In his account of Hezekiah's reign he had asserted that all of them had the right to worship at the Jerusalem shrine (30:1–12)—and the corresponding responsibility of supporting the temple workers (31:4–6). Here a theme similar to the latter is developed. The fabric of the temple needed refurbishing; in this case after earlier, unfaithful kings had "let" it "go to ruin" (34:11, RSV). If the instigation of the repair lay at the king's door, the financing of it rested with God's people. The Chronicler's spirituality included such a down-to-earth ingredient, which he hoped would not fall on deaf ears in his own day. Judah's religious snobbery that disdained northern believers meant a heavier financial liability than need be!

b. *Commitment to the Lord* (vv. 14–33). The Chronicler has regularly brought to the notice of his readers the habit of good leaders to hold a special service in which they and the people pledged their lives to God. It occurred in Asa's reign and during Jehoiada's regency; most recently it was instigated by King Hezekiah (15:9–12; 23:16; 29:10). Now Josiah was to take his place in this noble succession. In Chronicles it is always part of a larger reform program and is preceded and/or followed by elements of reform. This section, verses 14–33, has been by and large copied out from 2 Kings 22:8–23:3. The Chronicler has used it primarily because it fitted his pattern of covenant renewal, which he obviously considered an ideal of spirituality still relevant to his own age. The striking prelude to the ceremony also intrigued him because it coincided with his own spiritual wavelength in three respects: (1) a healthy respect for the Torah and its demand for exclusive worship of the Lord (v. 25), (2) inquiry for God's prophetic will, and (3) consequent self-humbling before the divine revelation of Law and Prophet(s). The inquiry or seeking (Hebrew *dāraš*) of the divine will through the prophetess Huldah (vv. 21, 26) echoes and develops the same verb used of the king's youthful commitment (v. 3). As to self-humbling, in verse 27 the single reference of 2 Kings 22:19 is doubled, so as to highlight Josiah's parallel role to that of Manasseh (33:12, 19). By virtue of these elements the passage was grist for the Chronicler's mill.

In the account of Manasseh's reign self-humbling was a pointer to the theology of 2 Chronicles 7, specifically to 7:14. Does the vocabulary of that chapter find any echoes here? Indeed, it does. The negative side of its theology is reflected in the forsaking of the Lord and the espousal of *"other gods"* (v. 25; cf. 7:19, 22), which result in *"all the calamity"* of verse 28 (cf. v. 24 and 7:22). However, the positive side of the theology of chapter 7 has opportunity to surface, not only in the self-humbling of the king before God but also in God's hearing of his penitent plea (v. 27; cf. 7:14). The upshot is that king and community resolve to keep God's *"commandments"* and *"statutes,"* acutely conscious that hitherto there had been failure in this area (v. 31; cf. 7:19). Once again the message is that grace can triumph over human sin and lead the wayward in paths of moral righteousness. The result of such grace is not license to sin again but, as Paul wrote, fresh allegiance *"from the heart to the standard of teaching to which you were committed"* (Rom. 6:17, RSV).

The *"Book of the Law"* (v. 14) found in the springcleaning of the temple is generally identified by scholars with some form of the Book of Deuteronomy. The overall Kings account furnishes sufficient indications to warrant this identification. Indeed, the Chronicler appears to disclose that he too has Deuteronomy in mind. In place of *"all the words of the book . . ."* (2 Kings 22:16) he particularizes *"all the curses that are written in the book"* (v. 24), borrowing from Deuteronomy 29:21, *"all the curses . . . that are written in this*

Book of the Law." The spirit of Deuteronomy is finely echoed in
the royal commitment to follow the Lord, in obedience that springs
from *"all his heart and all his soul"* (v. 31; cf. Deut. 13:3, 4; 26:16;
also 6:5; 10:12). It was a mark of the Chronicler's description of
Asa's covenanting (15:12) and appeared in a shorter form in his
thumbnail sketches of such models of excellence as Jehoshaphat and
Hezekiah (22:9; 31:21).

In contrast to his source the Chronicler wanted to single out that
"the inhabitants of Jerusalem" were participants in the covenant ceremony (v. 32). He was sensitive to the fact that they were the human
targets of God's prophetic judgment against Jerusalem (vv. 24, 27,
28). In 32:22 he had specified this very group as recipients of salvation "from the hand of Sennacherib . . . and from the hand of all
others." Sadly deliverance had stimulated no devotion, and now divine wrath loomed over them. In their desire to avert it they peni-
tently participated both in the pledge of commitment and in the
Passover celebration (35:18).

The king's initiative in getting them to make this commitment is
also emphasized (v. 32; contrast 2 Kings 23:3). It is echoed too in
verse 33, along with his continuing influence for good. The result
was that, just as the *"God of his father David"* became *"his God"* (vv. 3,
8), so the *"God of their fathers"* became *"their God"* (vv. 32, 33). The
process of making the traditional faith one's own is beautifully repeated. Josiah taught others the lesson of a living faith he had
learned earlier.

c. *Correct Worship* (35:1–19). The Kings account devotes merely
three verses to Josiah's celebration of the Passover (2 Kings 23:21–
23). The Chronicler expands that passage to nineteen verses, incor-
porating it into the beginning, middle, and end of his version (vv. 1a,
12, 18a, 19). This is the last opportunity he has to describe a religious festival; he makes the most of it for the edification of his readers and to emphasize his own standpoint. He presents his religious
swansong as a gala performance. Worship is described in rhetorical
terms as the giving of over forty thousand sacrificial victims,
donated by the king and religious leaders for the people to offer
(vv. 7–9; contrast 30:24). God is worth every single one of such gifts!

There are two particular emphases in this account. First, the
grounding of true worship in God's past revelation is brought to
the fore. The Passover ceremony, as described here, took over the

rulings of sacrificial worship laid down in the Torah (vv. 5, 6, 12, 13) and also the prescriptions for the organization of temple duties established by David and Solomon with prophetic authorization (vv. 4, 13). A blend of truths imparted in the old and new eras of revelation was honored in this celebration. Tribute was paid to both the Law and the Prophets. There was a concern to follow God's declared will in the area of worship. Guidelines had already been provided: to worship God was not to do one's own thing but to stay respectfully within the parameters of past revelation. To Christians, living in the post-temple era, the letter of the Law and the Prophets no longer applies, but none dare disregard their spirit. If precepts for Christian worship are comparatively minimal in number, biblical principles are of maximal importance.

The main basis for the Passover celebration is regarded as Deuteronomy 16, where it took the form of a congregational service of sacrifice rather than a home celebration, as Exodus 12 presented it. However, the preparation of the Passover lambs followed the prescription of Exodus 12:8–9 in that they were *roasted . . . with fire* (vv. 6, 13). Not only lambs or kids were to be offered, as in Exodus 12:5, but also bulls, as laid down in Deuteronomy 16:2 (vv. 7–9). The bulls, *"the other holy offerings"* of verse 13, were *"boiled"* in accord with Deuteronomy 16:7 (RSV). There was no prescription in the Torah for a sacrificial treatment of the Passover offerings: Leviticus 3 is taken as a precedent to follow. They are regarded as peace offerings, and their fat, liver, and kidneys are burnt on the altar as a token of worship. This is what is meant by the *"burnt offerings"* of verses 12, 14 (*"burnt offerings and* [= namely] *fat"*), and 16. Overall there is concern to honor God's scriptural will in the sphere of worship.

The Chronicler has another message, a more sensitive one, to deliver in his Passover story. The Levites are assigned a strikingly prominent role. Josiah's speech in verses 3–5 supplies the background to their new ministry. They were ministers of the Davidic era of revelation. Their old, Mosaic task of carrying the ark was over (v. 3 [perhaps replace *"Put"* with *"Leave"*]; cf. 1 Chron. 23:26). What was their new status to be? Hitherto in the temple era they had mainly a role as singers and gatekeepers (v. 15; cf. 1 Chron. 23:4, 5). Now a new type of ministry is proposed. Both the royal speech and the ensuing narrative assign to the Levites the role of killing and skinning the Passover victims. (In v. 6 read with RSV *"to do"* = "that you may do" for NKJV *"that they may do."*) Normally this was the lay person's responsibility (cf. Lev. 1:5, 6). In 30:16–17 it was allocated to the Levites only under emergency conditions. In this passage the Chronicler seems to be urging by dint of repetition that such preparatory work should be the regular prerogative of the Levites. Verses 6 and 11–15 portray the Levites discharging these preliminary activities and so playing a key role in the Passover ritual of the temple.

In closing, the Chronicles account picks up the Kings notice that an ancient precedent was only now being revived "since the days of the judges" (2 Kings 23:22). The Chronicler changes the reference to *"since the days of Samuel"* (v. 18). At first glance the alteration is easily explicable: Samuel was the last of the Judges. The pinpointing of Samuel seems to have had a deeper significance. Earlier in Chronicles Samuel was represented as adopted into the Levitical clan (1 Chron. 6:26–28, 33–38; cf. 1 Sam. 1:1; 8:2). A Levite led the nation's worship! This provided an old precedent for Levites taking a more prominent role and having a high status in religious worship. Carefully and sensitively the Chronicler is using narrative to argue a thesis dear to his heart.

It is an intriguing question to ask what the Chronicler's contention would be if he were writing today. I suggest that it would be the ministry of women. I can imagine him citing such a text as "there is neither male nor female; for you are all one in Christ Jesus" (Gal. 3:28). I can catch a reference to female prophets ministering in the early church (1 Cor. 11:5). I can hear him parading the contributions of women to the missionary enterprise. He would have left no stone unturned in researching his case and communicating his conviction.

d. *A catastrophic error* (vv. 20–27). The narrative in 34:8–35:19 has been set within the chronological framework of Josiah's eighteenth year, that is 622 B.C. The Chronicler now sums up the king's work in that narrative with the clause *"when Josiah had prepared the temple."* The Passover had functioned as a reinauguration of temple worship, a fitting sequel to his reforms and repairs. The resumption of the regular worship of God's people featured as a climax, the first striking of the renewed clock of temple ritual. So crucial were its institutional services to the Chronicler, as evidence of a spiritual response to God. Now, however, he has a less happy incident to record. He jumps thirteen years, from Josiah's eighteenth year to his final one,

609 B.C. The tragic account of the king's death was no surprise to his readers. They had already faced, in Kings, the embarrassment of a good king dying an incongruous death, even after the promise of a peaceful demise (2 Kings 22:20; 23:29, 30; cf. 2 Chron. 34:28). Could the Chronicler shed any light on the problem? A little, although he could not resolve it. In no way could he integrate the tragedy into his theme of ascents to glory. Human life has its share of bewildering turns and loose ends, and the Chronicler was too much of a realist to deny this unpalatable truth.

What was the historical background? Josiah was caught up in the death throes of a superpower, Assyria, and collided with the efforts of Egypt, the other superpower, to preserve its ally's life from the vigorous attacks of the Babylonians for as long as possible. The Chronicler has expanded the two shocked verses of 2 Kings 23 (vv. 29, 30) into a longer story, doubtless reflecting in part at least a separate tradition available to him. He contends that the king died at home in Jerusalem, in keeping with the letter, if not the spirit, of Huldah's prophecy (34:28; 35:24; contrast 2 Kings 23:29, 30). More importantly he insists that Necho had divine warrant for his military mission and that Josiah in opposing him cast himself in the villainous role of God's enemy.

The explanation seems to function more as a comfort to later generations than as a direct indictment of Josiah. The Chronicler must have known that it was not the first time a Judean king had heard such claims from a foreign superpower. In brazen tones Sennacherib had offered the same argument to Hezekiah according to 2 Kings 18:25. And there the reader was obviously meant to regard it as just another of Sennacherib's dirty tricks! With hindsight, however, the Chronicler is able to take Necho's claim at its face value. He goes so far as to describe Josiah as a second Ahab, who *"disguised himself"* (v. 22) in an attempt to prevent a prophetic word coming true (18:19, 29). In addition Josiah suffered the similar fate of a serious arrow wound which necessitated his removal from the fray (v. 23; cf. 18:33). If the death of Josiah must be admitted as out of keeping with his life, the Chronicler manages to salvage from the debacle a tribute to the word of God and a warning that to disregard God's revealed will is dire folly.

He does not want the aberration of Josiah's tragic end to overshadow the overwhelmingly positive contribution he made to the life of Judah. The triple mention of mourning not only caters to the shocked emotions of readers of Josiah's death but reflects a high regard for the king (cf. Jer. 22:11, 15–16). The Chronicler's own obituary notice is that Josiah was a good and pious king whose reign was characterized by the honoring of the Torah Scriptures. Who could have wanted a finer epitaph?

NOTE

1. This is a quotation from E. M. Blaiklock which I have in my notes. I cannot verify the source.

CHAPTER NINETEEN

Plunging to Ruin

2 Chronicles 36:1-23

John Bunyan ended his *Pilgrim's Progress* with the grim scene of Ignorance being turned away from the gate of the Celestial City because he willfully lacked a certificate of admission. Two Shining Ones were commanded by the King of the City "to go out and take Ignorance and bind him hand and foot and have him away." "Then I saw," added Christian, "that there was a way to hell even from the gates of heaven, as well as from the City of Destruction." In the New Testament the Sermon on the Mount, addressed to disciples, ends with a sinister warning: ". . . and it fell, and great was its fall" (Matt. 7:27). The Chronicler concludes his work on the same warning note and with language similar in some respects to that of *Pilgrim's Progress.* He surveyed the last two tragic decades of the monarchy. Exile was for him not only a historical event that took place in the sixth century B.C. It was also a type or key example of being out of fellowship with God, against which there certainly was—and is—need that God's people be warned. In Romans 8 the glorious message of liberation, life, and divine love realistically includes a warning of another, less welcome option: "If you live according to the flesh you will die" (Rom. 8:13).

The Chronicler's account of the monarchy ends as it began. In 1 Chronicles 10 he portrayed the overthrow of Saul's reign. Israel's troops fell slain before the Philistines, while other Israelites forsook their cities and fled. Saul perished and his armor was put in the Philistine temple. The cause of this catastrophe was the king's unfaithfulness. The same pattern of death, displacement, and dishonor reappears here, sadly during the reigns of Davidic kings. After the people "were unfaithful" (v. 14, RSV; NKJV "transgressed"), their young men were "killed . . . with the sword," while the rest were deported (vv. 17, 20). In dishonor the temple vessels or "articles" (v. 18)—the same Hebrew word is used as for Saul's armor in 1 Chronicles 10:9, 10—were put in Nebuchadnezzar's temple. Saul's experience and that of the last kings of Judah were the basis of the Chronicler's story-sermons, hellfire sermons which he preached to the people of God in his own day. He was rattling the skeletons in Judah's closet, to encourage them to take the high road of spirituality rather than the low road of nominalism, backsliding, and apostasy that leads to death.

His ultimate words veered to a positive tone. Just as Saul's disastrous reign gave way to David's reign of restoration and progress, and just as the Chronicler's fleeting mention in 1 Chronicles 9:1 of Judah's Exile "because of their unfaithfulness" was bracketed with mention of return—so here too there was a final message of hope and grace. It did not cancel out the description of judgment as "a tale . . . full of sound and fury, signifying nothing," but it did affirm that God's will for His people was their eventual blessing. At the end of the chapter the Chronicler seems to have had Jeremiah 29:10 in mind. He would certainly have agreed with the representation of the mind of God in Jeremiah 29:11: "I know the thoughts that I think toward you, says the Lord, thoughts of peace and not of evil, to give you a future and a hope."

FOREBODINGS OF DOOM

36:1 Then the people of the land took Jehoahaz the son of Josiah, and made him king in his father's place in Jerusalem.

2 Jehoahaz *was* twenty-three years old when he became king, and he reigned three months in Jerusalem.

3 Now the king of Egypt deposed him at Jerusalem; and he imposed on the land a tribute of one hundred talents of silver and a talent of gold.

4 Then the king of Egypt made *Jehoahaz's* brother Eliakim king over Judah and Jerusalem, and changed his name to Jehoiakim. And Necho took Jehoahaz his brother and carried him off to Egypt.

5 Jehoakim *was* twenty-five years old when he became king, and he reigned eleven years in Jerusalem. And he did evil in the sight of the LORD his God.

6 Nebuchadnezzar king of Babylon came up against him, and bound him in bronze *fetters* to carry him off to Babylon.

7 Nebuchadnezzar also carried off *some* of the articles from the house of the LORD to Babylon, and put them in his temple at Babylon.

8 Now the rest of the acts of Jehoiakim, the abominations which he did, and what was found against him, indeed they *are* written in the book of the kings of Israel and Judah. Then Jehoiachin his son reigned in his place.

9 Jehoiachin *was* eight years old when he became king, and he reigned in Jerusalem three months and ten days. And he did evil in the sight of the LORD.

10 At the turn of the year King Nebuchadnezzar summoned *him* and took him to Babylon, with the costly articles from the house of the LORD, and made Zedekiah, *Jehoiakim's* brother, king over Judah and Jerusalem.

2 Chron. 36:1-10

The pace of the narrative noticeably quickens in this passage. If chapters 33–35 depicted ascents to glory, here there is a rapid plunging to ruin. Like so many lemmings, king after king tumbles into exile. They topple to destruction as if possessed by the demons of the Gadarene swine. The pace of the Chronicler's source in 2 Kings 23:30b–24:18 is rapid, but this account is even more accelerated. Of course, he can assume knowledge of the Kings material. His intent is to emphasize the fate of exile suffered by each king in turn. It is like a series of clips of automobile crashes issued in a public service announcement to warn drivers against alcohol and drugs.

The message of the reigns of Jehoiakim and Jehoiachin in verses 5–10 is that the wages of evil is exile. Strangely, in the case of Jehoahaz in verses 1–4, although the account depends heavily on 2 Kings 23:30b–34, it omits the negative formula "And he did evil in the sight of the Lord." Did the Chronicler reason that Jehoahaz was caught up in the folly of Josiah? Certainly the termination of Jehoahaz's brief

435

reign was the historical tailpiece of Josiah's attempt to resist Egypt. Or was he thinking of the looming wrath of God which earlier chapters had mentioned as postponed by the virtues of particular kings (see 28:25; 32:25, 26; 34:24–38)? The Chronicler usually works within a doctrine of individual retribution whereby God keeps short accounts with both sinners and saints. Yet he does not seem to have abandoned the Kings notion of the stockpiling of guilt as a natural process until it toppled and engulfed the nation. What the Chronicler insists is that for the spiritually minded this process was not inexorable: divine resources of grace were available to break this syndrome and transcend it. Such evidently did not happen in the case of Jehoahaz. He was definitely not a Hezekiah or a Josiah who "did what was right in the sight of the Lord, and walked in the ways of his father David" (34:2; cf. 29:2).

The historical background is the period between 609 and 605 B.C., when the Egyptians had complete control over Syria and Palestine, before the Babylonians wrested it from them. The payment of tribute and the enforced change of king reflect this control. As the people's nominee, Jehoahaz was naturally suspect to Necho, and he was deposed in favor of his younger brother and exiled to Egypt, a hostage to ensure Judean loyalty. This dashing of Judah's hopes of independence is reflected in the pathos of a contemporary poem and in the peremptoriness of a divine oracle, recorded in Jeremiah 22:10–12. The political misfortune was the providential beginning of the end for Judah. It was a far cry from the glorious reigns of David and Solomon, when tribute money flowed into Jerusalem. Necho's heavyhandedness in taxing the people reminds the reader of another king of Egypt, Shishak, who rode roughshod over Judah and Jerusalem in an expression of God's wrath (12:1–12). Once more the Judeans are "servants" (12:8) to an Egyptian king. Their new monarch is devoid of power, despite being decked out with the trappings of traditional royalty, inasmuch as he is given a name which nominally celebrates Israel's God ("Jehoiakim"). We are far from an affirmation that "the Lord [or Yahweh or Jehovah] was God" (33:13).

The account of Jehoiakim's reign in verses 5–8 is an abbreviated version of 2 Kings 23:36–24:7, with the insertion of an independent tradition about his exile to Babylon, the new mistress of Palestine and Syria (vv. 6b–7). This exile was evidently temporary, like

Manasseh's, because 2 Kings 24:6 implies that he died in his home-land. This tradition of exile, also reflected in Daniel 1:2, may be based on the king's participation in a Babylonian victory procession celebrating imperial power. The Chronicler makes use of it because it supports his theme of recurring exile. The theological understanding of Jehoiakim's exile is clear. By his *"evil,"* defiance of the claims of *"his God"* (v. 5), and *"abominations"* (v. 8) the king exposed himself to the divine wrath being increasingly poured out on Judah (34:25). Jehoiakim is famous, or rather infamous, for the way he treated the scroll of Jeremiah's prophecies (Jer. 36:20–25). He insolently cut up the scroll and threw it into the fire, column by column.

Mention of the despoiling of the temple vessels or "articles" (v. 18) and their installation in a Babylonian temple broaches God's abandonment of His sanctuary, a theme in this chapter which rises to a crescendo in the destruction of the temple. It corresponds to Ezekiel's vision of the glory of the Lord gradually withdrawing from the temple and the holy city (Ezek. 9:3; 10:4, 18; 11:23). In turn, the eventual return of these vessels as the accrediting nucleus of a re-newed temple (see Ezra 1:7–11; 5:14, 15; 6:5) was to correspond to Ezekiel's description of the return of God's glory, filling the temple (Ezek. 43:1–5). Here, however, the negative phase of this saga of the vessels is firmly in view.

In verses 9–10 the brief account of Jehoiachin's reign, a curtail-ment of 2 Kings 24:8–17, selects simply the three motifs of evil, fur-ther loss of temple vessels and exile to Babylon. Historically he was caught up in a rebellion instigated by his father. Nebuchadnezzar's capture of Jerusalem in 597 B.C. marked the start of the last, weary lap for the Judean monarchy. The Chronicler does not mention the capture, yet he holds the same view of Jehoiachin's deportation, though from a theological perspective. Taught by the prophets, es-pecially by Jeremiah, he interprets the alien act as God's bringing of calamity in reprisal for spiritual defection (cf. 34:24). To do evil meant to lose the enjoyment of God's presence and of His land-centered blessings. The Chronicler considered the narrative still rele-vant to his readers as a strong metaphor for losing out in life. His thinking finds illustration in Psalm 126. Returned exiles celebrated the wonderful fact that "the Lord" had "restored the fortunes of Zion," but in their lack of blessing they prayed for a fuller restora-tion: "Restore our fortunes, O Lord" (Ps. 126:1, 4, RSV).

FINAL DISASTER

36:11 Zedekiah *was* twenty-one years old when he became king, and he reigned eleven years in Jerusalem.

12 He did evil in the sight of the LORD his God, *and* did not humble himself before Jeremiah the prophet, *who spoke* from the mouth of the LORD.

13 And he also rebelled against King Nebuchadnezzar, who had made him swear *an oath* by God; but he stiffened his neck and hardened his heart against turning to the LORD God of Israel.

14 Moreover all the leaders of the priests and the people transgressed more and more, *according* to all the abominations of the nations, and defiled the house of the LORD which He had consecrated in Jerusalem.

15 And the LORD God of their fathers sent *warnings* to them by His messengers, rising up early and sending *them,* because He had compassion on His people and on His dwelling place.

16 But they mocked the messengers of God, despised His words, and scoffed at His prophets, until the wrath of the LORD arose against His people, till *there was* no remedy.

17 Therefore He brought against them the king of the Chaldeans, who killed their young men with the sword in the house of their sanctuary, and had no compassion on young man or virgin, on the aged or the weak; He gave *them* all into his hand.

18 And all the articles from the house of God, great and small, the treasures of the house of the LORD, and the treasures of the king and of his leaders, all *these* he took to Babylon.

19 Then they burned the house of God, broke down the wall of Jerusalem, burned all its palaces with fire, and destroyed all its precious possessions.

20 And those who escaped from the sword he carried away to Babylon, where they became servants to him and his sons until the rule of the kingdom of Persia,

2 Chron. 36:11–20

Not surprisingly this climactic passage is written in an emotional vein. In Hebrew narrative it is indicated by a piling up of terms and clauses in a poetic manner. The downfall of Jerusalem, the destruction of the temple, and the deportation of the people have a Holocaust-like quality to which no post-exilic Jew could have reacted with dry eyes. The poignant poems of Psalms 74 and 79, as well as the Book of Lamentations, are contemporary reactions to the triple tragedy.

The Chronicler seems to have identified Zedekiah with a "brother" of Jehoiachin bearing that name (see the footnote in NKJV) who is mentioned in 1 Chronicles 3:16, whereas 2 Kings 24:17 equates him with the uncle of 1 Chronicles 3:15. Jeremiah 37–38 portrays Zedekiah as a Mr. Facing-both-ways, but his dominant attitude is summed up at the outset of that account: "Neither he nor his servants nor the people of the land gave heed to the words of the Lord which He spoke by the prophet Jeremiah" (Jer. 37:2). The Chronicler seemingly echoes that statement and its sentiment in the just condemnation of king, leaders, and people (vv. 12–16), though he lays the major blame on Zedekiah, in verse 12. 2 Kings 24:18–25:11 has supplied the barest skeleton of his account: he has dominant concerns of his own to pursue. Throughout his history of the monarchy after Solomon's reign he has kept a weather eye open for the temple theology of 2 Chronicles 7. Manasseh's experience in chapter 33 served as a testimony to the triumph of His grace. By contrast, the "*evil*" of Zedekiah's reign and the fate of his realm became a type of the human potential to resist God's will, to his own loss. And, in terms of Hebrews, one who has "insulted the Spirit of grace" is "worthy" of dire "punishment" (Heb. 10:29). "Departing from the living God" means "to fall into the hands of the living God," "a fearful thing" (Heb. 3:12; 10:31).

A basic principle of the temple theology of chapter 7 is a high regard for the temple itself. God had "*consecrated*" it as the place of His special presence (7:16, 20), as 36:14 affirms. However, in a matter where God said "yes," the community of Judah replied with a resounding "no." They "*defiled*" what God had "*consecrated.*" The reference to "*the abominations of the nations*" indicates a breaking of the Torah: it alludes to Deuteronomy 18:9, as the phrase did in 33:2. Here again a concern of chapter 7 was in view, specifically that of 7:19. God's people were treading a downward path, which was to

439

culminate in the withdrawal of His special presence. Chapter 7 had spelled out a sure consequence: He would cast the temple out of His sight and reduce it to a shocking condition (7:20, 21). God's word came true in Zedekiah's reign, when *"the house of God"* was first despoiled and then *"burned"* (vv. 18, 19).

Of course, 2 Chronicles 7 contains another great principle, God's offer of a fresh start. Here too Zedekiah and his subjects were unresponsive. Verses 12–13 illustrate in two respects the king's rejection of the offer made first in 7:14. He *"did not humble himself"* before God's prophetic word and resisted *"turning"* from his wicked ways. His role as an apostate is illustrated in verse 13 by reference to the contemporary charge of Ezekiel 17:18–19. Zedekiah's political rebellion involved the breaking of an oath made in the very name of God. The Chronicler borrows the expression *"he stiffened his neck"* from the Book of Jeremiah, where it is associated with rejecting the prophetic word of God (Jer. 7:26; 17:23; 19:15). So verses 12–13 possess a ABA'B' pattern, doubling references to the king's basic sin and his compounding of that sin by rejecting a call to repent.

Zedekiah's twofold rejection of God was reproduced in the community as a whole. Initially they "were unfaithful" (RSV; NKJV *"transgressed,"* v. 14) in the extreme: the Chronicler labels their failure with his cardinal term, as wanton estrangement from God. All was not yet lost: it is sinners who qualify for the grace of God. Unfortunately the overtures of 7:14 found no welcome. The phrase *"His people"* in verses 15–16 poignantly echoes "My people" in that golden text. The Chronicler understood its plea for repentance in terms of prophetic mediation, as 24:19 and 33:18 illustrate. Prophets were certainly sent. Again the Chronicler borrows from the testimony of Jeremiah's book: *"rising up early and sending them"* (v. 15) was the phrase used there for God's persistence in giving the people chance after chance (e.g. Jer. 7:25; 35:14). Ominously it is always associated with the failure of God's prophetic mission, as here. The upshot was that the promise of 7:14 was blocked and could not come into effect. *"There was no remedy"* (v. 16) or healing: God's compassionate longing to forgive and "heal" (7:14) was frustrated. The "accepted time" (2 Cor. 6:2) came and went. Could not God have tried again? No, at last even God has to desist. "I believe," wrote C. S. Lewis of such divine finality, "that if a million chances are likely to do good, they would be given. But a master often knows, when boys and parents do not, that it is really useless to send a boy in for a certain examination again. Finality must come sometime, and it does not require a very robust faith to believe that omniscience knows when."[1]

Have you noticed that the Chronicler is not tied to any legalistic mode of thinking? The Exile comes about primarily not because of a broken law but because of the rejection of God's offers of forgiveness and a second chance. It is the spurning of the gospel invitation that is the sin of sins in the Chronicler's book (cf. John 16:9). For him the breaking of God's standards drives no one beyond the pale. What does so is the refusal of the sinner to repent and start all over again with God. Lest Christians smugly agree and complacently contrast their security with the state and destiny of unbelievers, it is well to remember that the Chronicler was essentially thinking of falling away from within the believing community. Repentance is a Christian quality: the letters to the churches in Revelation 2–3 commend it to their readers no less than eight times. It is urged too in 1 John 1:9, which may be regarded as the New Testament equivalent of 2 Chronicles 7:14.

In the absence of repentance there inevitably had to follow in verses 17–20 the traumatic description of suffering and loss. In verse 17 the Chronicler appears to be using Lamentations 2:21 to help him convey the poignancy of the event. The most prized and most frail sectors of the community were cruelly cut down—and the long shadow of the invader was the dark figure of God Himself. The totality of the catastrophe is emphasized in two parallel clauses at the end of adjacent sentences: *"He gave them all into his hand"* and *"all these he took to Babylon"* (vv. 17–18). It appears too in the stark alternatives of verse 20—death or deportation.

Traumatic and total as the Chronicler's description of the Exile is, its significance as a perennial theological truth was also vital for him. In this chapter it is the last, if worst, of a recurring series of banishments from the land. The effect of setting it in a context of repeated exiles is to devalue it somewhat. The Chronicler lists one Egyptian exile and four Babylonian ones, including Manasseh's in 33:11. And there were others earlier in his history. The final one differed from the others in degree but not in kind. The result is that the Exile does not demarcate the post-exilic community from a pre-exilic one. Rather, in principle there are deep troughs to which the people of God descend—and from which they may rise by God's grace. Life has its vales of misery which seem inescapable to its victims but from which one may climb to live again for God, by humbly taking hold of His outstretched hand.

A Favorable Denouement

36:21 to fulfill the word of the LORD by the mouth of Jeremiah, until the land had enjoyed her Sabbaths. As long as she lay desolate she kept Sabbath, to fulfill seventy years.

22 Now in the first year of Cyrus king of Persia, that the word of the LORD by the mouth of Jeremiah might be fulfilled, the LORD stirred up the spirit of Cyrus king of Persia, so that he made a proclamation throughout all his kingdom, and also *put it* in writing, saying,

23 Thus says Cyrus king of Persia: All the kingdoms of the earth the LORD God of heaven has given me. And He has commanded me to build Him a house at Jerusalem which is in Judah. Who *is* among you of all His people? May the LORD his God *be* with him, and let him go up!

2 Chron. 36:21–23

The narrative glides into a positive conclusion in the course of verse 20. It is heralded by the happy term *"until."* "How long?" was the wistful question of the sufferers in the psalms, straining to see a light at the end of their dark tunnel (e.g. Pss. 6:3; 13:1, 2; 74:9, 10; cf. Zech. 1:12). The Chronicler and his post-exilic readers knew that the Exile came to an end, but that did not stifle a thrill of appreciation in response to God's grace. They prized in the books of the pre-exilic prophets the comparatively few but definite references to the salvation that was to follow the judgment of God. They regarded themselves as a doubly redeemed people, once at the Exodus and once from the Exile (Exod. 15:13; Ps. 107:2). Beyond all reasonableness God turned tragedy into triumph, suffering into glory.

It is the triumph of a *"word"* of grace. The divine word might be that of Jeremiah 25:11–12, which combines the theme of service with a seventy-year limit to Judah's sentence. More likely Jeremiah 29:10, with its more positive sentiments, is in view. In favor of this basis is its contextual stress on the exiles' seeking and finding God, praying and hearing His answer (Jer. 29:12–14), which the Chronicler seems to have had in mind as the prelude to return. The Chronicler does not throw to the winds the gospel logic of 7:14 ("If . . ."). His use of Manasseh as a role model in 33:11–13 revealed his high view of repentance as a trigger of God's grace. Zechariah had a similar conviction; he stressed that exilic repentance required the sequel of post-exilic repentance (Zech. 1:2–6).

With the prophetic word the Chronicler intertwined the covenant curse of Leviticus 26:34, which he cited word for word, simply changing the tenses from future to past to indicate fulfillment. Jeremiah 29:10 and Leviticus 26:34 both take God's judgment seriously but they are open to a positive future by setting a time limit for the Exile. The latter text speaks of the sabbath year, a seventh year of fallow land after six years of cultivation. The paralleling of the two texts envisages a period of 490 years—presumably the period of the monarchy, although the Chronicler does not tell us—which required a rest period of seventy years. Unused, the land was to mark time until the missing years were made up. One could deduce an ecological principle from the Leviticus text, that the land has its God-given rights, which its human users disregard at their peril. The Chronicler's own point is that both the Law and the Prophets affirmed that restoration follows exile in God's economy. This closing observation reflects his tremendous regard for the Word of God as he knew it. "The word of our God stands forever" (Isa. 40:8). Indeed, "the word of God is not chained" (2 Tim. 2:9), and in its sovereign freedom lies promise of freedom and favor for His people.

What follows in verses 22–23 is a quotation from Ezra 1:1–3a, which serves to express in plainer terms the promise of verse 21. It is perhaps best taken as the Chronicler's own quotation from the earlier book of Ezra. He had allowed himself to stray into the later period in 1 Chronicles 9:2, to bring out the continuity of God's purposes. His task has been to present the history of the Judean monarchy as a series of sermons to his post-exilic readers. That task is done and he breaks off his quotation, as if to say "But that's another story." There is a change of reading at the end. In place of "May his God be with him" (Ezra 1:3) the text reads literally "The Lord his God with him," which is probably to be interpreted ". . . will be with him" (cf. Ps. 91:15). The mandate to God's exiles to possess their possessions (1 Chron. 9:2; cf. Obad. 17) was backed by the promise of His enabling presence. God's supportive presence with His recommitted people was a certain promise for the Chronicler. The heroes of Chronicles, David and Solomon, had known this presence (1 Chron. 11:9; 28:20; 2 Chron. 1:2). Nor were the good kings Abijah, Asa, Jehoshaphat, and Hezekiah strangers to it (2 Chron. 13:12; 15:2; 17:3; 20:17; 32:8). It was a temple blessing still available to the post-exilic community. In the Christian era too it continues as a rich blessing. At the heart of the Christian faith is enthroned an Immanuel, "God with us." The Gospel of Matthew, like Chronicles, exults in this powerful truth (Matt. 1:23; 18:20; 28:20).

> Still, still with Thee, as to each new-born morning
> A fresh and solemn splendor still is given,
> So doth this blessed consciousness awakening,
> Breathe, each day, nearness unto Thee and heaven.[2]
> > Harriet Beecher Stowe

NOTE

1. C. S. Lewis, *Problem of Pain* (New York: Macmillan, 1947), p. 112.
2. Harriet Beecher Stowe, "When I Awake I Am Still with Thee."

Bibliography

Ackroyd, P. R. *I & II Chronicles, Ezra, Nehemiah.* Torch Bible Commentaries. London: SCM, 1973.

Coggins, R. J. *The First and Second Book of the Chronicles.* Cambridge Bible Commentary. Cambridge: CUP, 1976.

Curtis, E. L., and Madsen, A. A. *A Critical and Exegetical Commentary on the Books of Chronicles.* International Critical Commentary. Edinburgh: T. & T. Clark, 1910.

Keil, C. F. *The Books of the Chronicles.* Biblical Commentary on the Old Testament. Edinburgh: T. & T. Clark, 1872; reprinted Grand Rapids: Eerdmans, 1950.

Mangan, C. *1-2 Chronicles, Ezra, Nehemiah.* Old Testament Message. Wilmington, Delaware: Glazier, 1982.

McConville, J. G. *I & II Chronicles.* Daily Study Bible. Philadelphia: Westminster, 1984.

Myers, J. M. *I Chronicles, II Chronicles.* Anchor Bible. Garden City, NY: Doubleday, 1965.

Slotki, I. W. *Chronicles.* Soncino Books of the Bible. London, Jerusalem, and New York: Soncino, 1952.

Williamson, H. G. M. *1 & 2 Chronicles.* New Century Bible Commentary. Grand Rapids: Eerdmans, 1982.